CERTIFIED PROFESSION

EXAMINATION REVIEW SERIES

FINANCE & BUSINESS LAW

Fourth Edition

Betty L. Schroeder, Ph.D., Editor
Northern Illinois University

John Lewis, Ph.D.
Northern Illinois University

Sally A. Webber, Ph.D., CPA
Northern Illinois University

Lawrence S. Clark, J.D., L.L.M.
Sonoma State University

Philip DiMarzio, J.D., L.L.M.
Sycamore, Illinois

A joint publication of
International Association of Administrative Professionals™

I A A P
International Association of Administrative Professionals™

and PRENTICE HALL
Upper Saddle River, New Jersey 07458

Library of Congress Cataloging-in-Publication Data
Finance and business law / Betty L. Schroeder, editor ... [et al.].—
4th ed.
p. cm. – (Certified professional secretary examination
review series)
ISBN 0-13-084314-8
1. Secretaries–United States–Examinations, questions, etc.
2. Corporations–Accounting–Examinations, questions, etc.
3. Corporations–Finance–Examinations, questions, etc.
4. Commercial law–United States–Examinations, questions, etc.
I. Schroeder, Betty L. II. Series.
HF5547.5.C443 2000 99-25884
651.3′74′076–dc21 CIP

Acquisitions Editor: *Elizabeth Sugg*
Production Editor: *Lori Harvey, Carlisle Publishers Services*
Production Liaison: *Eileen O'Sullivan*
Managing Editor: *Mary Carnis*
Editorial Assistant: *Brian Hyland*
Development Editor: *Judy Casillo*
Manufacturing Manager: *Ed O'Dougherty*
Director of Manufacturing & Production: *Bruce Johnson*
Marketing Manager: *Shannon Simonsen*
Compositor/Interior Design: *Carlisle Communications, Ltd.*
Cover Design: *Joe Sengotta*
Printer/Binder: *Banta Harrisonburg*

Printed in the United States of America

10 9 8 7 6

ISBN 0-13-084314-8

Prentice-Hall International (UK) Limited, *London*
Prentice-Hall of Australia Pty, Limited, *Sydney*
Prentice-Hall Canada, Inc., *Toronto*
Prentice-Hall Hispanoamericana, S.A., *Mexico*
Prentice-Hall of India Private Limited, *New Delhi*
Prentice-Hall of Japan, Inc., *Tokyo*
Pearson Education Asia, Pte. Ltd., *Singapore*
Editora Prentice-Hall do Brasil, Ltda., *Rio de Janeiro*

Contents

Preface

The Certified Professional Secretary Examination® (CPS®) Review Series, review manuals and their corresponding Study Guides for each of the three parts of the Certified Professional Secretary Examination, is a joint publication of Prentice Hall and the International Association of Administrative Professionals™ (IAAP™). The content of each module is based on the current CPS Examination Review Guide published by IAAP.

CPS Examination

The rewards for achieving the Certified Professional Secretary (CPS) rating are numerous, as attested to by the more than 55,000 CPS holders. These include: pride in accomplishment, increased self-esteem, greater respect from employers and peers, and confidence to assume greater responsibilities as well as possible college credit toward a degree, pay increases, bonuses, and opportunities for advancement. In today's workplace, having the CPS credential can be assurance of employability.

The CPS Examination is a one-day, three-part examination based on the premise that a professional secretary should know how to apply the principles of good human relations and have basic knowledge of finance, business law, economics, communication, and management. It is expected that a competent secretary is thoroughly familiar with current techniques in office practice and procedures and is aware of developments in office systems and technology. **To apply for approval to take the CPS Examination, request the "Capstone" from IAAP. The "Capstone" provides detailed information about the examination and an application form.**

CPS Examination Review Series

The CPS Examination Review Series provides valuable assistance to the administrative professional preparing for the CPS Examination, whether it is used for group review sessions or for self-study. The series provides an excellent learning tool that is focused on key topics that are necessary for passing the exam.

The format used for each of the manuals in the series is identical. The CPS Examination Review Series provides as much relevant information as possible to help in preparing for the CPS Examination. **However, this does not imply that all information presented in the series will be included on the examinations.**

Each chapter contains:

- An overview introducing the reader to the chapter and its content
- Text in outline form, with examples highlighted in italics, to enhance the explanation given in the text
- Illustrations to aid understanding of concepts

- Review questions at the end of each chapter, developed in formats *similar* to those found in the CPS Examination
- Solutions to the review questions, with some explanation of correct answers, where needed, and references to portions of the outline that explains the answer more fully. For example:

  1. *(b)* *[A-2]*
  The outline reference pertains to: Section A, Point 2 in the chapter.

When a solution seems unclear, it is recommended that the section be reviewed for further clarification.

A complete Glossary of terms and definitions is included at the end of each manual. A reference is made to the chapter where the term may be found in context.

CPS Examination Review Series Self-Study Guides

Each manual has a corresponding Self-Study Guide written as a companion tool rather than a formally structured workbook. These guides enhance material presented in CPS Examination Review manuals and may be used for independent study and in accelerated, short-term group review courses.

The question arises as to why this series is formatted in this particular way. The response is simple: We want you to have a thorough, efficient review of the content that *may* appear on the CPS Examination. The purpose of the Self-Study Guide is to assist you in researching and building your own information bank.

CPS Examination Review Guide

The current CPS Examination Review Guide should be used to direct any course of study. The Guide includes the examination outline, sample questions, bibliography of recommended study materials, and suggestions on exam review. The CPS Examination Review Guide is available for purchase through the IAAP Distribution Department: 10502 NW Ambassador Drive, PO Box 20404, Kansas City, MO 64195-0404; phone 816-891-6600; fax 816-891-9118; e-mail distribution@iaap-hq.org

Acknowledgments

Through the sincere and dedicated efforts of a number of individuals interested in the certification of professional secretaries, the fourth edition of the *Certified Professional Secretary® Examination Review for Finance and Business Law* was prepared to complement the current study outline for the Certified Professional Secretary® Examination. Like the other two reviews in the series, *Finance and Business Law* will be a successful review tool because of the critiques and contributions of the following people.

The International Association of Administrative Professionals, through the Institute for Certification, has provided not only the incentive for the development of the fourth edition of this review but also valuable input during the review process. We are sincerely grateful and thank IAAP and the Institute for their continued support and enthusiasm for the development and revision of the series.

Specifically, we acknowledge the many contributions of Paulette Gladis CSJ, Ph.D., Dean, Institute for Certification; Dr. Katherene P. Terrell, University of Central Oklahoma, member, Institute for Certification; and Kathy L. Schoneboom CPS, Certification Manager, IAAP for their extremely helpful reviews and critiques of the manuscripts.

Another special acknowledgment recognizes the Illinois Division of IAAP and, in particular, those members of the Kishwaukee Chapter, DeKalb, Illinois, who are pursuing or have received their professional certification. These groups have continued to be extremely supportive and positive about this review series; their friendship is very much appreciated.

A very special "thank you" is given to Charnelle Lewis, Sycamore, Illinois, for her excellent writing and editing assistance with the economics manuscript.

Lastly, we are most appreciative of the assistance and leadership demonstrated by Elizabeth Sugg and Judy Casillo of Prentice Hall and for their continued support of this series. It is a joy to work with individuals so professional in their judgment of what administrative professionals need to prepare appropriately for the CPS Examination.

We hope that all the input provided by professionals throughout the revision process will continue to make this review series the "leader" in preparing professional secretaries everywhere for the CPS Examination in the future.

Betty L. Schroeder, Ph.D., John L. Lewis, Ph.D., Sally A. Webber, Ph.D., CPA,
Lawrence S. Clark, J.D., LL.M., Philip DiMarzio, J.D., LL.M.

CHAPTER 1 Basic Concepts of Economics

OVERVIEW

Economics is one of the many social sciences that attempt to analyze our complex society. Economics deals with understanding and predicting human behavior in an effort to solve the universal economic problem of scarcity. As a study of human behavior, economics analyzes decisions relative to consumption, production, distribution, and the exchange of goods and services in a society.

In this chapter we develop basic concepts used by economists to study human behavior. These concepts include types of economic systems, the demand for and supply of goods and services, markets for goods and services, and the structural environment in which firms operate. These concepts provide a basis for understanding such questions as: How will people react to an increase in the price of goods? or How will the agricultural community react to declining crop prices?

KEY TERMS

Capital
Command economy
Complementary goods
Consumption
Demand
Economic efficiency
Economic equity
Economic freedom
Economic security
Economic stability
Elasticity
Entrepreneur
Entrepreneurial ability
Equilibrium price
Explicit costs
Factors of production
Imperfect competition
Implicit costs
Inelastic demand
Inelastic supply
Labor
Laissez-faire
Land
Law of demand
Law of supply
Market
Mixed economy
Opportunity cost
Perfect competition
Private goods
Private property
Production possibility curve
Profit
Public goods
Scarcity
Shortage
Substitute goods
Supply
Surplus
Utility
Wants

A. The Basis of Economics

The basis of economics is the existence of scarcity. Scarcity exists whenever society's desire for goods and services exceeds society's ability to produce these goods and services, or whenever wants exceed resources. The consequences of scarcity are that choices must be made. Scarcity affects individuals in much the same manner as it affects society. When individuals must choose between paying bills and taking a vacation, scarcity is the reason a decision must be made.

The government must also deal with scarcity and choices. The Department of Defense may want to increase expenditures at the same time that the Department of Agriculture wants to increase support for agricultural commodities. Since the resources available are limited, the government must also make choices.

It is sometimes convenient to distinguish between individual choices and societal choices. Societal choices are limited by the availability of technology and resources, which set the boundaries for the production possibilities of an economy. Within these bounds, decisions must be made concerning how much of each type of good will be produced. A typical societal choice is the decision concerning how many public goods versus private goods should be produced.

EXAMPLE: Society must decide whether to use its scarce resources for public parks or to devote these resources to the production of private goods.

1. *Scarcity:* In economics, the concept of scarcity is derived from the idea that individuals and societies have unlimited wants and limited resources. As a result of scarcity, society makes choices among alternative uses of its resources. If no conflict between wants and resources exists, choices do not have to be made, and no economic problem exists.

   a. *Unlimited wants:* Economists accept the fact that society desires a vast amount of goods and services that provide utility (a measure of satisfaction) to the consumers within society. Taken together, the desires for all goods and services are so great they could be considered unlimited. It is assumed that as people satisfy more of their wants, they will continue to work and to make decisions in an attempt to satisfy additional wants. There is no limit to the wants that individuals within society wish to have satisfied.

   b. *Limited resources:* At any given point in time, the resources of society are limited. Resources, as classified by economists, include land, labor, capital, and entrepreneurial ability.

   (1) *Land:* All land, waterways, and natural resources that come from them.

   (2) *Labor:* Human resources; the ability of individuals to perform labor services in society.

   (3) *Capital:* Those human-made resources that are used in the production of other goods and services. Capital is defined somewhat uniquely by economists and in a substantially different way from the definition used by accountants.

   EXAMPLE: The machines on an assembly line that are used to produce automobiles are capital.

   (4) *Entrepreneurial ability:* The ability and risk taken to organize the factors of production (land, labor, and capital) to produce goods in such a way as to make a profit.

2. *Societal Choices:* As a result of scarcity, societies must make choices. With the given state of technology and limited resources, society can produce only a finite number of goods and services at a particular point in time. The maximum amount of goods and services that a society can produce at any given point in time is called its *production possibilities curve.*

a. *Production possibility:* The production possibilities of an economy can be illustrated graphically by using a simplified economy in which only two types of goods are produced. The maximum quantities of each type of good that can be produced are measured on horizontal and vertical axes (see Figure 1–1).

EXAMPLE: In Figure 1–1, if a society uses all its resources to produce capital goods (e.g., tractors), it can produce no consumer goods (e.g., cars). This is illustrated by point A on the figure, where 25 tractors and no cars are produced.

Society could use all its resources to produce cars (consumer goods) and no tractors. This is illustrated by point B, showing society producing 100 cars and no tractors.

In addition to these possibilities, a society could choose to produce anywhere along the curve between points A and B. If a society is producing on the production possibility curve, it is using all its available resources in an efficient manner. If it is producing inside the curve (e.g. , point C), it is not using all its resources efficiently and can increase its output of tractors and cars, or both, without reducing the output of the other.

The production possibility curve also illustrates the necessity of choice. If society uses all its resources fully (full employment), it will produce somewhere on the production possibility curve. However, once society has achieved a point on the production possibility curve (e.g., combination D) to get more tractors, it must give up cars and vice versa.

In this example, if society wanted to move from point D to point E, it must give up 5 tractors to get 30 additional cars.

b. *Opportunity costs:* Opportunity cost is the value of the opportunity forgone when a decision is made. The movement from point E to point D in Figure 1–1 illustrates the principle of opportunity cost.

Figure 1–1 Production Possibility Curve

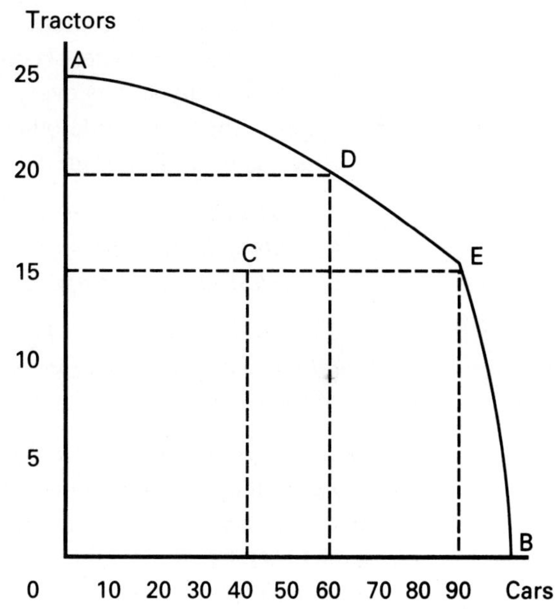

EXAMPLE: In Figure 1–1, if society changed the use of its resources and produced 15 tractors and 90 cars as opposed to 20 tractors and 60 cars, the opportunity costs of the 30 additional cars would be the 5 tractors that could no longer be produced.

A basic principle in economics is: There is no such thing as a free lunch. This statement attests to the fact that scarcity exists and there are insufficient resources to satisfy all of society's wants. If society wants to increase production of one good or service, it must reduce production of another good or service.

c. *Fundamental problems of economic systems:* The existence of scarcity and thus the necessity of making choices presents three fundamental, independent questions that every economic system must answer. This is true no matter what type of organization exists within the economic system. The three basic questions are what to produce, how to produce, and for whom to produce.

(1) *What to produce:* The question of what goods and services to produce and the quantity to produce is determined by societal demand. Society must choose among consumer goods, capital goods, and present and future consumption. In effect, if all resources are fully employed, a society is choosing a unique point on the production possibility curve at which to produce.

EXAMPLE: Should more automobiles or more airplanes be produced with our limited resources? Should more resources be used to produce military goods or social services?

(2) *How to produce:* Deciding how to produce involves choosing among different combinations of resources to produce a particular good or service. The problem is to find the most efficient combination of resources to produce a given level of output.

EXAMPLE: A choice has to be made regarding how to produce electricity. Should we use petroleum, energy from the sun, or nuclear power to fulfill our needs for electricity?

(3) *For whom to produce:* The question concerning for whom to produce is basically a distribution problem. The solution to this problem will determine how the total output of society is distributed among its members. Output can be distributed equally among everyone, or large portions of output can be directed to certain subgroups while others receive very little. To a large extent, politics, ethics, and economics are all involved in deciding for whom to produce.

EXAMPLE: The concept of welfare and progressive income taxes are attempts to address the issue of for whom to produce by reducing the purchasing power of the top income groups and increasing the purchasing power of the low-income groups.

3. *Individual Choices:* Just as society must make choices, individuals also live within limited resources and must make choices.

a. *Consumption:* Consumers have limited incomes; thus, each individual must choose what goods and services to purchase with that limited income. If an individual consumer purchases more of one good (good X), then less of another good (good Y) can be purchased. Therefore, the opportunity cost of increasing the consumption of good X is the value of good Y that must be forgone.

EXAMPLE: If Johnson has $15 to spend on refreshments, and the choice is between buying a hot dog for $1.50 or a soft drink for 75 cents, the choices are limited to 10 hot dogs and no soft drinks, 20 soft drinks and no hot dogs, or some combination of the two. Using this example, the opportunity cost of one hot dog would be two soft drinks, or the opportunity cost of two soft drinks would be one hot dog.

b. *Employment:* Individuals in society own productive resources and must decide how to use these resources. A decision must be made about how much of these resources to sell (a choice between work and leisure) and to whom the resources should be sold (a decision about what type of work to perform and who to work for).

c. *Saving:* Another important personal decision-making application is the use of current income versus future income. Individuals can increase consumption now at the expense of future consumption or can save now and have additional income for future consumption. The opportunity cost of saving is the value of present consumption that is forgone.

B. Organization of an Economic System

Different societies attempt to solve the universal problem of scarcity and address the basic questions of what to produce, how to produce, and for whom to produce in different ways. Some societies do this through custom, some through decree, and some through the price and/or market system. Historically, the United States has relied primarily on price and markets to answer the basic questions of what, how, and for whom to produce.

1. *Types of Economic Organization:* Different types of economic systems have often been classified as "isms" (e.g., socialism, communism, capitalism, and market socialism). Each of these "ism" systems can be classified as a combination of alternative forms of economic organization: authoritarian, individualistic, traditional, and mixed economy. Capitalism has traditionally been identified with the individualistic type of economic organization; socialism and communism are identified with authoritarian types of economic organizations. In reality, all economic systems are a combination of authoritarian (command) and individualistic (market) types of economic systems.

a. *Authoritarian (command) system:* An authoritarian economic organization is one within which people respond without choice to the commands of the state (government).

(1) An authoritarian type of economic organization is characterized by centralized state (government) control over the direction of economic activity. The questions of what to produce, how to produce, and for whom to produce are answered by the state. This can be done through very structured central planning or by a dictator simply making the decisions.

EXAMPLES: Communism, authoritarian socialism, and fascism.

(2) Citizens of the country have little freedom to choose among various occupations.

(3) The choice of consumer goods is limited.

b. *Individualistic (market) system:* In an individualistic economic system, people respond by choice to the dictates of their own self-interests. Individualistic economic organization allows the basic economic decisions and activities to be carried out by individuals and businesses without substantial interference by the government. An individualistic (or market) system is often referred to as *laissez-faire* capitalism.

(1) Decisions of what to produce (how to use society's resources) are made through the market, and its resources are used in the production of those goods and services that derive the most profit.

(2) The question of how to produce is also answered by market forces. Producers organize resources in the production process to make the maximum profit.

(3) The question of for whom to produce is answered through the market as individuals express their choices by buying. Individuals who are willing and able to purchase what is produced answer the question of what to produce. An increase in consumer preferences for a good or a service leads to increases in profit from producing that good or service, with additional resources being devoted to the production of the particular good or service.

c. *Traditional system:* People respond on the basis of past practice and custom in a traditional economic organization. This mode is based on procedures devised in the distant past and solidified by a long process of historical trial and error. In many cases the traditions are sustained by belief, custom, and, in some cases, law. Many underdeveloped countries have traditional economies.

(1) Occupational choices of children are often determined by the family's occupation.

(2) Decisions on what to produce are based on what has been produced in the past.

(3) The traditional type of economic organization leads to very little change or economic growth.

d. *Mixed economy:* In a mixed economy individuals within the system and the government have an impact on basic decisions of what to produce, how to produce, and for whom to produce. People respond to a mixture of both coercion and economic incentives.

(1) Mixed types of economic systems can be almost totally authoritarian, almost completely individualistic or market economy, or anywhere between.

(2) In the recent past, economies labeled as democratic or market socialism have developed wherein the state owns the means of production and, therefore, determines what is produced. However, the decision of for whom production takes place may still remain in the hands of the people through the operation of the market.

2. *Institutions of Modern Capitalism:* The fundamental concepts of modern capitalism include private ownership of property, freedom of contract, freedom of choice in enterprise, a relatively competitive free market, and some limited government responsibilities. Government responsibility comes about because markets cannot satisfy all of a society's goals. While markets may be very effective in satisfying such goals as economic freedom and economic efficiency, markets are less able to meet goals of economic stability, equity, and economic security. In most countries the government has the responsibility to implement policies that will aid in meeting the latter goals. It is important to remember, however, that the goals mentioned above are often competing. Societies are continually making choices that reduce economic efficiency but increase economic security or stability, or they are establishing policies that reduce stability to improve economic freedom.

a. *Private property:* The concept of private property is fundamental to a capitalistic (individualistic or market) economic system. Private property is the right of individuals to own the factors of production and to do with these resources what they see fit. Private property is distinguished from public property by the form of ownership. Public property implies ownership by the government or state.

b. *Freedom of contract:* Coupled with private property rights, freedom of contract allows owners of resources, goods, and services to obtain, control, and dispose of economic resources within rather broad legal limits. Freedom of contract is important in a capitalistic system since it ensures that individuals may dispose of personal property as they want.

c. *Government's responsibilities:* Government has the responsibility for providing public services, maintaining general economic stability and security, and preventing economic abuses. Historically, laissez-faire capitalism did not meet the goals of all people within society. Thus, the role of government has been extended to meet economic goals such as stability, equity, and security in addition to the goals of economic freedom, efficiency, and growth that a market-oriented system would meet.

(1) *Economic freedom:* The right and the ability to choose how to use income to buy goods and services and use owned resources in the production process. This includes freedom to work for whom one chooses to work and to enter any occupation.

(2) *Economic efficiency:* The production of goods and services in the most efficient (least costly) manner.

(3) *Economic growth:* An increase in the output of goods and services per capita over a period of time.

(4) *Economic stability:* The existence of low rates of inflation (price increases) and low rates of unemployment within the society.

(5) *Economic equity:* The distribution of resources in society and the degree of equality that is proper for the distribution of resources and income.

(6) *Economic security:* The absence of fear of losing possessions as a result of unexpected events.

d. *Goals not met by economic system:* Goals generally not met by market-oriented economic systems are stability, equity, and security. Typically, government assumes the responsibility for meeting these goals.

3. *Structure of Modern Capitalism:* When discussing modern capitalism, it is helpful to look at the economic system in terms of a model utilizing a circular flow of income that shows input and output flows and how they interrelate within the economy. This simple model visually illustrates how markets operate and the interaction of households, businesses, and governments within a market economy. As shown in Figure 1–2, the three major institutions within modern capitalism are households, business, and government. Modern capitalism is an example of a mixed economy.

a. *Households:* Households are units within the economic system. Under modern capitalism, households are the owners of the factors of production. Households make these resources available to business firms and to government. In return, households receive income in the form of wages (the payment to labor), rents (the

Figure 1–2 Circular Flow of an Economic System

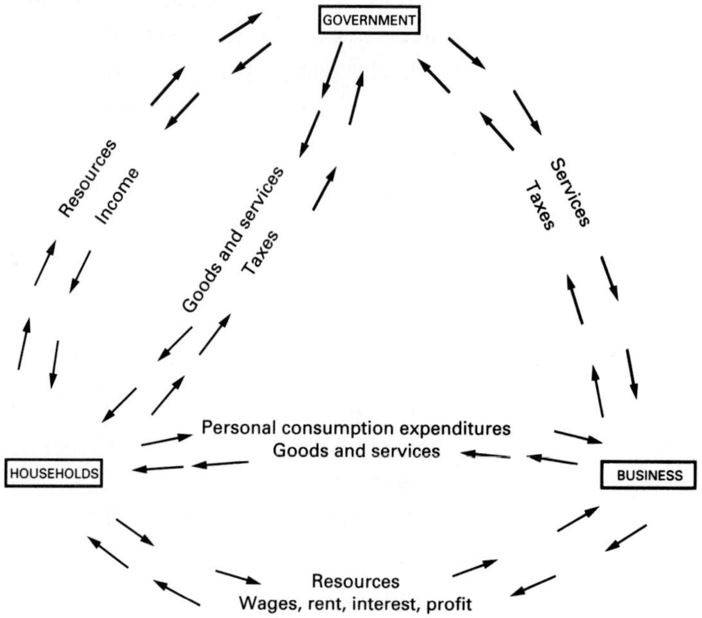

payment to land), interest (the payment to capital), and profits (the payment to entrepreneurial ability). Households use the income earned from selling their resources to buy the final goods and services or to pay taxes in return for services provided by government.

b. *Business firms:* Business firms are organizations that buy a variety of resources from households and organize them to produce goods and services that households or government want to purchase. In modern capitalism, business firms can be sole proprietors (one person owning a business), partnerships (at least two people owning a business), or corporations (ownership of the firm is in the hands of many people known as stockholders). Business firms make the ultimate decision on how goods and services are produced and buy resources from households, organizing them in such a way as to make a product that households want to buy—at a profit. Businesses also sell goods and services to the government.

c. *Government:* The role of government is one of maintaining law and order, providing social services desired by the public, and providing national defense. To make these services available, the government has to buy resources from the household sector (as business firms do) and, in return, produce services that are desired by individuals. Restrictions that government places on the markets are attempts to meet goals that markets do not meet.

C. Markets

Markets are fundamental to the functioning of a market economy. Markets exist for goods and services as well as for resources, and firms operate under varying competitive conditions often referred to as *market conditions.*

1. *Basic Components of a Market:* The basic components of any market are demand, supply, and equilibrium.

a. *Demand:* Demand is the relationship between a series of prices and corresponding quantities that individuals are able and willing to purchase at these prices.

b. *Supply:* Every market needs suppliers of goods and services. Supply is the relationship between a series of prices and the associated quantities that producers will be able and willing to make available at those prices.

c. *Equilibrium:* Supply and demand yield an equilibrium in quantity when considered together. Since the demand curve is downward sloping and the supply curve is upward sloping, they will intersect at some point. This intersection will establish a price at which all goods supplied at a given price will be purchased.

(1) *Price below equilibrium:* If the price of a good is below equilibrium, the quantity demanded will be greater than the quantity supplied. This shortage will result in an upward pressure on price to restore equilibrium.

(2) *Price above equilibrium:* If the price is above equilibrium, the quantity supplied will be greater than the quantity demanded. There will be pressure for prices to fall, again approaching equilibrium.

In reality, this equilibrium is seldom obtained. Market forces constantly affect the shifting of demand and/or supply. Thus, the market is constantly moving toward an equilibrium. This is most obvious in purely competitive markets, such as the grain market, where the quotes on the board of trade change on a minute-by-minute and day-by-day basis.

2. *The Price System:* The price system is synonymous with the market system in explaining economic behavior. The equilibrium price established by the market performs basic functions for a market-oriented economic system. Not only does the system ration goods and services, but it also allocates resources to the most productive use.

a. *The demand for goods and services:* Inherent in the price system is the demand for goods and services.

(1) *The law of demand:* The law of demand is a very important relationship in economics. This law states that as price decreases, individuals will buy more of a good or a service, and as price increases, individuals will buy less of a good or a service.

(a) *Income effects:* As price increases, the real purchasing power of individuals declines; therefore, they are able to purchase fewer goods and services.

(b) *Substitution effects:* Substitution effects relate to the consumer's desire to get the best buy. If the price of good A increases and the price of good B stays the same, then A becomes relatively more expensive than B, and some consumers are likely to shift their consumption patterns to B.

(2) *Individual demand:* Demand is the quantity of goods that an individual is willing and able to buy at a variety of prices within a given period of time. As the price of a good decreases, the consumer will purchase a greater quantity of that good. As price increases, the consumer will purchase less of that good. This inverse relationship between the price of a good and the quantity of that good demanded is referred to as the *law of demand.* The following example shows this demand relationship.

EXAMPLE: In Figure 1–3, if the price of shoes is $80 a pair and Donaldson is willing to pay $80 for shoes this year, he will be willing to buy only one pair of shoes this year. If the price is $40, Donaldson will be willing to buy two pairs. However, if the price drops to $20, he may be willing to purchase four pairs of shoes this year.

Figure 1–3 Individual Demand Curve

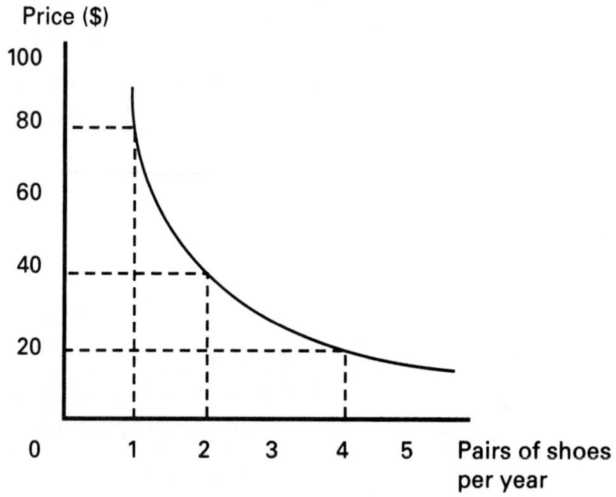

It is important to note that the demand schedule does not indicate or reflect the market price of a good. It simply indicates the quantity of a commodity that a person is willing to buy at various prices.

(3) *Market demand:* The total market demand for goods is the summation of all individual demands for that good. To find the market demand, one must add the quantity that will be bought by all individuals at a specific price. This total becomes the total market demand for the commodity at that given price level.

EXAMPLE: If there were 40,000 consumers, each with a demand curve equivalent to that pictured in Figure 1–3, at a price of $80, 40,000 pairs of shoes would be bought within a year. If the price of shoes were $40, 80,000 pairs of shoes would be purchased. If the price of shoes were $20, 160,000 pairs of shoes would be purchased. The market demand would then resemble Figure 1–4. It is unlikely that all 40,000 consumers would have the same demand curve as that pictured in Figure 1–3. Thus, to find the market demand, you would have to add the number of pairs of shoes each of the 40,000 consumers would purchase at a price of $80.

(4) *Determinants of demand:* While the price of the good will affect the quantity that individuals will purchase, other changes in our economic system will affect the amount that people purchase at all prices. These factors include consumer tastes and preferences, consumer income, prices of related goods, and expectations.

(a) *Consumer tastes and preferences:* People alter the goods and services that they desire over a period of time. As members of a society perceive that a good is something that they want to purchase, the demand increases, and as society moves away from that good, the demand decreases. Tastes and preferences are also influenced by sections of the country and, to some extent, by the ethnic or religious background of individuals.

EXAMPLES OF CHANGING PREFERENCES: Clothing fashions, automobile styles, and popular-music groups.

Figure 1–4 Market Demand Curve

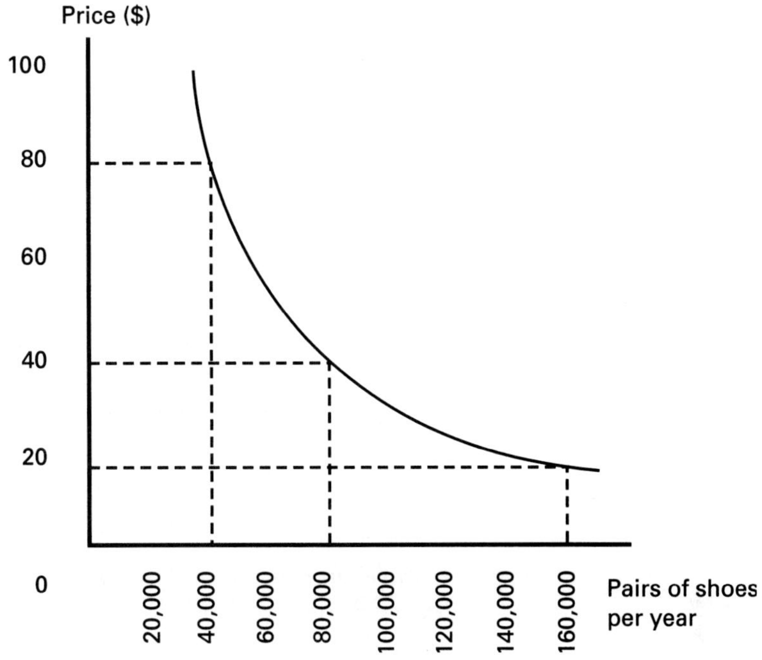

(b) *Income of consumers:* Income definitely has an impact on the demand for goods and services. As an individual's income increases, the demand for most goods and services will increase. When income and the demand for a good are positively related, economists refer to the good as a *normal* good. However, in a few cases income and demand for a good are inversely related; that is, an increase in income will result in a decrease in demand for a good. This type of good is labeled as an *inferior* good.

EXAMPLE: A good typically classified as an inferior good would be hamburger. As income increases, individuals consume less hamburger and consume more of other types of meat.

(c) *Prices of related goods:* The prices of related goods also have an impact on the demand for goods and services. Two types of relationships are common. A good may be a substitute for another type of good, or a good may be complementary to another good.

If two goods are substitutes, that implies that both goods, to some extent, satisfy the same want of an individual. Therefore, they can substitute one for the other. If the price of a substitute increases, the demand for the original good would increase.

EXAMPLES OF SUBSTITUTES: If the price of Coca-Cola increases, the demand for other types of cola would also increase. As a result of the Coca-Cola price increase, people would start substituting other colas because of the new price of Coca-Cola relative to its substitutes.

A rise in the price of beef could cause an increase in the demand for chicken since beef and chicken are both meats and can substitute for each another.

If two goods are complementary (goods that are used together), an increase in the price of one good will cause a decrease in the demand for the other.

EXAMPLES OF COMPLEMENTARY GOODS: Gasoline and automobile tires: As the price of gasoline goes up, the demand for automobile tires goes down since they are complementary goods. As the price of gasoline goes up, people will drive fewer miles and, therefore, need (or demand) fewer automobile tires. Other examples are tennis racquets and tennis balls and golf clubs and golf balls.

(d) *Buyers' expectations:* Individual expectations on the future of the market also have an impact on the demand for goods and services. An individual who expects future prices to increase is inclined to purchase now instead of paying the higher prices later. This leads to an increase in demand during the current period.

(e) *Population:* As the population increases, the total number of consumers increases. This results in an increase in demand.

(5) *Changes in demand and changes in quantity demanded:* Several factors affecting the demand for a good or service have been discussed. It is important to distinguish changes in quantity demanded from changes in demand. Changes in quantity demanded are changes in the amount of goods resulting from changes in price.

EXAMPLE: A movement from point A to point B on demand curve D1 in Figure 1–5 is an example of a change in quantity demanded. As the price goes down, the quantity demanded increases.

Changes in demand indicate changes in the quantity bought at all prices. A movement from one demand curve to another indicates a change in demand.

Figure 1–5 Shift in Demand

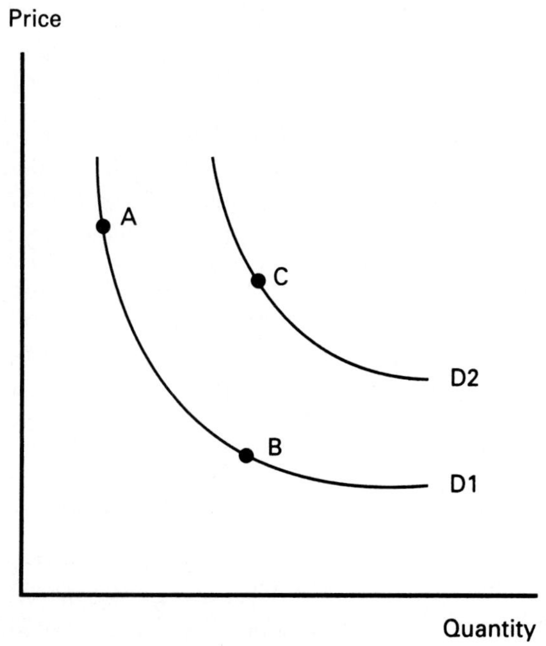

EXAMPLE: A movement from demand curve D1 to demand curve D2 in Figure 1–5 is an example of a change in demand. Changes in demand can be caused by changes in one of the determinants of demand: tastes and preferences, income, price of related goods, or expectations. A shift in demand for hamburger would result from the price of steaks increasing.

b. *The supply of goods and services:* The price system is also concerned with the supply of goods and services.

(1) *The law of supply:* The law of supply states that as price increases, the quantity of a good or a service produced by a business in a given period of time increases.

(2) *The supply curve of a firm:* Supply is defined as the maximum quantity of a good that a firm or supplier will make available at various prices over a certain period of time. Like demand, supply is a schedule of price–quantity relationships. Figure 1–6 represents a typical supply curve. The supply curve is upward sloping, whereas a demand curve is always downward sloping. The reason for the upward slope can be explained in this way. If a producer is to increase the quantity of a good or a service, the producer must receive a higher price. This is a result of increases in output requiring additional resources. If a firm needs additional resources in a competitive market, it will have to pay a higher price for those resources than the ones currently being used. (This relationship is also referred to as the *law of increasing costs.*)

EXAMPLE: In Figure 1–6 the supplier is willing to make 200 units (pairs of shoes) available at a price of $20 and 1,600 units (pairs of shoes) available

Figure 1–6 The Supply Curve of a Firm

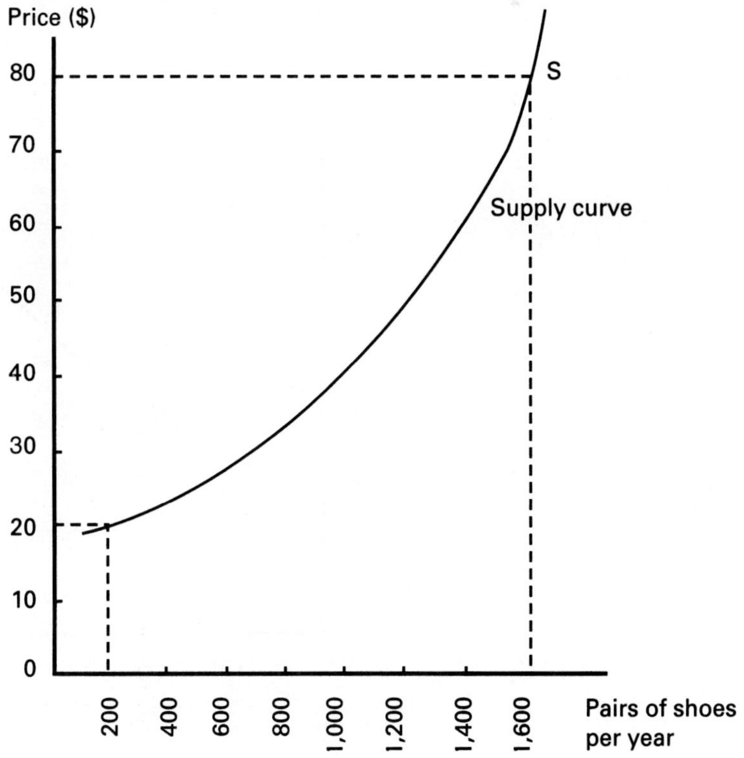

at a price of $80. The quantity made available is measured within a given time period, in this case, a year.

(3) *The market supply curve:* The total market supply curve of an industry is the horizontal summation of the supply curves of all the firms within the industry; that is, the number of units each firm is willing to make available at a given price is added to quantities other firms are willing to make available to arrive at the market supply. Figure 1–7 represents the market supply if 100 producers are in the industry, all facing identical costs.

EXAMPLE: Referring to Figure 1–7, at a price of $20, suppliers would make available 10,000 units in any given year. If the price were $40, there would be 110,000 units made available.

The process of developing the market supply curve is thus very similar to the process of developing the market demand curve.

(4) *Quantity supplied:* As price changes the quantity demanded, price also changes the quantity supplied. Changes in quantity supplied are movements along a supply curve, as in movement from point A to point B in Figure 1–7.

(5) *Changes in supply:* As other determinants cause a change in demand (a shift in the total curve), there are determinants that result in a shift in supply (a change in the quantity made available at all possible prices). The five determinants of supply are technology, resource prices, number of suppliers, price

Figure 1–7 The Market Supply Curve

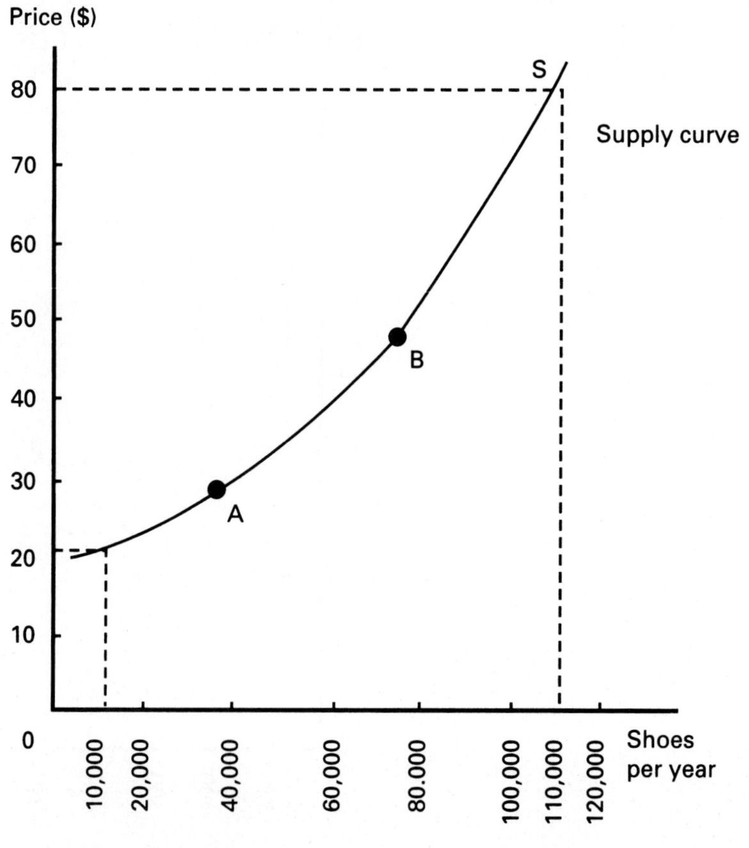

of related goods, and expectations. A change in one or more of the determinants will cause a shift in supply.

(a) *Technology:* Since technology affects the cost of production, it also affects supply. An improvement in technology suggests a more efficient means of production. Thus, producers can make more units available at lower prices. This would cause an increase in supply and shift the supply curve to the right, as shown in Figure 1–8 in the movement from supply curve S1 to supply curve S2.

(b) *Resource prices:* As the cost of resources used in production decreases, the supply of a certain number of goods can be made at a lower cost. This would result in an increase in supply, as shown in the move from S1 to S2 in Figure 1–8. The opposite, of course, would be true if a firm experienced an increase in resource costs.

(c) *Number of suppliers:* The number of firms in the market also affects the market supply of goods and services. As the number of producers of a good increases, the market supply would increase and vice versa.

(d) *Price of related goods:* As the price of related goods affects the demand curve, prices of related goods also affect the supply curve. If the price of related goods increases and the production of those goods appears more profitable, firms will reduce their supply of one good to increase the supply of the good whose price has increased.

EXAMPLE: This may be illustrated by the basic decision a farmer has to make each year concerning what crops to plant. If the market price of corn is high, corn is expected to be a profitable crop; the farmer would use a larger portion of land for corn and a smaller amount for beans for the following year. This would cause an increase in the supply for corn and a decrease in the supply for beans. If the market prices for corn

Figure 1–8 Shift in Supply

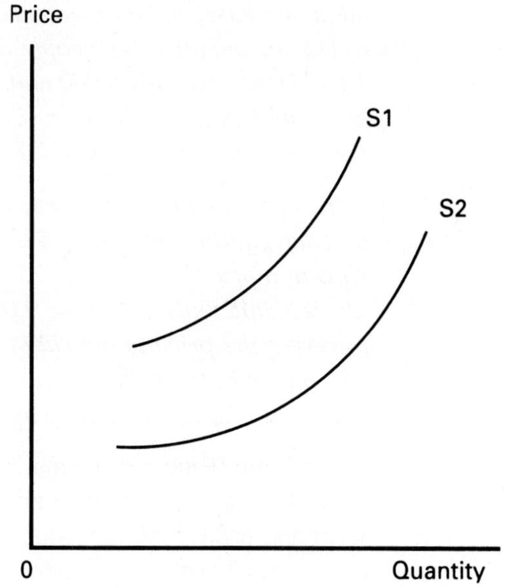

decreased, beans would become relatively more profitable, and the supply of beans would increase.

(e) *Expectations:* Similar to the role they play in determining demand, expectations play a role in determining supply. If prices are expected to rise, suppliers will attempt to supply less now in the hope that more can be supplied when prices increase, thus increasing profits.

c. *Elasticity:* An additional feature of demand and supply is elasticity. Elasticity measures the degree of responsiveness of buyers (sellers) to changes in the price of a commodity. If a small reduction in price results in a large change in the quantity bought (supplied), the demand (supply) is *elastic.* This means that the consumers (producers) are responsive to price changes.

EXAMPLE: The price of Crest toothpaste goes up. Since many brands of toothpaste are currently on the market, consumers will tend to switch to a lower-priced brand; thus, demand is fairly elastic.

If a large change in price results in a small change in quantity bought (supplied), the demand (supply) is *inelastic.* This means that the consumers (producers) are unresponsive to price changes.

EXAMPLE: If the price of salt increases, the amount of salt purchased would decline very little, thus an inelastic demand.

d. *Equilibrium:* A market is in equilibrium when all goods and services that consumers want to purchase at a given price are willingly supplied by producers. At this point both the suppliers and the demanders are satisfied. As long as the determinants of supply and demand are constant, there is a tendency for price and quantity demanded and supplied to remain at the same point. Changes in the determinants of demand and/or supply will stimulate market adjustments and bring the price toward a new equilibrium.

EXAMPLE: Figure 1–9 illustrates market equilibrium. At a price of $10, consumers are willing to purchase 8,000 units of the good, and producers are willing to make available 8,000 units. This equilibrium will be maintained unless the demand or supply changes. For example, if individual incomes increase, demand for the good might increase, and the demand curve would shift to D2. As the demand curve shifts to D2, the quantity that people would now buy at a price of $10 would increase to 10,000 units, but only 8,000 units would be made available by suppliers. This shortage would indicate to businesses that people were willing to pay a higher price, and the price would move toward the new equilibrium of $11 and a quantity of 9,000.

If the opposite had happened, similar results would take place. Suppose that the original equilibrium was at $11 and 9,000 and the demand declined from D2 to D. Now at a price of $11, only 7,000 units would be bought by consumers, and suppliers would make available 9,000. This surplus would be eliminated by suppliers lowering the price to get rid of excess inventory, and a new equilibrium price of $10 and quantity of 8,000 would be established. Similar effects can be traced by analyzing changes in supply and their impact on equilibrium price and quantity.

One unique feature of the market is that it will automatically adjust to an equilibrium. With private property and the freedom of consumers to purchase what they want and producers to produce what they want, price will provide the proper incentive for market adjustments to take place.

Figure 1–9 Market Equilibrium

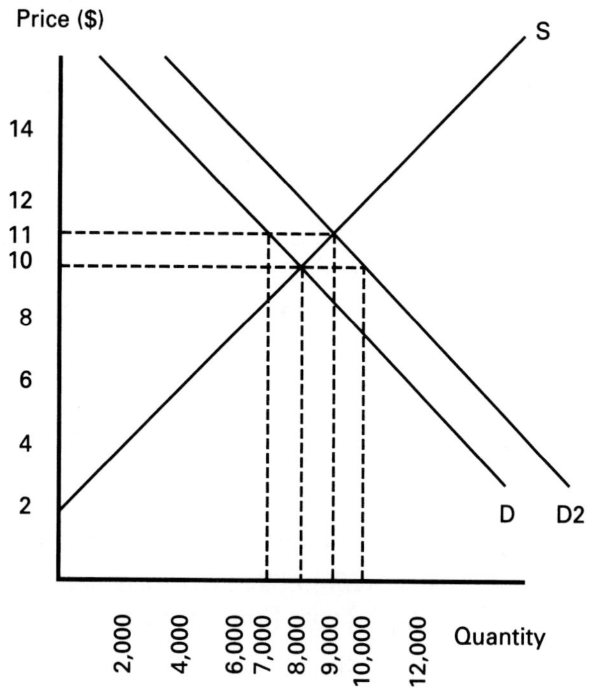

e. *Functions of prices:* Prices in an economic system have a variety of functions. One function is providing signals to consumers and producers that result in the clearing of the market. Another way of saying this is that prices allocate resources among alternative uses and ration goods and services.

(1) *The distribution function of prices:* Because society's wants exceed its scarce resources, there must be some way to ration the available goods and services. Price serves the rationing function by distributing goods to anyone capable of paying and willing to pay the market price. If a good becomes scarce, its price increases until the quantity demanded and the quantity supplied are equal. Thus, a price increase eliminates the shortage. Price adjustments are automatic and need no direction from government agencies or institutions.

(2) *The allocation function of prices:* Along with distributing goods and services, price also performs the function of allocating scarce resources. If one type of good is more valuable to society than another, consumers are willing to pay more for a given quantity of the more valued good. As consumers are willing to pay more for a more valued good, the profit for producing that good will increase. This is the signal to producers to use resources to produce more of that good relative to other goods. Therefore, producers seek to maximize profits by responding to the desires of consumers and to use productive resources in a way that fulfills societal wants. If the producer fails to heed consumer demand, competitive firms will meet this need; an unresponsive firm will lose money and be forced out of business. This allocation function of prices is what Adam Smith (the father of economics) referred to as "the invisible hand."

EXAMPLE: As a resource such as petroleum becomes scarce, its price increases relative to other forms of energy. As the price of petroleum increases, some users will find other forms of energy more economical to use. Therefore, the higher prices will provide an incentive to reallocate resource use from petroleum to other forms of energy.

3. *Types of Markets:* The discussion of markets would not be complete without a review of the types of markets within which producers operate.

a. *Competitive markets:* If a market economic system is to be effective, there must be competition among producers. Competition results in products being manufactured at the lowest possible price and in the most efficient manner. The equilibrium market price, determined by the intersection of supply and demand, not only determines the market price that a consumer must pay for a good or a service but also has an influence on the industry that produces the good. The industry that produces the good can be characterized as one that is competitive or that contains elements of monopoly power. For perfect competition to exist, several characteristics must be fulfilled:

(1) *Homogeneous products:* All producers within a market (industry) offer products that are identical; quality and other aspects of the good are all the same.

EXAMPLE: Grains produced by farmers are homogeneous products. Number 2 corn is number 2 corn, no matter what farmer happened to produce it.

Since all products are exactly the same, one interesting aspect of homogeneous products is that producers find it unnecessary to advertise their product. Therefore, advertising plays a very minor role. The only role advertising would play would be to inform consumers of the availability of a good or of the market for the good.

Brand-name products represent nonhomogeneous products since they are packaged differently. There can be an allegiance to the brand even though it is similar or identical to other products.

(2) *Many buyers and sellers:* Another characteristic of perfect competition is that there are many buyers and sellers. Many people want to buy the product, and many producers are making the product available for sale. *Many,* in this case, is defined as a sufficient number so that no one buyer or seller could have any impact on the market price for the good.

EXAMPLE: The market for grain is an industry that characterizes many buyers and sellers. Many farmers are producing grain, and any one farmer could substantially increase the amount of acreage of corn without affecting the market price. By the same token, there are many buyers of grain, and no one buyer can substantially affect the market for grain. With many buyers and sellers, no single producer or consumer can influence the market.

(3) *Freedom of entry and exit:* For a market to be competitive, there must be freedom of entry into and exit from the industry. Firms should be able to begin producing a given product at any time they see fit, and they should also be able to leave the industry at any point in time they see fit. There are three common barriers to a firm's freedom of entry and exit into an industry:

(a) *Restricted entry:* Existing firms or groups of firms may restrict entry to an industry. Historically, this has been the case where existing firms use cutthroat competition to prevent new firms from becoming established in the industry. Also, if one firm or a few firms have exclusive ownership of raw materials or patent rights, this exclusive ownership allows control of the flow of firms into the industry.

(b) *Government action:* Legislation often limits entry and exit by establishing rates, prices, and conditions of operation in many industries, including utilities, transportation, and communications. In addition, governments may require some type of accreditation or licensing before a firm can enter into an industry.

EXAMPLE: The government may require licensing to practice a particular occupation. Teachers, accountants, and other professionals must acquire some license to practice their professions. Requiring licenses allows a certain control over the market.

(c) *Mobility of resources:* Entry into an industry may require large cash outlay because of heavy fixed investments to initiate production. In the case of the steel industry and the automobile industry, the amount of cash necessary to begin the industry is substantial.

(4) *Sufficient information:* Buyers and sellers need sufficient information to enable them to make good judgments. This condition provides for complete information to be available on production, technology, and investment opportunities so that one firm does not have an advantage over another firm. All buyers and sellers would know the price and quality of goods that are available in the market.

EXAMPLE: The New York Stock Exchange, which records and distributes, almost instantly, prices and quantities of stocks sold.

In most markets this information is dispensed through advertising, which provides buyer and seller identity, reliability, price, terms of sale, overall quality, and so on. In perfect competition, however, there would be no persuasive advertising of the "ours is better than yours" variety. This would not be necessary because of product homogeneity.

Economists have set perfect competition as the ideal by which to judge the structure of industry. This is true because under perfect competition the producer of a product would have to accept the prevailing market price and produce as efficiently as other producers, or not make a profit. As a result, products would be made available at the lowest possible costs, and the price charged to the consumer would be equivalent to the cost of production for the producer. One cost of production is a normal rate of return (or normal profit) to the producer.

b. *Noncompetitive markets:* The term *noncompetitive* is used to describe those industries that do not fit the definition of the perfect competition model. Noncompetitive markets typically result because one of the conditions of perfect competition is not met, and the result is monopoly power.

Since the perfect competition model is used as the ideal by economists and most market systems, government attempts to ensure that the impact of noncompetitive markets on society is minimized. These actions include the passage of various laws to limit the amount of monopoly power that a firm can obtain. In the U.S.

economy this has been done through a series of antitrust laws and through government regulation of some industries. In noncompetitive markets, one or more of the following characteristics exist:

(1) *Concentration of buyers and sellers:* When noncompetitive markets exist, there is typically some concentration of buyers and sellers. This concentration is sufficient when buyers or sellers have some impact on the price of the good that they are buying or producing. If this is the case, the buyer or the seller will charge a higher price and provide a smaller quantity of the good for sale than if the market was competitive. In many instances, this will result in the producers earning a profit greater than the normal profit, thus making monopoly profits. In any case, the welfare of the buyer is reduced since the price will be higher and the product less available.

   EXAMPLE: In a town with only one grocery store, that store would have the ability to charge prices higher than the competitive level because of a lack of competition.

(2) *Product differentiation:* Product differentiation is an attempt to make consumers partial to a given product. Therefore, the producer is able to charge a slightly higher price for one product than for another product by packaging it differently or changing it slightly.

   EXAMPLES: Toothpaste, soft drinks, and other such commodities.

   Producers often package similar products differently or make small ingredient changes to develop brand loyalty. While the increase in selection made available to consumers may have some benefit, product differentiation also results in a slightly higher price than under conditions of perfect competition. Product differentiation also leads to promotional advertising rather than informational advertising described under perfect competition. The goal of promotional advertising is to create an image that a particular product is better than other similar products.

(3) *Lack of product information:* Under perfect competition, it is assumed that buyers and sellers have adequate information concerning price and quality of products in the market. In noncompetitive markets, buyers may lack information; therefore, producers are able to exploit this lack of information to avoid normal price competition. Thus, the firm operating in the nonperfect competitive market is able to exert greater control over the market than the competitive firm.

(4) *Barriers to entry:* In noncompetitive markets barriers to entry may exist. These entry barriers can be the result of the use of a variety of techniques:

   (a) *Cutthroat competition:* A firm using this technique cuts prices when a new firm enters the industry so that the new firm is unable to make a profit and is rapidly forced out of business.

   (b) *High entry cost:* A second barrier is high entry cost, which may prohibit firms from entering a particular industry. These costs could include high capital costs or high promotional costs of making a product known.

   (c) *Patents and other exclusive rights granted to products:* Although a patent protects a product developer against other people benefiting from the fruits of the developer's time and effort, it also gives a legal monopoly to the patent owner. A firm's exclusive right to all materials also precludes other firms from entering into the production of a good or a service.

(d) *Ownership of resources:* A firm's exclusive right to raw materials also precludes other firms from beginning production of a good or a service.

EXAMPLE: At one point, Alcoa owned rights to all bauxite deposits in the world. Since bauxite is necessary for the production of aluminum, Alcoa had a monopoly in the production of aluminum.

c. *Types of noncompetitive markets:* The three basic types of noncompetitive markets are monopoly, oligopoly, and monopolistic competition.

(1) *Monopoly:* A market consisting of only one producer of a product with no competition is known as a monopoly. Since there is only one firm in the industry, the industry and the monopolist are one and the same. In the United States the only pure monopolies are those created by government, which we refer to as natural monopolies (local electric companies, local telephone companies, and other types of utilities). Where these natural monopolies exist, a regulatory commission is usually established to control the price rate charged.

(2) *Oligopoly:* In an oligopoly a few sellers control the majority of the market. A balanced oligopoly is characterized by several firms, all with equal market power. An unbalanced oligopoly consists of one or two firms with substantial power.

EXAMPLES IN THE UNITED STATES: Automobiles (balanced), breakfast cereals (unbalanced), cigarettes (balanced), and appliances (balanced).

With only a few producers in the market, it is easy for these firms to charge a slightly higher price and earn a higher profit than would be charged in a competitive situation.

(3) *Monopolistic competition:* In monopolistic competition there are many producers, but each firm has a slight degree of monopoly power because its product is slightly different from other products in its group. (Product difference may be in the service that is offered.) While the perfectly competitive firm must accept the market price for a good, a monopolistically competitive firm may be able to charge slightly above the market price because it has slightly differentiated its product.

EXAMPLES: Toothpaste, soft drinks, and soaps.

Review Questions

Directions: Select the best answer from the four alternatives. Write your answer in the blank to the left of the number.

_______________ **1.** The distinguishing characteristic of an economic good is that

a. it is scarce.
b. it is sold in the marketplace.
c. it possesses utility.
d. the consumer derives utility from owning it.

_______________ **2.** The law of demand implies that people would

a. never choose work over leisure.
b. buy less gas if the gasoline tax were raised 6 cents.
c. buy as much milk at 90 cents per half gallon as at 75 cents per half gallon.
d. eat more beef if the price of beef were increased.

_______________ **3.** Which of the following statements is consistent with the law of demand?

a. Farmers produce fewer bushels of wheat because the price of wheat has recently increased.
b. A politician votes against a proposal because most constituents oppose it.
c. More students attend lectures in an introductory economics class because attendance counts 20 percent of the grade.
d. People drive less because of higher gas prices.

_______________ **4.** Goods are

a. scarce for the poor but not for the rich.
b. scarce neither for the poor nor for the rich.
c. scarcer for the poor than for the rich.
d. scarce for both poor and rich.

_______________ **5.** Scarcity means that

a. human desires will never be satisfied.
b. human desire for a good is greater than the amount that is freely available.
c. temporarily, some good is in short supply.
d. humans have failed to achieve a basic standard of living.

_______________ **6.** Which of the following is not a basic question faced by each economy?

a. What goods are subject to the law of demand?
b. What will be produced?
c. To whom will the goods that are produced be allocated?
d. How will the goods be produced?

______________ **7.** Which of the following factors would not affect the supply of computers?

a. Higher wage rates for workers in the electronics industry
b. Higher prices for resources used to produce computers
c. Technological improvement reducing the cost of production of computers
d. Increase in consumer income

______________ **8.** Which of the following was not a result of the higher prices of gasoline and petroleum-derived products in early 1974?

a. The demand for small cars expanded.
b. The incentive to use solar heating units increased.
c. The demand for used Cadillac and Lincoln Continental automobiles increased.
d. Tourism in Florida declined relative to that in 1973.

______________ **9.** Criteria for rationing goods and resources must be established because of

a. the law of comparative advantage.
b. capitalist economic organizations.
c. the scarcity imposed by nature.
d. the inability of political entrepreneurs to develop efficient forms of economic organizations.

______________ **10.** The law of demand refers to

a. the phenomenon that prices decrease as more units of a product are demanded and more are produced.
b. the increase in price that results from an increase in demand.
c. the inverse relationship between the price of a good and the quantity of the good demanded.
d. the increase in the quantity of a good available as the price of the good increases.

______________ **11.** Profit can be defined as

a. the difference between the revenue derived from the sale of a product and the opportunity cost of employing the resources required to produce the product.
b. the difference between the income and disbursements of a firm.
c. the difference between the price of a product and the cost of the raw materials used to produce it.
d. the total compensation received by the firm's owners.

______________ **12.** According to the law of supply,

a. more of a good is supplied as the price of the resources rise.
b. there is a positive relationship between the price of a good and the amount that buyers choose to purchase.
c. there is a positive relationship between the price of a good and the amount of it offered for sale by suppliers.
d. there is a negative relationship between the price of a good and the amount of it purchased by suppliers.

_______________ **13.** Technological advancements in the production of computer products will cause

a. the supply curve for computer products to shift to the right.
b. the supply curve for computer products to shift to the left.
c. the quantity supplied to increase along the existing supply curve.
d. little change since the computer industry is controlled by a few corporations.

_______________ **14.** When a shortage of a good exists,

a. the amount demanded is greater than the amount supplied at all prices except the existing price.
b. price must be controlled to avoid the need for rationing.
c. only an increase in production will eliminate the shortage.
d. if the price is not permitted to rise, nonprice factors, such as quality deterioration, will play more of a role in the allocation process.

_______________ **15.** Under competitive conditions, market prices

a. are always in long-run equilibrium.
b. can be determined only after a detailed study of supply and demand conditions has been made.
c. are incapable of coordinating the actions of buyers and sellers.
d. generally bring the self-interest of individual consumers and producers into harmony with the general welfare (economic efficiency).

_______________ **16.** Which of the following exists in a market in which producers have monopoly power?

a. Free entry and exit
b. Product differentiation
c. Large numbers of buyers and sellers
d. Complete information

_______________ **17.** Fisher said, "If I didn't have a date tonight, I would save $20 and spend this evening playing chess." The opportunity cost of the date is

a. $20.
b. $20 plus the cost of forgoing a night playing chess.
c. dependent on how pleasant a time one has on the date.
d. the cost of forgoing a night playing chess.

_______________ **18.** A new hospital is being built in your home town. The opportunity cost of building the new hospital would be

a. the money cost of constructing the hospital.
b. the highest-valued bundle of other goods and services that might be forgone because of the hospital construction.
c. the necessary increase in tax revenues to finance the construction.
d. increased if the money cost of building the hospital decreases.

_______________ **19.** In this diagram, point A is

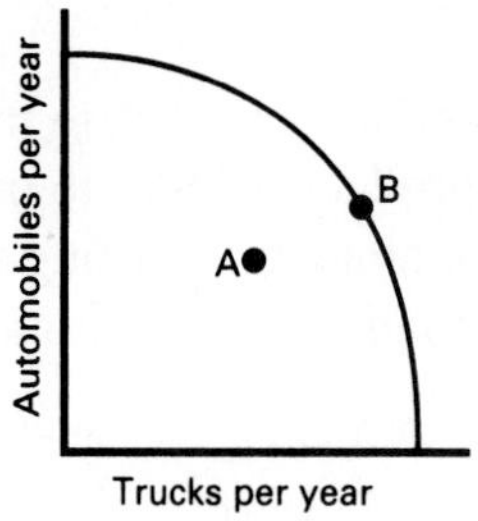

a. unattainable.
b. inefficient.
c. efficient.
d. preferred to point B.

_______________ **20.** Which of the following conditions would be most likely to cause the production possibility curve for corn and beans to shift from AA to BB?

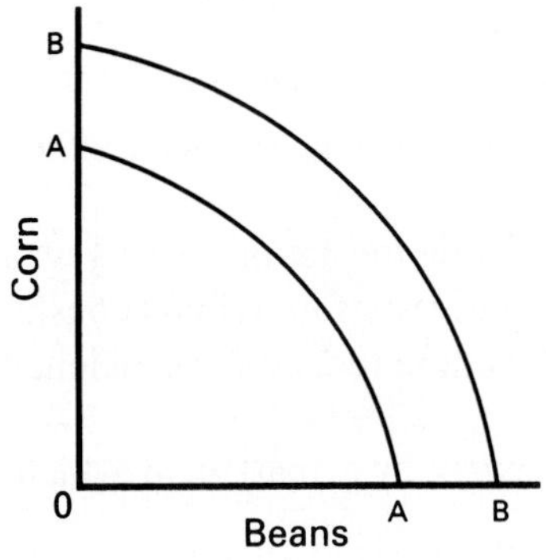

a. Reducing the labor force
b. Choosing more corn and less beans
c. Choosing more beans and less corn
d. Increasing the capital used to produce corn and beans

_______________ **21.** Based on the graph below, if the current price of beef was \$4 per pound, which of the following conditions would be accurate?

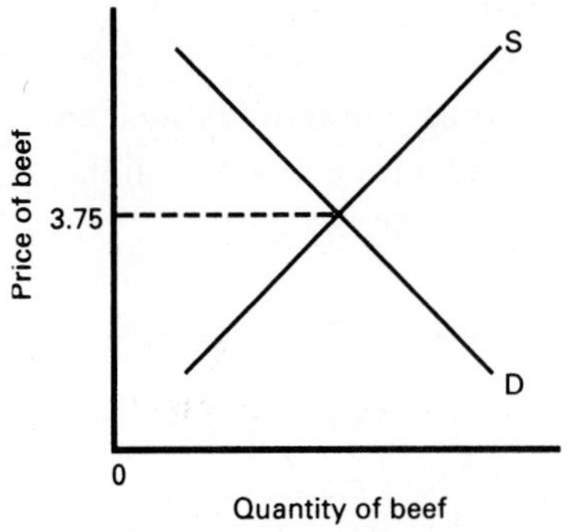

a. Producers would want to supply more beef than consumers would wish to buy.
b. Producers would be supplying less than the equilibrium quantity of beef.
c. Equilibrium could be reached only if demand increased.
d. The price of beef would have to rise to establish equilibrium.

Solutions

Answer	*Refer to:*
1. (a)	[A-1] The concept of scarcity is derived from the idea that individuals and societies have unlimited wants and limited resources.
2. (b)	[C-2-a] The law of demand states that as price increases, individuals will buy less of a good or a service.
3. (d)	[C-2-a] As the price of gas increases, people will buy less gas and travel less if possible.
4. (d)	[A-1] Scarcity of goods affects everyone, rich or poor.
5. (b)	[A-1-a] Scarcity of goods means that there is more demand than supply.
6. (a)	[A-2-c] What to produce, for whom to produce, and how to produce are the three basic questions an economic system must answer.
7. (d)	[C-2-b] Answers (a), (b), and (c) all affect the supply, while answer (d) affects the demand.
8. (c)	[C-2-b] Answers (a), (b), and (d) all describe the proper relationship between substitute goods: As price increases, demand for substitutes will increase. The demand for cars with low mileage per gallon of gas decreased at that time.
9. (c)	[C-2-e(1)] Society's wants exceed its scarce resources. Therefore, there must be a way to ration available goods and services.
10. (c)	[C-2-a(1)] The law of demand states that as price decreases, individuals will buy more of a good or a service, and as price increases, individuals will buy less of a good or a service.
11. (a)	[C-2-b] Answers (b) and (c) refer only to explicit costs and do not take into consideration opportunity costs. Answer (d) refers to cost only.
12. (c)	[C-1-b] The law of supply states that as price increases, the individual or firm will be willing to sell a greater quantity of goods and services.
13. (a)	[C-2-b] Improvements in computer technology suggest more efficient production and possibly lower prices. This would cause an increase in supply and shift the supply curve to the right.
14. (d)	[C-2-e] Price also performs the function of allocating scarce resources.
15. (d)	[C-3-a] Competition results in products being manufactured at the lowest possible price and in the most efficient manner.

16. (b) [C-3] Answers (a), (c), and (d) are requirements of perfect competition and would not be present if monopoly power were present.

17. (b) [A-2-b] Opportunity cost is the value of the opportunity forgone when a decision is made. In this case, one would spend $20 on the date and forgo a night of chess.

18. (b) [A-2-a, b] Opportunity cost is the value of the opportunity forgone when a decision is made. The opportunity cost of building the hospital would be the value of any goods or services that will not be offered because of the new construction.

19. (b) [A-2-a] Point A is inside the curve. Therefore, not all the resources available are being used efficiently. Output of one product can be increased without increasing the output of the other product.

20. (d) [A-2-a] Once a specific point on the production possibility curve is achieved, more capital must be invested to get more output.

21. (a) [C-2-c] Producers are responsive to price changes. As the price increases, producers may want to produce more, but consumers might not be willing to purchase more at the increased price.

CHAPTER 2

National Income and Its Determinants

OVERVIEW

From an economist's standpoint, the study of national income and its determinants has a variety of implications. National income and its determinants allow us to take a look at the economy, analyze the growth that has taken place in past years, identify weaknesses or strengths in our economy that will lead to future growth or recession, and identify the impact of changes in economic policy by either the federal government or monetary authorities.

In this chapter we will develop measures for economic performance and discuss policy issues, such as unemployment and inflation. The solutions to these policy issues will be analyzed, and the role of fiscal and monetary policy will be discussed.

KEY TERMS

- Aggregate demand (aggregate expenditures)
- Aggregate supply
- Average propensity to consume (APC)
- Built-in stabilizers
- Capital consumption allowance
- Ceteris paribus
- Classical school of economics
- Consumer price index (CPI)
- Consumption
- Cost-push inflation
- Cyclical unemployment
- Demand-pull inflation (inflationary gap)
- Disposable personal income (DPI)
- Economic growth
- Factors of production
- Fiscal policy
- Frictional unemployment
- GDP implicit price deflator index
- Gross domestic product (GDP)
- Inflation
- Investment
- Keynesian economics
- Marginal propensity to consume (MPC)
- Marginal tax rate
- Monetary policy
- National income
- Net national product (NNP)
- Output per capita
- Personal income (PI)
- Producer price index (PPI)
- Production possibility curve (PPC)
- Real income (purchasing power)
- Structural unemployment
- Supply-side economics
- Technological unemployment
- Transfer payments

A. Economic Growth

Economic growth is an increase in the per capita output of an economy. Economic growth involves both benefits and costs to a society. Although the concept has been challenged in recent years, economic growth is essential if society is to experience increased capacity to produce and to consume goods and services. National income measures whether economic growth has taken place. The average rate of growth in the United States was extremely high, by most measures, until the mid to late 1970s but slowed substantially from then until the early 1990s. Since then, the growth rate has been close to its historical average of 3 to 4 percent annually.

1. *Maintaining Economic Growth:* To maintain economic growth, a society must be able to increase the availability of goods and services to individuals within that society. A system of national income accounting has been devised to provide a yardstick for measuring economic growth. For a society to have continued economic growth, however, it is necessary from time to time to investigate those factors that control economic activity to stimulate economic growth.

a. *Factors controlling economic activity:*

(1) *Production:* The transformation of resources within the society into goods and services is the process of production.

(2) *Income:* Income is the flow of net production of goods and services over a period of time (e.g., a year).

EXAMPLES: Basic income concepts used to measure economic well-being are:

Gross domestic product (GDP)

Net national product (NNP)

National income (NI)

Personal income (PI)

Disposable personal income (DPI)

(3) *Wealth:* The net assets on hand at any given point in time are considered the wealth of an economy. If an economy is not growing at the desired rate, policy can be implemented to affect wealth and to move the economy toward its production possibility curve rather than operating at less than full employment or with high rates of inflation.

b. *Other factors affecting the level of economic activity:* The level of gross domestic product and other economic variables is affected by the level of employment and the level of inflation within our society. These variables in turn affect the level of consumption, level of investment, and level of government activity necessary for society to operate at its full-employment equilibrium. If society is not functioning efficiently, then resources remain unused and/or inflation is at an undesirable rate. The levels of consumption, investment, and government spending can affect the level at which the economy is operating and the level of employment and inflation.

c. *The need for consistent economic policy:* For society to grow, there must be an economic policy consistent with the growth rate of gross domestic product, the rate of unemployment existing within society, and the rate of inflation within society.

(1) *The classical school of economic theory:* The first writings by economists (commonly referred to as the *classical school*) developed a philosophy wherein any fluctuations in the economy would be self-correcting. These economists included Adam Smith, David Ricardo, and Alfred Marshall, among others. They believed that if inflation was at a higher rate than desir-

able, the real value of wages would decline, leading to declines in demand for goods and services. Therefore, a reduction of pressure on prices occurred. Conversely, if the rate of unemployment became higher than desirable, individuals would offer their services for less than the existing market wage. The reduction in the market wage would cause an increase in the number of people employed and reduce unemployment.

(2) *Keynesian economic theory:* In the mid-1930s a new philosophy of economics was developed that did not rely on market self-adjusting mechanisms to achieve economic stability. John Maynard Keynes, a British economist, developed the concept of employment theory relying on government to take an active step in the economic stabilization of a country.

(3) *Supply-side economic theory:* In the 1970s and early 1980s, Keynes's assumptions were challenged. A new school of thought, referred to as *supply-side economics,* emerged. Supply-side economics gives consideration not only to affecting the aggregate *demand* for goods and services but also to those factors affecting aggregate *supply* of goods and services. The supply-side economist argues that we should rely more on natural market mechanisms and provide sufficient incentives for these market mechanisms to solve societal problems of unemployment, inflation, and economic growth.

2. *Measuring Economic Growth:* Economic growth may be based on changes in the standard of living, output per capita, real income, or gross domestic product of individuals within a society.

a. *Standard of living as a measure of economic growth:* Historically, standard of living has been measured by the per capita consumption of individuals within society, the literacy rate of society, and measures of other types of amenities available to people in the society.

b. *Output per capita as a measure of economic growth:* In terms of pure economic growth, societies tend to look at the *output per capita* (society's output divided by its population) as a measure of the standard of living in society.

(1) If output per capita of a country increases, then economic growth is taking place.

(2) If output per capita declines or remains constant, then there is either a declining rate of growth or a zero rate of growth, respectively.

c. *Real income as a measure of economic growth: Real income* is income measured in constant dollars. The primary drawback is that there is no reference to the distribution of income within the society. Thus, a society can be extremely wealthy on a per capita basis, but wealth is actually held by only a small percentage of the population, while the standard of living for the general population may not be very high.

d. *Total aggregate output or gross domestic product as a measure of economic growth:* The basic yardstick for measuring economic growth is gross domestic product (GDP), which is the market value of the nation's total output of new final goods and services within a period of time, usually one year. Although this measure for economic growth does not take into consideration all aspects of the economy and, therefore, does not indicate the welfare of a society, GDP does give an indication of the direction in which a society is advancing. This type of measurement does not identify how much output is available per person or the distribution of the output among individuals in society.

3. *Economic Growth and Economic Welfare:* It is important to distinguish between economic growth and increases in economic welfare. When we use increases in output per capita or some other measure of GDP to indicate that economic growth has taken place, this says nothing about the types of goods and services that are being produced or the possible negative aspects of experiencing economic growth.

a. *Effects of increased production output:* As economic growth takes place, society tends to use scarce resources at a more rapid rate. Thus, increased production can have a negative result.

EXAMPLES: As production increases, pollution increases.

Increases in production may cause increases in urbanization, which may lead to increases in crime.

b. *Net economic welfare as an indication of economic growth:* Instead of using GDP to indicate economic growth, some economists have proposed using a net economic welfare measure. This net measure would subtract the increased cost of pollution, crime, and so on from the GDP to arrive at a net economic welfare.

4. *Factors Affecting Economic Growth:* For economic growth to occur, there must be net production of goods and services over a period of time, typically a year. *Net production* refers to the fact that, in production, resources must be used up. For *growth* to take place, the value of the goods and services produced must exceed the value of the resources used up in the production process. This may be accomplished by increased efficiency or by advances in the level of technology. In measuring economic growth, it is necessary to distinguish between net production from a *dollar* standpoint and net production from a *real goods and services* standpoint.

EXAMPLE: If GDP is used to measure the economic growth of a country, an increase in GDP this year over last year does not necessarily indicate whether the increase in GDP is attributed to (1) an increase in the quantity of goods and services produced, (2) an increase in the price level, or (3) a combination of these two.

To measure the impact of increases in prices, a series of price indices has been developed so that we can subtract the impact of price increases on GDP. Real growth takes place only when real income changes over time.

a. *Effects of factors of production on growth:* The growth of society over time is affected by the factors of production: land, labor, capital, and entrepreneurial ability. As these factors of production are used more efficiently, more output can be produced for the same quantity of resources.

(1) *Land:* The more productive land a country possesses and the more resources the land contains, the more rapidly that country can grow over time.

(2) *Labor:* The size and composition of the labor force also has a strong impact on the growth of a country over a period of time.

(a) Size of the labor force simply accounts for increases in the number of people who work or are willing to work at prevailing wages in the production process.

(b) Quality of the labor force is another important factor. As the average education of the labor force increases, the labor force typically becomes more productive and adds to the potential growth rates for a country.

(c) If the age distribution of the population moves toward a higher percentage in the prime working years, the output of that society will be greater.

(d) As the average hours of work per week change, the output of a society will be affected.

(e) The degree of specialization of the labor force will also affect the total production.

(3) *Capital:* The capital stock of a country includes resources such as buildings, equipment, and assets other than money that are used in the production process. If the capital stock of a country is large relative to other countries, that country will possess a greater ability to grow since it has greater productive capacity.

(4) *Entrepreneurial ability:* The unique talents individuals have of combining resources to produce goods or services more efficiently than other individuals is called *entrepreneurial ability.* The human resources needed to manage the development of new goods and services, continue to expand output, and accept the risks of business ownership are very important parts of the production process.

b. *Effects of other factors on growth:* Economic growth is also affected by such factors as technology and the sociopolitical framework of the country.

(1) A country's level of technology influences methods of production and the applicability of scientific principles utilized in the production process. As technology enables production to increase, efficiency typically increases, and economic growth takes place.

(2) The sociopolitical framework of the country provides the economic incentives within that country for growth to take place. If society provides incentives for businesses to invest and to increase capital stock, a foundation for future economic growth is developed.

B. National Income Measurement

National income accounting provides the system for measuring production, income, and wealth of a society (refer to Section A-1-a for definitions of the terms *production, income,* and *wealth*). As a result, fluctuations in economic activity can be monitored, and, if necessary, growth can be stimulated. The concepts of income and wealth are interrelated since both real wealth and real income result from production. The exception to this is natural wealth, which includes land, mineral deposits, lumber, and other resources taken from the land.

1. *Measuring Economic Variables:* Income and production may be measured using a variety of yardsticks: gross domestic product (GDP), net national product (NNP), national income (NI), personal income (PI), and disposable personal income (DPI). Figure 2–1 provides national income accounts for the United States for the year 1997.

a. *Gross domestic product (GDP):* GDP is the broadest concept of national income accounting and represents the aggregate money value, at market prices, of all the final goods and services produced within an economy in a given year. The use of final goods and services rules out double counting of values. If a good was counted both in the intermediate stages of production and at the time it was purchased for

Figure 2–1 Summary of National Income Accounts for 1997 (in Billions of Current Dollars)

Gross domestic product (GDP)	$	8,103
− Capital consumption allowance	−	872
= Net national product (NNP)	$	7,231
− Indirect business taxes	−	627
− Business transfer payments	−	35
+ Statistical discrepancy	+	56
+ Subsidies less current surplus of government enterprises	+	22
= National income	$	6,647
− Corporate profits	−	818
− Net interest	−	432
− Contributions to social security	−	724
+ Government transfer payments	+	1,083
+ Personal interest income	+	747
+ Personal dividend income	+	260
+ Business transfer payments	+	26
= Personal income	$	6,789
− Personal taxes	−	989
= Disposable personal income	$	5,800
− Personal outlays	−	5,674
= Personal savings	$	126

consumption, the value of net production would be exaggerated. GDP includes only market transactions.

(1) *Inclusion of government expenditures:* GDP includes all government expenditures except transfer payments. Transfer payments are disbursements from government or private firms for which no products or services are received in exchange.

EXAMPLES OF TRANSFER PAYMENTS: Social security payments, unemployment compensation, and government welfare programs.

(2) *Exclusion of nonmarket transactions:* Although GDP is a measure of all final goods and services produced for sale within a year, certain items are omitted. Nonmarket transactions, such as the value of a homemaker's services, the value of criminal activity, and the value of family production, are not included in the GDP of a country.

Note: Moreover, these figures are not counted in any of the national income accounting figures discussed below.

b. *Net national product (NNP):* Not all of a country's output within a given period of time is a net increase in output. Part of the output is used to replace the capital goods that were used during the production of other goods and services. These are called capital consumption allowances.

$$\text{net national product} = \text{gross domestic product} - \text{capital consumption allowances (depreciation)}$$

Net national product gives us a measure of the value of the goods and services available for consumption during a given time period.

c. *National income (NI):* Where GDP and NNP measure the value of the goods and services produced within an economy within a given period of time, national income (NI) measures the sum of payments to the factors of production that resulted from production that occurred. Each of the four factors of production (land, labor, capital, and entrepreneurial ability) has its own return: returns, wages, interest, and profit, respectively.

$$\text{national income} = \text{net national product} - \text{indirect business taxes}$$

EXAMPLES OF INDIRECT BUSINESS TAXES: Sales taxes and excise taxes.

d. *Personal income (PI):* Not all income paid for the factors of production is retained by households in the form of personal income. The amount of income available to households is the national income minus earnings of factors of production that households do not receive from employers (e.g., corporate profits, corporate social security contributions, and corporate net interest). In addition, transfer payments and nonlabor income must be added to the national income figure to get personal income. Transfer payments are not direct payments to the factors of production but are transfers of income from the government and business to households. Transfer payments include unemployment compensation, welfare payments, and farm subsidy payments. Nonlabor income would include interest, dividend, and business transfer payments.

e. *Disposable personal income (DPI):* Not all national income is available to households, and not all income available to households can be used for consumption or saving. From personal income, one must deduct payment of personal income taxes, personal property taxes, and inheritance taxes to get disposable personal income. DPI is the amount that people have available to buy consumer goods, to save, and to pay interest. In the United States, approximately 93 percent of DPI is spent on consumption and interest, and about 6 to 8 percent goes into personal savings.

2. *Real versus Nominal Measures:* GDP, defined as the total value of all final goods and services produced within a society within a year, can also be explained using the following equation:

$$\text{GDP} = \Sigma\, P_i Q_i$$

where P is the price of a good and Q is the quantity.

This means that GDP equals the sum (Σ) of the value of all goods, or the price of a good times the quantity of goods, for all goods and services produced.

a. *Reasons for change in GDP:* GDP may change in the following circumstances:

(1) The quantity of goods and services increases (real increases in GDP).

(2) The price of goods and services increases (nominal increases in GDP).

To separate the impact of increases in GDP from these real and nominal phenomena, we use a measure of changes in the value of the dollar and deflate the GDP figures by the price index. To deflate GDP, the ratio of the price index of the base year to the price index of the year in question is computed and then the GDP (in money) is multiplied by that ratio.

EXAMPLE: If prices in 1989 were 100 and prices in l998 were 120, the 1998 GDP must be multiplied by 100/l20 to get the real output of 1998 in terms of 1989 dollars.

b. *Basic price indices used in United States:* The basic price indices used are the consumer price index, the producers price index, and the GDP implicit price deflator index.

(1) *Consumer price index (CPI):* The consumer price index compares the costs of a given market basket (a sampling) of goods and services at different points in time. The CPI is based on the food, housing, recreation, clothing, and other expenditures made by a typical suburban family. The cost of buying these items is calculated on a monthly basis, and the index is figured from these calculations. The CPI is the most common price index.

(2) *Producers price index (PPI):* The PPI is the calculation of the cost of goods at the producer level versus the retail level used for the CPI. The PPI is often used as an indicator for increases in the CPI for the future.

(3) *GDP implicit price deflator index:* The GDP implicit price deflator index is computed only once a year using the prices of all goods and services produced in the United States. This index gives the most accurate measure of increases in prices and is the most comprehensive index used. This index excludes prices of imports, whereas the consumer price index (CPI) and producers price index (PPI) do not.

C. Signposts for Economic Conditions

Gross domestic product and other measures of the state of the economy fluctuate from month to month and from year to year. While GDP gives a measure of the output of society, other measures help analyze how the economy is operating with respect to its efficiency and ability to meet consumer needs. These other measures include unemployment and inflation.

1. *Unemployment:* Unemployment is the result of an economic system operating below its maximum level of activity. To be unemployed, one must be a member of the labor force, that is, a person who is willing and able to work in a productive activity. This excludes people who are old and infirm, children under legal working age, students, and people who work without pay, such as volunteer workers, and who are not considered part of the labor force. Unemployment can be classified into four types:

a. *Cyclical unemployment:* Cyclical unemployment exists when people who are willing and able to work at prevailing wage rates do not have jobs and whose unemployment is not explained by one of the other types explained here.

b. *Frictional unemployment:* Frictional unemployment results when people are caught between jobs or are looking for their first job. This type of unemployment is a healthy sign for society since it indicates that people are moving up. Changing jobs typically means increasing one's status within a profession. A frictional unemployment rate of about 1 percent is considered normal for society.

c. *Technological unemployment:* Technological unemployment is typical of an industrialized society in which people are displaced temporarily as a result of technological advance. Technological unemployment ranges from 2 to 3 percent in the United States.

d. *Structural unemployment:* Structural unemployment (often referred to as "hard-core" unemployment) is the result of changes in consumer tastes and preferences and changes in types of labor needed. This type of unemployment is the most difficult since it usually means that retraining of workers is necessary. Government policies to affect the level of economic activity will not often change structural unemployment. Historically, programs to retrain workers have been a basic corrective measure for structural unemployment.

Given these four types of unemployment, economists have often assumed that a 4 percent unemployment rate is a "full employment level" of activity. The 4 percent would include an acceptable level of frictional, technological, and structural unemployment. Since the late 1960s the unemployment rate in the United States has typically averaged above the 4 percent level. This is the result of a variety of circumstances. Foremost is the increase in the number of women in the workforce. As the number of families with two working members increases, the rate of frictional, technological, and structural unemployment may increase somewhat. In the 1980s many economists argued that a 6 or 7 percent unemployment rate should be considered a full employment rate. However, the economy of the 1990s has reestablished the 4 percent unemployment rate as the benchmark for full employment.

2. *Inflation:* Inflation is the increase in prices of goods and services. Historically, inflation has been the greatest problem when a society is producing at or near full employment. Inflation can be discouraged by reducing the demand for goods and services or by increasing the amount of goods and services supplied by the business sector.

a. *Effects of inflation on the economy:* Inflation has adverse effects on different sectors of the economy. It is believed that debtors benefit from inflation. As inflation takes place, the purchasing power of a dollar declines. Debtors would be paying off loans made now with dollars that will have lower purchasing power in the future. People on fixed incomes are often hurt by inflation. An individual with a fixed income has no way to protect against inflation. Similarly, creditors are hurt by inflation since they are being repaid in less valuable dollars.

b. *Types of inflation:* The two types of inflation are demand-pull inflation and cost-push inflation.

(1) *Demand-pull inflation:* The classical version of inflation is demand-pull inflation, caused by excessive aggregate demand. It is often expressed as "too much money chasing too few goods."

(2) *Cost-push (or seller's) inflation:* Cost-push inflation is caused by increases in the cost of factors of production, resulting in reductions of aggregate supply and, therefore, increases in prices. One common cause of cost-push inflation is the increase in wages in excess of labor productivity.

EXAMPLE: In the 1980s there were major advances in health care technology. The new technology improved medical care but used expensive technology. This led to cost-push inflation in society.

The impact of both types of inflation on society is the same. However, the cures for the inflation differ, depending on the type of inflation. If the inflation is demand-pull, the proper cure is to decrease the demand for goods and services. This could be done by increased taxation, reduction in government spending, or other measures that would affect the demand for goods and services. If the inflation type is cost-push, the solutions have to come as a result of increasing the productive capacity of the economy.

D. Determinants of National Income

The level of national income for the economy is determined by demand for goods and services within the economic system. This aggregate demand for goods and services is dependent on the levels of consumption by households, investment by businesses, spending by government, and the level of net exports. Each of these factors has an impact on national income through aggregate demand.

For an economy to be in equilibrium, the level of aggregate demand must be equal to the level of aggregate supply. Aggregate supply is the quantity of goods and services that a society can make available within a specific period of time. Aggregate supply is determined by the productivity of labor, the amount and quality of land available, technology, and the stock of capital that a country has available for use.

1. *Aggregate Demand:* In a market-oriented economic system, the activities within a society are carried out through the interaction of households and business, with some activities by government. This interaction of households and business generates demand for goods and services that results in expenditures for resources and consumption of goods and services. Changes in the level of these aggregate expenditures by households, business, government, and foreign countries have an impact on the total demand for goods and services for society and on the expenditures for goods and services made by each unit.

a. *Consumption:* Consumption is the expenditure incurred by households for final goods and services that yield direct satisfaction to consumers. Household consumption is the most stable of the various components of aggregate expenditures. The level of household expenditures (or consumption expenditures) is determined by several factors that influence individual decision making.

(1) *Stock of goods owned:* The existing stock of goods owned by consumers affects future consumption. The larger the stock of goods, *ceteris paribus* (all other things remaining equal), the smaller is the amount of consumption that will take place in the near future.

(2) *Rate of interest:* The rate of interest may have an impact on the rate of consumption. If the interest rate is high, people who are saving for a desired goal in the future will have to save fewer dollars to reach that goal. With high interest rates, the rate of return on investments will be greater, and people can reach their goals by saving less money. With this reduction in the rate of savings, there is an increase in the amount of money available for consumption. It is also true that with a higher interest rate, saving becomes more attractive. Therefore, an increase in the incentive to save exists. It is unclear which of these influences is stronger. Thus, it is difficult to predict the impact that the interest rate has on consumption. In our society it appears that consumption increases as interest rates remain high.

(3) *Level of taxes:* Individuals can dispose of their income in basically three ways:

(a) Consume goods and services

(b) Save (postponed consumption)

(c) Pay taxes

As the level of taxes individuals are required to pay increases, the money available for saving and consumption decreases. There is an inverse relationship between tax rates and consumption. The rate of taxation is a variable that can be controlled by the government, and changing the level of taxation to affect the level of consumption is one type of fiscal policy.

(4) *Level of personal income:* The major determinant of consumption expenditures is the level of personal income. As personal income increases, individuals will increase their purchases of goods and services, and increases in the level of consumption expenditures will occur. Most individuals, however, will not increase their level of consumption by the total amount of their increase in income.

EXAMPLE: If an individual's income increases by $1,000 per year, this will not necessarily lead to a $1,000 increase in consumption expenditures. Part of the $1,000 increase will be saved for future consumption.

The ratio of increases in consumption expenditures to increases in disposable income is referred to as the marginal propensity to consume (MPC). The marginal propensity to consume is the change in consumption resulting from a given change in disposable income.

EXAMPLE: If an individual's personal income (PI) increases by $1,000 and, as a result, taxes (T) increase by $300, the disposable personal income (DPI) would be $700. If an individual increases consumption expenditures by $560, the marginal propensity to consume (MPC) would be 0.8 ($560 divided by $700). The marginal propensity to save, the change in savings from a given change in disposable income, is equal to 1 minus the marginal propensity to consume (1 − MPC), or the marginal propensity to save is 0.2.

A corresponding relationship to the marginal propensity to consume is the level of consumption divided by the level of income. This is distinguished from marginal propensity, which refers to changes in consumption as a result of changes in income. This relationship is referred to as the *average propensity to consume* (APC).

b. *Investment:* Another variable that affects the level of income in society is the level of investment by business firms. Investment is defined as expenditures for capital goods. Net investment does not include replacement of existing capital stock or depreciation but includes only those expenditures that are intended to lead to new productive capacity (e.g., investments in new equipment, new buildings, and new production capacity). While investment affects the level of national income, several variables determine the level of investment at a given point in time. Investment is the *most volatile* GDP component.

(1) *Interest rate:* The interest rate is the price firms must pay for the privilege of using someone else's money. It is important to remember that the interest rate affects business decisions to invest even when the business is financing the investment project from undistributed corporate profits or some other form of internal financing. The interest rate, then, represents the income given up by

not taking the undistributed corporate profits and investing them elsewhere at a given rate of return. When a firm is making an investment decision, the interest rate is important, in terms of either the actual cost of borrowing money or the opportunity cost of using its money for the investment versus some other type of project. In general, the lower the interest rate, the larger the amount of investment that business firms are willing to undertake. For business to invest, the interest rate must be less than the expected return on the investment project. Thus, as the interest rate lowers, more projects become profitable.

(2) *Expectations:* A second factor that has a major influence on the level of investment is expectations. As business firms expect the future outlook of the economic situation to be positive, they will increase their investments to be able to meet the expected increase in demand. Things that change the expectations of business include changes in population growth or changes in the behavior of consumers or government, leading to a change in demand for specific products.

(3) *Corporate taxation:* The level of corporate taxation also has a major impact on investment decisions. Corporate taxation takes many forms, including corporate income tax and various types of investment taxes and/or tax credits. These taxes provide an incentive or deterrent for businesses to undertake investment projects. If the corporate income tax is high, there is less income after taxes for paying dividends. During the 1980s the U.S. government passed a series of investment tax credit laws that allow for increased depreciation of capital equipment. This, in essence, reduced the level of taxation for corporations. It was intended that, through investment tax credits, the demand for investment by firms would be stimulated.

c. *Government expenditures:* The level of government expenditures within an economic system is, to some extent, determined by budgets developed by the president and approved by Congress. Government expenditures include those expenditures incurred by federal, state, and local governments.

EXAMPLES OF GOVERNMENT EXPENDITURES: National defense expenditures; cost of administration of the government; education, training for employment, and social services; health care for senior citizens and the poor; and agriculture support programs.

It is important to note, however, that certain transfer payments do not count as government expenditures because they do not represent current production. These transfer payments simply transfer expenditures from one time period to another.

EXAMPLES OF TRANSFER PAYMENTS (payment not for GDP): Interest on the national debt, social security benefits, and pensions.

Historically, the level of government expenditures in the United States has increased both absolutely and relatively in regard to consumption and investment. There has been a trend in recent years to reduce that rate of growth. An additional factor considered very important is that government expenditures are, to some extent, tied to taxation. However, these expenditures are not limited to the level of taxation imposed on the people. In any given year the level of government expenditures may be greater than or less than the level of taxes. Depending on the particular situation, the government may have either a surplus or a deficit at the end of the year. The level of government expenditures includes federal, state, and local expenditures.

EXAMPLE: In the 1980s the level of state government expenditures increased at a more rapid rate than the level of federal government expenditures, primarily because of increases in the cost of providing public education and a reduction in federal government support for such programs.

d. *Net exports:* The portion of national income designated as net exports is the difference between the value of goods and services produced in the United States and exported overseas and the value of goods and services produced overseas and imported into the United States. The level of net foreign trade, relatively small in the past, has had little impact on the level of national income until the early 1980s. Since then, negative net exports have been increasing. (Additional information on the determinants is presented in Chapter 5.)

2. *Aggregate Supply:* Just as consumption, investment, government expenditures, and net export affect the total demand for goods and services, other factors affect the supply of goods and services made available within the society. These factors include productivity of labor, level of taxation, technology, and natural resources available to a country.

a. *Productivity of labor:* Productivity is defined as the output per worker during a given period of time. As the output per worker increases, the quantity of goods and services made available also increases, depending on the supply of labor resources. Productivity is influenced dramatically by the worker's level of education in society. A large portion of the growth in aggregate supply of goods and services within the United States has been attributed to increased productivity of labor.

b. *Level of taxation:* The level of taxation has an impact on aggregate supply from a dual standpoint. Taxes affect the incentive of individuals to work and the incentive of businesses to invest in capital goods that increase productive capacities in the future.

(1) *Impact on individual incentives:* As the marginal tax rate on income increases, the net take-home pay for working additional hours declines. This influences the incentive of the individual to work and to engage in nonmarket transactions (transactions that are not taxable).

EXAMPLE: Fixing a friend's car in exchange for help in painting the house is a nonmarket transaction.

If individuals engage in nontaxable activities, those individuals are withholding a portion of their labor from the market, thereby not increasing the supply of goods and services counted in the GDP. Thus, aggregate supply does not expand at as rapid a rate.

(2) *Impact on business incentives:* By the same token, corporate taxation has an impact on decisions to invest in capital goods that will increase future productive capacity. As tax rates on profits increase, the amount of money available for investment is reduced, and capital stock will not grow as rapidly.

c. *Level of technology:* As technology increases, firms will be able to produce more goods and services with a given set of resources, thus increasing society's output or producing a given quantity of goods and services at a lower cost. Increasing the output and lowering production costs enables the aggregate supply of goods and services available to society to increase.

d. *Availability of natural resources:* The quantity and quality of natural resources available for a country's use also have an impact on the aggregate supply of goods and services. Resources include land, labor, capital, and entrepreneurial ability.

(1) *Land:* Countries with an ample stock of land, including natural resources and capital, will have a larger aggregate supply than will countries with fewer of the factors of production.

(2) *Labor:* As the quality of labor increases, so does the productivity of labor and thus the aggregate supply.

(3) *Capital:* In combination with other resources, availability of capital affects a country's aggregate supply of goods and services.

(4) *Entrepreneurial ability:* A country must have appropriate incentives for entrepreneurs to take risks and ultimately to expand output and develop new goods and services. If these incentives exist, there will be a long-term impact on the productivity of the country and the aggregate supply of goods and services. If these incentives do not exist, the ability of a country to produce goods and services at a constant or increasing rate is greatly reduced.

E. Fluctuations in National Income

An economy is not always operating at its full employment level. There are times when it is operating below its full employment level and economic activity is declining. These time periods are referred to as periods of *recession.* When a country is producing at full employment and growing, the time period is referred to as *prosperity.*

EXAMPLES: The worst economic recession or depression was the period from 1929 to 1938. This was the longest prolonged period of depression that the U.S. economy has known, resulting in unemployment rates as high as 25 to 30 percent in some groups and even higher among certain other groups of people.

The period of the 1950s through the 1970s was a period of intermittent prosperity with slight recessions.

The period from the late 1980s through 1998 has been the longest sustained period of growth in recent history.

For a country to be operating at full employment, the amount paid to produce goods and services must be received back when those same goods and services are sold. In other words, the value of consumption (C) plus savings (S) plus government taxes (T) must equal the value of consumption (C) plus investment (I) plus government spending (G):

$$C + S + T = C + I + G$$

Both self-correcting and government policy measures can minimize the fluctuations of economic activities. These self-correcting aspects are "built-in" stabilizers that occur in the economy. They include unemployment compensation, welfare payments, and other government payments that fluctuate inversely to the level of economic activity. Other government policies that can be instituted are those affecting consumption, investment, and the level of government spending to stimulate or retard the economy.

The overall purpose of government policies to affect fluctuations in national income is to create a stable economy—an economy with a low level of unemployment and inflation. If the national income is not at a sufficient level, unemployment will be relatively high. If the economy is at full employment and still trying to grow, we will experience high rates of inflation.

1. *Natural Forces to Moderate Fluctuations:* In our economy today "built-in" stabilizers help offset downturns in business activity and moderate recovery. These stabilizers moderate the fluctuations in business cycles and the level of inflation and unemployment that society experiences. Stabilizers that reverse an economic downturn are unemployment compensation or welfare benefits, among others, which require increased government expenditures during periods of decline in economic activity.

   EXAMPLES: As economic activity declines, the unemployment rate rises, and unemployment insurance payments increase.

   As the economy declines, various welfare programs increase.

   As the economic conditions decline, some people will experience decreased work hours versus layoffs. As a result of moving into a lower marginal tax bracket, these people will not experience a decline in salaries equivalent to the decline in the value of the hours they are working.

   If the economy becomes very competitive during an economic downturn and firms try to counteract decreased sales or increased inventories by reducing prices, these changes will result in a relatively rapid change in the cycle.

   If labor is willing to accept lower wage rates, the impact of the downturn will be minimized and will result in a faster recovery.

2. *Policies to Moderate Economic Fluctuations:* Policies that alleviate pressure on inflation or moderate downturns in the business cycle can be classified as *fiscal* policy or *monetary* policy. These policies can be used to correct either inflation or unemployment.

   a. *Fiscal policy measures to counteract business cycles:* While some factors automatically operate within an economy to counteract business cycles, on occasion the government intervenes to stimulate activity or to reduce pressure on inflation. The impact of government occurs because of policies implemented to affect consumption, investment, or level of government spending.

      (1) *Effect on consumption:* The level of consumption is changed by a number of different variables. One variable is the level of taxation. As the level of taxation increases, the level of disposable personal income declines and vice versa. During periods of economic recession, the intent of government policy is to stimulate the demand for goods and services, leading to increased employment and a recovery from the recession. By reducing tax rates, government can increase the level of individual consumption, thus having an impact on the long-term equilibrium level of the economy.

      (2) *Effect on investment:* In much the same way, government can affect the level of investment.

         (a) *Tax incentives:* During periods of recession, government can provide incentives for business, through investment tax credits and reductions in the corporate income tax rate, to expand and continue appropriate levels of employment. Similarly, during a period of prosperity, the government may eliminate the tax credits and increase the rate of corporate income tax.

(b) *Financing the government deficit:* In periods of prosperity, with high rates of interest and inflation, the government can finance the government deficit by competing with private firms for money available for investments. During periods of recession, however, the government may want a deficit so that the borrowed money would provide more money to the economy and thus stimulate economic recovery.

b. *Monetary policy:* While the level of government spending can have an impact on business cycles, so can the amount of money that is in our economic system. The amount of money is controlled by the Federal Reserve System and can be increased or decreased, depending on the actions of that institution. The Federal Reserve System is independent of the federal government and can follow policies complementary or contradictory to the federal government administration.

(1) *Control of money supply during economic recession:* During periods of economic recession, one way to stimulate the economy is simply to make more money available to people. If people have more money, they will have a tendency to spend more and reverse the decline in business activity.

(2) *Control of money supply during periods of prosperity and inflation:* By taking money out of circulation during periods of prosperity and inflation, the pressure on inflation can be reduced.

(3) *Monetary controls:* Monetary authorities have a variety of controls that help to affect the money supply.

(a) *Reserve ratio for banks:* This ratio represents the percentage of a bank's assets that must be held in reserve with the Federal Reserve System. If the reserve ratio is reduced, the money that banks can lend increases, thus increasing the money supply.

(b) *Discount rate:* The cost to banks for borrowing from the Federal Reserve System is known as the *discount rate.* Higher discount rates discourage borrowing and limit the money supply.

(c) *Open-market operations:* These controls refer to buying or selling domestic government securities by the Federal Reserve System. If the Federal Reserve System sells securities, money is received in exchange for the securities. This reduces the money supply.

3. *Supply-Side Economics:* Supply-side economics involves those factors that influence the supply of goods and services available in society. If the United States is experiencing an economic recession, one possible remedy is to increase the demand for goods and services. During a period of high unemployment with high inflation, traditional demand management policy may not work. To reverse the recession, there must be increases in the supply of goods and services as well as increases in the demand. Supply-side economists use basically the same tools that demand management economists use; however, the outcome is somewhat different.

a. *Marginal tax rates:* The supply-side economists argue that if a society has *high* marginal tax rates, the incentives for individuals to work are reduced. As incentives are reduced, the hours people are willing to work and the total quantity of resources available for society are also reduced. With the lowering of the marginal tax rates, incentives to work and the output of the labor force are increased, and as a result of the increased number of working hours, the revenues collected through taxation may actually increase as well.

EXAMPLE: This philosophy was used to sell the 1963 tax cuts under the Kennedy administration and did have the desired impact of increasing output and tax revenues at the same time.

b. *Encouragement of investment and savings:* An additional component of supply-side economics is equivalent to that of the demand side. Under supply-side economics, the emphasis would be on encouraging investment and savings, resulting in increasing the capacity and productive potential of the economy. Measures used to encourage investment and saving include investment tax credits, corporate income tax reductions, tax credit incentives on individual savings accounts, and other stimuli for the investment sector.

F. Sources of Economic Information

For current economic information, a variety of reference material is available through public and business libraries. Here is a brief list of some of the major sources:

1. *Challenge:* A bimonthly periodical covering stories about the U.S. economy written for the layperson.
2. *Economic Indicators:* Prepared by the Council of Economic Advisors, published by the Joint Economic Committee.
3. *Economic Report of the President:* Published annually by the U.S. Government Printing Office.
4. *Federal Reserve Bulletin:* Published monthly by the Board of Governors of the Federal Reserve System.
5. *Survey of Current Business:* Published monthly by the Bureau of Economic Analysis, U.S. Department of Commerce.
6. *Wall Street Journal:* A daily newspaper covering economic events and activities in the business world.

Review Questions

Directions: Select the best answer from the four alternatives. Write your answer in the blank to the left of the number.

_______________ **1.** In contrast to nominal GDP, real GDP refers to

a. nominal GDP minus exports.
b. nominal GDP minus personal income taxes.
c. nominal GDP corrected for price changes.
d. nominal GDP corrected for depreciation.

_______________ **2.** The consumer price index (CPI) is a tool designed to measure the extent to which

a. the cost of a typical bundle ("market basket") of consumer goods has changed over time.
b. consumers have increased their spending over time.
c. GDP is allocated to consumers, not business or government, over time.
d. prices paid by employers to resource owners have changed over time.

_______________ **3.** Which of the following is *not* included in the calculation of net national product (NNP)?

a. Depreciation
b. Net exports
c. Government purchases
d. Net investment

_______________ **4.** Disposable income is equal to

a. national income minus personal income minus federal taxes.
b. personal income minus personal taxes.
c. net national product per capita minus personal taxes.
d. national income minus social security minus taxes plus dividends.

_______________ **5.** The real output of goods and services and the real income of resource suppliers

a. must increase at the same rate for prices to be stable.
b. will be constant during periods of price stability.
c. will never increase at the same rate.
d. are generally determined by the rate of inflation.

_______________ **6.** Structural unemployment is a result of

a. an inadequate matching of qualified workers and available jobs.
b. inaccurate and costly information about job opportunities.
c. insufficient employment in the building trades.
d. not enough employees.

_____________ **7.** Inflation

a. occurs whenever any price in the economy rises.
b. has been more severe in the United States than for other Western nations.
c. is measured by changes in the cost of a typical "market basket" of goods at different times.
d. causes the purchasing power of a dollar to rise.

_____________ **8.** The portion of disposable income a consumer does not spend on current consumption is called

a. investment.
b. saving.
c. supply.
d. temporary income.

_____________ **9.** Aggregate demand is equal to

a. consumption plus saving minus government spending.
b. consumption plus saving minus taxes.
c. consumption plus saving plus investment.
d. consumption plus investment plus government spending.

_____________ **10.** The marginal propensity to consume (MPC) is

a. consumption expenditures divided by saving.
b. consumption expenditures divided by disposable income.
c. consumption expenditures divided by personal income.
d. additional current consumption expenditures divided by additional current disposable income.

_____________ **11.** Consumption is equal to

a. disposable income minus taxes.
b. disposable income minus saving.
c. investment plus saving.
d. saving minus disposable income.

_____________ **12.** Which of the following would be considered an investment by an economist?

a. A corporation buying a car for its sales staff
b. A new television set bought by a household
c. A corporate bond purchased by a financial investor
d. Purchase of a corporate stock

_____________ **13.** A planned deficit

a. would stimulate aggregate demand more than the same level of expenditures with a balanced budget.
b. is rejected by most Keynesians as acceptable fiscal policy.

c. became widely accepted as a policy tool just before the Great Depression.
d. means that tax revenues exceed the level of government spending.

_______ **14.** Which of the following is not a built-in stabilizer?

a. Unemployment compensation
b. The investment multiplier
c. Corporate profit tax
d. Progressive income tax

_______ **15.** According to the supply-side view,

a. aggregate demand is the major determinant of real output and aggregate employment.
b. tax rates are a major determinant of real output and aggregate employment.
c. an increase in government expenditures and taxes will cause real income to rise.
d. expansionary monetary policy will cause real output to expand without causing the rate of inflation to accelerate.

_______ **16.** Which of the following would a supply-side fiscalist be most likely to propose as a current policy for effectively promoting economic growth and halting inflation?

a. An increase in government expenditures coupled with a tax increase
b. An across-the-board reduction in tax rates coupled with a reduction in government expenditures
c. An increase in taxes to attain a budget surplus
d. A large budget deficit coupled with an acceleration in the growth of the money supply

_______ **17.** The balanced-budget rule would require Congress to establish tax rates such that

a. the saving on the part of households and the investment of business decision makers were in balance.
b. the consumption expenditures and savings of households were in balance.
c. government expenditures and tax revenues were balanced annually.
d. the Federal Reserve System expanded the money supply at a noninflationary rate.

_______ **18.** You have been asked to study the production of the economy over the past five years. Why would you use the real GDP series rather than the nominal series?

a. The real series is less complicated than the nominal series because the exports are not included.
b. The real series is more precise because it accounts for imports, whereas the nominal series does not.
c. The nominal series fails to account for transfer payments, whereas the real series does not.
d. The nominal series reflects changes in both output and prices, whereas the real series reflects changes in output.

_______ **19.** Suppose that U.S. policymakers decide that to stimulate the growth rate of GDP, investment must be increased. What is needed, they conclude, is a reallocation of resources *away* from the production of consumer goods and *toward* the production of capital goods. Which of the following policy alternatives would be most likely to accomplish that objective?

a. A reduction in personal income taxes
b. A reduction in state sales taxes
c. A higher tax credit allowance for business investment in capital equipment
d. A restrictive monetary policy

_____________ **20.** An economy is currently experiencing a high rate of unemployment as the result of deficient aggregate demand. Which of the following policy alternatives would be most likely to push the economy toward full employment?

a. A tax cut coupled with an equal reduction in government expenditures
b. An increase in government expenditures, coupled with an increase in taxes
c. A decrease in corporate tax rates, leaving government expenditures unchanged
d. A level of taxes and government spending that keeps the budget in balance

Solutions

Answer	*Refer to:*
1. (c)	[B-2] Real GDP refers to nominal GDP corrected for price changes.
2. (a)	[B-2-b] The CPI consists of the costs of a given sampling of goods and services at different points in time.
3. (a)	[B-1-b] The NNP is GDP minus depreciation. Although the other responses are all components of GDP, only depreciation is subtracted from GDP to obtain NNP.
4. (b)	[B-1-e] The definition of disposable income is personal income minus personal taxes.
5. (a)	[D-1 and D-2] For an economy to be in equilibrium, the level of aggregate demand must be equal to the level of aggregate supply.
6. (a)	[C-1-d] This is the definition of structural unemployment.
7. (c)	[C-2] Inflation is the increase in prices of goods and services during a given period of time.
8. (b)	[D-1-a] Disposable income minus consumption is the definition of saving.
9. (d)	[D-1] The definition of aggregate demand is consumption plus investment plus government spending.
10. (d)	[D-1-a] The definition of marginal propensity to consume is change in consumption divided by the change in disposable income.
11. (b)	[D-1-a] Consumption is defined as disposable income minus saving.
12. (a)	[D-1-b] Investment is defined as an expenditure for capital goods. An economist would view the purchase of corporate cars for business use an investment.
13. (a)	[E-2-a] The government can affect the level of investment through planned deficits.
14. (b)	[E-1] The investment multiplier is not an automatic stabilizer since it helps perpetuate economic cycles.
15. (d)	[E-3] Under supply-side economics, investment and savings are encouraged, resulting in increased capacity and productive potential of the economy.

16. (b) [E-3] Lowering of marginal tax rates will provide more opportunity for incentives to work to increase, and thus the output of the labor force is increased as well as revenues from taxation.

17. (c) [E-2] This is the correct definition of a balanced budget.

18. (d) [B-2-a] Real increases or decreases in GDP reflect changes in the quantity of goods and services produced.

19. (c) [E-2-a] Government can provide incentives for business, through investment tax credits, to produce more capital goods.

20. (c) [E-2] Reductions in the corporate income tax rate are incentives to business to expand and continue appropriate levels of employment.

CHAPTER 3

Money and Banking

OVERVIEW

Money and its availability are prime determinants of the level of economic activity within our country. Money serves as a standard of value, a medium of exchange, a store of value, and a standard of deferred payment.

Financial markets in the United States are complex and represent very fluid markets. The financial markets, always extremely competitive, have become even more so as a result of changes in banking laws over the past several years.

The basis for the financial system is the Federal Reserve System, the country's central bank. The Federal Reserve System (the "Fed") controls the supply of money and develops regulations under which banks and other financial institutions (savings and loan associations, credit unions, and thrift institutions) must operate. The Federal Reserve System is independent of the U.S. government and acts independently of the executive and legislative branches of the government.

Modern fractional reserve banking stems from the experiences of early goldsmiths who found that 100 percent reserves were not needed to carry on daily business and to hold money for individuals. With the reserve requirement of less than 100 percent, financial institutions can expand the money supply at a multiple of the reserve requirement. The Fed has control over this reserve requirement and thus the financial institution's ability to create money.

KEY TERMS

Currency
Discount rate
Excess reserves
Federal Deposit Insurance Corporation (FDIC)
Federal Housing Administration (FHA)
Federal Reserve note
Federal Reserve System (FED)
Gresham's law
Margin requirements
Monetary policy
Money
Moral suasion
NOW account
Open-market operations
Primary deposit
Required reserves
Reserve ratio
Secondary deposit
Small Business Administration (SBA)
Supply of money
Transaction account
Usury laws

A. The Nature and Value of Money

Money and its availability are prime determinants of the level of economic activity within our country. Money serves as a standard of value, a medium of exchange, a store of value, and a standard of deferred payment. For money to serve its functions adequately, *the commodity value of money* (the value of the materials from which money is made) must be less than the exchange value of money. This is certainly the case with paper money and coins that are in existence in the United States today. If, on occasion, the value of coins in exchange is less than the value of the commodities that make up the coins, the coins are withdrawn from the market and replaced with ones of less commodity value.

1. *Money:* Money refers to the coins, currency, and checking account balances that people have available for use. This definition stems from the use of money as a medium of exchange. In the United States, coins, currency, and instruments drawn on transaction accounts are commonly accepted as money.

2. *Components of the Money Supply:*

a. *Coins and currency:* Currency represents about 27 percent of the money supply.

b. *Transaction deposits:* Transaction deposits (about 73 percent of the money supply) include deposits in checking accounts at commercial banks, deposits in NOW accounts in savings and loan associations and savings banks, and deposits in share draft accounts in credit unions.

c. *"Near monies":* "Near monies" consist of balances in savings accounts and other instruments that can be converted easily into money. However, in their present form they do not serve as money since near monies are not acceptable as payment for most transactions.

In addition, short-term government securities are often classified as near monies because they have to be converted into money before they can be used in exchange. These securities are highly liquid and can be converted to money in a relatively short period of time.

EXAMPLE: Groceries cannot be bought with a U.S. government bond or with a savings account, but both of these instruments are easily convertible into money; thus, they are classified as near monies.

d. *Credit cards:* A credit card is, in essence, a line of credit issued by a credit card company to an individual. When a credit card is used to purchase goods or services, a debt is incurred or a loan made. The credit card itself is not money but is access to credit.

3. *Functions of Money:* Money performs four important functions in any economic system:

a. *Standard of value:* Money serves as a common denominator in expressing the value of other goods or services. If money did not exist, we would have to express the value of items in terms of other commodities.

EXAMPLE: The value of wheat, clothes, or household goods is expressed in terms of money rather than relative to other goods and services. The value of a coat might be four pairs of shoes, or the value of a steak would be one-half of a shoe if the standard of value were shoes.

By using money as the standard of value, we eliminate the problem of comparing one commodity to another by expressing the value of goods in a manner easily understood by all.

b. *Medium of exchange:* Money is accepted in all transactions of goods bought and sold and for the discharging of debts. When a unit of money is no longer accepted as a medium of exchange, it no longer performs its primary function and is usually replaced by another medium of exchange.

c. *Store of value:* Money provides a mechanism by which a given dollar amount may be reserved for the future.

EXAMPLE: If you put $100 into a savings account today, 10 years from now you will still have $100 plus interest. However, if the price level changes, the purchasing power of that $100 in the future would be less than the purchasing power today. This does not mean that you do not have $100; it simply means that the purchasing power of that $100 has changed.

d. *Standard of deferred payment:* Money also allows agreements to be made for future payments. Thus, it becomes a standard of deferred payment. Without money, deferred payment would have to be made in terms of commodities rather than money. Again, money increases the efficiency with which exchange takes place and allows for agreements between individuals in regard to both current and future transactions.

4. *The Value of Money:* The value of money is determined by the quantity of goods and services that a given amount of money will purchase. To say that the value of money has declined means that the purchasing power of money has declined. The dollar is still worth a dollar, but the amount of goods and services that the dollar will purchase has decreased.

a. *Changes in the value of money:* The value of money has changed in the United States as well as in most of the world. Since World War II, the purchasing power of a dollar in the United States has continually declined because of inflation. There are three explanations for the fluctuation in the value of money:

(1) *The commodity theory of money:* The value of money depends on the value and quantity of materials (e.g., gold and silver) contained in the unit of money. The commodity theory of money has lost prominence in the United States, especially since the use of fiat money (paper money and demand deposits are not backed by any commodity at the present time).

(2) *The quantity theory:* A second explanation for changes in the value of money, the quantity theory, emphasizes the principle that the larger the quantity of money, the less valuable each unit will be. This theory hypothesizes that the stock of money is equal to some constant times the price level. If the stock of money increases, prices will go up automatically. The quantity theory, however, better explains periods of full employment. If the economy is operating at less than full employment, the relationship between quantity of money and the price level is not as consistent.

(3) *The income theory:* Another theory, the income theory, attempts to explain the fluctuation in the value of money. The income theory emphasizes that the value of money depends on the growth of money income and real income or the value of total spending in the economy. This theory reasons that an increase in the quantity of money will not necessarily cause an increase in prices, production, and employment but will cause an increase in production and employment if the increase in the quantity of money stimulates total

spending. The increase in total spending will have an impact on prices, production, and employment.

b. *Decline in purchasing power of a dollar:* Decline in purchasing power tends to benefit debtors since the purchasing power of money used for paying debts is less than the purchasing power of money that was borrowed. Similarly, when prices rise, industrial profits tend to be high, stimulating output and employment.

EXAMPLES: In times of rising prices, creditors are hurt because they are being repaid in dollars with less purchasing power than the dollars that were loaned.

Individuals on fixed incomes are hurt because they must pay higher prices for goods and services, but their income does not change.

The average worker has usually not been hurt by rising prices (inflation) because wages usually increase at a rate equal to or higher than the rate of price increases. The real purchasing power of the worker's salary has increased over time.

B. The Supply of Money

The supply of money consists of coins, currency, and transaction accounts in financial institutions owned by the nonbanking public. One important aspect of money is that the commodity value of money must be less than the exchange value of money. If the commodity value becomes greater than the exchange value, people will keep their money for its real value and not for its exchange value. Referred to as *Gresham's law,* this may be stated another way: Bad money drives good money out of circulation.

EXAMPLE OF GRESHAM'S LAW: In the late 1960s, the value of silver in a quarter became greater than the exchange value of a quarter. People began keeping the quarter for its silver value, so the U.S. government began to replace the old quarter with a "sandwich" quarter, which included more copper, a metal of less value than the silver in the old quarter.

1. *Forms of Money:*

a. *Currency:* Currency consists of coins and paper money issued by the federal government. Today, paper money is in the form of federal reserve notes because the money is issued through the Federal Reserve System. Paper currency has been backed by 40 percent gold and later by 25 percent gold. However, today, federal reserve notes are not backed by any commodity. Historically, other kinds of paper money have been used in the United States besides federal reserve notes. These were called treasury currency and included treasury notes of the 1890s, U.S. notes (referred to as "greenbacks"), silver certificates, and gold certificates. The silver and gold certificates could be redeemed at the U.S. Treasury for an amount of gold or silver equal to the value of the paper money. Since 1968, no silver or gold certificates have been issued by the U.S. government. Today, all paper money can be redeemed at the U.S. Treasury or the Federal Reserve banks for an equivalent amount of currency or other federal reserve notes.

b. *Transaction accounts in financial institutions:* Prior to the Bank Regulation Act of 1980, commercial banks had a virtual monopoly on transaction accounts (checking accounts). With a checking account, an individual would have a bank balance against which checks could be written. With the Bank Regulation Act of 1980, savings and loan associations, savings banks, and credit unions could establish similar accounts. These are referred to as NOW accounts in savings-and-loan associations and savings banks and as share-draft accounts in credit unions. These accounts originate in these two ways:

(1) *Primary deposits:* The initial deposit into an account is called the primary deposit.

(2) *Secondary deposits:* Accounts can also be established with secondary deposits, created by a financial institution granting a loan and depositing the balance into an individual's account.

Financial institutions do not have to keep all their depositors' assets in the form of cash. The probability that all depositors would want to convert their accounts into cash at a given point in time is very small. The financial institution needs to keep cash on hand equivalent only to that portion of the deposits that is expected to be withdrawn at a given point in time. Reserve ratios are established by the Federal Reserve System. While ratios provide protection for depositors, their primary purpose is to give the Federal Reserve System the ability to regulate the money supply.

2. *Types of Financial Institutions:*

a. *Federal Reserve System:* The Federal Reserve System (Fed) was organized in 1913 with the passage of the Federal Reserve Act. This act divided the United States into 12 districts, with each district having its own Federal Reserve bank. The act gave the Fed the power to control the activities of commercial banks. With the Bank Regulation Act of 1980, the controlling authority of the Federal Reserve System expanded to other financial institutions. The Fed is a nonprofit organization, independent of the federal government. Its main purpose is to control and service financial institutions. Federal Reserve activities are coordinated by a seven-member board of governors chosen by the president of the United States. Their 14-year terms are staggered so that no president has a substantial impact on the board, thus keeping the operation of the system independent of the executive and judicial branches of the federal government.

b. *Other financial institutions:* Commercial banks, savings-and-loan associations, credit unions, thrift institutions, and insurance companies provide financial services to citizens in society. Each of these types of institutions has a unique function, with their activity limited to that function by law. With the Bank Regulation Act of 1980, the activities in which each of these institutions can engage became similar. Each type of institution is governed by a specific set of regulations enforced by this country's central bank, the Federal Reserve System.

EXAMPLES OF BANKING SERVICES: Transaction accounts[1]*, personal loans, savings accounts, consumer loans, credit cards in the name of the institution, financial planning services, estate planning services, and commercial loans.*

(1) *Commercial banks:* Historically, commercial banks have been the major financial institutions within society: making loans, accepting both transaction account balances and time deposit accounts, and providing the full services of a financial institution. Before the Bank Regulation Act of 1980, commercial banks were the only financial institutions that had transaction accounts and

[1]A financial institution's issuance of transaction accounts has a very direct impact on the economy.

were the only institutions able to expand the money supply through fractional reserves. Deposits up to $100,000 in banks are insured by the Federal Deposit Insurance Corporation (FDIC).

(2) *Savings-and-loan associations:* These institutions were originally established to make home loans. Loans could be made to the limit of the company's assets. People deposited savings that the association would, in turn, use to make home and home construction loans. Since the Bank Regulation Act of 1980, savings-and-loan associations have been permitted to issue checking privileges against savings accounts and offer other services previously available only through commercial banks.

Since deregulation, many savings-and-loan companies have experienced financial difficulties. In many cases the difficulties resulted from expansion into areas of business in which the company had little experience. Even with failure of some savings-and-loan associations, deposits were protected by the Federal Savings and Loan Insurance Corporation (FSLIC), which has recently been merged with the FDIC. This organization guarantees deposits up to $100,000 per depositor if the company has financial difficulties.

(3) *Credit unions:* Credit unions are organizations that receive money deposited into savings accounts and make loans. In the past, credit unions have made consumer loans at an interest rate equivalent to or slightly lower than bank interest rates and have paid dividends on savings accounts slightly higher than banks. Credit unions are owned by their depositors (members). Since the Bank Regulation Act of 1980, credit unions have expanded their sphere of operation to include issuance of drafts against savings accounts deposited with the credit union.

(4) *Insurance companies:* Insurance companies are a unique form of financial institution. Historically, they have provided substantial amounts of money for large investment. The premiums collected on policies are loaned out for investment purposes; thus, the insurance company can earn a rate of return on the money until it is paid out on life insurance policies. In addition, with standard life insurance, there is usually a clause that allows individuals to borrow against the cash value of the insurance policy. The Bank Regulation Act of 1980 did not have a substantial impact on insurance companies.

3. *Creation of Money:* A bank, like any business, attempts to make a profit by providing a service for which it receives payment. Banks have certain assets, and these assets must equal liabilities plus net worth. The assets of a bank are the value of anything the bank owns. The liabilities are the bank's debts to others, and the net worth is the difference between the bank's assets and the liabilities. For most banks, the majority of its liabilities are its transaction account deposits, which are payable on demand. Since the proportion of these liabilities that will be paid out at any point in time is predictable, only a fraction of the liabilities must be kept on hand at any point in time. This allows the bank to create money.

EXAMPLE: If a bank has $1,000,000 in liabilities in the form of transaction accounts and does not expect more than 20 percent of those balances to be demanded at any point in time, the bank has $800,000 that it can use for other purposes. The bank may use this $800,000 to make loans to its customers and thus put the deposits of other customers to work. When the bank makes loans in this manner, it is creating money.

Banks are required by law to keep a portion of their assets on reserve with the Federal Reserve Bank. This reserve and the cash kept in the bank's vault are termed the bank's *required reserves.* Monies available in excess of required reserves are *excess reserves.* The availability of excess reserves is what allows the bank to create money.

EXAMPLE: Assume that the legal reserves against transaction deposits is 20 percent. For every dollar in a transaction account, a bank must have 20 cents in reserves either with the Federal Reserve System or in vault cash. If Bank A had $10,000,000 deposited in transaction accounts, it would be required to have $2,000,000 in reserves.

(The actual reserve requirement for banks, historically, has ranged from 15 to 20 percent.)

EXAMPLE: Figure 3–1 demonstrates the ability of banks to create money. Assume that a bank must have 20 percent reserves on its demand deposits. These five transactions increased the money supply to $29,520. Of that amount, $19,520 was the result of the initial increase of $10,000. If this example were expanded to include additional loans based on excess reserves, the final level of money supply would be $50,000. Of this, $10,000 would be due to the initial transaction, and $40,000 would result from the loans the bank made as a result of having excess reserves.

As the example above illustrates, the banking system can expand the money supply by a multiple of its excess reserves. This multiple is equal to 1 divided by the reserve ratio. In the foregoing example, the multiple was 1 divided by 0.2, or 5. Thus, an initial $8,000 in excess reserves could result in a $40,000 increase in the money supply after banks had made loans based on excess reserves. As the reserve ratio of banks increases, the ability of banks to expand money through loaning excess reserves declines, and, vice versa, as the reserve ratio declines, the ability of the banking system to create money expands.

Figure 3–1 Ability of Banks to Create Money

	Banking System T-Account			
Transaction	Assets		Liabilities	
1. Bank A receives a new deposit for $10,000 in the form of a check issued by the Federal Reserve Board for bonds purchased. This is a $10,000 increase in the money supply.	1. Cash	$10,000	1. DD	$10,000
2. Bank A sends required reserves (RR) to Fed; the remainder of the cash assets are excess reserves (ER).	2. RR ER	2,000 8,000	2. DD	10,000
3. Bank A loans its excess reserves. (The result is: DD, 18,000; RR, 3,600; and ER, 6,400.) Money Supply (MS) is now increased by $8,000.	3. RR ER Loans	3,600 6,400 8,000	3. DD	18,000
4. Bank A now loans its current ER (6,400), increasing DD to 24,400 and changing RR to 4,880. MS is increased by $6,400.	4. RR ER Loans	4,880 5,120 14,400	4. DD	24,400
5. Bank A now loans its ER of 5,120. This increases DD to 29,520; RR becomes 5,904; ER equals 4,096; and total loans equal 19,520. MS has again increased by the amount of ER of the bank.	5. RR ER Loans	5,904 4,096 19,520	5. DD	29,520

DD, demand deposit; RR, required reserves; ER, excess reserves; MS, money supply.

4. *The Banking System and Monetary Policy:* The actions of the Federal Reserve System determine the monetary policy of the country. Monetary policy is activity that would have an impact on the availability of money in society. Monetary policy could have an impact on economic fluctuations since increases in the money supply tend to stimulate the economy, and declines in the money supply tend to retard the economy. During periods of inflation, the appropriate monetary policy would be to restrict the growth of the money supply, whereas in times of high unemployment the appropriate monetary policy would be to expand the money supply. The Federal Reserve System has a variety of weapons that can be used to assist in stabilizing the economy: open-market operations, discount rate, changes in the reserve requirement, moral suasion, selective controls over margin requirements for loans made to purchase stocks and bonds, selective controls over installment contracts and other forms of consumer credit, and selective controls over the terms of home mortgage contracts.

   a. *Open-market operations:* The most important set of policies used by the Fed to control the money supply is open-market operations. These involve the buying and selling of government securities by the open-market committee of the Federal Reserve Board. Open-market operations occur daily in New York City with the objective of tightening or loosening member banks' reserve positions. In periods of inflation, the committee sells securities. In periods of recession, it buys securities.

      EXAMPLE: If the Fed sells $1,000 worth of bonds to the public and the public pays for the bonds in cash, the Fed has exchanged $1,000 worth of government securities for $1,000 worth of cash, and the money supply has been reduced by $1,000. (Cash held by the Fed is not part of the money supply.) If the payment for the securities issued by the Fed is in the form of a check (assuming a reserve requirement of 0.2), a 5:1 reduction in the money supply of member banks will take place as the excess reserve positions of the banks are altered. Thus, in the case of selling $1,000 worth of bonds, the total money supply could be reduced by $5,000 (the initial $1,000 plus $4,000 as a result of changes in excess reserves).

   b. *Discount rate:* The rate that the Federal Reserve Bank charges if member banks want to borrow from the Fed is known as the *discount rate.* To increase reserves, a bank can discount its assets, such as loans and securities, to the Fed. The Federal Reserve Bank will pay the borrowing bank a fraction of the face value of the assets. This discount, usually in the range of 5 to 10 percent, would affect the willingness of banks to borrow money from the Fed. If the discount rate is extremely high, banks will not want to borrow money and will maintain a reserve position that will guarantee they will not have to borrow. This, in turn, has the impact of reducing the banking system's willingness to create money. Similarly, if the discount rate is extremely low, banks will be encouraged to discount some of their assets and thus to expand the money supply.

   c. *Changing the reserve requirement:* A powerful tool that the Federal Reserve System has available is the changing of the reserve requirement. Although this tool is used infrequently, its impact is both dramatic and immediate. Changes in the reserve requirement, in essence, change the banking system's ability to create money.

      EXAMPLE: If the reserve requirement were 20 percent, the banking system would have the potential to expand the money supply by a 5:1 ratio. If the reserve requirement were 25 percent, however, the expansion would be only by a 4:1 ratio.

Thus, by changing the reserve requirement from 20 to 25 percent, a dramatic 25 percent increase of reserves would be necessary to back the deposits of banks. To comply with this, the banks would have to reduce their loans or excess reserves would become required reserves. Each of these would have the effect of reducing the supply of money in the economy. Similarly, if the reserve requirement changed from 25 to 20 percent, the banks would have a 20 percent increase in excess reserves and thus could expand the money supply.

d. *Moral suasion ("jawboning"):* Historically, the Federal Reserve System has used moral suasion to promote certain socially beneficial policies. Moral suasion does not involve actual policy action but simply tries to encourage member banks to follow a policy that the Fed prefers member banks to follow. Although the use of a moral-suasion approach lacks the clout of open-market operations, the discount rate, and reserve requirements, it has occasionally provided some success over short periods of time.

e. *Margin requirements on loans for purchases of securities:* Margin requirements necessary on loans for securities (stocks and bonds) are controlled by the Federal Reserve System. Margin requirements refer to the percentage of the stock purchase price an individual must deposit with a broker or a bank before the difference can be made up by a loan. Margin requirements have ranged from 25 to 100 percent since 1964. At the present time, margin requirements are in the 50 to 60 percent range. As margin requirements increase, the money supply is reduced since people need more cash to buy securities. A reduction in the margin requirements allows people to purchase more stocks and bonds with a limited amount of cash, which increases the money supply.

f. *Other selective controls:* The Federal Reserve System's remaining selective controls are designed to affect two specific markets: installment contract buying and home mortgage rates. The Fed has imposed restrictions on these markets at different points in time, especially during war. At present, the Fed places limited restrictions on installment contracts and home mortgages since they are controlled by state usury laws or other types of legislation.

The Federal Reserve System can implement a variety of controls to change the level of the money supply. These tools are used to help stabilize the economy and minimize the rate of inflation and unemployment.

C. The Involvement of Government in Availability of Credit

The federal government intervenes in the credit market by providing a series of regulations that affect individuals wanting credit. These regulations are administered through a variety of government agencies, including the Federal Housing Authority (FHA), the Federal Deposit Insurance Corporation (FDIC), and the Small Business Administration (SBA).

1. *Federal Housing Authority (FHA):* The Federal Housing Authority (FHA) is a government agency that helps finance housing projects for low-income families and makes loans available to families at lower-than-market interest rates. On occasion, the FHA will simply guarantee the home loans as opposed to providing the loan. The FHA obtains revenue by selling bonds to the public. The revenue from the bonds is used to finance housing projects. The bonds are retired by borrowers paying off their debt to the agency.

2. *Federal Deposit Insurance Corporation (FDIC):* The FDIC was developed after bank failures in the early 1930s. The FDIC insures an individual's deposits, up to $100,000, against bank failure. An association similar to the FDIC, the Federal Savings and Loan Insurance Corporation (FSLIC) was formed to guarantee deposits in savings-and-loan associations to a maximum of $100,000. In the late 1980s and early 1990s, much attention was given to the cost of the savings-and-loan bailout. During that time many savings-and-loan associations failed. Since deposits were insured by the FSLIC, the government had to augment the FSLIC assets to meet obligations. Recently, the FSLIC was merged into the FDIC.

3. *Small Business Administration (SBA):* The SBA provides small business services similar to the FHA. In essence, the SBA provides loans at a low market interest rate to small businesses to help maintain small business as a viable unit within society. The SBA, like the FHA, sells bonds to the public and uses the revenue from the bonds to operate the agency and make loans to businesses. These bonds are then retired by repayment of the loans.

Review Questions

Directions: Select the best answer from the four alternatives. Write your answer in the blank to the left of the number.

______________ **1.** Which of the following is not a function of money?

a. Measure of output
b. Medium of exchange
c. Standard of value
d. Store of value

______________ **2.** The most frequently used monetary tool of the Federal Reserve System is

a. changes in the discount rate.
b. changes in reserve requirements.
c. moral suasion.
d. open-market operations.

______________ **3.** The value (purchasing power) of each unit of money

a. is largely independent of the money supply.
b. tends to increase as the money supply expands.
c. increases as the level of prices rises.
d. tends to decline as the money supply expands relative to the availability of goods and services.

______________ **4.** As a medium of exchange, money

a. provides the opportunity for a given dollar amount to be reserved for future use.
b. is accepted in all transactions of goods bought and sold.
c. earns income for its holders.
d. serves as a common denominator in expressing the value of goods and services.

______________ **5.** The major income-earning asset of financial institutions is

a. demand deposits.
b. time deposits.
c. reserve deposits with the Federal Reserve System.
d. loans outstanding.

______________ **6.** Which of the following constitute the required reserves of financial institutions?

a. Demand deposits and time deposits
b. Vault cash and deposits of the bank with the Federal Reserve System
c. U.S. securities and stock equity
d. Cash and U.S. securities

_______________ **7.** Uncertainty in general business conditions will cause financial institutions to hold excess reserves. Other things constant, this will

a. have no effect on the money supply.
b. tend to reduce the money supply.
c. tend to increase the money supply.
d. tend to reduce the money supply during a period of inflation while increasing it under recessionary conditions.

_______________ **8.** Excess reserves of financial institutions are

a. actual reserves minus required reserves.
b. federal reserves held by banks minus their liabilities.
c. assets minus the liabilities of banks.
d. actual reserves minus demand deposits.

_______________ **9.** A reserve requirement of 20 percent

a. implies a potential money deposit multiplier of 20.
b. implies a potential money deposit multiplier of 5.
c. implies a potential money deposit multiplier of 4.
d. is mandatory at all times, according to Federal Reserve policy.

_______________ **10.** The establishment of a stable monetary environment is

a. the responsibility of the U.S. Treasury.
b. the responsibility of the Federal Reserve System.
c. the joint responsibility of the Treasury and the Federal Reserve System.
d. the result of an automatic mechanism built into the independent decision making of our commercial banking system.

_______________ **11.** Which of the following is not a function of the Federal Reserve System?

a. Limiting the national debt
b. Setting the reserve required for deposit holdings of member banks
c. Buying and selling government bonds to control the size of the money supply
d. Establishing a money supply consistent with the business stability of the entire economy

_______________ **12.** The major purpose of the Federal Reserve System is to

a. keep the discount rate flexible.
b. be a lender of last resort.
c. regulate the money supply and thereby provide a monetary climate in the best interest of the economy.
d. regulate the levels of excess reserves held by member banks.

_______________ **13.** Monetary policy

a. is determined by commercial banks.
b. is determined by the U.S. Treasury.

c. is the major concern of the Federal Reserve System.
d. is a responsibility shared equally by the U.S. Treasury and the Federal Reserve System.

______________ **14.** Open-market operations are

a. the tool most often used by the Federal Reserve System to alter the money supply.
b. the least effective tool the Federal Reserve System has to alter the money supply.
c. the tool used by the Treasury to raise tax revenues.
d. the tool used by the Federal Reserve System to regulate stock market activities.

______________ **15.** In recent years the primary tool used by the Federal Reserve System to control the money supply has been

a. jawboning.
b. open-market operations.
c. changes in the discount rate.
d. changes in reserve requirements.

______________ **16.** An expansion in the money supply is desired as part of an antirecession policy. The Federal Reserve Board might

a. increase reserve requirements.
b. buy U.S. securities.
c. increase the discount rate.
d. urge the U.S. Treasury to sell more U.S. securities.

______________ **17.** Suppose that a member bank of the Federal Reserve System has $8,000 in demand deposits and is able to loan out $5,000 of this amount and still keep $1,000 in excess reserves in the bank. What is the legal reserve requirement?

a. 62.5 percent
b. 75 percent
c. 37.5 percent
d. 25 percent

______________ **18.** The Federal Reserve System wants to reduce the supply of money as part of an anti-inflation policy. The Federal Reserve System might

a. reduce reserve requirements.
b. sell U.S. securities.
c. reduce the discount rate.
d. urge the Treasury to sell more U.S. securities.

Solutions

Answer	*Refer to:*
1. (a)	[A-3] The four functions of money are standard of value, medium of exchange, store of value, and standard of deferred payment. Answer (a) is the only option that is not a function of money.
2. (d)	[B-4-a] Open-market operations are engaged in daily by the Fed, while reserve requirements are seldom changed and discount rates rarely change more than once every two months.
3. (d)	[A-4] The money supply is a prime determinant of the value of money. The impact of changes in money supply or value of money is dependent on corresponding changes in output of goods and services.
4. (b)	[A-3-b] When money is used as a medium of exchange, it is accepted as payment in all transactions of goods bought and sold and for the discharging of debts.
5. (d)	[B-2-b] Financial institutions lend money to individuals and businesses as income-earning ventures.
6. (b)	[B-3] This is the definition of required reserves.
7. (b)	[B-4] If a financial institution holds excess reserves, it is not expanding the money supply to its potential. This will result in a reduced money supply.
8. (a)	[B-3] This is the definition of excess reserves.
9. (b)	[B-3] The multiplier is found by using the formula: 1 divided by the reserve requirement. If the reserve requirement is 0.2, the multiplier is 1/0.2, or 5.
10. (b)	[B-2] All monetary policy is the responsibility of the Federal Reserve System.
11. (a)	[B-2-a] Answers (b), (c), and (d) all refer to monetary policy, which is controlled by the Fed. The national debt is controlled by Congress.
12. (c)	[B-2-a] Answers (a), (b), and (d) refer to measures the Fed can use to control the money supply, not the purpose of the Fed.
13. (c)	[B-2] The Federal Reserve System has sole responsibility for monetary policy.
14. (a)	[B-4-a] Open-market operations are most often used by the Fed to alter the money supply.

15. (b) [B-4-a] Open-market operations are the primary tool for controlling the money supply.

16. (b) [B-4-a] Buying U.S. securities would expand the money supply. Selling securities cannot be done by the Treasury.

17. (d) [B-3] If $5,000 is loaned and $1,000 is excess reserves, $2,000 is left for required reserves. $2,000/8,000 = 25 percent, which is the reserve ratio.

18. (b) [B-4-e] This is the only means identified here that would *reduce* the money supply.

CHAPTER 4 Business Involvement in Current Social and Economic Programs

OVERVIEW

The degree to which business has a responsibility to assist in solving current social problems is an issue that is often discussed. Trying to define exactly what responsibility business has in finding solutions to social problems and what responsibility individuals and government have in solving these social problems is difficult.

One solution is a laissez-faire type of capitalism in which business has no responsibility in solving social problems. In a laissez-faire society, solving social problems would be the responsibility of private individuals or groups, not business or government. For example, unemployment insurance or social security would be organized by private groups.

Another solution is that business must share the responsibility in solving social problems. Such problems as pollution and conservation of natural resources cannot be solved solely through the efforts of private individuals and groups. Individuals who believe that the government has a responsibility to impose regulations on the private sector that would result in solutions of social problems support this argument.

In this chapter, four social problems, their significance, and related economic issues are reviewed. These problems are conservation of natural resources, consumerism, pollution control, and equal employment opportunity.

KEY TERMS

- Age Discrimination in Employment Act of 1967
- Americans with Disabilities Act (ADA)
- Antitrust laws
- Civil Rights Act of 1964
- Consumerism
- Discrimination
- Economics of pollution
- Environmental Protection Agency (EPA)
- Equal Employment Opportunity Act of 1972
- Equal Employment Opportunity Commission (EEOC)
- Federal Aviation Administration (FAA)
- Federal Food and Drug Administration (FDA)
- Federal Power Commission (FPC)
- Federal Trade Commission (FTC)
- Pollution
- Price ceiling
- Productivity
- Vocational Rehabilitation Act of 1973

A. Conservation of Natural Resources

Conservation of natural resources can be examined best as a problem of current versus future consumption. If a society engages in large amounts of current consumption, resources are depleted, reducing the amount of resources available for future production and thus future consumption. A variety of methods can be utilized to encourage the conservation of natural resources.

1. *Using Minimum Quantity of Resources for Production:* For businesses to produce goods and services efficiently, markets must be able to operate without restrictions. Restrictions promote inefficiency.

   EXAMPLE: If the government imposes import quotas or import tariffs on foreign steel, this action encourages the use of domestic steel in production. In turn, the use of domestic steel encourages the extraction of more iron ore within the United States. This process increases the price of iron ore and depletes the supply of domestic ore. The increased use of domestic resources might be reversed if the import duties were eliminated, but other social problems, such as higher unemployment in the domestic steel industry, might be the result.

2. *Deterring Use of Natural Resources:* If resources are to be conserved in the short run, policies must be enacted to deter their use. One such policy might be excise taxes placed on some resources to discourage their use. As the price of the resource increases, business would attempt to find a different resource to make their products in an efficient manner. This would result in the conservation of a given natural resource.

   EXAMPLE: If the United States placed an excise tax on domestic crude oil, the price of domestic crude oil would increase relative to foreign crude oil as well as the price of crude oil relative to other forms of energy. Business firms would then have two choices: (1) Use foreign crude oil to produce petroleum products or (2) find an alternative form of energy to continue their production processes.

   The long-term impact would be to reduce the demand for domestic petroleum and conserve domestic petroleum reserves. This would increase the price for goods and services since cost of energy would increase.

3. *Voluntary Conservation by Business:* Another argument often heard is that business has a responsibility to conserve natural resources and should introduce conservation programs voluntarily. The basic problem is one of cooperation.

   EXAMPLE: If one firm within an industry attempts to conserve a natural resource, the production costs for that firm will increase. The firm will be placed in a position where the cost of using their production methods and resources is greater than that of competing firms. Therefore, either the business profits will decline or their product prices will be higher.

   Consumers must be willing to pay a higher price for goods produced using resource conservation methods. Firms cannot be expected to use expensive conservation methods "out of the goodness of their hearts." If some business firms cooperated to ensure conservation of natural resources, other problems might develop. For example, the cooperative firms might run the risk of violating antitrust laws as a result of the cooperative effort.

   When considering future conservation of natural resources in the United States, consumers must consider the way in which the markets function and either accept the results of such market operations or impose restrictions to change the results. If we accept the market results, we allow prices of resources to increase and/or decrease as demand dictates. The elimination of such government policies as price ceilings on natural gas, gasoline, and other resources would allow the prices of those resources to increase to a point where consumers and producers would actively search for alternative resources to conserve natural resources.

B. Consumerism

Consumerism is a movement shared by a large number of people who believe that society is not always getting "a fair shake" in the economic system. The primary economic reason for consumerism is the enhancement of consumer welfare.

1. *Business Practices Adverse to Consumer Interests:* Some of these business practices include the following:

a. Unsafe, impure, and low-quality products

b. Deceptive advertising of goods and services

c. Techniques that obscure or hide real prices

d. Poor or inadequate servicing of products

Each of these practices provides, at minimum, inconvenience to the consumer and, at maximum, increased expenditures for goods and services that may or may not be needed. In addition, the availability of unsafe, impure, and low-quality products can result in personal injury or even death.

2. *The Consumer's Bill of Rights:* At the core of consumerism is the Consumer's Bill of Rights, first declared by President John F. Kennedy. The original draft of consumers' rights included the following:

a. The right to safety

b. The right to be informed

c. The right to choose

d. The right to be heard

Since Kennedy's original declaration, two others have been added:

e. The right to recourse and redress

f. The right to a physical environment that will enhance the quality of life

3. *The Economics of Consumerism:* The primary economic reason for consumerism is the enhancement of consumer welfare. When looking at the overall activities of the country relative to consumerism, one must look at the benefits as well as the costs to the consumer of having that protection available.

a. *Economic benefits of consumerism:* Possible avenues through which consumerism may help improve consumer welfare include:

(1) *Improvements in product and service information:* To obtain the greatest satisfaction from a limited income, the consumer must have information on the prices and quality of a variety of goods and services to make rational decisions.

EXAMPLE: We expect that weights and measures will be represented correctly by sellers. This information is essential in making appropriate buying decisions.

It is helpful to know the ingredients comprising a product, the product's uses, how it operates, and how long it is expected to last, assuming average usage. This type of information is essential for the consumer to make informed purchasing decisions.

EXAMPLE: If someone wanted to purchase a saw for home use, the price might range from $30 to $70. By having accurate information about the different intensity of use, one might find that a less expensive saw was fine for home use.

(2) *Reduction in deceptive advertising:* Everyone at some time or another has been taken in by a deceptive sales promotion. While a reduction in deceptive sales activities increases consumer welfare, the cost of enforcing these reductions cannot be ignored. Deceptive sales tactics are the opposite of informational advertising and generate "fog" or confusion to the consumer. One problem with deceptive sales practices is that it is difficult to draw the line between what is a deceptive practice and what is not. A sales promotion considered useless and deceptive by one consumer may not be considered so by another consumer.

(3) *Increased consumer protection:* The largest part of consumerism activities is directed toward the protection of the consumer rather than the education of the consumer. These activities are directed toward protecting consumers from unsafe, impure, and low-quality products and from unfair practices. Results of consumerism activities in this area include the following:

(a) Laws preventing smoking in elevators and other public places

(b) Regulations requiring seat belts and shoulder harnesses in automobiles

(c) Laws requiring the wearing of helmets by motorcycle riders

(d) Government inspection of meat

(e) Licensing of professionals, such as medical doctors, before they can provide services

Other consumerism measures are intended to protect consumers from unscrupulous sellers. Price controls on gasoline and maximum rents for housing units fall into this category. Consumers who can get as much at the controlled price as they would be able to purchase at an uncontrolled price clearly gain. However, other consumers who might like to purchase some of the good may be unable to do so because of the lower quantity supplied.

b. *The economic costs:* In economic terms, all goods and services have a cost. Consumerism activities and legislative measures are not a free service to consumers. Two sets of costs can be readily identified:

(1) *The cost to consumers for providing protection to other consumers:* Direct costs to consumers for consumerism activities consist of the reduction in well-being experienced by some consumers as the presumed benefits of these activities are extended to others.

EXAMPLE: As a result of the consumerism movement, seat belts are now required in all automobiles. People purchasing a new car must pay the seat belt costs whether they want to use the seat belts or not. Therefore, the values of those involved in the consumerism movement—in this case, seat belts are beneficial—are imposed on all society by forcing all persons who own cars to bear the costs.

(2) *Costs of resources used in consumerism activities:* The costs of resources used in affecting any given consumerism activity must be taken into consideration. The resources used by the Federal Trade Commission, the Federal Aviation Administration, the Federal Food and Drug Administration, and other consumer protection agencies could be used elsewhere if they were not being used to protect the consumer. In recent years, the annual cost of operating federal agencies whose sole responsibility was providing consumer protection exceeded $3 billion.

4. *Consumerism Activities and Measures:* Specific types of activities, stemming from the Consumer's Bill of Rights, are employed to bolster the consumer's position with respect to producers and sellers. These activities include consumer information and educational services, performed by such organizations as Consumers Union; the investigation of practices thought to be adverse to consumer interests; the publication of reports by a number of consumer-oriented groups; and the extension of regular activities by government agencies for the purpose of protecting the consumer.

a. *Providing informational services:* Most individuals agree that the provision of information as a form of consumerism has positive benefits at a minimum cost. There is virtually no economic argument against consumerism measures that require truth in advertising or a listing of ingredients on labels. The benefits of these activities are obvious, and the costs are no more than the cost of providing false or misleading advertising.

b. *Minimizing risk to the consumer:* Consumerism measures that attempt to minimize the impact on individuals from actions of others are relatively easy to justify on a cost-benefit basis.

EXAMPLE: In the absence of regulation, people would drive automobiles with defective brakes or without headlights, imposing substantial risk on other people who happened to be driving on the highway. Legislation that regulates automobile safety increases the benefit to society as a whole, and the cost of this regulation is somewhat minimal.

c. *Protection from business manipulation:* Protection of the individual from business manipulation is probably the most questionable set of consumerism activities. Manipulation of individual consumers means that a business firm can do with the consumer whatever it desires. To protect a consumer from business manipulation, one has to assume that the consumer can be manipulated by businesses. Business can be prevented from manipulating consumers if societal measures are available that provide information to individual consumers or that enable individual consumers to be protected from such activities by other consumers.

5. *Government Support for Consumerism:* Much of the consumer's power and thrust comes from government support through legislation. Several government agencies on the federal level are actively engaged in consumer affairs: Federal Trade Commission, Food and Drug Administration, Interstate Commerce Commission, Federal Aviation Administration, Department of Agriculture Consumer and Marketing

Services, Federal Power Commission, Occupational Safety and Health Administration, and Securities and Exchange Commission, to name a few. The function of these agencies (as well as state and local consumer affairs agencies) is to protect the consumer from unfair business practices.

C. Pollution Control

Economic analysis of pollution provides a perspective on its causes and effects. The absence of property rights to our shared resources of air, land, and water provides the major incentive to pollute. The elimination of pollution can be accomplished through three primary avenues: direct controls that eliminate pollution, indirect controls that would tax polluters for the right to pollute, and the establishment of property rights to whatever is being polluted, typically air, land, and water. Each of these avenues has advantages and disadvantages and must be evaluated carefully before effective and efficient pollution controls can be implemented.

1. *Pollution:* Pollution is present in all industrial societies—capitalist, socialist and communist countries alike. In general, pollution is a result of increased economic growth. Pollution is defined as the use of the environment by producers and consumers as a dumping ground for waste. The environment is able to recycle some degree of pollution, but pollution becomes a problem when the quantity of pollutants is greater than what the environment can recycle. The three common forms of pollution are air pollution, water pollution, and land pollution.

a. *Air pollution:* Air pollution is the emission of waste, such as carbon monoxide, sulfa oxides, nitrogen oxides, hydrocarbons, and particulates into the air. These waste materials typically come from the production and consumption processes in our economic system.

b. *Water pollution:* Water pollution is ordinarily measured in terms of the capacity of water to support aquatic life. This capacity depends on the level of dissolved oxygen in the water and the presence of matters or materials injurious to plant and animal life existing in the water. The capacity of the water to support aquatic life is reduced when various kinds of materials and matters are dumped into it. Among these are toxins that do not settle out of the water and are not easily broken down by biological means.

EXAMPLES OF TOXINS: Mercury, dioxins, herbicides, and pesticides.

In recent years, questions have been raised about the oceans being used for the dumping of nuclear wastes or for undersea nuclear explosions.

c. *Land pollution:* Land pollution results from the dumping of a wide variety of wastes onto the terrain and from tearing up the earth's surface through such activities as strip mining. Garbage dumps and landfills grow as cities dispose of waste. The strip mining of the land for coal has, in the past, left unsightly blemishes on the countryside and has taken productive land out of use in some cases.

2. *The Economics of Pollution:* In general, pollution occurs in areas where no well-defined property rights exist. Air, water, and land pollution occurs when the rights to the air, water, or land are not well defined.

EXAMPLE: Air is unlike other resources—no one owns air. Since air is not owned, it can be used without being paid for. As a result, business can minimize the cost of production by eliminating waste into the air rather than using expensive recycling technology.

a. *Reducing pollution costs:* From a business standpoint, production costs can be reduced by using air, water, and land, which have no property owners. By disposing of pollutants into the air or water, business does not have to pay the cost of recycling or cleanup technology. Thus, the costs of production are reduced, and goods are made available to consumers at a lower cost. From a societal point of view, if industries put too much pollution into the environment, the quality of air is reduced, and all society members must then bear the cleanup costs.

EXAMPLES:In a residential area close to a steel plant, the particulates from the steel blast furnace cause the paint on homes and automobiles to deteriorate faster.

If a firm pollutes a stream, the quality of the water as well as the surrounding area is reduced. The quality and quantity of fish in the stream may also be reduced, thereby reducing the satisfaction people who use the stream receive.

b. *The cost of eliminating pollution:* The consumer's initial reaction to pollution is that it should be eliminated totally. However, substantial costs are involved in pollution elimination.

EXAMPLES: If steel companies were required not to pollute, they would have to invest large amounts of capital to collect the particulates from the blast furnaces before these pollutants were emitted into the air.

Similarly, if producers were required not to emit pollutants into streams, they would have to install some type of waste treatment system for the water before it would be allowed to enter a stream.

If producers were required to eliminate all pollution, the result would be an increase in the cost of production and an increase in the cost of any products made by the producer or, as in the case of steel, products made from the original product produced.

c. *Factors for analyzing effects of pollution:* In analyzing the economics of pollution, three factors are important:

(1) The environment can recycle some pollution: we do not need to reduce the level of pollution to zero.

(2) Eliminating pollution benefits society.

(3) Eliminating pollution costs society. These costs will be in the form of higher prices for goods and services due to increased production costs.

3. *Control of Pollution:* Pollution can be reduced through the use of direct and indirect controls and through the establishment of property rights.

a. *Direct controls:* Direct controls involve government banning of activities that result in pollution. These controls are most useful for types of pollution that nature cannot recycle. Such items as plastic bags or tires will not disintegrate on their own. To control the disposal of these items, direct controls may be necessary.

EXAMPLE: Government's banning the use of pesticides such as DDT.

Such policies are enforced by the Environmental Protection Agency (EPA) at the federal level and by various state and local agencies established for this purpose. Some problems that may arise from the use of such direct controls include the following:

(1) Using direct controls does not always consider that the use of certain polluting products (e.g., pesticides) might be necessary to obtain a saleable crop.

(2) The benefits from using the pollutants are not the same for all producers. If outright prohibition of pollutants takes place, this prohibition imposes higher costs on some producers than on others.

EXAMPLE: Abolishing the use of DDT may have substantial effects on the cost to farmers of growing grain but have a minimal effect on the cost to groundskeepers for maintaining golf courses.

(3) A third problem with direct controls is the enforcement that becomes necessary. Since direct controls fail to provide incentive to polluters not to pollute, it is necessary for some type of enforcement to ensure that the controls are not violated.

b. *Indirect controls:* A second method used to control pollution is through indirect controls. Typically, indirect controls include taxing for pollution activities. Producers or individuals would pay a tax for the right to pollute. This method is especially useful in cases where the amount of pollution can be measured. However, substantial problems occur if the pollution cannot be measured directly.

EXAMPLE OF INDIRECT CONTROLS: Taxes or deposits on bottles and cans are imposed to encourage recycling. The high tax or deposit placed on these (1) provides an incentive to recycle and (2) makes it profitable for some individuals to clean up discarded containers.

This process could also be used for firms that emit pollutants into the air or water simply by taxing those firms for the emission of pollutants and then using the tax dollars to clean up the water or to install devices that would minimize the impact of pollution on the environment.

c. *Use of property rights:* A third solution to pollution elimination is to assign property rights to the air and water. By assigning property rights, individuals who own the property (air and water) could charge for the use of the air and water. Therefore, the water and air would become a private good and susceptible to supply and demand conditions for resources that exist in other parts of the market.

D. Employment Opportunities

Substantial attention has been given to discrimination in the labor market. Laws have been passed in an attempt to alleviate this discrimination and to provide equal employment opportunity for all. The major employment law passed in recent years is the Equal Employment Opportunity Act of 1972. Previous legislation included the Civil Rights Act of 1964 and the Age Discrimination Act of 1967. Other major employment legislation targets certain segments of the workforce. The Vocational Rehabilitation Act of 1973 responded to the employment of handicapped persons, and the Americans with Disabilities Act made employment accommodations for physically and mentally disabled persons a reality. Each of these laws attempted in some way to alleviate discrimination in the labor market.

1. *Discrimination:* The term *discrimination* means that equals are treated unequally or that unequals are treated equally. More specifically, discrimination exists in the labor market when persons with equal productivity are paid different wages or persons with differences in productivity are paid equal wages. Some types of discrimination found in labor markets are the following:

a. *Wage discrimination:* In 1985 the average income of males between the ages of 35 and 44 was $25,886, and those between 45 and 54 earned an average of $26,702 annually. At the same time the average annual income of females between the ages of 35 and 44 was $16,114 (62 percent of the average annual income of males). Between 1985 and 1996, some changes occurred in the income differentials between males and females. The median income for white females in 1996 was $24,160 compared to $32,966 for white males. Thus, in 1996 female income was 73.3 percent of male income.

On the surface, this would indicate that females have been discriminated against in terms of salaries, even though the average income for females has been increasing steadily. However, before a case for discrimination can be justified, jobs held by men and those held by women must be examined to discover whether production is at equal levels in the same types of jobs. It is very difficult to talk about wage discrimination on an aggregate scale instead of talking about wage discrimination on the basis of equal pay for equal work.

b. *Employment discrimination:* Employment discrimination means that some people are not hired because of noneconomic characteristics, such as race or gender. Employment discrimination, like wage discrimination, is difficult to identify. Differences among employment rates comparing Caucasians and minority groups or males and females may suggest discrimination but may not prove it exists.

EXAMPLE: When productivity is examined, it may be discovered that unemployment rates are much higher among some particular ethnic groups. Or when educational level is examined and individuals are compared who have identical educational levels, unemployment rates may be much higher among some ethnic groups when compared with other ethnic groups.

Such evidence for employment discrimination becomes more conclusive.

c. *Occupational discrimination:* Another type of discrimination in the labor market is occupational discrimination. Certain occupations may be more available to people of one gender or race. Several studies have been completed recently that show that more high-paying occupations are held by men and that women are often relegated to lower-paying occupations. This would indicate that occupational discrimination exists.

2. *The Costs of Discrimination:* Discrimination represents a substantial loss not only to individuals but also to society. To individuals, the loss may be less income and the inaccessibility of occupations in which they would like to be employed. The social loss is in terms of a lower output and lower productivity than if discrimination did not exist. This lower output is a result of high unemployment of certain groups that results in a smaller production possibility curve for society than would otherwise be possible.

3. *Legislation Regulating Discrimination Practices:* Five basic laws have been passed to minimize discrimination within the labor market in the United States.

a. *The Civil Rights Act of 1964:* Instrumental in eliminating many forms of discrimination, this act was the first legislation of its kind. Title VII was concerned with equal employment opportunities and specified that employees or labor organizations with

25 or more employees must treat all persons equally, regardless of gender, race, national origin, or religion. It also provided for the creation of the Equal Employment Opportunity Commission to help with enforcement of the act.

b. *The Age Discrimination in Employment Act of 1967:* This legislation applies to private employers of 20 or more persons and all federal, state, and local governments, regardless of the number of people employed. This act prohibits discrimination based on the age of the applicant. Specifically, it prohibits discrimination against individuals between the ages of 40 and 65 in the hiring, compensation, working conditions, and privileges of employment. This act also made it illegal for an employer to request an applicant's age on an employment application form or in the advertising of employment opportunities.

c. *The Equal Employment Opportunity Act of 1972:* This Act involves a series of amendments to the Civil Rights Act of 1964. Perhaps the most significant amendment provided an independent agency for the first time at the federal level—the Equal Employment Opportunity Commission (EEOC). The EEOC was empowered to enforce laws prohibiting discrimination based on gender, race, national origin, or religion. In addition, the EEOC received the power to institute civil action as a means of eliminating discrimination in employment. As a result of this act, coverage was also extended to state and local government employees and employees of labor organizations with 15 or more members.

d. *The Vocational Rehabilitation Act of 1973:* Job-related discrimination against handicapped individuals was specifically eliminated in the Vocational Rehabilitation Act of 1973.

e. *The Americans with Disabilities Act:* The Civil Rights Act of 1964 was extended in 1992 to cover the physically and mentally disabled, including AIDS patients; cancer patients; and treated, recovering substance abusers. Individuals with emotional disorders, however, were excluded. Businesses are required to make reasonable accommodations to workers and job applicants with disabilities unless the required changes present an undue hardship for the business. The act is considered the most comprehensive civil rights legislation in 30 years.

Each of these federal laws relates to economic discrimination in the labor market and attempts to minimize the amount of discrimination that might take place. The EEOC is the major enforcer of the various laws and is empowered to initiate civil proceedings against firms, labor unions, and government agencies that have violated one of these acts.

Review Questions

Directions: Select the best answer from the four alternatives. Write your answer in the blank to the left of the number.

______ **1.** Which of the following statements describes a choice that involves conservation?

a. Produce wheat or corn
b. Use resources for current or future consumption
c. Have private industry or government pay for education
d. Produce automobiles

______ **2.** Of the following statements, which business practices are generally thought to be adverse to consumer interests?

a. Advertising goods or services in local newspapers
b. Many firms making similar products
c. Production of low-quality products
d. Production of high-cost products

______ **3.** Which of the following is generally not assumed to be a consumer right?

a. Right to safety
b. Right to choose
c. Right to low-priced products
d. Right to be heard

______ **4.** With respect to consumerism, there are

a. neither costs nor benefits to the consumer.
b. both costs and benefits to the consumer.
c. only benefits to the consumer.
d. only costs to the consumer.

______ **5.** Increased information about the quality of a product will

a. leave no impact on the economic costs of the item.
b. result in a lower price for the product to the consumer.
c. help consumers make decisions that result in increasing their welfare.
d. confuse consumers and thus result in irrational decisions being made.

______ **6.** Which of the following is not generally considered a regulation aimed at protecting the consumer?

a. Inspection of meat
b. Prohibition of smoking in elevators
c. Seat belts in cars
d. Licensing of accountants

_______________ **7.** The economic costs of regulation do not include

a. costs of government agencies that enforce regulations.
b. the licensing of professionals who provide specific services.
c. value of resources used to meet regulations that could be available for another use.
d. loss of freedom to engage in those activities prohibited by regulation.

_______________ **8.** Which of the following activities is not considered an activity to help consumers?

a. Providing information
b. Regulations minimizing risk to consumers of products
c. Providing national defense by government
d. Protection from business manipulation

_______________ **9.** Which of the following government agencies is most actively engaged in consumer affairs?

a. Bureau of the Budget
b. Department of Commerce
c. Food and Drug Administration
d. U.S. Congress

_______________ **10.** The major reason for pollution is

a. lack of social conscience of business.
b. lack of property rights.
c. greediness of consumers.
d. absence of government regulations.

_______________ **11.** Three general ways to control pollution are the uses of

a. direct controls, extension of property rights, and government regulation.
b. indirect controls, extension of property rights, and tax placed on polluters.
c. elimination of property rights, indirect controls, and government regulation.
d. direct controls, indirect controls, and extension of property rights.

_______________ **12.** Which of the following best describes discrimination?

a. Equals are treated equally.
b. Persons with the same productivity are paid the same.
c. Unequals are treated unequally.
d. Equals are treated unequally.

_______________ **13.** A specific example of discrimination in the labor market is

a. a man is employed in an occupation for which he does not meet the basic qualifications.
b. an employee receives a wage commensurate with education and experience.
c. a worker is displaced by technology.

d. a woman is denied a promotion to manager even though she has the basic qualifications for the position.

______ **14.** Costs of discrimination are borne by

a. individuals only.
b. individuals and society together.
c. society alone.
d. producers alone.

______ **15.** The Americans with Disabilities Act requires that

a. businesses make reasonable accommodations for workers and job applicants with disabilities.
b. job-related discrimination of handicapped individuals be eliminated.
c. discrimination based on the age of the individual be prohibited.
d. employers treat all employees equally on the basis of gender, race, national origin, and religion.

______ **16.** In a market-oriented economic system, discrimination

a. can be eliminated, but the costs are high.
b. would never exist.
c. should be eliminated since the costs are very low.
d. can never be eliminated.

______ **17.** In an office building a number of signs can be found posted in various corridors. Which one is the result of consumer action designed to protect the consumer?

a. "Directions for tornado watches/warnings"
b. "Building hours 7 a.m. to 10 p.m."
c. "No smoking in elevator"
d. "Caution—wet floors!"

______ **18.** ABC Autos, Inc., is a retail automobile dealership. A series of sales promotions are being developed and considered for use in promoting the sale of new automobiles. Which of the following statements most likely represents deceptive advertising?

a. "The new Rally is the best car you'll ever own!"
b. "The moment you sit behind the wheel, you will want to drive it away!"
c. "More miles to the gallon!"
d. "No money down! You can drive it away for $199 a month plus a moderate finance charge!"

Solutions

Answer	*Refer to:*
1. (b)	[A-1] Answers (a), (c), and (d) all involve choices on current resource use, not conservation of resources for the future.
2. (c)	[B-1] The production and marketing of low-quality products are thought of as practices adverse to the consumer's interest. Firms that are making similar products are typically competitive and therefore beneficial to consumers. Advertising goods and services keeps consumers informed about products coming onto the market.
3. (c)	[B-2] Answers (a), (b), and (d) state some of the rights of consumers. Answer (c) is something consumers might like to have but has not been declared a right.
4. (b)	[B-3] For any decision involving the use of scarce resources, there are costs and benefits to both the consumer and the producer.
5. (c)	[B-3-a(1)] The consumer must have information about the prices and quality of a variety of goods and services to make rational decisions.
6. (d)	[B-3-a(3)] Answers (a), (b), and (c) all relate to areas that affect the consumer directly. Answer (d) affects the consumer only indirectly.
7. (b)	[B-3-b] The licensing of professionals is considered an economic benefit of consumerism rather than an economic cost to consumers.
8. (c)	[B-3] The provision of national defense by the government is usually considered necessary since it is impossible for business to provide national defense. Providing national defense is not considered an activity that helps consumers.
9. (c)	[B-5] Answer (c) is correct since it is the only alternative that lists a government agency engaged in consumer affairs.
10. (b)	[C-1] Although some pollution may be caused by answers (a), (c), and (d), the major reason for pollution is lack of property rights.
11. (d)	[C-3] Answer (d) lists the three general methods of controlling pollution. Answers (a), (b), and (c) all have a specific policy listed with the general method.
12. (d)	[D-1] If equals were treated unequally, some individuals would be discriminated against for one reason or another.

13. (d) [D-1-c] This is the only situation that appears to be discriminatory. A woman who has the basic qualifications for a managerial position who is denied the promotion may have just cause to believe that discrimination has taken place.

14. (b) [D-2] If discrimination exists, the individual loses, but society also loses the potential output of the person being discriminated against.

15. (a) [D-3-e] The Americans with Disabilities Act supports primarily persons with disabilities.

16. (d) [D-3] A market requires choices to be made, and choices will always result in some form of discrimination. The role of society is to define what criteria can be used to discriminate.

17. (c) [B-3-a(3)] A large part of consumerism activities is directed toward the protection of the consumer.

18. (d) [B-3-a(2)] The statement is vague, not stating a definite finance charge or any other "hidden" costs in purchasing the automobile.

CHAPTER 5
International Trade

OVERVIEW

The United States is involved in substantial amounts of international trade. In 1997 over $965 billion worth of goods and services were exported from the United States, that is, sold to other countries around the world. In addition, U.S. citizens bought slightly over $1,059 billion in foreign goods and services (imports) in 1997. This resulted in a negative balance of trade of close to $94 billion.

All countries in the world engage in some form of international trade. In relation to the total level of production in society, the United States engages in a relatively small amount of trade. However, in absolute dollars, the total amount of trade is substantial for the country. The reasons countries engage in trade are numerous, but one principle is always present: The country is better off *after* trade than it was *before* trade.

In this chapter we review the fundamentals of international trade, the economic basis of international trade (especially geographic specialization, absolute advantage, and comparative advantage), and special problems of international trade. The balance of payments in international finance and international exchange is also discussed. The effects of tariffs and quotas as policies established by individual countries are emphasized as an important part of international trade.

KEY TERMS

Absolute advantage
Ad valorem
Balance of payments
Common market (European Economic Community)
Comparative advantage
Compound tariff
Embargo
Foreign exchange rate
Geographic specialization
Import quota
Import tariff
International finance
Nationalism
Protective tariff
Revenue tariff
Specific tariff
Tariff
Tariff quota

A. Fundamentals of International Trade

In addition to economic concepts, international trade encompasses the political economy and the sociocultural climate of different nations. These determine the movement of goods, services, people, and capital across national political boundaries and thus set the stage for international trade. The fundamentals of international trade involve its economic theory and importance in our society.

1. *Theory of International Trade:* To explain the basic theory of international trade, we must look at each of the following questions:

Why does international trade take place?

What determines the composition, pattern, and direction of international trade?

On what kinds of terms does international trade take place?

What are the economic results of international trade?

a. *The need for international trade:* International trade exists because of differences in the productive capacities of various countries. These differences lead to differences in production costs for goods. Thus, it becomes mutually advantageous for countries to trade with one another. For trade among countries to become beneficial, geographic specialization must take place on the basis of the comparative advantages of producing a different commodity.

b. *Composition, pattern, and direction of international trade:* Three primary factors determine the composition, pattern, and direction of international trade:

(1) *The relative endowments of factors of production:* The term *relative endowments* refers to the amount of land, capital, available labor, and skills possessed by the labor force in any particular country. Countries have unequal endowments of these factors; thus, they will differ in their abilities to produce certain types of goods.

(2) *Economics of large-scale production:* The economics of large-scale production deals with the relationship of the average cost of production to the amount produced. For some goods, as the output increases, the average cost of production declines. If countries have small internal or domestic markets, they would be unable to produce in an efficient manner. Through international trade and marketing products overseas, the output of goods can increase, and the average cost of production can be reduced, resulting in more efficient production.

(3) *Minimization of transportation costs:* In a free market, industries tend to locate where the costs of transportation are minimized. In some cases it is advantageous for a country to specialize in a particular commodity because the transportation costs for getting the resources to the place of production or the finished products from production to the final markets will be minimized.

c. *Terms of trade:* The terms of trade at which exchange takes place are often referred to as the foreign exchange rate for currency. Foreign exchange refers to the monetary means for making payments in currencies other than a country's own currency. The rate of exchange is the price of foreign currency in terms of domestic currency.

EXAMPLE: In the United States, the exchange rate indicates the number of U.S. dollars per unit of foreign currency. If the British pound sterling is quoted as $2.50, this means that one pound sterling is worth $2.50 in U.S. money.

The demand for foreign exchange stems from countries buying foreign goods.

EXAMPLE: If Americans buy more Japanese products, Americans have a demand for Japanese yen to pay for these products. This also increases the supply of American dollars in Japan.

d. *Economic results of international trade:* Through international trade, each country gains as the gap between prices of goods and services and the prices of factors of production are narrowed among countries. International trade reduces the opportunity cost of obtaining certain commodities in which a country has a comparative cost disadvantage.

2. *The Importance of International Trade:* Commodity and service trade comes to 7 to 12 percent of world income. However, for some countries trade is much more important.

EXAMPLE: As a percentage of gross domestic product, exports are around 30 to 35 percent for the Netherlands; about 15 percent for Germany, Great Britain, and Italy; and about 10 percent for France.

For a few countries, such as the United States, international trade is less important. The U. S. exports are usually around 6 to 10 percent of gross domestic product. Yet, trade contributes much to our standard of living.

a. *U.S. involvement in international trade:* While international trade represents a relatively small portion of the gross domestic product, the United States is the world's largest exporter and importer and the largest provider of international capital and grants.

(1) *Volume of imports:* The volume of U.S. imports is of vital significance to other countries. These sales provide the dollar earnings that other countries need to pay for the importation of American goods. The volume of U.S. imports is closely related to the level of national income. The higher the level of national income in the United States, the greater the quantity of imports we consume. This fact results in close ties between the U.S. economy and economies of foreign countries.

EXAMPLE: If the U.S. economy enters a period of recession, the demand for imports is decreased, and the quantity of dollars that foreign countries have to purchase goods from the United States is reduced. Along with the decreased demand for foreign goods is reduced income (in U.S. dollars) to buy American goods and services that foreign countries do not produce domestically.

(2) *Volume of exports:* The U.S. exports are lower than the world average (usually around 7 to 12 percent of the gross domestic product). However, international trade is important to the United States because of its contribution to our standard of living. International trade is the product of a world in which countries are dependent on one another to maintain their respective standards of living.

B. Economic Basis of International Trade

The economic basis of international trade involves an analysis of geographic specialization, absolute advantage, and comparative advantage. These three concepts are explained in this section, along with specific problems relating to international trade, domestic policies leading to restrictions in trade, the idea of nationalism, and artificial barriers that interfere with international trade.

1. *Geographic Specialization:* Geographic specialization is based on the premise that differences in production capabilities lead to differences in comparative costs for production. Geographic specialization is also the basis for mutually beneficial international or interregional trade. Two conditions are the foundation for specialization and trade: (1) the relative prices of the factors of production and (2) differences in the level of technology in various countries. Both of these factors lead to differences in relative costs of production. Countries gain from trade by specializing in the production of goods they can produce at a low cost and importing commodities that are expensive to produce domestically. Production specialization in which the country or area has a cost advantage is referred to as *geographic specialization.*

The basis for trade among regions within a country or among different countries is the same. Each region within a country has comparative advantages for producing particular goods and services because of the presence of soil, climate, topography, natural resources, labor supply, and capital supply best suited to produce those goods or services.

EXAMPLES: In the United States, Florida and California have a comparative advantage in producing citrus fruits; the Plains states, in grain and pork; the north-central and northeastern states, in heavy manufacturing; and the East Coast, in fresh fish.

Historically, in international trade, the United States has had an advantage in agriculture and technology; Canada, in wheat and wood pulp; Japan, in textiles; Australia, in wool; and France, in wine and perfumes.

Through geographic specialization, world production efficiency is increased and standards of living improved.

2. *Absolute Advantage and Comparative Advantage:* The principles of absolute advantage and comparative advantage are the basis for international trade and interregional economics. The principles by which geographic specialization takes place stem from the concepts of absolute advantage and comparative advantage:

a. *Principle of absolute advantage:* The principle of absolute advantage, in relation to the concept of comparative advantage, illustrates the benefits of interregional and international trade.

EXAMPLE: Figure 5–1 provides information about two manufacturers of electronic products, each with an identical quantity of land, equipment, and quality of labor available. The U.S. manufacturer can produce 200 television sets or 400 stereo systems with the same resources that the manufacturer in Japan needs to produce only 20 television sets or 200 stereos.

The U.S. producer can manufacture more of each product—television sets and stereo systems—with a given amount of resources. We say that the United States has an absolute advantage in producing both television sets and stereo systems.

Figure 5–1 Televisions/Stereos—U.S./Japan

	Television Sets	Stereo Systems
U.S. producer	200	400
Japanese producer	20	200
Opportunity cost		
Television sets (U.S.)	1	2
Television sets (Japan)	1	10

Initially, it might seem that the U.S. manufacturer should produce both products and that the Japanese manufacturer should find something else to produce. However, this would not result in efficient production of television sets and stereo systems.

b. *Principle of comparative advantage:* The principle of comparative advantage refers to the ability of a particular country to produce a good at a lower opportunity cost, compared to the opportunity costs of other goods, than can other countries with whom it trades. This principle emphasizes that each country tends to specialize in production and exportation of commodities in which it has a comparative advantage and to import those commodities in which it has a comparative disadvantage.

EXAMPLE: Use the example illustrated in Figure 5–1 to analyze the opportunity costs for a U.S. manufacturer and a Japanese producer. When analyzing the opportunity costs for the U.S. manufacturer, the opportunity cost of producing television sets must first be considered. If the U.S. producer can manufacture 200 television sets with the same resources, some of both products can be produced by diverting resources from televisions to stereos. In the extreme case, 200 televisions and no stereos or 400 stereos and no televisions could be produced with the same resources. If the U.S. producer started manufacturing only televisions and then changed to producing only stereos, 200 televisions would be forgone to produce 400 stereos. The U.S. producer would be giving up one-half of a television set for every stereo system produced. The opportunity cost of producing a stereo system would be one-half that of a television set. This opportunity cost represents the real cost of producing stereo systems.

A similar analysis can be used for the Japanese producer. If only television sets were produced, production would be 20 television sets. If the manufacturer then moves from producing only televisions to producing only stereos, 20 televisions must be given up to produce 200 stereos. The Japanese producer is giving up one-tenth of a television set for every stereo produced. The opportunity cost to the manufacturer for producing television sets is one-tenth of a stereo system. Therefore, the cost of producing stereos by the Japanese producer is less than the cost of producing stereos by the U.S. producer (the cost to the Japanese producer is one-tenth of a television set compared to the cost to the U.S. producer, one-half of a television set).

Result: Since the cost of producing stereos is less, the Japanese producer would want to specialize in stereo production.

A similar analysis could be completed for the production of television sets. The cost of producing television sets to the U.S. producer is one television set for two stereo systems. For the Japanese producer, one television set is equal to 10 stereo systems. The U.S. producer has a comparative advantage in the production of television sets since what must be forgone in terms of stereo systems is less.

Result: The U.S. producer has an absolute advantage in the production of both television sets and stereo systems. However, the real cost of producing television sets and stereo systems is different for the two companies. As a result, the U.S. producer should specialize in producing televisions, and the Japanese manufacturer should specialize in producing stereo systems.

3. *The Establishment of Trade:* Once specialization takes place, the profitability for the two countries (United States and Japan) to establish trade would be determined by the terms of trade.

   EXAMPLE: Continuing the U.S./Japan example, for the U.S. manufacturer to produce televisions, 10 stereos must be forgone for every television set produced. If televisions can be purchased from the United States for an amount equivalent to less than 10 stereos, the U.S. producer would gain from the trade. On the other hand, for every television set the U.S. producer forgoes, only two stereos can be produced. The U.S. producer would gain if the value of two stereos were traded for the value of one television set. Using that knowledge as the basis for trade, the U.S. producer will give up televisions for stereos if the value of the televisions exceeds that of two stereos. Similarly, the Japanese producer will give up stereos for televisions if a television set can be obtained by giving up less than 10 stereos. Thus, each producer can benefit from specialization and trade.

   The principles in this example can be used to understand the establishment of international trade as well as interregional trade. Trade between two countries takes place in a manner similar to that of trade between regions within a country.

   EXAMPLE: Figure 5–2 shows that the United States produces 100 bushels of wheat or 50 gallons of wine with a given set of resources. With those same resources, France can produce 50 bushels of wheat or 40 gallons of wine. Assuming that the quality of wheat and the quality of wine are the same, the United States has an absolute advantage in the production of both wheat and wine. However, according to the principle of comparative advantage, the United States must give up only one-half gallon of wine to produce a bushel of wheat, whereas France must give up four-fifths of a gallon of wine to produce a bushel of wheat. The United States has a comparative advantage in wheat production, and trade will take place as long as the United States has to give up less than two bushels of wheat for every gallon of wine. In return, France would receive more than four-fifths of a bushel of wheat for every gallon of wine. If the terms of trade were within this range, both countries could gain, and efficiency in the production of both wheat and wine would be attained.

4. *The Value of Establishing Trade:* The establishment of trade between two countries provides the opportunity for the following cooperative efforts to occur:

   a. *Reallocation of resources:* Resources will be reallocated as each country expands employment of those resources needed for the production of goods for which that country holds a comparative advantage.

   b. *Equalization of cost and commodity price differentials:* Relative price and cost differentials are a primary reason for trade, but trade will result only if these differences tend to be eliminated in the international market. The equalization of commodity prices and factor cost must be gained from international trade. As long

Figure 5–2 Wheat/Wine—U.S./France

	Wheat (bushels)	Wine (barrels)
United States	100	50
France	50	40

as price and cost disparities exist among nations, there will be the opportunity cost for gain by engaging in international trade.

C. Special Problems of International Trade

While the international trade theory presented above explains how countries gain from trade, particular circumstances often lead countries into minimizing the amount of international trade involvement. These circumstances can be classified as domestic policy and nationalism.

1. *Domestic Policy:* Traditionally, independent countries have monetary and fiscal controls that cause some exchange rate problems. If a country is attempting to reduce its rate of unemployment by expanding its economy through increased money supply, this has an adverse effect on that country's international trade position. Domestic inflation would increase the demand for imports and reduce the demand for exports. A country may want to follow an official policy of restricting imports during that period of time, so it can achieve domestic stability even though it does not gain as much from trade as possible. Barriers that a country imposes to achieve domestic goals include tariffs (taxes placed on imported commodities), quotas, and embargoes.

2. *Nationalism:* Nationalism is a belief that one's country should be self-sufficient and should not depend on other countries for goods and services. Nationalism often interferes with and restricts international trade.

   EXAMPLE: The common market in Europe is an example of the spirit of nationalism among countries in a region of the world. Among the common market countries, there is relatively free trade. However, trade restrictions do exist among members of the common market and the rest of the world. This is an attempt by the members of the common market to expand the ability of common market countries to be self-sufficient at the expense of international trade.

D. Elements of International Finance

International finance is the movement of monies from one country to another. Basic balance sheet accounting is used to analyze the flow of monies among countries. This balance sheet is referred to as the *balance of payments.*

1. *The Balance of Payments:* The balance of payments is an international summary statement of all economic and financial transactions between one country and the rest of the world for one year. The balance of payments distinguishes between debit payments and credits and receipts. Because of the double-entry nature of the accounting system, the debits must be equal to the credits in any balance-of-payments statement.

   a. *Debit:* A debit is any transaction that gives rise to a claim for payment against a resident of a country.

      EXAMPLE: Anderson receives wine from France as a purchase or a gift. The fact that the wine from France enters the United States gives rise to a claim for payment from the United States to France. Thus, the value of the wine coming into the country is a debit item to the U.S. balance of payments.

      Any commodity or service coming into a country is a debit whether payment is made or not. Similarly, a cash outflow would be a capital outflow and a debit on the U.S. balance of payments.

      EXAMPLES: The purchase of a foreign corporation's stocks and bonds by an American citizen would be a debit on the U.S. balance of payments.

Payments to U.S. military overseas represent debits to the U.S. balance-of-payments account.

b. *Credit:* A credit to the balance-of-payments account would be a claim of the United States against a foreign country.

EXAMPLES: The export of any good or service, the purchase of U.S. stocks and bonds by a citizen of a foreign country, and any foreign investment in U.S. companies.

c. *Categories of debits and credits:* The debits and credits are divided into five categories within the balance-of-payments account:

(1) *Current account:* Commodities and services imports and exports.

(2) *Net remittances and pensions:* Unilateral transfer or private gifts or grants between countries.

(3) *Net government transactions:* Loans and grants made between countries.

(4) *Net capital movements:* U.S. investment in foreign countries minus foreign countries' investments in the United States.

(5) *Financing transactions:* Involvement of international reserves to make the balance of payments balance.

A nation's balance of payments is considered in disequilibrium when the nation's autonomous payments are not sufficient to meet its autonomous receipts, thereby necessitating corresponding balancing, financing, or accommodating transactions, including foreign money sales and increases in nonresident liquid liabilities.

2. *International Exchange:* International exchange can be summarized in terms of payment for imports, export of goods and services, import surplus/unfavorable balance of trade, and long-term international capital movements.

a. *Payment for imports:* To pay for its imports, a country must have foreign monies (foreign exchange) that will be demanded by the exporters. The possible sources for this exchange are the following:

(1) The export of goods and services from one country to another

(2) The borrowing of money from abroad

(3) The receipt of gifts from abroad

(4) The liquidation of home-owned foreign assets

b. *Export of goods and services:* The export of goods and services is the only way that will result in the acquisition of foreign dollars by a country over a long-term basis. Other forms of obtaining foreign capital can be used only temporarily or over short periods of time.

EXAMPLE: When O'Connor borrows from abroad, this loan must be repaid at some point in time. Similarly, gifts from abroad cannot continue indefinitely.

The export of goods and services is necessary for a country to have the long-term ability to trade.

c. *Import surplus or unfavorable balance of trade:* Over short periods of time, a country may have an import surplus, also called an *unfavorable balance of trade.*

The normal method of financing a persistent import surplus over several years is through long-term borrowing or long-term capital movement into the country.

d. *Long-term international capital movements:* Most developed countries obtain capital through long-term international capital investments without reducing consumption. These capital movements rank second in importance to international imports and exports.

International finance is simply a financial accounting of international transactions. The two important aspects of international finance are the balance of trade (the difference between the value of exports and the value of imports) and the balance of movement of capital. For a country to participate continually in the international market, it must have a balance, or surplus balance, trade account to finance other types of transactions.

E. Commercial Policies

Countries may occasionally want to engage in activities that may restrict international trade. These commercial policies are usually import tariffs, export tariffs, transit tariffs, and quotas. Tariffs and quotas are discussed in this section along with the economic effect and some arguments for these types of protection.

1. *Tariffs:* Tariffs are taxes levied on commodities as they move through a custom boundary.

a. *Purposes of tariffs:* The two general purposes of tariffs are protection and revenue.

(1) *Protective tariffs:* Protective tariffs are typically import tariffs levied to protect domestic industry against foreign competition. The use of protective tariffs increases the cost of imported products, making it easier for domestic producers to compete. Most tariffs in the United States today are protective tariffs.

(2) *Revenue tariffs:* Revenue tariffs are levied to benefit the country levying the tariff. Early tariffs levied in the continental United States, and some developing countries' tariffs levied in recent years, were based on revenue considerations. The impact of revenue tariffs on trade gains is less than that of the protective tariff. If revenue tariffs restricted trade, they would defeat their primary purpose—to gain revenue—since revenue could not be received if trade for the commodities ceased.

b. *Types of tariffs:* There are three different types of tariffs: *ad valorem* tariffs, specific tariffs, and compound tariffs.

(1) *Ad valorem tariffs: Ad valorem* tariffs are based on the value of the commodity.

EXAMPLE: A tariff of 10 percent of the price of the goods or some percentage of the price of the goods.

(2) *Specific tariffs:* Specific tariffs are charges per physical unit of the good.

EXAMPLE: A tariff of 10 cents per pound on imported beef.

(3) *Compound tariffs:* Compound tariffs are based on *ad valorem* and physical units.

EXAMPLE: A tariff of $100 per ton of steel plus 50 percent of its value.

Each of these tariffs increases the price of the foreign good in the country imposing the tariff.

2. *Quotas:* Another form of commercial policy to restrict the amount of international trade is the *quota.* The two types of quotas used are import quotas and tariff quotas.

a. *Import quota:* An import quota puts a limit on the amount or value that can be imported into a country.

EXAMPLE: An import quota could be initiated allowing only 500,000 tons of beef into the country in any given year. Once that quota is reached, no more beef may come in until the next quota period.

b. *Tariff quota:* A tariff quota puts a low tariff or no tariff on goods imported into the country up to a certain amount. After that quota is reached, a higher tariff goes into effect. Tariffs provide revenues, while quotas benefit only those with import licenses.

EXAMPLE: There may be no tariff on imported beef for the first 100,000 pounds and a tariff of 50 cents per pound after that quota has been reached.

Quotas are generally considered to be more harmful than tariffs since quotas completely sever the price-cost relationship. Tariffs merely distort this relationship.

c. *Embargo:* A unique form of quota is an embargo. During an embargo, no units of a particular commodity can be imported or, in some cases, exported.

EXAMPLE: The United States placed an export embargo on all exports to Iraq in 1990.

3. *General Restrictive Devices:* A country can choose to place general restrictions on goods imported into or exported from the country.

EXAMPLES: Sanitary regulations, administrative protection, milling regulations, and marks of origin.

These practices would, in essence, restrict the amount of trade with a given country. The commercial history of the United States shows wide swings between extremely high protective tariffs, such as those used in the 1930s, to low tariffs in the 1960s and 1970s. In general, vested self-interest groups have lobbied for tariffs that, though harmful to the country, benefit some workers in the protected industries.

4. *Economic Effects of Tariffs and Quotas:* The immediate impact of a tariff is to change the price-cost conditions of the importing and exporting countries. The price of the commodity in competitive equilibrium must be higher by exactly the amount of the tariff in the levying country compared to the exporting country. Free trade tends to equalize prices.

a. *Economic effects of tariffs:* A tariff creates a price differential that, in competitive equilibrium, is exactly equal to the tariff. The differential can be achieved in three ways:

(1) The price of the good can stay the same in the exporting country but rise in the importing country by the full amount of the tariff.

EXAMPLE: An English bicycle costs $100, and an import tariff of $25 is levied by the United States. In this instance, the price of the bicycle in England and in the international market would be $100, while in the United States the price would be $125.

(2) The price in the exporting country would fall by the full amount of the tariff and stay the same in the importing country.

EXAMPLE: In the example above, the price of the bicycle might fall to $75 in England and remain at $100 in the United States.

(3) The price would fall some in the exporting country and rise some in the importing country.

EXAMPLE: The price of the bicycle in the United States would be between $100 and $125 or, in England, between $75 and $100, with the differential being $25.

Which country would bear the brunt of the tariff depends on the elasticity of the demand for the item and the supply of the item. A country with the judicious use of tariffs can improve its terms of trade and make foreigners pay part, or the major portion, of the tariff.

b. *Economic effects of quotas:* The imposition of a quota tends to lower the supply, quantity demanded, and thus the price for the importing country, thereby improving its terms of trade.

(1) A quota has no limits to its price effect; in contrast, a tariff has price-effect limits.

(2) With a tariff, government gets the price differential; with a quota, the importer gets the price differential. When a quota is imposed, the availability of the goods demanded is reduced, resulting in a higher price being paid by the consumer. The difference between the competitive price and the higher price is received by the importer.

c. *Arguments against tariffs:* The economic argument against tariffs is that they prevent full realization of potential benefits from specialization in trade. The basis for a mutual gain in trade is the relative cost differences between countries. These differences narrow and eventually disappear with free trade as the world achieves more efficient allocation of its scarce resources. If protective tariffs or quotas are imposed, the movement toward the production cost differences is eliminated and, therefore, the need for countries to trade.

d. *Arguments for protective tariffs:* There are five basic arguments for protective tariffs: protecting terms of trade, protecting infant industries, preventing unemployment, increasing military or political security, and protecting domestic wage levels.

(1) *Protecting terms of trade:* A country could have lower prices as a result of imposing import tariffs. This is especially true if the country is a large importer of goods or services and the country exporting the good depends on that as a substantial market. Thus, the exporting country would have to reduce its prices to an extent where the tariff had no negative effect on sales in the importing country. This is much like the monopolist who raises prices above the competitive level and gains monopoly profits. Of course, any gain realized with the country imposing the tariff is at the direct expense of the exporting country. The possibility of a country improving its terms of trade with a tariff depends heavily on that country being a world power in the importing of goods and services. That country must also be strong enough to prevent any retaliation on these types of tariffs from other countries.

(2) *Protecting infant industries:* Tariffs can also encourage economic growth and industrialization. Newly emerging industries sometimes have difficulty developing in the face of competition from already established foreign firms in the same industries. Granting protection to infant industries allows them to become established.

EXAMPLE: The infant industry thesis was developed in the United States by Alexander Hamilton, the first Secretary of the Treasury. This thesis argued that new countries with newly developed industries could not compete with the same industries in established countries without protection during their "growing-up," or infancy, period. Once the infancy period was completed, the protective tariffs would be eliminated.

While the infant industry argument has validity, it is difficult to determine which particular industries fit into the "infant" category. What happens in actual practice is that protection continues indefinitely, and the protected industry continues to argue for protection indefinitely.

(3) *Preventing unemployment:* One way to reduce unemployment is to raise import tariffs and decrease imports. This decrease in imports would cause an increase in the demand for domestic goods and services and increase employment. The use of tariffs for prevention of unemployment simply transfers the unemployment in the country imposing the tariffs to other countries around the world. The imposition of tariffs for preservation of employment can also be answered by retaliation from foreign countries by imposing similar tariffs that would reduce the ability to export.

(4) *Increasing military or political security:* The military and political security argument has been the most popular argument for tariffs in recent years. This argument states that a country should continue to produce items essential for military security regardless of its inefficiency in that area.

EXAMPLE: During the 1973 Arab oil embargo, many people argued that the United States should become energy self-sufficient from a military protection standpoint. If the United States were not energy self-sufficient, we would be at the mercy of foreign countries to provide us with sources of energy during periods of war, and our ability to wage war would be reduced substantially.

One problem with limiting imports of foreign products to ensure domestic production is that the desired results may not be achieved. If restrictions were placed on importation of foreign crude oil, domestic reserves would have to be used. This would deplete a nonrenewable domestic resource faster than if foreign oil were imported.

EXAMPLE: If the United States becomes energy self-sufficient, we will be using domestic resource deposits of oil, uranium, and other energy forms more rapidly than we would if we also imported some of these energies from other countries.

(5) *Protecting domestic wage levels:* Proponents of this theory argue that high-priced home labor will have to compete with low-priced foreign labor. As a result, home labor may be unemployed and/or have to accept lower wages if industries in which these home laborers work are not protected. Individuals who are pro-tariff often cite the low wage levels that allow goods to be produced inexpensively in Hong Kong as an example of low-priced foreign labor.

This argument often confuses wage rates with wage costs. Wage rates are the wages per unit of labor, while wage costs are the wages per unit of output. The only meaningful comparison for international trade purposes is the wage cost.

> If labor productivity in the United States is five times higher than that in a foreign country, the wages in the United States could be as much as five times greater without any difference in wage costs.

Although each argument has some validity in terms of restriction of international trade, each will also prevent the efficient operation of a world economy. Another consequence would be higher costs and less output than free trade would produce. When considering policies that restrict trade, the real cost to a society and whether those costs are offset by domestic gains must be taken into account.

Review Questions

Directions: Select the best answer from the four alternatives. Write your answer in the blank to the left of the number.

________ **1.** An increase in the tariff on foreign-produced automobiles would be least likely to benefit

a. producers of automobiles.
b. domestic consumers of automobiles.
c. workers in the automobile industry.
d. steel producers, if steel were used to produce domestic automobiles.

________ **2.** Each trading nation can gain by specializing in the production of those items for which they are low-opportunity-cost producers while trading for those things for which they are high-opportunity-cost producers. This statement best describes the implications of

a. the export-import link.
b. the industrial diversity argument.
c. the law of comparative advantage.
d. the equation of exchange.

________ **3.** A trade policy that reduces government-imposed restrictions preventing foreign goods from freely entering the U.S. market (e.g., a reduction in tariffs) will

a. reduce the demand for U.S. export goods.
b. benefit producers at the expense of consumers.
c. reduce the nation's income by failing to protect domestic jobs from foreign competition.
d. enhance economic efficiency by allocating more resources to the areas of their greatest comparative advantage.

________ **4.** Which of the following is not an argument for protecting certain domestic industries from foreign competitors?

a. The law of comparative advantage
b. The national defense for protection argument
c. The present unemployment argument
d. The infant industry argument

________ **5.** The share of gross domestic product (GDP) in the United States that results from exports is approximately

a. 25 percent.
b. 10 percent.
c. 15 percent.
d. 20 percent.

_______________ **6.** Specialization and trade, according to comparative advantage, tend to reduce cost while directing each output toward its highest valued use. Thus, total benefits increase while total output

a. is reduced as a cost of specialization.
b. is reduced in physical terms, not in value.
c. increases in the region gaining most and is reduced to the region gaining least.
d. increases in the trading regions.

_______________ **7.** The law of comparative advantage explains why a nation will benefit from trade when

a. it exports more than it imports.
b. its trading partners are experiencing offsetting losses.
c. it exports goods for which it is a high-opportunity-cost producer while importing those for which it is a low-opportunity-cost producer.
d. it exports goods for which it is a low-opportunity-cost producer while importing those for which it is a high-opportunity-cost producer.

_______________ **8.** Which of the following is a credit to a government's balance of payments?

a. U.S. citizen's purchase of stock in a British company
b. Purchase of U.S. stock by a British citizen
c. Payment to U.S. military personnel in Asia
d. Value of a gift given by a U.S. citizen to a Canadian citizen

_______________ **9.** For which of the following reasons do producers export goods to other nations?

a. They export goods because they believe in the law of comparative advantage.
b. They export goods because they seek to increase the standard of living of persons in other countries.
c. They export goods because they plan to use the compensation received as payment for resources to produce more goods and services and to purchase imports.
d. They export goods so that they can obtain the currency of other nations, which they will attempt to hold indefinitely.

_______________ **10.** Which of the following does not restrict the volume of international trade?

a. Quotas
b. Tariffs
c. High transportation cost
d. A stable international monetary framework

_______________ **11.** A tariff differs from a quota in that

a. a tariff is levied on imports, whereas a quota is imposed on exports.
b. a tariff is levied on exports, whereas a quota is imposed on imports.
c. a tariff is a tax levied by a foreign country, whereas a quota is a limit on the total trade allowed.
d. a tariff is a tax imposed on imports, whereas a quota is an absolute limit to the number of units of a good that can be imported.

_______________ **12.** The infant industry argument about tariffs states that

a. it is unfair to levy tariffs on items intended for use by infants.
b. tariffs should be levied on foreign products that compete with new domestic industries.
c. tariffs should be levied on items intended for infants to protect domestic infant industries.
d. permanent tariffs should be levied on foreign products that compete with those produced by domestic industries.

_______________ **13.** Suppose that the United States imposed a tariff on television sets, preventing foreign-produced television sets from freely entering the U.S. market. Which of the following would be most likely to occur?

a. The price of television sets to U.S. consumers would increase, and the demand for U.S. export products would rise.
b. The price of television sets to U.S. consumers would fall, and the demand for U.S. export products would fall.
c. The price of television sets to U.S. consumers would increase, and the demand for U.S. export products would fall.
d. The price of television sets to U.S. consumers would fall, and the demand for U.S. export products would rise.

_______________ **14.** Suppose that the Swiss government subsidized the watchmaking industry, enabling Swiss producers to undersell foreign watch producers. A watch-importing nation would take best advantage of the Swiss subsidization policy by

a. setting a tariff high enough to discourage foreign competition against its domestic watchmaking industry.
b. setting a declining quota on the import of Swiss watches such that its domestic watchmaking industry would continue to grow at the same rate as the rest of the economy.
c. setting a tariff such that the prices of Swiss and domestic watches to the consumer are equal.
d. gladly accepting the subsidy of the Swiss government, displacing the appropriate adjustment for the resources temporarily from the domestic watchmaking industry.

_______________ **15.** A no-trade situation exists in which the United States exports wheat to a foreign country. The U.S. domestic price

a. and output of wheat would decline.
b. and output of wheat would rise.
c. of wheat would rise, but the domestic output would fall.
d. of wheat would decline, but the domestic output would rise.

_______________ **16.** A situation exists where labor-intensive textile products can be produced less expensively in low-wage countries than in the United States. The United States would gain if it

a. levied a tariff on the goods produced by the less expensive foreign labor.
b. subsidized the domestic textile industry so that it could compete in international markets.
c. used its resources to produce other items while importing textiles from foreigners.
d. levied a tax on the domestic textile products to penalize the industry for inefficiency.

Solutions

Answer	*Refer to:*
1. (b)	[E-1] Domestic consumers of foreign-produced automobiles would most likely experience the higher prices placed on the imported automobiles.
2. (c)	[B-2] The law of comparative advantage is based on specialization according to opportunity cost.
3. (d)	[E-1] A reduction in trade restrictions will increase imports and make more dollars available for foreigners to buy U.S. exports, thus increasing the demand for exports. In turn, this trade policy will make it possible for the United States as well as other countries to allocate resources to goods that can be produced to the greatest comparative advantage.
4. (a)	[E-4] Answers (b), (c) and (d) are all arguments for restricting trade, while (a) is the basis for trade.
5. (b)	[A-2] The figure for U.S. exports as a percentage of GDP averages between 6 and 10 percent.
6. (d)	[B-2] Physical output is increased with specialization and trade.
7. (d)	[B-2] The principle of comparative advantage explains why one country would specialize in producing certain goods and importing others rather than producing all goods domestically.
8. (b)	[D-1] A purchase of U.S. stock by a British citizen would result in money moving into the United States from England and thus would be a credit to that government's balance of payments.
9. (c)	[A-1, B-2-b] The law of comparative advantage provides a rationale for specialization and trade, but belief in it alone does not justify exports. Producers export goods to market their products, thus receiving payment that can be invested in future production.
10. (d)	[E-1, E-2] A stable international monetary framework would encourage the increase in international trade. Quotas place restrictions on imports. Tariffs increase prices, thus reducing quantity demand and the level of imports.
11. (d)	[E-1, E-2] This statement identifies a primary difference between tariffs and quotas.
12. (b)	[E-4-d(2)] The infant industry agreement applies to the short run only. Tariffs are imposed only on foreign products that, in the long run, will compete with new domestic industries.

13. (c) [E-1] Restrictions on imports would increase cost of imports, leading to increased demand for domestic television sets that would result in price increases. In addition, since sales of foreign television sets would decrease, the supply of U.S. dollars in foreign countries would fall and reduce the demand for U.S. exports.

14. (d) [E-4] Accepting the subsidy of the Swiss government would enable trade to continue between the countries, and the watchmaking industry would certainly benefit over time within both countries.

15. (b) [A-1] A no-trade situation would result in a rise in domestic prices, and producers would want to increase output. The export of wheat will reduce the domestic supply and cause prices to increase.

16. (c) [E-4] Those products that could be produced more inexpensively in low-wage countries should be imported by the United States so that resources could be used more wisely for the production of other goods.

CHAPTER 6 Review of Accounting

OVERVIEW

This chapter is designed to introduce the candidate to the study of accounting. Understanding the basic concepts, principles, and functions of accounting should aid the candidate in preparing for the CPS Examination.

KEY TERMS

Accounting
Accounting entity
Assets
Audit (independent external)
Bookkeeping
Conservatism
Consistency
Corporation
Estimation
External financial reports
External users
Full disclosure
Generally accepted accounting principles (GAAP)
Going concern
Historical cost
Internal financial reports
Internal users
Materiality
Money measurement
Objectivity
Partnership
Periodicity

A. Accounting Process

Accounting is the process of recording, measuring, summarizing, analyzing, and interpreting financial information and communicating this information to various users for decision-making purposes.

1. *Accounting Entity:* Accounting information is recorded separately for each accounting entity. An accounting entity is any business, individual, or not-for-profit organization whose financial affairs can be viewed as distinct from those of any other entity or unit.

   EXAMPLE: Jones owns and operates a small grocery store. Jones is one accounting entity, and the grocery store is an entirely separate business entity. Separate accounting records should be kept for Jones and the store. If Jones mixes the recording of personal and business expenses, Jones will be unable to make valid decisions about the profitability of the business.

2. *Types of Business Entities:* Accountants are concerned primarily with three basic types of business entities: the sole proprietorship, the partnership, and the corporation.

   a. *Sole proprietorship:* A business owned by one individual. A sole proprietorship is not a separate legal entity from its owner; however, it is a separate accounting entity.

b. *Partnership:* A business with two or more owners who have agreed to operate as co-owners and who share the profits and losses of the business in an agreed-on proportion. For most purposes a partnership is not a separate legal entity from its owners; however, it is a separate accounting entity.

c. *Corporation:* A separate legal entity created by state or federal law. Corporations usually have the same legal rights and obligations as individuals. To form a corporation, a corporate charter must be obtained from the state where the business is formed. A corporation issues shares of capital stock in exchange for money, assets, or services. Owners of the capital stock are called *stockholders* or *shareholders* of the company; stockholders are the owners of the corporation.

Corporations are both separate legal entities and separate accounting entities. Characteristics of corporations as well as the advantages and disadvantages of the three types of business entities are discussed further in Chapter 16.

3. *Recording Financial Information:* Financial information is normally recorded when an economic transaction takes place.

a. *Money measurement:* A common unit of measure must be used for recording economic events. In accounting, money is that unit of measure. This is known as the *money measurement or monetary unit principle.*

EXAMPLE: A business has $500 in the bank and owns a building. If the business wants to determine the total value of its assets, a monetary value must first be assigned to the building.

b. *Historical cost:* If accountants are to record the building in the previous example as a monetary value, it is necessary to make an assumption in determining that value. There are a number of possible alternatives for valuation. For example, the cost of replacing the building, the potential selling price of the building, the owner's estimation of the fair market value, or the original purchase cost might be used to value the building. In accounting, the original purchase (historical) cost should be used to value assets.

(1) Historical cost was chosen because it can be determined with objectivity. The term *objective* in accounting refers to valuations that can be factually substantiated and can be verified by an independent party. Historical cost is determined in a market transaction, and it is easily verifiable. At the time an asset is acquired, the cost represents the fair market value of the asset. The other valuation methods suggested result in subjective estimates of value that are changing constantly.

(2) As time passes, historical cost may not represent the current fair market value of the asset. Because operational assets are not intended for resale, however, current market value may not be relevant to accounting purposes.

c. *Stable dollar:* Another assumption of accounting is the *stable dollar concept.* The stable dollar concept assumes that a dollar today is worth the same amount as a dollar used to buy an asset in the past.

4. *Classifying Financial Information:* After financial information is recorded, it must be classified according to the areas that are affected. This is done by recording information in different accounts.

5. *Summarizing Financial Information:* Because of the large number of economic transactions that are recorded, the information must be summarized into reports for decision makers to be able to use it effectively.

   EXAMPLE: Ajax Company recorded 5,000 transactions in June. These transactions related to purchases of materials; sales of goods to customers; payments for utilities, rent, and services; salaries paid to employees; and various other business activities. Accountants summarize the financial data into reports before providing the information to decision makers.

6. *Using Accounting Information:* A number of different groups use accounting information. Such users may be *internal* or *external* users of accounting information.

   a. *Internal users:* The managers of a business represent one important group of users of accounting information. Managers are generally referred to as *internal users* of accounting data.

   b. *External users:* A number of users of accounting data are external to the company's management. A business would be unable to issue one set of financial statements that meets the specific needs of all groups of external users. General-purpose financial statements are prepared and issued for use by external users of accounting data.

      EXAMPLES OF EXTERNAL USERS: Bankers, creditors, investors, stockholders, employees, customers, and government agencies.

B. Reporting Accounting Information

1. *External Financial Statements:* The standard general-purpose reports (financial statements) that are issued are the balance sheet (the statement of financial position), the income statement, the statement of retained earnings, and the statement of cash flows.

   a. *Generally accepted accounting principles:* The format of these financial statements and the methods of recording the data summarized within them are governed by a set of rules called *generally accepted accounting principles.* These rules are considered necessary because external users do not normally have access to financial information other than that provided by management of the company. Generally accepted accounting principles (GAAP) consist of pronouncements issued by the accounting profession, industry-wide practices, and other methods developed over the history of accounting that have authoritative support. GAAP are currently set by a private-sector organization called the Financial Accounting Standards Board (FASB). The rules comprising generally accepted accounting principles will be discussed throughout the rest of the accounting section of this examination review manual.

   b. *Audits:* So that external users may have more confidence in external financial reports, these reports may be audited by an independent certified public accountant (CPA). An audit consists of an independent auditor (CPA) reviewing the financial statements to determine their conformity with generally accepted accounting principles. The auditor then issues an opinion regarding the fairness of the financial statements. A CPA might also perform a number of accounting services for a business, such as management advising or tax return preparation. The major function of a CPA is to perform an audit of the financial statements.

2. *Internal Financial Reports:* Internal reports generated for use by managers within the particular accounting entity do not need to follow generally accepted accounting principles. Internal users have access to the entity's accounting information system and are able to request reports in any form they desire. Internal financial reports are generally more detailed than external reports. Certain accounting reports and techniques are frequently used by managerial accountants (these are discussed in more detail in Chapter 19). Managers of the business also use the financial statements generated for external users in making decisions about the operations of the company.

C. Basic Concepts and Principles

Some of the basic concepts, principles, and methods used in accounting are introduced here. Many of them will be elaborated on in later chapters.

1. *Going Concern:* In accounting, the going-concern assumption states that the accountant assumes that the entity is going to exist for an indefinite period of time. The going-concern assumption is often used to justify the historical cost concept. Since we assume that the business entity will continue in existence for an indefinite period of time, the fixed assets of the entity will be needed to continue its operations. The fixed assets cannot be sold without disrupting the operations of the business. Thus, historical cost is a relevant measure of the value of the fixed assets being used by the business.
2. *Relevance:* Accounting information must make a difference in the specific decisions that are to be made from the information.
3. *Periodicity:* The life of an entity is divided into time intervals for reporting purposes. The only time an *exact* accounting of the financial affairs of an entity can be made is at the end of the life of the entity. If an entity is a going concern, decision makers need accounting information about the entity prior to its termination to make decisions. The accountant must make periodic reports about the economic affairs of the entity. The traditional time period for financial reporting is one year. An accounting period that consists of 12 consecutive months is called a *fiscal year.* When a fiscal year ends on December 31, it is called a *calendar year end.* A fiscal period may also follow the natural business year and end when inventories are at their lowest point and business activities are at their lowest level.
4. *Estimation:* The student of accounting needs to realize that much of what is included in financial reports is an estimate. Since accountants divide the life of an entity into arbitrary periodic time intervals, many of the amounts included in the periodic financial reports must be estimated.
5. *Consistency:* Consistency is the accounting principle that requires that once an accounting or reporting method is selected, it should be used from one period to another. This ensures that financial reports of an entity will be comparable from period to period. If a change in accounting method is made, the consistency principle requires that the change be disclosed in the financial statements.
6. *Conservatism:* The principle of conservatism requires that when doubt exists about the valuation of an asset or the recording of an accounting transaction, the accounting method that is the least likely to overstate income and financial position should be chosen. An overstatement of financial position would result from overstating assets or understating liabilities.
7. *Full Disclosure:* The full disclosure principle requires that all information that may be relevant to decision makers be communicated to them through the financial statements.

8. *Materiality:* Materiality refers to the relative importance of an item or event to the decisions that users will be making. If an item is very insignificant compared to other items, it is not necessary to follow accounting theory precisely. In determining materiality, the important consideration is whether knowledge of the item would influence the decisions of users. Materiality is a relative concept.

   EXAMPLE: For a company with sales of $100,000, $10,000 would be material, whereas $10,000 would be immaterial for a company with $10,000,000 in sales.

Review Questions

Directions: Select the correct answer from the four alternatives. Write your answer in the blank to the left of the number.

______ **1.** The process that involves identifying, recording, measuring, and communicating financial information is

a. accounting.
b. estimation.
c. generally accepted accounting principles.
d. bookkeeping.

______ **2.** The principle that requires that the accounting method used be the one least likely to overstate income and financial position is called

a. the conservatism principle.
b. the objectivity principle.
c. the consistency principle.
d. the materiality principle.

______ **3.** The accounting concept that states that accounting information should pertain to the problem at hand and provide useful information about the problem is

a. full disclosure.
b. materiality.
c. going concern principle.
d. relevancy.

______ **4.** The accounting principle that requires that once an accounting or reporting method is selected it should be used from one period to another is

a. periodicity.
b. consistency.
c. comparability.
d. objectivity.

______ **5.** Accounting reports issued solely for use by the management of a company are called

a. external reports.
b. balance sheets.
c. internal reports.
d. income statements.

_______________ **6.** The going-concern assumption

a. states that the accountant assumes that the entity will exist for an indefinite period of time.
b. requires that assets be written up to market value when market value is higher than the cost of the asset.
c. requires that the accounting method least likely to overstate income and financial position be chosen.
d. states that the life of an entity is limited.

_______________ **7.** Generally accepted accounting principles

a. are currently set by the Securities Exchange Commission.
b. must be followed when reporting to internal financial statement users.
c. consist only of pronouncements issued by the accounting profession.
d. are currently set by the Financial Accounting Standards Board.

_______________ **8.** Which one of the following forms of business is considered a separate legal entity?

a. Sole proprietorship.
b. Merger.
c. Partnership.
d. Corporation.

_______________ **9.** The principal function of an independent CPA is to

a. prepare tax returns.
b. conduct an audit, the purpose of which is to guarantee that the financial statements are free of fraud.
c. conduct an audit to determine whether the company's financial statements are presented fairly in accordance with generally accepted accounting principles.
d. provide advisory services to management.

_______________ **10.** Tiller Co. purchased a plot of land for $195,000 five years ago. The appraised value of the land at that time was $200,000. Land in this area is generally worth about 50 percent more today than it was five years ago. The value of the land on Tiller Co.'s current records should be

a. $200,000.
b. $292,500.
c. $195,000.
d. $300,000.

Solutions

Answer	*Refer to:*
1. (a)	[A]
2. (a)	[C-6]
3. (d)	[C-2]
4. (b)	[C-5]
5. (c)	[B-2]
6. (a)	[C-1]
7. (d)	[B-1-a]
8. (d)	[A-2-c]
9. (c)	[B-1-b]
10. (c)	[A-3-b]

CHAPTER 7 Theory and Classification of Accounts

OVERVIEW

The theory and classification of accounts is the most fundamental area in accounting. The candidate must thoroughly understand the recording of debits and credits in asset, liability, owners' equity, revenue, and expense accounts in order to understand the discipline of accounting.

The candidate should understand the definitions of asset, liability, owners' equity, revenue, and expense accounts; how to record transactions in the accounts; and the accounting equation and its relationship to debits and credits in the accounts.

KEY TERMS

Account
Account balance
Accounting equation
Accounts payable
Accounts receivable
Accrual
Assets
Capital stock
Credit
Debit
Dividend
Double-entry accounting
Expenses
Inventory
Journal
Ledger
Liability
Matching
Net income
Owners' equity
Permanent accounts
Posting
Retained earnings
Revenue
Revenue realization
Source document
Stockholders' equity
T-account
Temporary accounts

A. Accounts

Accounts are used for the collection and summarization of data resulting from economic transactions. An account is a device used to collect and summarize information. Accounts are sometimes called *ledger accounts.*

1. *Recording Information in Accounts:* The data comprising an account may be recorded in a number of forms.

a. *Computerized systems:* Many companies keep their accounting records on a computer; their accounts are recorded in the form of magnetic tape or disks.

b. *Manual systems:* A company using a manual accounting system might use a three-column account format (see Figure 7–1).

2. *Using T-Accounts:* The easiest way to represent an account for instructional or problem-solving purposes is to use a T-account. A T-account resembles a capital T.

Figure 7–1 Three-Column Account: Cash Account

Date	*Explanation*	*Ref*	*Receipts (dr)*	*Payments (cr)*	*Balance*
1/1	Beginning balance	√			100.00
1/5	Purchased materials	CD #1		50.00	
1/10	Sold materials	CR #2	25.00		75.00

Figure 7–2 Cash Account

Cash

	dr	cr	
Balance 1/1	100.00		
1/10 Sold merchandise	25.00	50.00	1/5 Purchasec merchandise
Balance 1/10	75.00		

T-accounts are *teaching tools* and are not used in the actual recording of data by businesses.

EXAMPLE:

Name of the Account

Debit side (abbreviated *dr*)	Credit side (abbreviated *cr*)

3. *Recording Debits and Credits:* A debit is an entry recorded on the left side of a T-account. A credit is an entry recorded on the right side of a T-account. The terms *debit* and *credit* refer simply to the left and right sides of an account, respectively. Debits and credits also connote adding to or subtracting from an account.
4. *Recording Entries:* Entries for individual transactions are recorded in the various accounts. Each account serves as a summary of a particular type of transaction during a period of time.
5. *Calculating the Account Balances:* The difference between the total debits and total credits recorded in an account is called the *account* balance. (Note that the T-account in Figure 7–2 is a record of the information in Figure 7–1.)
6. *The Ledger:* A record of all the accounts maintained by an entity is called the *ledger.*

B. Classification of Permanent Accounts

1. *Assets:* Assets are economic resources from which an owner can expect to receive benefits now or in the future. Here is another way of defining the term *assets:* things of value that are owned by the entity.
   a. *Asset accounts:* Some asset accounts are cash, accounts receivable, notes receivable, inventory, prepaid expenses, land, buildings, equipment, supplies, investments, patents, copyrights, and goodwill. The term *receivable* refers to an asset

that is an amount the business has the right to collect in the future from another party.

b. *Debits and credits:* Increases in assets are recorded as *debits.* Decreases in assets are recorded as *credits.* Asset accounts normally have debit balances. The normal balance of any account falls on the increase side of the account.

EXAMPLE:

Asset Account

dr	*cr*
Normal Balance	
Increases are recorded as debits (+)	Decreases are recorded as credits (−)

c. *Recording of assets:* As discussed earlier, assets are recorded at cost following the money measurement, stable dollar, and historical cost conventions of accounting. This is done because costs can be objectively determined and verified.

2. *Liabilities:* Liabilities are obligations or debts of an entity that are owed to other parties. Liabilities come about from purchasing goods or services on credit, borrowing cash to finance the operations of the business, receipt of payment in advance of providing a product or service, and the adjustment process discussed in Chapter 9, Section F. Accounts payable constitute one of the liabilities of a business. Accounts payable arise when a company purchases merchandise on credit for use in its business.

a. *Liability accounts:* Some liability accounts are accounts payable, notes payable, mortgages payable, bonds payable, wages payable, and unearned income. The term *payable* refers to an obligation the entity owes another party.

b. *Debits and credits:* Increases in liabilities are recorded as *credits.* Decreases in liabilities are recorded as *debits.* Liability accounts normally have credit balances.

EXAMPLE:

Liability Account

dr	*cr*
	Normal Balance
Decreases are recorded as debits (−)	Increases are recorded as credits (+)

3. *Owners' Equity (Stockholders' Equity):* Owners' equity represents the resources invested in the business by owners. Owners' equity is a residual claim. This means that, legally, the claims of creditors (liabilities) come first and that owners are entitled to whatever remains after creditors are paid.

$$\text{owners' equity} = \text{total assets} - \text{total liabilities}$$

EXAMPLE: The ABC Company has total assets equaling $5,000. The firm owes suppliers $1,000 for goods purchased on credit (accounts payable) and has a $2,000 note owed to the bank. Therefore, total liabilities at this time are $3,000.

Owners' equity is the residual amount of $2,000 ($5,000 total assets minus $3,000 total liabilities).

a. *Sole proprietorship:* In a sole proprietorship, owner's equity is recorded in the owner's capital account.

EXAMPLE: Jones owns a sole proprietorship. His owner's equity account is called Jones, Capital.

b. *Partnership:* In a partnership, each owner has a separate capital account.

c. *Corporation:* In a corporation, owners' equity is divided into two categories. Investment by owners of the corporation is classified as contributed capital, and earnings of the company that have been retained in the business are classified as retained earnings.

d. *Increases in owners' equity:* Owners' equity may be increased in two ways:

(1) From investment by owners

(2) From retention of earnings generated by the business

e. *Decreases in owners' equity:* Owners' equity may be decreased in two ways:

(1) Through distribution of cash or other assets of the business to its owners

(2) Through losses incurred in the operation of the business

f. *Debits and credits to owners' equity:* Increases in owners' equity are recorded as *credits.* Decreases in owners' equity are recorded as *debits.* The normal balance of owners' equity is a credit.

EXAMPLE:

Owners' Equity Account

dr	*cr*
	Normal Balance
Decreases are recorded as debits (−)	Increases are recorded as credits (+)

4. *Balance Sheet Accounts:* Asset, liability, and owners' equity accounts are included on the *balance sheet* of an entity. These are called balance sheet, permanent, or real accounts. These accounts remain on the books of the business permanently. The balance sheet is also known as the *statement of financial position.* (The balance sheet is discussed in Chapter 8.)

C. The Accounting Equation

The accounting equation is a representation of the following relationship: Assets are equal to liabilities plus owners' equity.

$$\text{assets} = \text{liabilities} + \text{owners' equity}$$

1. *Equality Represented:* This equality must always hold true in accounting since assets must always be equal to the rights or claims associated with the assets.

2. *Sources of Assets:* Another way of looking at the liabilities and owners' equity side of the equation is to view liabilities and owners' equity as sources of the assets. All the resources used to obtain assets are provided either through creditors' holdings (liabilities) or through owners' investments (owners' equity).

EXAMPLE: Stone has started Stone's Bicycles, a business that sells bicycles. purchased 20 bicycles for $2,000 on June 1. Stone used $1,000 of her own money to buy the bicycles and borrowed $1,000 from the bank. Stone gave the bank a six-month note payable in exchange for the $1,000. Stone's Bicycles has $2,000 worth of assets represented by the bicycles. Stone has ownership rights (owner's equity) in the amount of $1,000, which she contributed toward the purchase of the bicycles. Since Stone used $1,000 of borrowed money to purchase the bicycles, she does not have owner's equity equal to the total amount of the cost of the bicycles. The bank owns some of the equity in the bicycles in the form of a claim against the assets (a liability). The bank's claim is the right to be repaid $1,000 six months from now. The accounting equation for Stone's Bicycles would appear as follows:

$$\text{assets} = \text{liabilities} + \text{owner's equity}$$
$$\$2{,}000 = \$1{,}000 + \$1{,}000$$

3. *Continual Changes in Composition:* The composition of the assets, liabilities, and owners' equity of a business changes continually. However, the equality of the basic equation must always be maintained.

4. *Residual Aspect of Owners' Equity:* The accounting equation may be written as follows:

$$\text{assets} - \text{liabilities} = \text{owner's equity}$$

When written in this way, the equation emphasizes the residual aspect of owners' equity.

5. *Double-Entry Accounting:* Whenever an accounting transaction is recorded, the total dollar amount of the debits recorded must equal the total dollar amount of the credits recorded. If a larger amount of debits were recorded than credits, or vice versa, the accounting equation would be out of balance. This recording of an equal amount of debits and credits is called *double-entry accounting.* It is also sometimes referred to as the *duality concept.* By recording data in this fashion, a periodic check of the equality of the total debit and credit balances in the accounts can be made and used to help discover errors made in recording transactions.

D. Recording Accounting Transactions

1. *Journalization:* Accounting transactions are first recorded in *journals,* or books of original entry. This is called journalization. Transactions are recorded in a journal in chronological order.

   a. *Source document:* When accounting transactions occur, some sort of document is usually prepared. This document is called a *source document.* Source documents serve as the source of information for recording transactions in the journal. Examples of source documents include checks, sales invoices, purchase orders, and receipts. Source documents are often called *business papers.*

   b. *General journal:* The most common type of journal is the general journal. When a business keeps only a general journal, all types of transactions are recorded in the general journal. (Some businesses may keep special journals as well as a general journal. Special journals are discussed in Chapter 10.)

(1) The general journal serves as a complete record of each accounting transaction since both sides of the transaction are recorded in one place.

(2) The general journal entry contains the following elements:

(a) Date of the transaction

(b) Ledger account to be debited and the amount

(c) Ledger account to be credited and the amount

(d) An explanation of the transaction, including an identification of the source document

EXAMPLE: ABC Company purchased a machine for $2,000 cash on August 8. This transaction would be recorded in the general journal as shown in Figure 7–3. The account (or accounts) to be debited is listed first, and the amount is recorded in the debit column. The account (or accounts) to be credited is listed next, and the amount is recorded in the credit column. Note that the account to be credited is indented. This indentation is used to indicate that the account is credited. Following the debit and credit entries is an explanation of the transaction. The reference column is provided so that the journal entry may be cross-indexed to the ledger account.

To conserve space, the journal entries throughout the rest of the book will be presented in the following format:

		dr	*cr*
Aug. 8	Machinery	2,000	
	Cash		2,000
Purchased stamping machine, check number 112			

Note that the position of the accounts indicates which account is to be debited and which is to be credited. The explanation may be omitted from journal entries when the transaction is routine and the entry is clear without the explanation.

2. *Posting to the Ledger:* Information that is recorded in the journal is transferred periodically to the ledger accounts. The transfer of information from the journal to the ledger is called *posting.*

Figure 7–3 General Journal

Page 10

Date	*Explanation*	*Ref*	*Debit*	*Credit*
Aug. 8	Machinery		2,000	
	Cash			2,000
	Purchased stamping machine, check number 112			

Figure 7–4 shows the posting of the transaction journalized in Figure 7–3 to the ledger. The debit side of the journal entry is posted first. The machinery ledger account is located, the debit amount from the journal entry is recorded in the debit column, the date of the transaction is recorded, and the journal page number from which the entry was taken is recorded in the reference column. The ledger account number is then recorded in the reference column of the journal to cross-reference the entry and to record that the transaction has been posted. The referencing procedure may be somewhat different, depending on the business involved. Some sort of referencing is necessary to provide an *audit trail,* which is the information that makes it possible for the accountant to trace each transaction back to its source document to determine that it was recorded properly. The same procedure would be followed for transferring the credit entry to the cash account.

3. *Typical Accounting Transactions:* In the following examples, journal entries are shown, and the amounts are posted to T-accounts. The T-accounts represent the general ledger. The explanations will be omitted from the journal entries, although in reality they would be included.

a. Smith starts a small business repairing television sets. On August 1, Smith invests $1,000 of his own money in the business. This transaction results in an increase in the asset *cash* of $1,000 and an increase in *owner's equity* of $1,000. The journal entry would be as follows:

		dr	*cr*
Aug. 1	Cash	1,000	
	Owner's equity (Smith capital)		1,000

This is posted as transaction A in the T-accounts in Figure 7–5.

b. Smith borrowed $2,000 from the bank on August 3. He gave the bank a note payable. As a result of this transaction, the asset *cash* is increased by $2,000, and the liability *notes payable* is increased by $2,000. The journal entry would be as follows:

		dr	*cr*
Aug. 3	Cash	2,000	
	Notes payable		2,000

See transaction B in the T-accounts in Figure 7–5.

Figure 7–4 Cash/Machinery Accounts

Acct. #01 Cash

Date	*Explanation*	*Ref*	*Debit*	*Credit*	*Balance*
					10,000
Aug. 8		10		2,000	8,000

Acct. #10 Machinery

Date	*Explanation*	*Ref*	*Debit*	*Credit*	*Balance*
					100,000
Aug. 8		10	2,000		102,000

Figure 7–5 Cash/Equipment Accounts

dr Cash cr

A. Aug. 1	1,000		
B. Aug. 3	2,000	C. Aug. 8	1,500
		D. Aug. 10	500
		E. Aug. 20	250
Bal. Aug. 20	750		

Equipment and Tools

C. Aug. 8	1,500		
Bal. Aug. 20	1,500		

Notes Payable

		B. Aug. 3	2,000
		Bal. Aug. 20	2,000

Inventory of Parts

D. Aug. 10	750		
Bal. Aug. 20	750		

Accounts Payable

E. Aug. 20	250	D. Aug. 10	250
		Bal. Aug. 20	-0-

Owner's Equity

		A. Aug. 1	1,000
		Bal. Aug. 20	1,000

c. Smith purchased testing equipment and tools for use in his business for $1,500 on August 8. He paid for the equipment in cash. This transaction resulted in an increase in the asset *equipment and tools* of $1,500 and a decrease in the asset *cash* of $1,500. The journal entry would be as follows:

		dr	*cr*
Aug. 8	Equipment and tools	1,500	
	Cash		1,500

See transaction C in the T-accounts in Figure 7–5.

d. Smith purchased $750 worth of parts to use in repairing television sets on August 10. He paid for the parts by using $500 cash and charging the other $250 on open account. This transaction resulted in an increase of $750 in the asset *inventory of parts,* a decrease of $500 in the asset *cash,* and an increase of $250 in the liability *accounts payable.* The journal entry would be as follows:

		dr	*cr*
Aug. 10	Inventory of parts	750	
	Cash		500
	Accounts payable		250

This journal entry is called a *compound journal entry* because more than two accounts are affected by the transaction. This transaction is posted as transaction D in Figure 7–5.

e. Smith paid the $250 account payable on August 20 using cash. As a result of this transaction, the asset *cash* decreased by $250, and the liability *accounts payable* decreased by $250. The journal entry would be as follows:

		dr	*cr*
Aug. 20	Accounts payable	250	
	Cash		250

See transaction E in the T-accounts in Figure 7–5.

f. After recording transactions A through E, the T-accounts have been totaled to determine the account balances. When the increases and decreases recorded in an account are separately added and the sum of the decreases is subtracted from the sum of the increases, the procedure is called *determining the account balance.* Note that the asset accounts *cash, inventory of parts,* and *equipment and tools* all have debit balances. The liability *accounts payable* has a zero balance, and the liability *notes payable* has a credit balance. The *owner's equity* account also has a credit balance.

Total Assets		Total Liabilities and Owner's Equity	
Cash	750	Notes payable	2,000
Inventory of parts	750	Owner's equity	1,000
Equipment and tools	1,500		
Total	3,000	Total	3,000

Total Assets = Total Liabilities and Owners' Equity
Total Debits = Total Credits

E. Classification of Temporary Accounts

1. *Revenues:* Revenues are earnings resulting from the receipt of cash or other assets (or the reduction of a liability) in exchange for goods sold by an entity or services performed by an entity.

a. *Revenue realization principle:* Revenue is usually recognized only after exchange has taken place or a service has been rendered.

EXAMPLES: Smith repaired his neighbor's television set and received $85 for his services. The $85 represents revenue earned by Smith in exchange for services. The account used to record revenue from services is called service fees *or* service revenue.

Stone's Bicycles sold two bicycles for a total of $250. The person who purchased the bicycles promised to pay for them within 30 days. The $250 represents revenue earned from the sale of goods. The fact that the $250 has not yet been received in cash does not affect the recording of revenue since an exchange has taken place. The account used to record revenue from the sale of goods is called sales.

b. *Increases and decreases in revenues:* Increases in revenues are recorded as credits. Decreases in revenues are recorded as debits. Revenue accounts normally have a credit balance.

EXAMPLE:

Revenue Account

dr	*cr*
Normal Balance	
Decreases are recorded as debits (−)	Increases are recorded as credits (+)

2. *Expenses:* Expenses are the costs of goods and services consumed (used up) by the entity as a result of earning revenue.

   a. *Incurring expenses:* To earn revenue, it is necessary to incur expenses.

   EXAMPLES: The cost of the parts Smith used in repairing his neighbor's television set represents an expense or cost used up in earning revenue.

   The rent for the building where Stone stores her bicycles represents an expense. It is a cost incurred to produce revenue.

   b. *Increases and decreases in expenses:* Increases in expenses are recorded as debits. Decreases in expenses are recorded as credits. Expense accounts normally have a debit balance.

   EXAMPLE:

Expense Account

dr	*cr*
Normal Balance	
Increases are recorded as debits (+)	Decreases are recorded as credits (−)

3. *Net Income:* The excess of total revenues over total expenses of an entity represents the *net income* of the entity. Net income is measured over a specific period of time. If total expenses exceed total revenues, a *net loss* is incurred:

$$\text{revenues} - \text{expenses} = \text{net income or net loss}$$

   a. *Reporting net income:* Net income is reported periodically on the income statement.

   b. *Accrual concept:* Revenues should be reported when earned rather than when the cash is received, and expenses should be reported when incurred rather than when paid.

   EXAMPLE: The previous example, where Stone's Bicycles sold two bicycles in exchange for an account receivable, illustrates the accrual concept. The revenue was reported when earned (at the time of the sale) rather than when the cash was received.

   c. *Matching principle:* The matching principle states that expenses incurred in earning revenues should be matched with those revenues to determine net income. Expenses should be reported in the same period as the revenues to which they correspond.

EXAMPLE: Arnold is a sales representative for the ABC Company. During July, he sold merchandise totaling $100,000. His sales commission will be included as part of his August paycheck. The sales commission should be reported as an expense on ABC's records in July. In this way the sales revenue and sales commission expense are matched.

d. *Increases in owners' equity:* Net income represents an increase in owners' equity. A net loss represents a decrease in owners' equity.

e. *Income summary account:* At the end of an accounting period, revenues and expenses are closed to an income summary account, which is then closed to owners' equity. Revenue, expenses, income summary, and drawing accounts are called *temporary accounts* since they are periodically closed to owners' equity. The closing process will be discussed in Chapter 9.

4. *Investments by Owners:*

a. *Increases in assets and owners' equity:* Additional investments by owners of a business are not revenue. They are recorded as increases in assets and increases in owners' equity.

b. *Sale of stock:* If a corporation sells shares of stock, the resulting cash obtained is not revenue but an additional investment by owners. The sale of stock is recorded as an increase in the asset *cash* and an increase in the owners' equity account *capital stock.*

5. *Withdrawals and Dividends:*

a. *Withdrawal of assets:* Withdrawals of assets from a business by the owners are not expenses. They are a decrease in the owners' equity in the business. A withdrawal is recorded as a decrease in cash and a decrease in owners' equity.

b. *Dividends:* Dividends represent distributions of assets by a corporation to its owners (stockholders).

(1) Dividends are paid to stockholders when declared by the corporation's board of directors.

(2) Payment of a dividend is not an expense. It is a distribution of assets, similar to a withdrawal of assets by owners in a sole proprietorship.

6. *Typical Transactions Including Revenues and Expenses:* In the following examples, journal entries are shown as well as postings to T-accounts. The T-accounts are shown in Figure 7–6. Waldorf Corporation sells widgets. The following are some of the transactions for Waldorf Corporation for the month of January.

a. Waldorf Corporation sold 10,000 widgets during January. Of the total sales, 2,000 widgets were sold for cash, and 8,000 widgets were sold on account. Widgets sell for $10 each. As a result of this transaction, sales revenue was increased by $100,000 (10,000 units sold × $10 per unit), cash was increased by $20,000 (2,000 units sold for cash × $10 per unit), and accounts receivable was increased by $80,000 (8,000 units sold on open account × $10 per unit). The journal entry to record this transaction would be as follows:

	dr	*cr*
Cash	20,000	
Accounts receivable	80,000	
Sales revenue		100,000

Figure 7–6 T-Accounts for Waldorf Corporation

dr *Cash* *cr*

Bal. Jan. 1	$30,000	D.	$20,000
A.	20,000	F.	7,000
C.	50,000	H.	40,000
		I.	5,000

Accounts Receivable

Bal. Jan. 1	$50,000		
A.	80,000	C.	$50,000

Inventory of Widgets

Bal. Jan. 1	$50,000		
G.	90,000	B.	$50,000

Accounts Payable

		45,000 Bal.	Jan. 1
H.	$40,000	G.	$90,000

Sales Commissions Payable

		7,000 Bal.	Jan. 1
F.	$7,000	E.	$8,000

Sales Revenue

		A.	$100,000

Salaries Expense

D.	$20,000		

Sales Commission Expense

E.	$8,000		

Cost of Goods Sold

B.	$50,000		

Rent Expense

I.	$5,000		

This transaction was recorded as transaction A in the T-account in Figure 7–6.

b. The cost of the widgets sold during January was $50,000. This cost represents an expense in the period the widgets were sold. When the widgets were purchased, the asset account *inventory* was debited. *Expensing* of the cost of the widgets in the same period they are sold results in proper matching of revenues and expenses. As a result of this transaction, the asset *inventory of widgets* decreased by $50,000 and the expense *cost of goods sold* increased by $50,000. The journal entry for this transaction would be as follows:

	dr	*cr*
Cost of goods sold	50,000	
Inventory		50,000

Note: This is the entry that would be prepared using the *perpetual inventory method.* Another method of recording inventory transactions is called the *periodic method.* Both the perpetual and periodic methods are discussed in Chapter 12. This transaction was recorded as transaction B in Figure 7–6.

c. Waldorf Corporation collected $50,000 for widgets sold on account in December. The revenue from the sales of these widgets was recorded in December when the sale took place (revenue realization). At that time, an account receivable was set up for the $50,000. Now Waldorf Corporation will record the collection of that account receivable. As a result of this transaction, cash was increased by $50,000, and accounts receivable was decreased by $50,000. The journal entry to record this transaction would be as follows:

	dr	*cr*
Cash	50,000	
Accounts receivable		50,000

See transaction C in the T-account in Figure 7–6.

d. Waldorf Corporation paid the sales representatives $20,000 in salaries for the month of January. This payment represents an expense incurred in generating the revenue from sales of widgets. As a result of this transaction, salaries expense was increased by $20,000, and cash was decreased by $20,000. The journal entry to record this transaction would be as follows:

	dr	*cr*
Salaries expense	20,000	
Cash		20,000

This transaction was recorded as transaction D in the T-accounts in Figure 7–6.

e. The sales representatives earned $8,000 in selling commissions related to the January sales. These selling commissions will be paid in February. The selling commissions relate to January revenue and should be expensed in January according to the matching principle. To record the expense in January, a liability account *sales commissions payable* must be set up. As a result of this transaction, sales commissions expense was increased by $8,000, and sales commissions payable was increased by $8,000. The journal entry to record this transaction would be as follows:

	dr	*cr*
Sales commissions expense	8,000	
Sales commissions payable		8,000

This transaction was recorded as transaction E in Figure 7–6.

f. Sales commissions incurred in December were $7,000. These commissions were paid to the sales representatives in January. The sales commissions expense related to this transaction was recorded in December according to the matching principle. When the expense was recorded in December, sales commissions payable was increased by $7,000. This transaction represents payment of that

$7,000 liability. As a result of this transaction, sales commissions payable was decreased by $7,000, and cash was decreased by $7,000. The journal entry to record this transaction would be as follows::

	dr	*cr*
Sales commissions payable	7,000	
Cash		7,000

This transaction was recorded as transaction F in the T-accounts in Figure 7–6.

g. During the month of January, Waldorf Corporation purchased $90,000 worth of widgets from its suppliers on account. As a result of this transaction, the asset *inventory of widgets* was increased by $90,000, and the liability *accounts payable* was increased by $90,000. The journal entry to record this transaction would be as follows:

	dr	*cr*
Inventory of widgets	90,000	
Accounts payable		90,000

This transaction was recorded as transaction G in the T-accounts in Figure 7–6.

h. During January, Waldorf Corporation paid for $40,000 worth of widgets that had been purchased on open account previously. As a result of this transaction, the liability *accounts payable* decreased by $40,000, and the asset *cash* decreased by $40,000. The journal entry for this transaction would be as follows:

	dr	*cr*
Accounts payable	40,000	
Cash		40,000

This transaction was recorded as transaction H in the T-accounts in Figure 7–6.

i. During January, Waldorf Corporation paid $5,000 rent on the building used for operations. The rent on the building represents an expense of doing business. It is necessary to have a building to operate from in order to earn revenue. The rental expense cannot be matched with any specific revenues. Therefore, the rent expense is matched with the revenues earned in the same accounting period that the expense is incurred. As a result of this transaction, the rent expense account increased by $5,000, and the cash account decreased by $5,000. The journal entry to record this transaction would be as follows:

	dr	*cr*
Rent expense	5,000	
Cash		5,000

This transaction was recorded as transaction I in the T-accounts in Figure 7–6.

Review Questions

Directions: Select the best answer from the four alternatives. Write your answer in the blank to the left of the number.

______ **1.** The device used to collect and summarize information resulting from economic transactions is called a/an

a. debit.
b. account.
c. credit.
d. magnetic tape.

______ **2.** In accounting, the term *credit* means

a. an entry made on the left side of an account.
b. increases in accounts.
c. decreases in accounts.
d. an entry made on the right side of an account.

______ **3.** The left side of an account is called

a. the credit side.
b. the debit side.
c. the asset side.
d. the liability side.

______ **4.** The difference between total debits and total credits recorded in an account is called

a. the accounting equation.
b. the balance.
c. the inventory.
d. owners' equity.

______ **5.** The normal balance of an account is indicated by

a. the increase side.
b. the decrease side.
c. the debit side for liabilities.
d. the credit side for assets.

______ **6.** An obligation or debt of an entity owed to one of its creditors is called

a. an expense.
b. an asset.
c. owners' equity.
d. a liability.

_______________ **7.** Which of the following accounts would be classified as a temporary account?

a. Inventory
b. Notes payable
c. Accounts receivable
d. Wage expense

_______________ **8.** Economic resources from which future benefits can be received are called

a. dividends.
b. receivables.
c. capital.
d. assets.

_______________ **9.** Which of the following is a correct form of the accounting equation?

a. Assets = liabilities + owners' equity
b. Assets + liabilities = owners' equity
c. Assets + owners' equity = liabilities
d. Assets = liabilities + contributed capital

_______________ **10.** Net income results in

a. a decrease in owners' equity.
b. an increase in owners' equity.
c. no change in owners' equity.
d. a credit to the capital account.

_______________ **11.** Accounting transactions are first recorded in

a. the journal.
b. a T-account.
c. the general ledger.
d. alphabetical order.

_______________ **12.** The stock of goods that an entity holds for future sale is called

a. accounts receivable.
b. cost of goods sold.
c. property, plant, and equipment.
d. inventory.

_______________ **13.** The periodic transfer of information from the journal to the ledger is called

a. journalizing.
b. transferring.
c. posting.
d. debiting.

_______________ **14.** Which one of the following transactions results in recording an increase in a liability account?

a. Purchasing goods on credit
b. Repaying a loan to the bank

c. Selling common stock
d. Collecting cash from a customer

_______________ **15.** Total assets minus total liabilities is called

a. owners' equity.
b. capital stock.
c. net income.
d. intangibles.

_______________ **16.** Owners' equity can be decreased through

a. withdrawals made by owners.
b. payment of a long-term liability.
c. retention of earnings generated by the business.
d. investments made by owners.

_______________ **17.** In double-entry bookkeeping, a debit refers to

a. an increase in a liability account.
b. an entry recorded on the left side of an account.
c. a decrease in an asset account.
d. an entry recorded on the right side of an account.

_______________ **18.** The accounting principle which states that expenses should be recorded in the same period as the revenues to which they correspond is the

a. going concern principle.
b. recording principle.
c. accrual concept.
d. matching concept.

_______________ **19.** Revenues should normally be recognized (recorded) when

a. cash is received in payment of a customer's account receivable.
b. an exchange has taken place or a service has been performed.
c. a customer sends a purchase order to the selling company.
d. a company produces merchandise.

_______________ **20.** Net income may be represented by

a. assets minus expenses.
b. revenues minus expenses.
c. assets minus liabilities.
d. liabilities minus revenues.

_______________ **21.** Investments made in the entity by owners

a. are revenue to the entity.
b. are recorded in the capital account in a sole proprietorship.

c. decrease owners' equity.
d. are recorded as debits in the investments account.

_____________ **22.** Payment of a cash dividend by a corporation represents a/an

a. expense.
b. distribution of assets to owners.
c. increase in owner's equity.
d. reduction in net income.

_____________ **23.** Accounting transactions are first recorded in a

a. ledger.
b. balance sheet.
c. financial statement.
d. journal.

_____________ **24.** When an account receivable is collected,

a. total assets remain unchanged.
b. total assets decrease.
c. total assets increase.
d. total owners' equity decreases.

_____________ **25.** Which of the following items could result from the correct recording of a transaction?

a. A decrease in assets and an increase in owners' equity
b. A decrease in an asset and an increase in a liability
c. An increase in an asset and a decrease in a liability
d. An increase in an asset and an increase in a liability

_____________ **26.** The journal entry to record the purchase of office supplies on account could be

a. debit supplies expense; credit office supplies.
b. debit accounts payable; credit supplies expense.
c. debit office supplies; credit accounts payable.
d. debit office supplies; credit cash.

_____________ **27.** A computer printer with a list price of $1,200 was purchased by Jones Co. for $1,100 cash. Which of the following entries represents the correct recording of the transaction?

a. Office equipment	1,200	
Jones capital		1,200
b. Cash	1,100	
Office equipment		1,100
c. Office equipment	1,100	
Accounts payable		1,100
d. Office equipment	1,100	
Cash		1,100

_______________ **28.** Arnold Co. purchased a building in exchange for $20,000 cash and an $80,000 note payable that will come due in four years. Which of the following journal entries records the transaction correctly?

a. Building	80,000	
Note payable		80,000
b. Building	80,000	
Cash	20,000	
Note payable		100,000
c. Building	100,000	
Cash		20,000
Note payable		80,000
d. Building	20,000	
Cash		20,000

Solutions

Answer	*Refer to:*
1. (b)	[A]
2. (d)	[A-3]
3. (b)	[A-3]
4. (b)	[A-5]
5. (a)	[B-1-b, B-2-b]
6. (d)	[B-2]
7. (d)	[E-3-e]
8. (d)	[B-1]
9. (a)	[C]
10. (b)	[B-3-e]
11. (a)	[D-1]
12. (d)	[B-1]
13. (c)	[D-2]
14. (a)	[B-2]
15. (a)	[B-3]
16. (a)	[B-3-e]
17. (b)	[C-5]
18. (d)	[E-2, E-3-c]
19. (b)	[E-1]
20. (b)	[E-3-a]
21. (b)	[B-3-a, E-4-a]
22. (b)	[E-5]

23. (d) [D-1]

24. (a) [E-6-c]

25. (d) [C]

26. (c) [D-3-d]

27. (d) [D-3-c, A-3-b]

28. (c) [D-3-d]

CHAPTER 8

Basic Financial Statements

OVERVIEW

This chapter is designed to introduce the candidate to the basic financial statements of accounting. These statements are the final product of financial accounting.

The candidate should know the format and classification of the balance sheet and what is included in the various asset, liability, and owners' equity accounts. The candidate should know the classified forms of the income statement and the nature of revenue, expense, gain, and loss accounts. The candidate should also know how the statement of retained earnings shows the changes in the retained earnings account from one period to the next.

KEY TERMS

Allowance for uncollectible accounts
Balance sheet
Bonds payable
Book value or carrying value
Common stock
Comprehensive income
Contra-asset account
Cost of goods sold
Current assets
Current liabilities
Depreciation
Earnings per share
Fixed assets
Gains
Gross margin (or gross profit)
Income statement
Intangible assets
Investments
Liquidity
Long-term liabilities
Losses
Mortgage
Notes payable
Notes receivable
Operating cycle
Other assets
Other liabilities
Preferred stock
Prepaid expenses
Statement of cash flows
Statement of changes in capital
Statement of retained earnings
Temporary investments

A. Balance Sheet

The balance sheet is a financial statement that shows the financial position of an entity as of a specific time. The balance sheet lists all the assets, liabilities, and owners' equity of an entity. The balance sheet is formally called the *statement of financial position.*

1. *Accounting Equation:* The balance sheet is a formal statement that shows the accounting equation (assets = liabilities + owners' equity) at a specific time.
2. *Heading:* Every balance sheet should have a proper heading. The heading includes the following information:
   a. The name of the company

b. The title of the statement

c. The date of the statement (the balance sheet is dated as of a specific day)

EXAMPLE:

Stone's Bicycles
Statement of Financial Position
December 31, 20XA

3. *Classification of Assets on Balance Sheet:* Assets are typically classified as current assets, investments, fixed assets, intangible assets, and other assets.

a. *Current assets:* The first category of assets shown on the balance sheet is current assets. Current assets are those assets expected to be used in the operations of an entity within its operating cycle or one year, whichever is longer. The operating cycle is defined as the period of time it takes a firm to buy merchandise (or produce it), sell the merchandise, collect the customers' accounts receivable resulting from sale of the merchandise, and pay the accounts payable of the firm. This cycle will vary, depending on the nature of the business. Most businesses have an operating cycle shorter than one year, and they use a period of one year for the purpose of classifying current assets.

Within the category of current assets, the individual asset accounts are listed according to their degree of liquidity. *Liquidity* is a measure of the speed with which an asset can be converted into cash. The more easily an asset can be converted into cash, the more liquid it is considered to be. The normal order in which current assets are listed is as follows:

(1) *Cash:* Cash includes coins, paper money, checks, money orders, and money on deposit in banks.

(2) *Temporary investments:* Temporary investments consist of government bonds, corporate securities, or other securities that can be converted into cash very quickly. These may also be called *short-term marketable securities.* Temporary investments are expected to be held for less than one year or one operating cycle. Accounting for both temporary and long-term investments is covered in chapter 11.

(3) *Notes receivable:* Notes receivable are promissory notes given to a business by its customers. These notes normally indicate the amount of the future payment, the interest rate, and the time at which payment is to be made by the customers. Notes receivable are signed documents that are transferable.

(4) *Accounts receivable:* Accounts receivable are amounts owed to a business by customers for sales made on open account.

(a) *Uncollectible accounts receivable:* It is usually not realistic to assume that the total amount of the accounts receivable will be collected. Some portion of the accounts receivable will normally prove to be uncollectible.

(b) *Allowance for uncollectible accounts:* The amount of the accounts receivable that is estimated to be uncollectible is recorded in the allowance for uncollectible (or doubtful) accounts.

(c) *Contra-assets:* The allowance for uncollectible accounts is a contra-asset account. Contra-asset accounts have credit balances and are shown as deductions from their related asset accounts on the balance sheet. The allowance account is shown as a deduction from the total account receivable balance on the balance sheet, showing the *net* amount that is expected to be collected (see disclosure in Figure 8–2).

EXAMPLE: ABC Company has accounts receivable totaling $100,000. Of this amount it is estimated that $10,000 will be uncollectible. The balance in the allowance for uncollectible accounts before recording the $10,000 uncollectible estimate is zero. The entry to record the estimate of the uncollectible accounts would be made as follows:

	dr	*cr*
Bad debt expense	10,000	
Allowance for uncollectible accounts		10,000

(5) *Inventory:* Inventory is an asset that consists of goods or merchandise on hand held by a business for future sale.

(a) Merchandising firms normally have one inventory control account.

(b) Manufacturing firms normally have three types of inventory control accounts:

Raw materials: Raw materials inventory is made up of the store of raw materials a company holds for use in producing goods.

Work in process: Work-in-process inventory consists of goods on hand that are still in the process of being completed.

Finished goods: Finished goods inventory consists of products completed and on hand awaiting sale to customers.

(6) *Prepaid expenses:* Prepaid or deferred expenses consist of the cost of goods or services bought for use in the business that are not used up by the end of the accounting period. Prepaid expenses are assets for as long as future benefits may be obtained from them. Examples of prepaid expense accounts are supplies, prepaid rent, and prepaid insurance.

EXAMPLE: A company pays rent one year in advance on a building used in operating the business. The payment of the rent in advance results in an asset called prepaid rent expense. *The prepaid rent is an asset because the company has the right to use the building for 12 months without paying rent.*

The amounts in the prepaid expense accounts are written off to expense as their potential for future benefit is consumed.

b. *Investments:* The second category of assets listed on the balance sheet is investments. Investments are assets held by the company for investment purposes, not for use in the operations of the business. The investments category is used for assets that are expected to be held for longer than one year. Chapter 11 discusses the classification of long-term investments into available-for-sale securities, held-to-maturity securities, and investments.

EXAMPLES OF INVESTMENTS: Stocks of other corporations, cash surrender value of life insurance, savings accounts kept for a specific purpose (e.g., debt retirement or construction of a new building), and bonds of other corporations.

c. *Fixed assets:* The third category of assets listed on the balance sheet is fixed assets. Fixed assets are often called *plant and equipment.* Fixed assets are long-lived assets used in the operations of the business and not held for sale to customers.

(1) *Tangible nature of fixed assets:* Fixed assets are *tangible property,* such as land, machinery, equipment, buildings, furniture, and fixtures.

(2) *Depreciation:* Depreciation is the systematic and rational allocation of the original cost of an asset over its expected useful life. Depreciation takes place even though an asset is not in use, such as during a strike. Depreciation is the process of allocating the cost of an asset to the periods in which it is used. Fixed assets normally wear out, or deteriorate, with time and use. Land is an example of a fixed asset that does not deteriorate. However, machinery, equipment, buildings, furniture, and fixtures do deteriorate. These types of assets are subject to depreciation. The depreciation of an asset is recorded in an account called *accumulated depreciation.*

EXAMPLE: ABC Company purchased a machine for $12,000. The machine is expected to last for six years. The decision has been made to depreciate the asset an equal amount during each year of its life. After the first year of use, the following entry is made to record depreciation:

	dr	*cr*
Depreciation expense	2,000	
Accumulated depreciation		2,000
To record depreciation on machine		
($12,000/6 years = $2,000 per year).		

There are a number of different methods of computing depreciation expense. These methods are discussed in Chapter 13, Section B–1.

(3) *Accumulated depreciation account:* The accumulated depreciation account is a contra-asset account. Accumulated depreciation is shown as a deduction from the related fixed asset account on the balance sheet. The fixed asset account contains the original cost of the asset (see disclosure in Figure 8–2).

(4) *Book value:* The original cost of an operational asset less the accumulated depreciation related to that asset is equal to the book value, or carrying value, of the asset.

(5) *Depletion*: Assets that are natural resources such as timber or iron ore are subject to depletion since the total quantity available will eventually be used up. Depletion is discussed in Chapter 13, Section B–2.

d. *Intangible assets:* The fourth category of assets listed on the balance sheet is intangible assets. Intangible assets are long-lived assets that do not have any tangible existence. Intangible assets represent rights that the company owns.

EXAMPLES: Patents, copyrights, trademarks, franchises, leaseholds, and goodwill.

e. *Other assets:* The last category of assets listed on the balance sheet is other assets. Other assets include long-lived assets that do not fit the criteria for classification in another area.

4. *Classification of Liabilities on the Balance Sheet:* Liabilities are typically classified as current liabilities, long-term liabilities, and other liabilities.

a. *Current liabilities:* Current liabilities are obligations of a business that are due to be paid within the next operating cycle or one year, whichever is longer.

EXAMPLES OF CURRENT LIABILITIES: Accounts payable, short-term notes payable, wages payable, taxes payable, unearned revenue, interest payable, and the current portion of principal due on long-term debt.

b. *Long-term liabilities:* Long-term liabilities are obligations of a business that will not come due during the next operating cycle.

EXAMPLES OF LONG-TERM LIABILITIES: Mortgages payable, bonds payable, and long-term notes payable.

(1) *Mortgage:* A mortgage is a long-term obligation that is usually secured by real estate and is usually repaid in installments made up partially of interest and partially of a repayment of the principal of the loan.

(2) *Bond:* A bond is a security issued by an entity wanting to borrow a large sum of money. Bonds are issued in stated denominations, and they pay a stated rate of interest.

(3) *Long-term notes payable:* A note payable is an obligation of an entity consisting of a signed document that promises to pay a specific amount of money plus interest at a specific time in the future. Ordinarily, a long-term note payable does not come due within the next operating cycle.

The current portion of long-term liabilities should be classified as a current liability.

EXAMPLE: ABC Company has a $200,000 note on an office building. Yearly payments of $20,000 are made on this note. The company will have to reclassify $20,000 of this long-term liability as a current liability on the balance sheet since the $20,000 comes due within the next year.

c. *Other liabilities:* Other liabilities is the category used in some balance sheets to classify long-term liabilities that do not fit the criteria for classification in another area.

5. *Classification of Owners' Equity on the Balance Sheet:* Owners' equity is classified in the accounts differently, depending on the form of the ownership of the business.

a. *Sole proprietorship:* In a sole proprietorship, there is one owner's equity account called *capital.* This account reflects all increases and decreases in the owner's equity.

b. *Partnership:* In a partnership, there is a separate owner's equity (capital) account for each partner. This account shows an individual partner's contributions of capital to the business, any distribution of assets to the partner from the business, and the partner's share of any profits or losses incurred by the business. The sum of all the individual partners' equity accounts would equal the total owners' equity of the partnership.

c. *Corporation:* The stockholders' equity in a corporation is disclosed in two amounts: the amount invested by stockholders of the corporation and the amount generated by retention of earnings from the business.

(1) *Capital stock:* Investments in the business by stockholders are shown in the contributed capital section. When stockholders invest in a corporation, they receive capital stock. There may be two classes of capital stock: common stock and preferred stock.

(a) *Common stock:* All corporations *must* issue common stock. Common stock is sold to owners who receive no assurance of income from ownership of their stock. They have the rights to all residual assets left after

Figure 8–1 Balance Sheet Presentations of Owners' Equity

Sole proprietor:	Owner's equity		
	Jones, capital		20,000
Partnership:	Partners' equity		
	Smith, capital	10,000	
	Adams, capital	8,000	
	Total partners' equity		18,000
Corporation:	Stockholders' equity		
	Capital stock	1,000,000	
	Retained earnings	523,000	
	Total stockholders' equity		1,523,000

creditors' and preferred stockholders' claims have been met. Common stockholders have the right to vote.

(b) *Preferred stock:* Preferred stock is issued mostly by large corporations. Preferred stock has a preference over common stock. Preferred stockholders often have the right to receive a specified but limited amount of dividends before any distribution of dividends may be made to common shareholders. Preferred stockholders usually do not have the right to vote. (Preferred and common stock are discussed further in Chapter 16.)

(2) *Retained earnings:* The amount generated by retention of earnings is called *retained earnings.* Retained earnings consist of the cumulative income and losses of a corporation less any dividends declared.

Figure 8–1 shows the balance sheet presentation of owners' equity for a sole proprietorship, a partnership, and a corporation. Figure 8–2 shows a balance sheet for a corporation.

B. Income Statement

The income statement is a financial report that summarizes the operations of the business resulting in revenues, expenses, gains, and losses. The income statement shows the increase or decrease in owners' equity resulting from the operation of the business over a period of time (the accounting period).

1. *Net Income Related to Revenues and Expenses:* This equation defines net income from normal operations of a business as revenues minus expenses:

$$\text{net income} = \text{revenues} - \text{expenses}$$

2. *Gains and Losses:* A business may earn revenues that are not part of the normal operations of the business (gains) or incur expenses that do not result from normal operations of the business (losses). Gains and losses result in increases and decreases in owners' equity and are a part of the net income of a company. Since gains and losses do not result from the normal operations of a business, they are usually reported separately on the income statement.

Figure 8–2 Statement of Financial Position

ABC Company
Statement of Financial Position
December 31, 20XB

Assets

Current assets		
Cash		25,000
Temporary investments		20,000
Notes receivable		10,000
Accounts receivable	100,000	
Less: Allowance for uncollectible accounts	10,000	90,000
Inventory		100,000
Prepaid insurance		2,000
Total current assets		247,000
Investments		
Investment in securities		80,000
Cash surrender value of life insurance		20,000
Total investments		100,000
Fixed assets		
Land		60,000
Buildings	900,000	
Less: Accumulated depreciation	200,000	700,000
Machinery and equipment	1,000,000	
Less: Accumulated depreciation	450,000	550,000
Total fixed assets		1,310,000
Intangible assets		
Patents		25,000
Total assets		1,682,000

Liabilities and Owners' Equity

Current liabilities		
Notes payable		5,000
Accounts payable		70,000
Salaries payable		10,000
Taxes payable		2,000
Current portion of mortgage		36,000
Total current liabilities		123,000
Long-term liabilities		
Mortgage payable	200,000	
Less: Current portion	36,000	164,000
Notes payable		50,000
Bonds payable 10% due 2000		150,000
Total long-term liabilities		364,000
Other liabilities		
Estimated warranty liability		56,000
Deferred income taxes		23,000
Total other liabilities		79,000
Total liabilities		566,000
Owners' equity		
Contributed capital		
Preferred stock, 7%, $100 per 500 shares outstanding		50,000
Common stock, 100,000 shares outstanding		616,000
Total contributed capital		666,000
Retained earnings		450,000
Total stockholders' equity		1,116,000
Total liabilities and stockholders' equity		1,682,000

a. *Gain:* A gain might be derived from the sale of a fixed asset for more than its book value.

EXAMPLE: Assume that the DEF Corporation owns land that cost $20,000 and is currently being used as a parking lot. DEF Corporation is in the business of selling lawnmowers. DEF sells this land for $30,000. The land did not constitute goods held for sale in the normal course of the business; therefore, the sale results in a gain.

Gains and losses are measured on a net basis. Rather than report revenue of $30,000 from the sale of the land and an expense of $20,000 for the cost of the land, accountants report only a gain of $10,000 (the net amount).

	Revenue from sale of land	$ 30,000
−	Cost of land	−20,000
	Net gain on sale of land	$ 10,000

b. *Loss:* A loss results when a fixed asset is sold for less than its book value.

EXAMPLE: Assume that DEF Corporation sold the parking lot land for $18,000 instead of $30,000. In this case a net loss of $2,000 would be incurred.

	Revenue from sale of land	$ 18,000
−	Cost of land	− 20,000
	Net loss on sale of land	−$ 2,000

Gains and losses may also occur as a result of uncontrollable events, such as fires, floods, or tornadoes. If the damages received from an insurance company exceed the book value of the property destroyed, a gain would result. If the damages received were less than the book value of the property lost, a loss would result.

3. *Net Income Related to Gains and Losses:* This equation describes the net income from normal operations of a business as well as revenues or expenses that are not a part of the business's normal operations:

$$\text{net income} = \text{revenues} - \text{expenses} + \text{gains} - \text{losses}$$

4. *Heading:* Every income statement should have a proper heading. The heading includes the following information:

a. The name of the company

b. The title of the statement

c. The period of time that the statement covers

(Note: The income statement is dated over a period of time while the balance sheet is as of a *specific* date.)

EXAMPLE:

Stone's Bicycles
Income Statement
For the Year Ending December 31, 20XA

5. *Basic Forms of the Income Statement:* An income statement may be reported in a classified form or an unclassified form. Figure 8–3 shows a classified income statement, and Figure 8–4 shows an unclassified income statement.

a. *Format of a classified income statement:*

(1) *Operating income:* Operating income consists of the revenues and expenses that result from the normal operations of the business. The expenses incurred in the normal operations of the business are subtracted from the revenues generated in the normal operations of the business to arrive at operating income. Operating income is the first section of a classified income statement.

(a) *Revenue:* Revenue from sales of goods or services is reported first in the operating income section.

Figure 8–3 Income Statement for a Corporation

ABC Company
Income Statement
For the Year Ending December 31, 20XB

Sales		5,000,000	
Less: Cost of goods sold		2,450,000	
Gross margin			2,550,000
Selling expenses			
Sales salaries	300,000		
Sales commissions	210,000		
Advertising	175,000		
Travel	25,000		
Total selling expense		710,000	
General and administrative expenses			
Salaries	458,000		
State and local taxes	47,600		
Telephone	8,400		
Legal and professional fees	9,200		
Insurance	12,450		
Depreciation	198,550		
Bad debt expense	10,000		
Total general and administrative expenses		744,200	
Total operating expenses			1,454,200
Operating income			1,095,800
Other income and expenses			
Investment revenue	98,000		
Gain on sale of land	12,000	110,000	
Interest expense (85,000)			
Loss on equipment due to fire	(8,500)	(93,500)	
Total other income			16,500
Net income before income taxes			1,112,300
Less: Applicable income taxes			444,920
Net income after income taxes			667,380
Earnings per share (on 100,000 shares)			6.67

Figure 8–4 Income Statement for a Partnership

XYZ Company
Income Statement
For the Year Ending December 31, 20XB

Revenues and gains		
Service fees		225,000
Gain on sale of equipment		7,500
Total revenues and gains		232,500
Less expenses and losses		
Salaries	120,000	
Rent for office building	30,000	
Supplies	2,500	
Depreciation	2,000	
Bad debts	1,800	
Interest	1,600	
Maintenance	500	
Total expenses and losses		158,400
Net income		74,100

Note: XYZ is a partnership. Therefore, there is no income tax expense shown on the income statement. On an unclassified income statement of a corporation, income taxes would be included under expenses and losses.

(b) *Cost of goods sold:* Next, the cost of goods sold is reported in the classified income statement of a merchandising firm. Cost of goods sold is the cost of merchandise sold to customers. Sales of goods minus cost of goods sold is called *gross margin* (or *gross profit*) on sales. In a firm that only provides services rather than selling a product, there is no cost of goods sold.

(c) *Operating expenses:* Operating expenses are divided into at least two categories: selling expenses and general and administrative expenses. Selling expenses are expenses that are directly related to the selling of a product. General and administrative expenses are expenses related to the office and administrative costs:

$$\text{gross profit} - \text{total operating expenses} = \text{operating income}$$

(2) *Other income and expenses:* Other income and expenses are reported after operating income. Other income and expenses consist of revenues and expenses that are not connected with the primary operations of the business. This category would include gains and losses, investment income (dividends received or interest earned on investments), interest expense, and incidental rental revenue. Interest expense is considered to be a financing expense rather than an operating expense and as such is included in the *other income and expense* category.

(3) *Net income before income taxes:* Operating income plus other income or minus other expenses results in net income before income taxes (corporate use only).

(4) *Net income after income taxes:* Income tax expense is deducted from *net income before income taxes* to arrive at *net income after income taxes.*

(a) *Corporations:* As separate legal entities, corporations pay taxes on their net income. The steps for reporting income taxes on the income statement refer only to corporations.

(b) *Sole proprietorships:* Because sole proprietorships are not separate legal entities, the business is not responsible for the payment of income taxes. The *owner* must include the income of the business on his or her personal tax return and pay the taxes individually; thus, income tax expense is not reported on the income statement of a sole proprietorship. Operating income plus other income or minus other expenses would result in the net income of the business, and the income statement would be complete.

(c) *Partnerships:* The individual partners are responsible for paying the taxes on their share of the income of the partnership. They report this income on their personal tax returns. The partnership pays no income taxes; thus, no income taxes are reported on the income statement of a partnership. As with a sole proprietorship, operating income plus/minus other income/expenses would result in the net income of the business, and the income statement would be complete.

(5) *Earnings per share:* A corporation also reports earnings per share on the income statement. Earnings per share is determined by dividing net income after taxes by the average number of shares of common stock held by owners during the period. *Earnings per share* is abbreviated EPS. The detailed calculation of earnings per share will not be discussed in this review manual (see the presentation of simple EPS in Figure 8–3).

Note: Partnerships and sole proprietorships do not issue common stock and, therefore, do not report earnings per share.

b. *Format of an unclassified income statement:* Figure 8–4 shows an income statement for a partnership in unclassified format.

(1) *Revenues and gains:* In an unclassified, or single-step, income statement all revenues and gains are grouped together first.

(2) *Expenses and losses:* Next, all expenses and losses are deducted from total revenues and gains to arrive at net income.

C. Comprehensive Income

Comprehensive income includes all changes in owners' equity during a period except those that result from investments by or distributions to owners.

1. *Types of Comprehensive Income:* Comprehensive income includes all revenues, expenses, gains, and losses included in net income as well as gains and losses that are reported in the stockholders' equity section. Unrealized holding gains and losses on securities classified as available for sale are examples of items that would be reported in the stockholders' equity section rather than the traditional income statement. (See Chapter 11, Section A-3-c.)

2. *Other Comprehensive Income:* Gains and losses that are not reported as part of net income but affect stockholders' equity are called *other comprehensive income.* Other

Figure 8–5 Statement of Retained Earnings

ABC Company
Statement of Retained Earnings
For the Year Ending December 31, 20XB

Retained earnings, December 31, 20XA	282,620
Add: Net income	667,380
Total	950,000
Less: Dividends	500,000
Retained earnings, December 31, 20XB	450,000

comprehensive income must be displayed in the financial statements in one of three ways:

a. A second separate income statement

b. A combined income statement of comprehensive income

c. As part of the statement of stockholders' equity

D. Statement of Retained Earnings

A corporation may present a statement of retained earnings. The statement of retained earnings shows the changes in retained earnings from one period to another. Figure 8–5 shows an example of a statement of retained earnings.

1. *Increases in Retained Earnings:* Net income results in an increase in retained earnings.
2. *Decreases in Retained Earnings:* Net loss results in a decrease in retained earnings. Dividends decrease retained earnings.

E. Statement of Changes in Capital

If the business is a sole proprietorship or a partnership, the company may present a statement of changes in capital. This statement shows the changes in the capital account from one period to another.

1. *Increases in Capital:* Increases in capital result from total net income and additional contributions.
2. *Decreases in Capital:* Decreases in capital result from total net losses and withdrawals.

F. Statement of Cash Flows

The final basic financial statement is the statement of cash flows. This statement shows the cash flows provided or used by the operating, investing, and financing activities of the business. This statement is discussed further in Chapter 18.

Review Questions

Directions: Select the correct answer from the four alternatives. Write your answer in the blank to the left of the number.

______ **1.** Which one of the following headings would be correct for the income statement of Morrison Company?

a. Morrison Company
   Income Statement
   December 31, 20XA
b. Morrison Company
   Income Statement
c. Income Statement
   For the year ending December 31, 20XA
d. Morrison Company
   Income Statement
   For the year ending December 31, 20XA

______ **2.** Current assets are listed on the balance sheet according to

a. liquidity.
b. alphabetical order.
c. order of acquisition.
d. size of dollar amount.

______ **3.** The financial statement that shows cash provided and used by operating, financing, and investing activities is called the

a. statement of financial position.
b. income statement.
c. statement of cash flows.
d. retained earnings statement.

______ **4.** In a classified (multiple-step) income statement, interest revenue would be reported

a. as an other income or expense item.
b. in the revenue section of the income statement.
c. in a separate section for financing and investing items.
d. after income tax expense.

______ **5.** Obligations of a business that will not come due after one year or the current operating cycle are called

a. other equities.
b. current liabilities.
c. intangible liabilities.
d. long-term liabilities.

______________ **6.** Net increases in income that are generated from incidental operations instead of the normal operations of the business are called

a. operating revenues.
b. gains.
c. losses.
d. intangible revenue.

______________ **7.** Which of the following transactions would result in the recording of a prepaid expense account?

a. Payment of a two-year insurance policy on January 1, 20XA. The policy expires on December 31, 20XB.
b. Payment of an account payable that resulted from the purchase of office supplies.
c. Payment of rent for June on June 30.
d. Purchase of stock in another corporation.

______________ **8.** Income tax expense would be shown on the income statement for

a. sole proprietorships.
b. corporations and sole proprietorships.
c. partnerships, corporations, and sole proprietorships.
d. corporations.

______________ **9.** The current portion of a long-term liability should be classified as a/an

a. trademark.
b. intangible liability.
c. long-term liability.
d. current liability.

______________ **10.** Total stockholders' equity in a corporation includes

a. capital stock (both common and preferred) and retained earnings.
b. only capital stock.
c. a separate capital account for each stockholder.
d. long-term bonds payable sold to fund expansion.

______________ **11.** Decreases in retained earnings result from

a. net income.
b. gains.
c. dividends declared.
d. repayment of loan principal amounts.

______________ **12.** In a classified (multiple-step) income statement operating expenses would typically include

a. interest expense.
b. income tax expense.

c. selling expenses.
d. dividends paid.

_____________ **13.** An account that is shown as a reduction from its related asset account on the balance sheet is called a/an

a. reducing account.
b. depreciating expense account.
c. debit account.
d. contra-asset account.

_____________ **14.** Rohas Corporation purchased a machine for $80,000. The post-closing balance in the accumulated depreciation account that relates to the machine was $20,000 on December 31, 20XA. The machine could be sold currently for $54,000. Depreciation expense for 20XA was $5,000. What is the book value of the machine?

a. $54,000
b. $55,000
c. $60,000
d. $80,000

_____________ **15.** During 20XA, the Corner Grocery, a sole proprietorship, had revenues of $700,000 and expenses of $400,000. Owner's equity was $150,000 on January 1, 20XA. Stevens, the owner, withdrew $50,000 cash from the business during 20XA. What was the balance in the capital account on December 31, 20XA?

a. $100,000
b. $400,000
c. $450,000
d. $700,000

Use the following information in answering Questions 16 and 17.

Miller Corporation had sales of $1,000,000 during 20XB. Cost of goods sold was $600,000; selling expenses were $100,000; general and administrative expenses were $60,000; other expenses were $10,000; and income taxes were $20,000.

_____________ **16.** What was Miller Corporation's gross profit for 20XB?

a. $210,000
b. $240,000
c. $400,000
d. $500,000

_____________ **17.** What was Miller Corporation's net income before tax for 20XB?

a. $210,000
b. $230,000
c. $240,000
d. $400,000

Solutions

Answer	*Refer to:*		
1. (d)	[B-4]		
2. (a)	[A-3-a]		
3. (c)	[E]		
4. (a)	[B-5-a(2)]		
5. (d)	[A-4-b]		
6. (b)	[B-2]		
7. (a)	[A-3-a(6)]		
8. (d)	[B-5-a(4)]		
9. (d)	[A-4-b(3)]		
10. (a)	[A-5-C]		
11. (c)	[A-5-C(2)]		
12. (c)	[B-5-a]		
13. (d)	[A-3-a(4)(c), A-3-c(3)]		
14. (c)	[A-3-c(4)]		
		Cost	$80,000
		− Accumulated depreciation (post-closing)	− 20,000
		Book value	$60,000
15. (b)	[E]		
		Capital 1/1/XA	$150,000
		+ Net income (revenues − expenses)	+300,000
		− Withdrawals	− 50,000
		Capital 12/31/XA	$400,000
16. (c)	[B-5-a(1)(b)]		
		Sales	$1,000,000
		− Cost of goods sold	− 600,000
		Gross profit	$ 400,000

17. (b) [B-5-a]

Sales		$1,000,000
− Cost of goods sold		− 600,000
Gross profit		$ 400,000
− Operating expenses:		
Selling expenses	$100,000	
General/adm. exp.	60,000	− 160,000
Net operating income		$ 240,000
− Other expenses		− 10,000
Net income before income tax		$ 230,000

CHAPTER 9

The Accounting Cycle

OVERVIEW

In this chapter we introduce the candidate to the steps involved in the accounting cycle. An understanding of the accounting cycle is necessary in understanding how transactions are recorded in the accounts and how financial statements are prepared.

The candidate should know the basic steps involved in the accounting cycle and how to complete each one of the steps. Journalizing and posting of transactions were discussed in Chapter 7, and financial statement format was discussed in Chapter 8.

KEY TERMS

Accounting cycle	Closing entry	Worksheet
Adjusting entries	Trial balance	

The accounting cycle consists of all the accounting procedures performed during each accounting period. The accounting period for most businesses is one year. The following are the steps in the accounting cycle.

A. Analyzing Transactions and Recording

Accounting transactions occur, and source documents are prepared. The transactions are recorded in the journal(s) as they occur.

EXAMPLE: Stone's Bicycles sold a bicycle for $90 cash. A sales invoice (source document) was prepared when the transaction occurred. From the sales invoice, the transaction was recorded in a journal.

B. Posting

The debits and credits recorded in the journal entries are posted to the appropriate ledger accounts.

C. Trial Balance

A trial balance is a listing of all the ledger account balances. Taking a trial balance is a process of summarizing all the ledger accounts.

1. *Equality of Debits and Credits:* The trial balance proves the equality of total debits and total credits in the accounts.
   a. If total debits do not equal total credits in the trial balance, an error has been made in recording and/or posting the transactions.

b. If total debits do equal total credits in the trial balance, this does *not* ensure that no errors have been made in recording and posting transactions. An entry could have been posted twice or posted to an incorrect account or for an incorrect amount, yet the trial balance could still balance.

2. *Preparation of Trial Balance:* A trial balance can be prepared at any time. Many companies prepare trial balances on a regular basis to provide a check on the equality of total debits and total credits in the accounts.

a. The first step in the end-of-period accounting process is to prepare an unadjusted trial balance from the ledger accounts.

b. This unadjusted trial balance can be included as a portion of the worksheet and might not be prepared as a separate step in the accounting cycle.

The accounts of PALS Partnership are presented in the following:

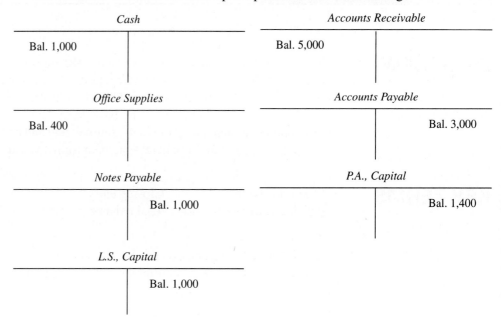

Cash	
Bal. 1,000	

Accounts Receivable	
Bal. 5,000	

Office Supplies	
Bal. 400	

Accounts Payable	
	Bal. 3,000

Notes Payable	
	Bal. 1,000

P.A., Capital	
	Bal. 1,400

L.S., Capital	
	Bal. 1,000

The trial balance of PALS Partnership is shown in Figure 9–1.

Figure 9–1 Trial Balance of PALS Partnership

PALS Partnership
Trial Balance
December 31, 20XB

	Debits	*Credits*
Cash	$1,000	
Accounts receivable	5,000	
Office supplies	400	
Accounts payable		$3,000
Notes payable		1,000
P.A., capital		1,400
L.S., capital		1,000
Totals	$6,400	$6,400

D. Worksheet

The worksheet is an accounting tool that makes the end-of-period processes of adjusting the accounts, closing the accounts, and preparing the financial statements easier (see Figure 9–4).

1. *Columns on the Worksheet:* A worksheet has columns for the unadjusted trial balance, the adjusting entries, the adjusted trial balance, the income statement, and the balance sheet.
2. *End-of-Period Adjustments:* The worksheet provides a place for recording all the end-of-period adjustments where errors may be detected and corrected easily.
3. *Journalizing and Posting:* After the worksheet has been completed, financial statements are prepared and the adjusting and closing entries are journalized and posted.

The end-of-period processes may be completed without the use of a worksheet. Using a worksheet, however, helps minimize the errors made in adjusting and closing the accounts and preparing the financial statements.

E. Preparing Financial Statements

The basic financial statements are prepared using the worksheet information. The financial statements are prepared following the formats discussed in Chapter 8.

F. Adjusting Entries

Adjusting entry information is taken from the worksheet, recorded in the journal, and posted to the ledger. Adjusting entries are necessary to bring accounts up to date that have incorrect balances as of the end of the accounting period. In preparing financial statements, it is necessary to follow the accounting principles of revenue realization, accrual accounting, and matching. Since we prepare financial statements at periodic intervals, some accounts have incorrect balances at year end. This occurs because an event that should be reported in accounting has occurred, but no formal transaction has occurred that resulted in preparation of a source document and recording of the transaction in the accounts. The following are basic types of adjusting entries:

1. *Estimates:*
   - **a.** *Depreciation expense:* Depreciation expense recorded for a machine is an example of one of these types of adjustments. The cost of the machine is capitalized, and this cost is apportioned systematically to each period of the asset's useful life. There is no source document to initiate the recording of depreciation expense. Therefore, an adjusting entry must be made to reflect properly the asset valuation and the depreciation expense at the end of each accounting period. See Chapter 13 for an example of the recording of depreciation expense.
   - **b.** *Allowance for uncollectible accounts:* The recording of the correct amount in the allowance for uncollectible accounts is also done through an adjusting entry at the end of the period. See Chapter 14 for an example of the recording of bad debt expense and the allowance for uncollectible accounts.
2. *Prepaid/Unearned Accounts:*
   - **a.** *Expenses:*
     - (1) *Expenses recorded initially as assets:* Goods or services purchased for future use and paid for in advance may be recorded initially as assets. This type of

asset represents a deferred expense that is commonly given the label *prepaid.* The adjustment process for expenses paid for in advance and recorded as assets is illustrated by some typical examples in (a) and (b), which follow.

(a) *Insurance expense:* Suppose that Company A purchased a fire insurance policy on March 1, 20XB, for $2,000. The policy had a two-year life. When the policy was purchased, Company A made the following journal entry:

	dr	*cr*
Prepaid insurance	2,000	
Cash		2,000

The end of Company A's fiscal year is August 31. On August 31, 20XB, the asset account *prepaid insurance* still has a $2,000 balance. An adjusting entry must be made to reflect the expiration of six months of insurance coverage benefits. Company A would make the following adjusting journal entry on August 31:

	dr	*cr*
Insurance expense	500	
Prepaid insurance		500
To record insurance expense for the period March 1 through August 31 ($2,000 × 6/24 months).		

If this adjusting entry were not made, the asset *prepaid insurance* would be overstated, and the amount of *insurance expense* would be understated, in the financial statements.

(b) *Supplies expense:* Another type of adjusting entry is the entry to record use of supplies when the original purchases of supplies were recorded in an asset account. Assume that GEF Company purchased $500 of office supplies on April 12. The following journal entry was made on that date:

	dr	*cr*
Office supplies inventory	500	
Cash		500

GEF Company wants to prepare financial statements on June 30. No entries were made between April 12 and June 30 to record the usage of office supplies. A physical count on June 30 reveals that there are $232 worth of office supplies left on hand. From this count, GEF Company can determine that $268 ($500 − $232) of office supplies were used. An adjusting entry must be made to record the expense and reduce the asset account *office supplies.* GEF Company would make the following adjusting entry on June 30:

	dr	*cr*
Office supplies expense	268	
Office supplies inventory		268

(2) *Expenses recorded initially as expenses:* Goods or services purchased for future use and paid for in advance might be recorded initially in an expense account rather than an asset account as discussed in Section F-2-a(1).

(a) *Supplies expense:* If GEF Company had originally recorded the purchase of the office supplies on April 12 as an expense, it would be necessary to record an adjusting entry to reflect that some of the office supplies are still on hand. Assume that GEF Company made the following journal entry on April 12:

	dr	*cr*
Office supplies expense	500	
Cash		500

Assume that the physical count still indicated that $232 of office supplies were on hand on June 30. If no adjusting entry were made, office supplies expense would be overstated, and assets would be understated. GEF Company would make the following adjusting entry on June 30:

	dr	*cr*
Office supplies inventory	232	
Office supplies expense		232
To record office supplies on hand on June 30.		

Figures 9–2 and 9–3 show two different methods of recording the same transaction. Whether a company originally records the purchase of office supplies as an asset or as an expense is up to the managers of the company. Regardless of whether office supplies are originally recorded as an asset or as an expense, the final end-of-period amounts recorded in the office supplies inventory and office supplies expense accounts should be the same.

(b) *Insurance expense:* When the purchase of an insurance policy is originally recorded as insurance expense and the life of the policy covers two or more accounting periods, an adjusting entry must be made to reduce the amount of expense recorded and to set up the asset *prepaid (*or *unexpired) insurance.* Assume that Company A made the following entry when the fire insurance policy was purchased for $2,000 on March 1:

	dr	*cr*
Insurance expense	2,000	
Cash		2,000

When the fiscal year ends on August 31, it would be necessary to record the following adjusting entry:

	dr	*cr*
Prepaid insurance	1,500	
Insurance expense		1,500

To record the portion of the fire insurance policy that is unexpired as of August 31, 20XB($2,000 × 18/24 months).

Figure 9–2 Office Supplies Inventory/Expense Accounts

Office Supplies Inventory

April 12	500		
		June 30	268
June 30	Bal. 232		

Office Supplies Expense

June 30	268		
June 30	Bal. 268		

Figure 9–3 Office Supplies Expense/Inventory Accounts

Office Supplies Expense

April 12	500		
		June 30	232
June 30	Bal. 268		

Office Supplies Inventory

June 30	232		
June 30	Bal. 232		

b. *Revenues:*

(1) *Revenues recorded initially as liabilities:* Revenue received in advance may be recorded initially in an unearned revenue (liability) account. This type of liability represents a deferred revenue item. The adjustment process for revenue received in advance and recorded as liabilities is illustrated in the following example.

(a) *Rental revenue:* Z Company received payment in advance for rental of a building for 12 months. The payment of $1,200 was received on June 1, 20XB, and the end of the company's accounting year is December 31, 20XB. Assume that Z Company made the following journal entry on June 1:

	dr	*cr*
Cash	1,200	
Unearned rental revenue		1,200

(b) *Adjusting entry:* As of December 31, the amount of seven months of the total rental revenue has been earned. If no adjusting entry were made, rental revenue would be understated, and unearned rental revenue would be overstated. Z Company would make the following adjusting entry on December 31:

	dr	*cr*
Unearned rental revenue	700	
Rental revenue		700
To record the portion of rent received in advance which has been earned through December 31.		

(2) *Revenues recorded initially as revenues:* Revenue received in advance might be initially recorded in a revenue account.

(a) *Rental revenue:* Z Company received payment in advance for rental of a building for 12 months. The payment of $1,200 was made on June 1, and the end of the company's accounting year is December 31, 20XB. Assume that Z Company made the following entry to record the transaction on June 1:

	dr	*cr*
Cash	1,200	
Rental revenue		1,200

(b) *Adjusting entry:* As of December 31, all of the rental revenue was not earned. If no adjusting entry were made on December 31, rental revenue would be overstated, and the liability unearned rental revenue would be understated. Z Company would make the following adjusting entry on December 31:

	dr	*cr*
Rental revenue	500	
Unearned rental revenue		500
To record the portion of rent received that has not yet been earned ($1,200 × 5/12 months).		

Examples b(1)(a) and b(2)(a) show two different ways of recording the same transactions. The end-of-period balances in the accounts are the same regardless of the method used.

3. *Accruals:*

a. *Accrued expenses:* Accrued expenses should be recorded when expenses have been incurred but have not yet been recorded as of the end of the accounting period. When an adjusting entry of this type is made, an accrued liability is recorded.

(1) *Accrued salaries:* Salaries have been earned by employees but have not yet been paid. Assume that Y Company's year end is November 30, 20XB, which is a Thursday. The employees of Y Company are paid weekly on Friday. As of November 30, the employees have earned salaries for four days' work that have not been paid or recorded. Assume that the amount earned by the employees from Monday through Thursday was $9,820. If no adjusting entry were made, *salaries expense* would be understated for the period, and the liability *salaries payable* would be understated. Y Company would make the following adjusting entry on November 30:

	dr	*cr*
Salaries expense	9,820	
Accrued salaries payable		9,820
To record salaries earned for the period ending November 30 that have not yet been paid.		

(2) *Accrued interest expense:* Interest expense on borrowed money accumulates on a day-to-day basis, but it is not normally recorded until it is paid. At the end of an accounting period, it is necessary to make an adjusting entry to record any interest expense incurred since the last payment date and to record the liability for payment of that interest at a future time. Assume that Z Company borrowed $5,000 from the bank on September 1, 20XB. Z Company signed a promissory note that stated that the note would be repaid on February 28, 20XC, with 15 percent interest. Z Company's year end is December 31. On September 1, Z Company made the following entry:

	dr	*cr*
Cash	5,000	
Note payable to bank		5,000
To record six-month 15 percent loan obtained from bank.		

Z Company must make the following adjusting entry on December 31 to record the interest expense accrued from September 1 through December 31:

	dr	*cr*
Interest expense	250	
Accrued interest payable		250
To record interest expense from September 1 through December 31 ($5,000 × 0.15 × 4/12 months).		

Note: Interest rates are always quoted on an annual basis. In this example, interest had accrued for four months, so it was necessary to multiply by 4/12 to determine the interest expense for the fraction of the year that had passed.

b. *Accrued revenues:* Accrued revenues should be recorded when revenues have been earned but have not yet been recorded as of the end of the accounting period. When an adjusting entry of this type is made, an accrued asset (receivable) and revenue are recorded.

(1) *Interest revenue:* Interest revenue is earned with the passage of time on notes receivable held by a company, but interest revenue is not normally recorded until it is received. At the end of an accounting period, it is necessary to make an adjusting entry to record any interest revenue earned that has not been received. Assume that Z Company accepted a four-month, 16 percent note receivable for $3,000 from a customer on November 1, 20XB. Z Company's year end is December 31. As of December 31, Z Company has earned two months of interest revenue that has not been recorded. It would be necessary for Z Company to make the following adjusting entry on December 31:

	dr	*cr*
Accrued interest receivable	80	
Interest revenue		80
To record interest earned on note receivable from November 1 through December 31 ($3,000 × 0.16 × 2/12 months).		

4. *Use of the Worksheet:* Figure 9–4 shows a typical worksheet that includes columns for the unadjusted trial balance, the adjustments, the adjusted trial balance, the income statement, and the balance sheet.

Columns 1 and 2 show the unadjusted trial balance of Handy Corporation. This trial balance was taken from Handy Corporation's general ledger.

Columns 3 and 4 show the adjustments necessary to bring the accounts in the unadjusted trial balance to the proper year-end amounts.

Adjustment a records the bad debt expense for the period and adjusts the allowance for uncollectible accounts balance. On December 31, 20XB, Handy Corporation estimated that $800 of the $10,000 accounts receivable balance would prove to be uncollectible. Since the allowance account had a credit balance of $40, it was necessary to make an adjusting entry crediting the allowance for uncollectible accounts for $760. The following adjusting entry was made on the worksheet:

	dr	*cr*
a. Bad debt expense	760	
Allowance for uncollectible accounts		760

Adjustment b records the amount of supplies used during the period. Handy Corporation records purchases of office supplies in the asset account *office supplies.* On December 31, 20XB, a physical count of the office supplies on hand was taken and $150 of supplies were on hand. The following adjusting entry was made to record the use of $400 ($550 − $150) of the supplies recorded in the office supplies account:

	dr	*cr*
b. Supplies expense	400	
Office supplies		400

Adjustment c records the portion of the asset *prepaid insurance* that has expired during the current period. Handy Corporation purchased a 20-month insurance policy on

Figure 9–4 Worksheet

Handy Corporation
Worksheet
Year Ending 12/31/XB

	Unadjusted Trial Balance		*Adjustments*		*Adjusted Trial Balance*		*Income Statement*		*Balance Sheet*	
	dr (1)	cr (2)	dr (3)	cr (4)	dr (5)	cr (6)	dr (7)	cr (8)	dr (9)	cr (10)
Cash	2,230				2,230				2,230	
Accounts receivable	10,000				10,000				10,000	
Allowance for uncollectible accounts		40		a. 760		800				800
Office supplies	550			b. 400	150				150	
Prepaid insurance	200			c. 80	120				120	
Furniture and fixtures	12,000				12,000				12,000	
Accumulated depreciation		2,200		d. 1,000		3,200				3,200
Accounts payable		5,400				5,400				5,400
Notes payable		2,000				2,000				2,000
Capital stock		5,000				5,000				5,000
Retained earnings 12/31/XB		5,920				5,920				5,920
Service revenue		65,700				65,700		65,700		
Loss of sales of equipment	2,420				2,420		2,420			
Salaries expense	57,860		e. 540		58,400		58,400			
Dividends	1,000				1,000				1,000	
Totals	86,260	86,260								
Bad debt expense			a. 760		760		760			
Supplies expense			b. 400		400		400			
Insurance expense			c. 80		80		80			
Depreciation expense			d. 1,000		1,000		1,000			
Salaries payable				e. 540		540				540
Interest expense			f. 50		50		50			
Interest payable				f. 50		50				50
Totals			2,830	2,830	88,610	88,610	63,110	65,700		
							2,590			2,590
Net income							65,700	65,700	25,500	25,500

May 1 and made full payment for the policy at that time. The payment on May 1 of $200 was recorded as follows:

	dr	*cr*
c. Prepaid insurance	200	
Cash		200

As of December 31, eight months of the life of the policy have expired. Handy Corporation made the adjusting entry to record the insurance expense and the reduction in the value of the insurance policy:

	dr	*cr*
c. Insurance expense	80	
Prepaid insurance		80
($200 × 8/20 months)		

Adjustment d records depreciation expense for the period. Handy Corporation estimated that the $12,000 of furniture and fixtures had a useful life of 12 years when purchased. The straight-line depreciation method is used. Depreciation expense for the year would be $1,000, calculated as follows:

$$\$12{,}000/12 \text{ years} = \$1{,}000 \text{ per year}$$

The following adjusting entry was made to record depreciation expense:

	dr	*cr*
d. Depreciation expense	1,000	
Accumulated depreciation		1,000

Adjustment e records the salaries earned by employees in the final week of December, 20XB, that have not yet been paid or recorded. Handy Corporation employees earned $540 that had not been paid. The following adjusting entry was made to reflect the year-end liability for salaries earned and not paid:

	dr	*cr*
e. Salaries expense	540	
Salaries payable		540

Adjustment f records the interest that has accrued on the note payable through December 31. Handy Corporation borrowed $2,000 from the bank on November 1, 20XB. The company agreed to pay the balance of the note plus 15 percent interest in 12 months. As of December 31, interest expense for two months has been incurred. The calculation of the interest expense was made as follows:

$$\$2{,}000 \times 0.15 \times 2/12 \text{ months} = \$50$$

Handy Corporation made the following adjusting entry to record the accrued interest expense:

	dr	*cr*
f. Interest expense	50	
Interest payable		50

Columns 5 and 6 show the adjusted trial balance with the account balances after adjustment. Column 5 or 6 is the sum of the account balance shown in column 1 or 2 plus or minus any adjustments made in column 3 or 4. Note that debits equal the credits in columns 1 and 2, 3 and 4, and 5 and 6.

Columns 7 and 8 show the accounts taken from the adjusted trial balance (columns 5 and 6) that make up the income statement. The amount needed to make debits equal credits in the income statement column is the amount of net income or loss. Note that in Figure 9–4 the net income is $2,590. This amount of net income is carried over to the balance sheet credit column (column 10) because it is a portion of the ending retained earnings balance.

Columns 9 and 10 show the accounts taken from the adjusted trial balance (columns 5 and 6) that make up the balance sheet. The new retained earnings balance as of December 31, 20XB, consists of the sum of the December 31, 20XA, retained earnings balance ($5,920 credit); the dividends balance ($1,000 debit); and the net income balance ($2,590 debit) carried over from the income statement.

G. Closing Entries

Entries must be prepared to close the temporary accounts at the end of the accounting period. Revenue, expense, gain, and loss accounts are summarized in the income statement, and net income is added to the owners' equity or retained earnings account. Thus, the revenue, expense, gain, and loss accounts are actually subdivisions of the owners' equity account that are used to accumulate information during the accounting period. At the end of the accounting period, they have served their purpose and should be closed, or *zeroed out.* The income summary account is used in the closing procedures to summarize the amounts of revenues and expenses. The following are the procedures used in closing the temporary accounts:

1. *Closing Revenue and Gain Accounts:* Revenue and gain accounts are closed by debiting the individual revenue/gain accounts and crediting the income summary account.
2. *Closing Expense and Loss Accounts:* Expense and loss accounts are closed by debiting the income summary account and crediting the individual expense/loss accounts.
3. *Closing the Income Summary Account:* The income summary account is closed to owners' equity in a partnership or sole proprietorship or to retained earnings in a corporation. If a profit was earned during the period, the income summary account is closed by debiting income summary and crediting owner's capital or retained earnings. If a loss was incurred during the period, the income summary account is closed by debiting owner's capital or retained earnings and crediting the income summary account.
4. *Closing Withdrawal and Dividend Accounts:* Withdrawal (or drawing) accounts and dividends declared accounts are also closed at the end of the period. They are temporary accounts. However, they are not income statement accounts. The withdrawal account is closed by debiting owner's capital and crediting withdrawals (drawings). The dividends declared account is closed by debiting retained earnings and crediting dividends declared. Not all firms create a separate dividend account when dividends are declared. Some firms would reduce retained earnings directly when recording a dividend declaration.
5. *Journalizing and Posting:* The closing entries are first journalized and then posted to the ledger. See Figure 9–5 for an illustration of the closing journal entries and the T-account posting of the closing entries.

Figure 9–5 Closing Journal Entries and T-Account Posting of Closing Entries for Handy Corporation

1. Service revenue	65,700	
Income summary		65,700
2. Income summary	63,110	
Salaries expense		58,400
Bad debt expense		760
Supplies expense		400
Insurance expense		80
Depreciation expense		1,000
Interest expense		50
Loss on sale of equipment		2,420
3. Income summary	2,590	
Retained earnings		2,590
4. Retained earnings	1,000	
Dividends declared		1,000

Service Revenue

	65,700 Bal.
65,700	
	-0- Bal.

Salaries Expense

Bal. 58,400	
	(2) 58,400
Bal. -0-	

Bad Debt Expense

Bal. 760	
	(2) 760
Bal. -0-	

Supplies Expense

Bal. 400	
	(2) 400
Bal. -0-	

Insurance Expense

Bal. 80	
	(2) 80
Bal. -0-	

Depreciation Expense

Bal. 1,000	
	(2) 1,000
Bal. -0-	

Interest Expense

Bal. 50	
	(2) 50
Bal. -0-	

Loss on Sale of Equipment

Bal. 2,420	
	(2) 2,420
Bal. -0-	

Income Summary

	(1) 65,700
(2) 63,110	
(3) 2,590	
Bal. -0-	

Retained Earnings

	5,920 Bal.
	(3) 2,590
(4) 1,000	
	7,510 Bal.

Dividends Declared

Bal. 1,000	
	(4) 1,000
Bal. -0-	

Figure 9–6 Post-closing Trial Balance

Handy Corporation
Post-closing Trial Balance
December 31, 20XB

	Debits	*Credits*
Cash	2,230	
Accounts receivable	10,000	
Allowance for uncollectible accounts		800
Office supplies	150	
Prepaid insurance	120	
Furniture and fixtures	12,000	
Accumulated depreciation		3,200
Accounts payable		5,400
Salaries payable		540
Interest payable		50
Notes payable		2,000
Capital stock		5,000
Retained earnings		7,510
Totals	24,500	24,500

H. Post-closing Trial Balance

The final step of the accounting cycle is to take a post-closing trial balance. This ensures that debits still equal credits in the accounts after the adjusting and closing entries have been journalized and posted and that all revenue and expense accounts have zero balances. The post-closing trial balance of Handy Corporation is shown in Figure 9–6. The post-closing trial balance includes only permanent accounts.

I. The Next Accounting Cycle

The accounting cycle begins again on the first day of the next accounting period. The opening balances for the next period are equal to the amounts on the post-closing trial balance.

Review Questions

Directions: Select the correct answer from the four alternatives. Write your answer in the blank to the left of the number.

______________ **1.** A trial balance that is prepared after all adjusting and closing entries have been posted is called

a. the balance sheet.
b. the unadjusted trial balance.
c. the adjusted trial balance.
d. the post-closing trial balance.

______________ **2.** The withdrawals account would normally be closed to

a. the owner's capital account.
b. the income summary account.
c. the retained earnings account.
d. the dividends account.

______________ **3.** The financial statements are normally prepared

a. after the worksheet is completed.
b. before beginning the worksheet.
c. using the post-closing trial balance.
d. from information taken from the unadjusted trial balance.

______________ **4.** Taking a trial balance means

a. making a listing of the account balances in the general journal.
b. adjusting the books of the company.
c. transferring the debits and credits from the journal to the ledger.
d. making a listing of the general ledger accounts and their balances.

______________ **5.** Which one of the following accounts would be included on a post-closing trial balance?

a. Prepaid insurance
b. Sales
c. Gain on sale of land
d. Interest expense

______________ **6.** Accounts that are closed at the end of each accounting period are called

a. permanent accounts.
b. owners' equity accounts.
c. temporary accounts.
d. real accounts.

_______________ **7.** Which one of the following is the first step in the accounting cycle?

a. Posting transactions
b. Analyzing and recording transactions in the journal
c. Taking a trial balance
d. Adjusting the accounts

_______________ **8.** On a worksheet, a positive net income amount is recorded

a. only in the income statement credit column.
b. only in the income statement debit column.
c. in both the income statement debit column and the balance sheet credit column.
d. in both the income statement credit column and the balance sheet debit column.

_______________ **9.** Failing to make an adjusting entry to record accrued wages payable would result in

a. an understatement of assets and an overstatement of net income.
b. an understatement of liabilities and an understatement of net income.
c. an understatement of liabilities and an overstatement of net income.
d. an overstatement of liabilities and an understatement of net income.

_______________ **10.** Little Company purchased an insurance policy that covers 18 months. At the time the policy was purchased, the payment was recorded as a debit in the prepaid insurance account. The adjusting entry at the end of the accounting period would require

a. a debit to insurance expense and a credit to the cash account.
b. a debit to prepaid insurance and a credit to the cash account.
c. a debit to prepaid insurance and a credit to the insurance expense account.
d. a debit to insurance expense and a credit to the prepaid insurance account.

_______________ **11.** Green Company originally recorded the purchase of office supplies in an expense account. At year end, Green Company counted the office supplies and found that $100 of supplies were still on hand. As a result of this,

a. no adjusting entry would be needed.
b. an adjusting entry debiting office supplies expense and crediting the asset office supplies should be made for $100.
c. an adjusting entry debiting the asset office supplies and crediting office supplies expense should be made for $100.
d. an adjusting entry debiting cash and crediting the asset office supplies should be made for $100.

_______________ **12.** Miller Company failed to record accrued rent receivable as of the end of the accounting period. As a result, total assets would be

a. overstated, and total net income would be overstated.
b. understated, and total net income would be unaffected.
c. understated, and total liabilities would be understated.
d. understated, and net income would be understated.

_______________ **13.** An accounting tool used to make the end-of-period process of adjusting the accounts, closing the accounts, and preparing the financial statements easier is called a/an

a. trial balance.
b. adjusting balance.
c. post-closing trial balance.
d. worksheet.

_______________ **14.** A listing of all accounts that shows total debits and total credits is called a/an

a. balance sheet.
b. income statement.
c. trial balance.
d. worksheet.

_______________ **15.** Adjusting entries are needed to

a. close out temporary accounts at year end.
b. bring accounts that have incorrect balances as of the end of the accounting period up to date.
c. bring the trial balance into balance.
d. correct errors made when initially recording a transaction.

_______________ **16.** Which one of the following entries would be considered an adjusting entry?

a. The recording of a note payable to Company Z
b. Sale of merchandise on account
c. The recording by Company Z of the expiration of a portion of the asset *prepaid rent*
d. Payment of interest expense

Use the following information in answering Questions 17 to 20.

Alex Company rented a building from Bates Co. for 36 months on June 1, 20XA. The amount of the rent was $3,600. Alex Company's year end is October 31. Alex Company recorded the payment of $3,600 as rent expense on June 1.

_______________ **17.** What is the amount of the rent expense related to this lease that should be reported on Alex Company's income statement for October 31, 19XA?

a. $500
b. $1,000
c. $3,100
d. $3,600

_______________ **18.** What is the amount of prepaid rent that should be shown on Alex Company's October 31, 20XA, balance sheet?

a. $500
b. $1,000

c. $3,100
d. $3,600

______________ **19.** On October 31, 20XA, the correct adjusting entry to record this transaction would be

a. debit rent expense and credit prepaid rent for $500.
b. debit prepaid rent and credit rent expense for $3,100.
c. debit prepaid rent and credit rent expense for $500.
d. debit rent expense and credit prepaid rent for $3,600.

______________ **20.** Using the same information in Questions 17 to 19, assume that Alex Company originally recorded the $3,600 payment as a debit to prepaid rent and a credit to cash. The necessary adjusting entry would be

a. debit rent expense and credit prepaid rent for $500.
b. debit prepaid rent and credit rent expense for $500.
c. debit rent expense and credit prepaid rent for $3,100.
d. debit prepaid rent and credit rent expense for $3,100.

Use the following information in answering Questions 21 to 24.

______________ The following accounts and balances appear on the adjusted trial balance of Stowe's Hair Salon. The accounts are not listed in chart of account order.

Accumulated depreciation expense	$ 600
Cash	1,764
Wages expense	1,700
Advertising expense	126
Revenue from services	3,917
Equipment	3,974
Rent expense	750
Stowe, capital	4,820
Stowe, drawing	1,200
Accounts receivable	721
Accounts payable	1,424
Supplies	416
Depreciation expense	110

______________ **21.** Total debits in the trial balance are

a. $9,261.
b. $10,161.
c. $10,461.
d. $10,761.

______________ **22.** Net income for Stowe's Hair Salon is

a. $31.
b. $931.
c. $1,041.
d. $1,231.

______________ **23.** Total assets as shown on the balance sheet are

a. $6,275.
b. $6,575.
c. $7,475.
d. $7,775.

______________ **24.** After closing entries are posted, the balance in the Stowe, capital account will be

a. $4,551.
b. $4,661.
c. $4,851.
d. $6,051.

Solutions

Answer	*Refer to:*
1. (d)	[H]
2. (a)	[G-4]
3. (a)	[E]
4. (d)	[C]
5. (a)	[H]
6. (c)	[G]
7. (b)	[A]
8. (c)	[Figure 9–4]
9. (c)	[F-3-a]
10. (d)	[F-2-a(1)(a)]
11. (c)	[F-2-a(2)(a)]
12. (d)	[F-3-b]
13. (d)	[D]
14. (c)	[C]
15. (b)	[F]
16. (c)	[F]
17. (a)	[F-2-a(2)] \$3,600/36 months = \$100/month \$100/month × 5 months = \$500 rent expense
18. (c)	[F-2-a(2)] \$3,600 − \$500 = \$3,100
19. (b)	[F-2-a(2)]
20. (a)	[F-2-a(1)]

21. (d) [C]

	dr	cr
Accumulated depreciation	$	$ 600
Cash	1,764	
Wages expense	1,700	
Advertising expense	126	
Revenue from services		3,917
Equipment	3,974	
Rent expense	750	
Stowe, capital		4,820
Stowe, drawing	1,200	
Accounts receivable	721	
Accounts payable		1,424
Supplies	416	
Depreciation expense	110	
Totals	$10,761	$10,761

22. (d) [Chapter 8, B-1]

Revenue from services		$ 3,917
Less expenses:		
Wages expense	$ 1,700	
Advertising expense	126	
Rent expense	750	
Depreciation expense	110	2,686
Net income		$ 1,231

23. (a) [Chapter 7, B-1]

Cash		$ 1,764
Accounts receivable		721
Supplies		416
Equipment	$ 3,974	
Less accumulated depreciation	(600)	3,374
		$ 6,275

24. (c) [Chapter 8, D]

Stowe, capital beginning	$ 4,820
Add: Net income	1,231
Less: Stowe, drawing	(1,200)
Stowe, capital ending	$ 4,851

CHAPTER

10

Accounting for Cash

OVERVIEW

Cash is an area of accounting with which candidates should be familiar. The procedures for performing a bank reconciliation for a business account are the same as those used to reconcile an individual's checking account. Other aspects of accounting for cash, such as internal control and the recording of transactions, may be less familiar to the candidates.

The candidate should understand the recording of cash receipts and cash disbursements, the procedures needed for proper internal control over cash, the treatment of trade and cash discounts, the handling of a petty cash fund, the use of a voucher system, and the procedures for reconciling a bank account and be familiar with the types of checks and the check register.

KEY TERMS

Bank reconciliation	Check register	Purchases journal
Cash	Control account	Sales journal
Cash disbursements journal	Deposits in transit	Special journal
Cash discount	Internal controls	Subsidiary account
Cash receipts journal	NSF check	Trade discount
Certified check	Outstanding checks	Voucher
	Petty cash fund	Voucher system

A. Cash Receipts

1. *Cash:* Coins, paper money, checks, money orders, and money on deposit in bank accounts are all classified as cash. An item accepted as a deposit by a bank should be considered part of the cash of the company.

2. *Major Types of Cash Receipts:* Cash may be received for the immediate sale of merchandise, performance of services, or for payment of a sale on credit.

3. *Internal Controls:* The procedures and rules used by a company to ensure that its assets are being used for legitimate business purposes are known as *internal controls.* Internal controls aid in the efficient operation of a business.

   a. *Procedures and rules:* The establishment of procedures and rules by a company usually fall into the following five categories:

      (1) *Adequate separation of duties among employees:* Custody of an asset and recordkeeping for it should be separated. This helps prevent an individual

from stealing assets and changing the accounting records to cover up the theft.

(2) *Proper authorization*

(3) *Maintenance of adequate documents and records*

(4) *Limiting access to assets and to accounting records*

(5) *Performing independent checks on the performance of individuals*

b. *Internal controls for cash receipts:* Cash is very easily misappropriated, so it is essential that a business maintain good internal controls over cash receipts and disbursements. The following items are examples of good internal control procedures for cash receipts:

(1) *Recording cash sales:* Cash sales should be recorded on a cash register.

(2) *Depositing cash receipts:* Cash receipts should be deposited intact daily.

(3) *Daily reconciliation of cash sales:* At the end of the day, an individual not involved in the collection of cash receipts should reconcile the total cash on hand with the record of cash sales for the day.

(4) *Endorsement of checks received:* Any checks received should be restrictively endorsed immediately.

(5) *Recording cash receipts:* Recording of cash receipts should be separated from custody of cash.

(6) *Opening mail cash receipts:* Responsibility should be assigned for opening mail receipts. Payments on outstanding accounts receivable balances are typically received in the mail.

(a) The person who is assigned the responsibility for opening mail receipts should restrictively endorse all checks and prepare a list of checks received.

(b) The individual opening the mail may prepare the bank deposit slip and make the deposit, or the checks may be forwarded to a cashier who deposits the receipts intact daily.

(c) A copy of the list of checks received [see Section (6)(a)] should be sent to the accounting department.

(d) The accounting department should receive a duplicate deposit slip that can be compared with the list of mail receipts. Any differences must be reconciled.

(e) The accounting department enters the amounts received in the accounting records.

(7) *Preparation of bank reconciliation:* An independent bank reconciliation should be prepared monthly. The individual preparing the bank reconciliation should not be involved in the cash depositing or recording functions.

B. Subsidiary Ledgers and Special Journals

1. *Control Account:* A control account has a balance that is the total of all the balances of a related subsidiary ledger. For example, the general ledger accounts receivable account is a control account because its balance shows the total amount owed to the company by its customers. The individual accounts for each customer are kept in the *subsidiary accounts receivable ledger*. The general ledger accounts payable account is also a control account.

2. *Subsidiary Account:* The detailed accounts of individual balances are kept in a subsidiary ledger.

a. *The subsidiary accounts receivable ledger:* The subsidiary accounts receivable ledger contains an account for each credit customer of the company. The total of all the individual accounts contained within the subsidiary accounts receivable ledger should be equal to the balance in the general ledger. The balance in a single account of the subsidiary accounts receivable ledger (if it is up to date) represents the amount owed to the business by that particular customer.

b. *The subsidiary accounts payable ledger:* A separate account for each supplier from whom the company has purchased on account is maintained in the subsidiary accounts payable ledger. The total of all the balances of the individual accounts contained within the subsidiary accounts payable ledger should be equal to the balance in the general ledger accounts payable control account. Each individual subsidiary accounts payable account shows all credit purchases made by the company from a particular supplier, all payments made to the supplier, and any adjustments made to the account. The balance in an individual subsidiary accounts payable account represents the amount owed by the company to that supplier.

3. *Special Journals:* Special journals may be used in the recording of transactions that occur very frequently. In earlier chapters, all transactions were assumed to be recorded in a general journal. In reality, it is more efficient to use special journals for recording routine transactions that occur often. Many businesses have special journals to record cash receipts, cash disbursements, sales of goods on account, and purchases of inventory on account. It is possible that a company might have more special journals than these. However, these are the four most common special journals.

a. *Cash receipts journal:* All receipts of cash are recorded in the cash receipts journal.

b. *Cash disbursements journal:* All payments of cash are recorded in the cash disbursements journal, sometimes called a *cash payments journal.*

c. *Sales journal:* Credit sales are recorded in the sales journal. Cash sales are recorded in the cash receipts journal.

d. *Purchases journal:* The purchases journal is used to record inventory purchases on account.

e. *General journal:* When special journals are used, the general journal is used to record any transaction that does not fit in a special journal. Adjusting entries, closing entries, sales returns, and purchases returns are examples of items that would be recorded in the general journal.

Note: Refer to an accounting principles textbook for examples of how to record transactions in special journals.

C. Cash Disbursements

1. *Cash Disbursement Records:* To ensure that proper control is maintained over cash disbursements, almost all cash disbursements should be made by check. Cash disbursements are usually recorded in a cash disbursements journal (see Section B-3-b).

2. *Trade and Cash Discounts:*

a. *Trade discounts:* Trade discounts are reductions from the retail list price of items in a catalog that are given by manufacturers or wholesalers to their dealers. Each dealer might have a specific discount (e.g., 25, 30, or 40 percent) on items the dealer buys from the catalog. Trade discounts are not recorded on the accounting records of the buyer or of the seller. Both companies record the sale at the reduced amount. The trade discount is simply a method of determining the sales price.

EXAMPLE: Jones Distributing Company is a dealer for Ajax Wholesaling Company. Jones Distributing Company is given a 30 percent trade discount on all purchases from Ajax Wholesaling Company's catalog. Jones purchased goods with a total catalog list price of $10,000 from Ajax. The amount of the sale would be computed as follows:

	List price	$10,000	
−	Trade discount	−3,000	($10,000 × 0.30)
	Selling/purchase price	$ 7,000	

b. *Cash discounts:* Cash discounts encourage customers to pay their accounts promptly. Cash discounts are stated on the invoice and tell the customer how much of a discount may be taken if the bill is paid within a certain period.

An invoice might have the terms 2/10, n/30. This means that the customer will get a 2 percent discount if the bill is paid within 10 days of the invoice date and that the net amount (the total amount) is due in 30 days.

The terms 3/15, n/30 mean that the customer will get a 3 percent discount if the bill is paid within 15 days and the net amount is due in 30 days.

The terms 3/15 EOM, n/60 mean that the customer may deduct a 3 percent discount if the invoice is paid within the first 15 days of the month following the month of the sale and that the net amount is due within 60 days from the date of the sales invoice.

EXAMPLE: Jones Company receives an invoice from Papper Company dated January 2, 20XA. The terms of the invoice are 2/10, n/30. The amount of the invoice is $100. If the invoice were paid on January 10, the amount due would be $98.

	Total invoice amount	$100
−	Cash discount (2% × $100)	−2
	Amount to be paid	$ 98

Using the gross method of recording cash discounts, Jones Company's journal entry to record payment of this invoice would be as follows:

	dr	*cr*
Accounts payable	100	
Cash		98
Purchase discounts		2

Papper Company's entry to record receipt of the payment would be as follows:

	dr	*cr*
Cash	98	
Sales discounts	2	
Accounts receivable		100

If the invoice were paid on January 15, the 10-day discount period would have passed, and the total invoice amount of $100 would be due.
Using the gross method of recording cash discounts, Jones Company's entry to record payment on January 15 would be as follows:

	dr	*cr*
Accounts payable	100	
Cash		100

Papper Company's entry to record the receipt would be as follows:

	dr	*cr*
Cash	100	
Accounts receivable		100

EXAMPLE: If an invoice is subject to both a trade and a cash discount, the cash discount is computed on the selling price after consideration of the trade discount. Jones Company received an invoice from Ajax Company. The list price of the goods purchased was $2,000. The trade discount is 30 percent, and the terms of the cash discount are 3/10, n/30. Jones Company paid the invoice within the 10-day discount period. The amount paid was $1,358, which was computed as follows:

List price	$2,000	
− Trade discount	− 600	($2,000 × 0.30)
	$1,400	
− Cash discount	− 42	($1,400 × 0.03)
Amount paid	$1,358	

3. *Impest Petty Cash:* It is not practical for a company to write checks for small expenditures. Some items, such as postage stamps, taxi fares, office supplies, and parking meter payments, can be made more easily from a special fund called a *petty cash fund.* An impest petty cash fund has one custodian, often a secretary, who is responsible for handling cash payments from the fund. The word *impest* means an advance of money for some specified business use.

a. *Establishing the petty cash fund:* The petty cash fund is established at some reasonable amount. Assume that a petty cash fund of $100 is to be established. A check for $100 would be written and cashed, and the money would be kept in a petty cash drawer or box. The journal entry to record the establishment of the fund is as follows:

	dr	*cr*
Petty cash	100	
Cash		100

The only times an entry is made to the petty cash fund are when the fund is established or when the total amount of money in the fund is increased or decreased.

b. *Making disbursements from the petty cash fund:* When disbursements are made from the fund, the custodian prepares a petty cash voucher. A petty cash voucher is a record of the expenditure that includes the date, the amount paid, the reason for the expenditure, and the signature of the person who received the money. The petty cash drawer should always contain cash and vouchers equal to the total amount of the fund. No journal entries are prepared when the disbursements are made. The entries to record the disbursements are made when the fund is replenished.

c. *Replenishing the petty cash fund:* When the fund becomes depleted, the petty cash custodian makes a list of the petty cash vouchers and requests reimbursement. Assume that the petty cash vouchers indicate that $83.78 was disbursed from the fund. A check would be made out to the petty cash fund for $83.78. This check would be cashed and the money placed in the petty cash drawer. A journal entry would be made to record the expenditures as indicated by the petty cash vouchers. A typical journal entry to record replenishment might be as follows:

	dr	*cr*
Postage expense	42.00	
Freight in	21.00	
Transportation expense	12.53	
Miscellaneous expense	8.25	
Cash		83.78

Note: The expense accounts are debited each time the fund is replenished. A variance between the total vouchers to be expensed and the cash necessary to replenish the petty cash fund to its full amount is charged to cash long or short.

d. *Reconciling petty cash:* At any time, the sum of the money and the petty cash vouchers in the petty cash drawer should equal the total amount of the fund. A periodic reconciliation should be made to ensure that this is the case. Occasional surprise audits (counts) of the fund should be made by a supervisor. This ensures that the petty cash custodian is using the fund for authorized expenditures and that vouchers are being properly completed.

4. *Checks and Check Registers:*

a. *Check:* A check is a written document that orders a bank to pay a specific amount from the depositor's account to the payee of the check. Checks come in many different forms. Many checks have a check stub attached to the check. This stub is filled out prior to writing the check and is kept by the company writing the check. The stub may serve as a source document for recording the transaction.

b. *Certified check:* A certified check is a check for which the bank guarantees that the depositor has enough funds in the bank account to cover the check when it is presented for payment. The depositor must take the check to the bank and have it certified prior to giving the check to the payee. The bank stamps "certified" on the check and removes the money from the depositor's account. A fee is usually charged for certifying a check. Certified checks might be issued when a large sum of money is involved.

c. *Check register:* Another term for cash disbursements journal is *check register.* The check register lists all the checks issued. When a voucher system is used, a simplified version of the cash disbursements journal may be used, and this journal is usually called a check register (see Section C-5 for further discussion of the check register).

5. *The Voucher System and Recording of Accounts Payable:* A voucher system is used to obtain the maximum amount of internal control over cash disbursements, purchasing, and receiving. A voucher system requires that a voucher be prepared and verified prior to making any payments.

a. *The voucher system:* A voucher is a document that is used to authorize payment of a liability. A voucher typically contains spaces for the voucher date, information from the supplier's invoice, the ledger accounts to be debited and credited, space for the approval signatures for each step of the verification process, and space for the signature for the approval of the liability. Vouchers are numbered consecutively, and a separate voucher is attached to each incoming invoice.

b. *Recording transactions in a voucher system:*

(1) An invoice is received and a voucher is prepared by transferring all the pertinent information from the invoice to the voucher.

(2) The voucher with the invoice attached is sent to the appropriate individuals for verification.

(3) After the verification process has been completed, an employee from the accounting department indicates the accounts to be debited and credited.

(4) The voucher is approved by an official who notes that the verification procedures have been completed and that the liability is valid.

(5) After approval, the voucher is entered in the voucher register. A voucher register is similar to a purchases journal, but it has more columns for the different types of asset and expense accounts to be debited. A purchases journal records only purchases of inventory and supplies on account. A voucher register is used to record all types of expenditures. (A voucher register replaces the purchases journal in companies using the voucher system.) All credits in the voucher register consist of a credit to the vouchers payable account.

(6) When payment is made, the date of the payment and the check number are recorded in the voucher register, and the check is recorded in the check register. When a voucher system is used, all entries in the check register consist of a debit to vouchers payable and a credit to cash. The check register contains columns for debits to vouchers payable, credits to cash, and credits to purchase discounts (for use when payment is made within the cash discount period).

(7) The column totals from the voucher register and the check register are posted to the general ledger periodically.

(8) Paid vouchers are filed numerically in a special file.

6. *Internal Control of Cash Disbursements:* To maintain adequate internal control over cash disbursements, these steps should be followed:

a. *Payments:* All cash disbursements should be made by check except for minor expenditures paid through a petty cash fund.

b. *Use of prenumbered checks:* Checks should be prenumbered, and any checks that are written incorrectly should be marked "void" and filed in numerical sequence with the other canceled checks. In this way, all check numbers will be accounted for.

c. *Authorized signatures:* The individual who is authorized to sign checks should not have the authority to approve invoices or vouchers for payment or to make entries in the accounting records.

d. *Access to cash:* The individual who records cash disbursements in the accounting records should not have access to cash.

e. *Approval of voucher or invoice:* Checks submitted for signature should be accompanied by an approved voucher or invoice that should be stamped "paid" at the time the check is signed. This eliminates the possibility of paying the same invoice twice.

7. *Cash Over and Short:* Small errors may occur in making change during over-the-counter sales to customers. When this happens, the total of the daily cash register tapes will not be equal to the total cash collected. If there is more cash available than that reported on the total cash register tape (overage), the cash-over-and-short account is credited. If there is less cash available than that reported on the total cash register tape (shortage), the cash-over-and-short account is debited.

EXAMPLE: Jones Company collected $1,010.25 in cash for over-the-counter sales on March 1. The total cash sales per the cash register tapes on March 1 were $1,011.38. The entry to record the day's sales would be as follows:

	dr	*cr*
Cash	1,010.25	
Cash over and short	1.13	
Sales		1,011.38

D. Bank Statements and Cash Balance

Every month the bank provides each depositor with a bank statement for the bank account. This bank statement includes any checks paid by the bank and charged to the depositor's account and any deposit slips showing amounts that have been credited to the depositor's account. The bank statement is the bank's record of its account payable to the depositor. See Figure 10–1 for an example of a bank statement.

1. *Reconciliation:* When the bank statement is received, the depositor should prepare a reconciliation that explains any differences between the bank statement and the cash account in the ledger. In most circumstances, the balance per the bank statement will not agree with the cash balance per the general ledger. Preparation of a bank reconciliation by a party independent of recording cash, handling cash, or preparing checks is an important internal control tool.

   a. *Transactions not recorded by bank:* Transactions could have been recorded by the depositor that have not yet been recorded by the bank. Examples of these types of transactions are the following:

      (1) *Deposits in transit:* Deposits recorded on the books of the depositor and sent to the bank that have not yet been recorded by the bank.

      (2) *Outstanding checks:* Checks written and recorded on the books of the depositor that have not yet been paid by the bank and recorded on the books of the bank.

   b. *Transactions not recorded by depositor:* Transactions could have been recorded by the bank that have not yet been recorded in the general ledger of the depositor. Examples of these types of transactions are the following:

Figure 10–1 Bank Statement

THE FIRST NATIONAL BANK

MONTHLY
STATEMENT
OF ACCOUNT

PAGE
1

Jones Company
6491 Alameda Drive
Chicago, IL 60101

ACCOUNT NUMBER
31-484-6
STATEMENT DATE
11/29/20XA
LAST STATEMENT DATE
10/31/20XA

YOUR LAST CHECKING STATEMENT BALANCE WAS	*From Which is Subtracted CHECKS/DEBITS/ PAYMENTS*	*And Added DEPOSITS/CREDITS/ ADVANCES*	*YOUR SERVICE CHARGE IS*	*RESULTING IN A CHECKING BALANCE OF*
$10,423.82	*$15,633.28*	*$16,752.44*	*$43.50*	*$11,499.48*

DATE	*CHECKS/DEBITS/PAYMENTS*		*DEPOSITS/CREDITS/ ADVANCES*	*BALANCE*
11/1	101.23			
11/2	1,320.24		2,423.82	
11/3	916.13	4,422.21		
11/5	212.10	33.24		
11/7	98.80			
11/8	100.00	893.26	4,513.17	
11/10	87.50			
11/12	3,212.10	105.40		
11/13	108.20		3,123.22	
11/14	56.43	157.22		
11/16	82.18			
11/18	99.50	3,310.12	2,100.10	
11/19	71.33			
11/21			1,822.16	
11/26	63.25 DM	182.84	2,769.97	
11/29	43.50 SC			

DM = Debit Memo, NFS Check.
SC = Service Charge.

(1) *Service charges:* The bank may charge a service charge for handling the depositor's account. Prior to receiving the bank statement, the depositor has no record of the amount of the service charge, and it will not have been recorded on the depositor's books.

(2) *Notes collected by the bank:* The bank might have collected a note receivable for the depositor. If this is done, the bank usually charges a collection fee.

(3) *NSF checks:* NSF checks are nonsufficient funds checks. An NSF check is a check that has been received by the depositor company and deposited in its account. This check was returned to the bank because the account on which the check was written did not contain sufficient funds to cover the amount of the check. The bank returns the check to the depositor along with a debit memo indicating that the depositor's account was reduced by the amount of the check the bank was unable to collect.

(4) *Miscellaneous debit or credit memos:* Other miscellaneous types of debit or credit memos, such as check printing costs or stop payment order charges, may not yet be recorded by the depositor.

2. *Detection and Correction of Errors:* The bank reconciliation may be complete after consideration of the reconciling items discussed in Section D-1. It is possible that the bank or the depositor may have made an error in recording the transactions for the month. If an error was made, the error must be corrected to reconcile the bank statement balance and the general ledger balance. Common types of errors are the following:

a. A check or a deposit is recorded with an incorrect amount.

b. The depositor has more than one bank account and records a check or a deposit in the wrong account.

c. The bank has made an error. The bank should be notified immediately so that the error can be corrected. There is no need to make an entry on the depositor's books, since they are correct.

If the depositor made an error in recording a transaction, a correcting journal entry must be made to bring the account balance to the proper amount.

3. *Preparation of a Bank Reconciliation:* A bank reconciliation is a report that explains the difference between the bank's balance shown on the bank statement issued by the bank and the balance shown in the general ledger cash account. Figure 10–2 shows a typical form used in preparing a bank reconciliation.

EXAMPLE OF BANK RECONCILIATION: Jones Company received the bank statement shown in Figure 10–1 on December 5, 20XA. An examination of the bank statement showed that the bank had not yet recorded a deposit of $1,322.93, which was mailed on November 28, and that five checks totaling $2,020.89 had not yet been presented to the bank for payment.

The outstanding checks were as follows:

Check Number	*Date*	*Amount*
1933	11/20	$ 33.25
1938	11/25	282.65
1941	11/29	1,050.87
1942	11/29	200.00
1943	11/29	454.12
		$2,020.89

The $63.25 debit memo was for an NSF check issued by G-Var Company to Jones Company. The bookkeeper of Jones Company had recorded check number 1930 to the gas company as $65.43 in the records. The correct amount of the check was $56.43. This type of error is called a transposition error *(when two figures of a number are transposed). The difference resulting from a transposition error is always divisible by 9, and this fact can be used to help locate errors. The bank reconciliation for Jones Company is shown in Figure 10–2.*

4. *Journal Entries to Record Reconciling Items:* The additions and deductions necessary to go from the balance per bank to the adjusted balance per bank and from the balance per books to the adjusted balance per books are called *reconciling items.* It is

Figure 10–2 Bank Reconciliation for Jones Company

Balance per bank statement	11,499.48		Balance per books		10,899.27
Add: Deposit in transit	1,322.93		Add: Transposition error		9.00
	12,822.41				
Less: Outstanding checks			Less: Service charge	43.50	
			NSF check	63.25	
No. 1933	$ 33.25				
No. 1938	282.65		Total		106.75
No. 1941	1,050.87				
No. 1942	200.00				
No. 1943	454.12	$ 2,020.89			
Adjusted bank balance		$10,801.52	Adjusted book balance		$10,801.52

necessary to record journal entries for all reconciling items under the balance per books. No journal entries are necessary for the reconciling items that relate to the balance per bank, since they refer to the bank's records rather than the company's records. The journal entries to record the reconciling items on the Jones Company bank reconciliation are as follows:

a. *Transposition errors:* The transposition error resulted in an overstatement of utilities expense of $9.00 and an understatement of cash of $9.00. The entry to correct the transposition error would be as follows:

	dr	*cr*
Cash	9.00	
Utilities expense		9.00

b. *Service charges:* The service charge was not yet recorded on the books of Jones Company. The entry to record the service charge would be as follows:

	dr	*cr*
Bank service charge expense	43.50	
Cash		43.50

c. *NSF check:* The NSF check was originally recorded as a cash receipt. Since there were not sufficient funds to cover the check, it is not really a cash receipt but an account receivable from the customer. Jones Company would make the following entry to record the receipt of the NSF check:

	dr	*cr*
Accounts receivable—G-Var	63.25	
Cash		63.25

Review Questions

Directions: Select the correct answer from the four alternatives. Write the letter of your answer in the blank to the left of the number.

______ **1.** The total amount owed by Jones Company to Company X is represented by

a. the balance in Jones Company's subsidiary accounts payable account for Company X.
b. the balance in Jones Company's subsidiary accounts receivable account for Company X.
c. the amount in the general ledger accounts payable control account.
d. the amount in the general ledger accounts receivable control account.

______ **2.** Trade discounts should be

a. recorded as a sales discount when cash is received for the merchandise.
b. allowed only if the invoice is paid within a specified time period.
c. treated as a reduction from the list price of goods used in determining the selling price.
d. recorded as a sales discount at the time the goods are shipped.

______ **3.** Which one of the following items should be classified as cash?

a. Money orders
b. Certificates of deposit
c. Marketable securities
d. Postage stamps

______ **4.** When the petty cash fund is reimbursed,

a. cash is debited.
b. expenses are debited.
c. petty cash is debited.
d. petty cash is credited.

______ **5.** Which of the following procedures would be considered a good internal control procedure for cash?

a. All cash receipts should be deposited monthly.
b. All disbursements should be made by check (except for minor items paid from petty cash).
c. The person who records the cash receipts should restrictively endorse all checks.
d. The bank reconciliation should be prepared by the same person who records cash receipts and disbursements, since this person is familiar with the records.

______ **6.** The terms 3/15, n/60 on an invoice mean that

a. a discount of 3 percent may be taken if the invoice is paid in 60 days.

b. a discount of 3 percent may be taken if the invoice is paid within 15 days of the invoice date and that the net amount of the invoice is due within 60 days.
c. if the invoice is paid within 60 days, 3/15 of the invoice may be deducted.
d. a discount of 3 percent may be taken if the invoice is paid by the 15th day of the month following the month of purchase.

_______________ **7.** Which one of the following procedures should be followed to ensure good internal control over cash disbursements?

a. Disbursements made from the petty cash fund should be recorded on petty cash vouchers that are signed by the recipient of the cash.
b. The same individual who signs checks should approve vouchers for payment.
c. The individual who signs the checks should also record them in the check register.
d. Vouchers should be stamped "paid" when the canceled check is returned with the bank statement.

_______________ **8.** Nonsufficient funds checks are

a. checks that have been canceled by the bank to show that they have been paid.
b. checks that are guaranteed by the depositor's bank.
c. checks written by a customer and returned by the bank as uncollectible because there were insufficient funds in the customer's account.
d. checks issued by a company that have not yet been presented to the bank for payment.

_______________ **9.** A business paper used in summarizing a transaction and approving it for recording and payment is called

a. an invoice.
b. a voucher.
c. a control account.
d. a special account.

_______________ **10.** The cash-over-and-short account might be used to record

a. a transposition error made in recording a check in the cash receipts journal.
b. an NSF check.
c. small errors made in making change in the petty cash fund.
d. a bank service charge.

_______________ **11.** When a voucher system is used,

a. an obligation should not be recorded as a liability until a check is written for payment.
b. vouchers are prepared only for large invoices.
c. petty cash is debited and vouchers payable is credited when the petty cash fund is reimbursed.
d. all credits in the voucher register are made to the vouchers payable account.

______________ **12.** Which one of the following would be considered a good internal control procedure for cash?

a. Payment of small expenses from the current day's cash receipts.
b. Avoiding too many people handling checks by having the same person open cash received by mail and record payments on accounts receivable.
c. Verification of the amount on an invoice before payment
d. Numbering of checks only after they have been written to avoid having a number assigned to a check written incorrectly

______________ **13.** After completing a bank reconciliation, journal entries need to be made to record

a. errors made by the bank.
b. all reconciling items.
c. the reconciling items that explain the difference between the balance per bank and the adjusted balance per bank.
d. the reconciling items that explain the difference between the balance per books and the adjusted balance per books.

______________ **14.** The correct journal entry to record a check returned as NSF by the bank would be

a. debit NSF expense, credit cash.
b. debit bad debt expense, credit cash.
c. debit cash, credit accounts receivable.
d. debit accounts receivable, credit cash.

______________ **15.** When a company uses special journals, a contribution of cash by the owner of a sole proprietorship should be recorded in the

a. cash receipts journal.
b. cash disbursements journal.
c. general journal.
d. purchases journal.

Use the following information in answering Questions 16 to 18.

Merry Co. purchased items with a list price of $10,000 on May 1, 20XA. Merry Co. was given trade discounts of 20 and 10 percent. The terms of the invoice were 3/10, n/30.

______________ **16.** Assuming that Merry Co. paid the invoice on May 9, the amount of the payment would be

a. $6,860.
b. $6,984.
c. $7,200.
d. $9,700.

_______________ **17.** Assuming that Merry Co. paid the invoice on June 10, 20XA, the amount of payment would be

a. $6,984.
b. $7,200.
c. $8,000.
d. $10,000.

_______________ **18.** Assuming that Merry Co. paid the invoice on May 9, the journal entry to record payment would include

a. a debit to accounts payable, a debit to purchase discounts, and a credit to cash.
b. a debit to accounts payable, a credit to purchase discounts, and a credit to cash.
c. a debit to cash, a credit to accounts payable, and a credit to purchase discounts.
d. a debit to accounts payable and a credit to cash.

Use the following information in answering Questions 19 to 21.

Good Company wrote a check for $370 to Jones Company in payment for office equipment. The bookkeeper erroneously recorded the check in the cash disbursements journal for $730. The accounts used were correct; only the amount recorded was in error. The error was discovered when the monthly bank reconciliation was prepared.

_______________ **19.** The item should be shown on the bank reconciliation as

a. an addition to the balance per books.
b. a deduction from the balance per books.
c. an addition to the balance per bank.
d. a deduction from the balance per bank.

_______________ **20.** The journal entry to correct the error would be

a. a debit to office equipment and a credit to cash for $360.
b. a debit to cash and a credit to office equipment for $360.
c. a debit to error correction and a credit to cash for $360.
d. a debit to cash and a credit to error correction for $360.

_______________ **21.** This type of error is called

a. a posting error.
b. a balancing error.
c. a transposition error.
d. a slide error.

Solutions

Answer	*Refer to:*
1. (a)	[B-2-b]
2. (c)	[C-2-a]
3. (a)	[A-1]
4. (b)	[C-3-c]
5. (b)	[A-3-b(7)]
6. (b)	[C-2-b]
7. (a)	[C-3-b]
8. (c)	[D-1-b(3)]
9. (b)	[C-5-a]
10. (c)	[C-7]
11. (d)	[C-5-b(5)]
12. (c)	[A-3, C-6-b]
13. (d)	[D-4]
14. (d)	[D-4-c]
15. (a)	[B-3-b]
16. (b)	[C-2-a, C-2-b] The correct solution is calculated as follows:

$10,000		
− 2,000	($10,000 × 0.20)	trade discount
$ 8,000		
− 800	($8,000 × 0.10)	trade discount
$ 7,200		
− 216	($7,200 × 0.03)	cash discount
$ 6,984		

17. (b)	[C-2-a, C-2-b]
18. (b)	[C-2-b]

19. (a) [D-3]

20. (b) [D-4-a]

21. (c) [D-4-a]

CHAPTER 11

Accounting for Investments

OVERVIEW

This chapter is intended to introduce the candidate to the basics of accounting for investments. Topics such as bond premium, discount amortization, and the equity method of accounting for investments in common stock are explained in the chapter. It is not important that the candidate fully understand these topics; however, knowledge that the various methods exist and when they are used will be useful.

The candidate should understand the three major categories of investments and the appropriate accounting procedures for each.

KEY TERMS

Available-for-sale securities	Consolidated statements	Parent company
Bond	Contract rate	Stock dividend
Bond discount	Equity method	Subsidiary company
Bond premium	Investment	Temporary investments
	Marketable securities	Trading securities

A. Introduction to Investments

Investments are assets held by a company that are not used in the operations of the business. These assets are held for investment purposes in the hope of earning a return or profit on the amount invested. The treatment of accounting for investments differs, depending on whether the investments are of a short-term or a long-term nature.

1. *Short-term Investments:* Short-term investments, which the company intends to hold for less than one operating cycle, are classified as *temporary* investments (or marketable securities). Marketable securities are classified as current assets on the balance sheet.

2. *Long-term Investments:* Long-term investments are investments intended to be held for longer than one operating cycle. Long-term investments are classified as *investments* on the balance sheet. There are three basic types of investments: real estate, bonds, and stocks. Bond sinking funds and cash surrender value of life insurance are also classified as long-term investments.

3. *Classification of Investments:* Investments in equity securities (not accounted for using the equity method [see Section D-1-b(2)] or the consolidation method [see Section D-1-b(1)]) and investments in debt securities should be grouped into one of three classifications: securities to be held to maturity, trading securities, and securities available for sale.

a. *Securities to be held to maturity:* Investments in debt securities that the owner intends to hold until they mature should be classified as *held-to-maturity.* These securities are accounted for using the amortized cost method (see Section C-3).

b. *Trading securities:* Investments in debt securities or investments in equity securities are classified as *trading securities* if they are bought and held principally for the purpose of selling them in the near term. These securities would be involved in active and frequent buying and selling, and the objective of holding these types of securities would generally be to generate profits on short-term differences in price. Trading securities are shown at market value on the financial statements, and any unrealized holding gain or loss is included in earnings on the income statement. Realized holding gains and losses are also included in earnings. An unrealized holding gain results when the market value of the security is higher than the cost paid for the security. An unrealized holding loss occurs when the market value of the security is lower than its cost. Holding gains or losses are realized when the security is sold and the owner receives the difference in value.

c. *Securities available for sale:* Investments in debt or equity securities that are not classified as held-to maturity or trading securities are classified as *available-for-sale* securities. Available-for-sale securities are shown at market value on the financial statements, and any unrealized holding gains or losses are not included in earnings but are shown in a separate shareholders' equity account until they are realized.

B. Real Estate

Investments in real estate are usually long term in nature. The accounting treatment for investments in real estate is the same whether the investments are of a short-term or a long-term nature. An example of a real estate investment would be land held for future development of the business. The land is not currently used in the business but is being held for future expansion. The land would be carried at cost on the records of the business. A gain or loss would be recorded when the land is sold if it is sold for an amount different from its cost.

EXAMPLE: Selzig Corp. holds 10 acres of land for investment purposes. The cost of the land was $100,000. The land is sold for $150,000. The entry to record the sale would be as follows:

	dr	*cr*
Cash	150,000	
Investment: land		100,000
Gain on sale of land		50,000
To record sale of 10 acres of land held for investment purposes.		

C. Bonds and Interest Income

Bonds are debt securities issued by the government or a corporation to raise large sums of money. Most individual bond certificates have a stated face value of $1,000. Bonds pay interest at a fixed rate, depending on the stated face value. Bond interest is normally paid every six months. The fixed interest rate paid by a bond is called the *contract rate.*

1. *Issuance of Bonds:* When bonds are issued, they may be sold for an amount greater or less than their face value. If a bond sells for less than its stated face value, it is selling at a *discount.* If it sells for more than its stated face value, it is selling at a *pre-*

mium. Bonds will sell for face value when the contract rate and the market rate are equal.

a. *Discount:* If the market rate of interest (for bonds of the same quality) at the time the bonds are sold is higher than the contract rate paid by the bonds, the bonds will sell at a discount.

b. *Premium:* If the market rate of interest at the time the bonds are sold is lower than the coupon (contract) rate paid by the bonds, the bonds will sell at a premium.

2. *Accounting for Bonds and Interest Income:*

a. *Short-term investments:* Short-term investments in bonds are classified as either trading securities or available-for-sale securities and accounted for as discussed in Section A-3.

b. *Purchase of bonds between interest dates:* The price paid for a bond includes a portion for purchased interest if the bond is purchased between interest dates. Commissions paid in acquiring a bond are considered a part of the cost.

(1) If a bond is purchased exactly on an interest payment date, the full purchase price is considered the cost of the bond (i.e., no "interest receivable" is purchased).

(2) If a bond is purchased between interest dates, the buyer must pay the seller for any interest that has accrued on the bond. The buyer then receives the full amount of the interest payment on the next interest payment date.

EXAMPLE: Assume that Petit Company purchased the Selzig Corp. bonds on February 1. Petit Company paid $9,658 for the bonds. Of this amount, $166.67 represented accrued interest. The interest portion was calculated as follows:

$10,000	Face value
× 0.10	Coupon rate
$1,000	Interest per year
× 2/12	Portion of year
$166.67	Interest for two months

The entry to record the purchase of the bonds would be as follows:

		dr	*cr*
Feb. 1	Investment in bonds	9,491.33	
	Interest receivable	166.67	
	Cash		9,658.00

When the semiannual interest payment is received, Petit Company would make the following entry:

		dr	*cr*
June 1	Cash	500.00	
	Interest receivable		166.67
	Interest income		333.33
To record semiannual interest receipt ($10,000 × 0.10 × 6/12 months).			

c. *Interest income:* The interest income earned on bonds accrues from day to day. Bond interest is paid every six months. Therefore, it might be necessary to record an adjusting entry to recognize accrued interest receivable at the end of the accounting period.

EXAMPLE: Assume that Petit Company's year end is October 31. The Selzig Corp. bonds pay interest on June 1 and December 1. Petit Company purchased the bonds on December 1. The journal entry to record the June 1 receipt of interest would be as follows:

	dr	*cr*
Cash	500.00	
Interest income		500.00
To record semiannual receipt of bond interest ($10,000 × 0.10 × 6/12 months).		

It would be necessary for Petit Company to record an adjusting entry to recognize the interest that has been earned from June 1 through October 31. The adjusting journal entry to record the interest accrual would be as follows:

	dr	*cr*
Accrued interest receivable	416.67	
Interest income		416.67
To record interest accrued on Selzig bond from June 1 through October 31 ($10,000 × 0.10 × 5/12 months).		

3. *Amortization of Premium or Discount on Long-Term Bonds:* Debt securities that a company intends to hold to maturity should appear on the balance sheet at amortized acquisition cost. A premium or discount is ignored in the measurement of interest revenue for short-term bonds since the bonds are not intended to be held to maturity. The effect of any premium or discount on interest revenue should be recognized when the bonds are to be held to maturity. A bond premium or discount results when the market rate of interest is different from the contract rate of interest. The premium or discount paid for the bond effectively adjusts the rate of interest received on the bond to the market rate. Amortization of bond premium or discount is used to adjust the interest received to approximate the effective amount of interest earned on the investment. Amortization of bond premium decreases interest income, and amortization of bond discount increases interest income.

a. *Amortizing bond premium or discount:* When long-term bonds are acquired at a premium or discount, they are recorded at cost. As interest is received over the life of a bond, any premium or discount is amortized. This brings the carrying value (book value) of the bond closer to its face value. By the maturity date of the bond, it will be valued at face value.

b. *Methods of bond premium or discount amortization:* There are two methods of bond premium or discount amortization: the straight-line method and the effective interest method. The effective interest method is more exact and should be used whenever the difference that results from using the straight-line method instead of the effective interest method is material.

D. Stocks and Dividend Income

1. *Recording Investment in Stock:* Purchases of stock are usually recorded at cost. Commissions paid in acquiring stocks are considered part of the cost of the stock.

a. *Short-term investment:* Short-term investments in stock of other companies are called *marketable equity securities.* Marketable equity securities are classified as trading securities or available-for-sale securities and are shown at market value on the balance sheet.

EXAMPLE: Jones Corporation has the following portfolio of marketable equity securities:

	Cost	Market
Equity security 1	$100,000	$ 90,000
Equity security 2	150,000	170,000
Equity security 3	50,000	30,000
Equity security 4	60,000	60,000
Totals	$360,000	$350,000

The marketable equity securities would be reported in the balance sheet at $350,000.

b. *Long-term investment:* Long-term investments in stock are accounted for differently, depending on the quantity of stock the investor owns and the resulting amount of control that the investor can exercise over the operations of the investee. This amount of control is measured by the percentage of the investee's voting common stock that is owned by the investor. The three classifications used in accounting for ownership of common stock are the following:

(1) *Ownership of more than 50 percent of common stock:* In this case, the investor is said to own a controlling interest in the investee, and the financial statements of the two companies are combined into a *consolidated* set of financial statements by the parent company. When financial statements are consolidated, the two accounting entities are treated as if they were one accounting entity for financial statement purposes. The investor company that owns more than 50 percent of the voting stock in the investee company is called the *parent company.* The investee company that is controlled by the parent company is called the *subsidiary company.* The procedures for consolidating financial statements are beyond the scope of this chapter.

(2) *Ownership of 20 to 50 percent of common stock:* In this case, the investor is *assumed* to have significant influence over the operations of the investee corporation. Because of the assumption of significant influence, the investor should account for the investment using the equity method. Under the equity method, the investment is originally recorded at cost. When the investee corporation reports earnings, the investor recognizes its share of the investee's reported earnings by debiting the investment account and crediting earnings. The amount recorded is based on the percentage of the stock held by the investor. Dividends and the investor's proportionate share of net losses are recorded as a reduction in the investment account. The earnings or loss account recorded by the investor for its proportionate share of the investee's income is shown on the income statement as investment income or loss.

EXAMPLE: In January, 20XA, James Co. purchased 2,000 shares (25 percent) of PRO, Inc. common stock for a total cost of $80,320. The entry to record the purchase on James Co.'s books is as follows:

		dr	*cr*
Jan. 1	Investment in PRO, Inc.	80,320	
	Cash		80,320
	Purchased 2,000 shares of stock.		

On December 31, 20XA, PRO, Inc. reported net income of $100,000. The entry to record James Co.'s share of PRO, Inc.'s net income is as follows:

		dr	*cr*
Dec. 31	Investment in PRO, Inc.	25,000	
	Earnings from investment in PRO, Inc.		25,000
	To record 25 percent equity in PRO, Inc.'s net income of $100,000.		

On January 20, 20XB, PRO, Inc. paid James Co. $5,000 in dividends. (The total dividend declaration was $20,000.) The entry to record the receipt of the dividend is as follows:

		dr	*cr*
Jan. 20	Cash	5,000	
	Investment in PRO, Inc.		5,000
	To record receipt of dividends paid by PRO, Inc.		

On December 31, 20XB, PRO, Inc. reported a net loss of $28,000. The entry to record James Co.'s share of PRO, Inc.'s net loss is as follows:

		dr	*cr*
Dec. 31	Loss from investment in PRO, Inc.	7,000	
	Investment in PRO, Inc.		7,000
	To record 25 percent equity in PRO, Inc.'s net loss of $28,000.		

(3) *Ownership of less than 20 percent of common stock:* When less than 20 percent of the common stock is owned, the investor is assumed to have little influence over the operations of the investee. In this case, the investment is classified as either trading or available-for-sale and accounted for accordingly.

Investments in preferred stock are accounted for as either trading or available-for-sale securities.

2. *Recording Dividend Income:*

a. *Recording receipt of dividends:* Dividend income does not accrue as interest income does. Dividends are income when received by the investor and are usually not recorded until they are received. The entry to record the receipt of dividends when stock ownership is less than 20 percent is as follows:

	dr	*cr*
Cash	XXX	
Dividend income		XXX

b. *Recording receipt of stock dividends:* Stock dividends are distributions in the form of additional shares of stock instead of cash. Stock dividends do not represent income to the recipient. The investor apportions the original cost of the shares over the new total amount of shares owned.

EXAMPLE: If XYZ Corp. owned 1,000 shares of Ajax Corp. common stock and a 5 percent stock dividend was paid by Ajax Corp., XYZ Corp. would receive an additional 50 shares of Ajax Corp. stock.

Assume that XYZ Corp. paid $10,000 for the 1,000 shares that it originally owned. After the stock dividend is received, that $10,000 is apportioned over the new number of shares owned ($10,000/1,050 shares = $9.524). The new cost per share of stock would be approximately $9.524 per share. If any of the shares of stock are sold after the stock dividend is received, the gain or loss on the sale must be computed using the new cost of $9.524 per share.

Review Questions

Directions: Select the correct answer from the four alternatives. Write the letter of your answer in the blank to the left of the number. (For simplicity, when calculating interest in this set of questions, assume 360 days per year and 30 days per month.)

______ **1.** A long-term debt security that normally has a face value of $1,000 and pays semiannual interest at a stated rate is called

a. a note receivable.
b. an account receivable.
c. a bond.
d. preferred stock.

______ **2.** If bonds are sold between interest dates,

a. the seller must pay the buyer the accrued interest to the date of sale.
b. the buyer must pay the seller the accrued interest to the date of sale.
c. the bonds will sell at a premium.
d. the seller is allowed to deduct the interest that accrued prior to the date of purchase from the next semiannual interest payment.

______ **3.** When a bond sells for more than its face value, the difference between the face value of the bond and the selling price is called

a. a bond discount.
b. a bond premium.
c. additional paid in debt.
d. amortization.

______ **4.** When bonds receivable that were purchased at a discount are classified as held to maturity,

a. the bond investment account should be debited for the face value of the bonds purchased.
b. the carrying value of the bonds (the book value in the investment account) will remain unchanged over the life of the bond.
c. any discount on the purchase of the bond should be amortized over the life of the bond.
d. accrual of bond interest at year end is not necessary.

______ **5.** Land held by a business for future sale should be valued in the balance sheet at

a. historical cost.
b. lower of cost or market.
c. market value.
d. replacement cost.

______________ **6.** Puscas Co. purchased 10 shares of Schmaus Co. common stock for $100 per share. Puscas Co. paid a $50 brokerage commission on this transaction. The investment account should be debited for

a. $150.
b. $950.
c. $1,000.
d. $1,050.

______________ **7.** Short-term marketable equity securities classified as trading or available-for-sale securities should be reported in the balance sheet at

a. cost.
b. market value.
c. lower of cost or market.
d. amortized historical cost.

______________ **8.** A real estate investment that had a book value of $20,000 was sold for $22,000. The journal entry to record the sale would include

a. a credit to cash for $22,000.
b. a credit to a gain account for $2,000.
c. a debit to the investment account for $20,000.
d. a debit to cash for $20,000.

______________ **9.** When the equity method is used to account for an investment in another company,

a. the investor is assumed to have significant influence over the operations of the investee.
b. dividends are recorded as income.
c. the basis of the investment on the company's books remains at cost.
d. dividends are recorded by the investor company as an increase in the investment account.

______________ **10.** A company that owns more than 50 percent of the voting stock of another corporation is called

a. the primary company.
b. the subsidiary company.
c. the parent company.
d. the investee company.

______________ **11.** Financial statements that combine the results of a parent company with its subsidiaries for financial reporting purposes are called

a. parent statements.
b. consolidated statements.
c. entity statements.
d. subsidiary statements.

_____________ **12.** Which one of the following items would be classified as a long-term investment?

a. Bond sinking fund
b. An investment in bonds that is expected to be held for less than one year
c. A building used in the business
d. Land used in the business

_____________ **13.** Dividends received from an investee corporation should be recorded as

a. income regardless of the percentage of the voting stock of the investee held by the investor.
b. income if the investor owns less than 30 percent of the voting shares of the investee.
c. a reduction of the investment account if the investor owns 20 percent or more of the voting shares of the investee.
d. a decrease in cash on the books of the investor company.

_____________ **14.** Axel Co. owned 400 shares of common stock that were purchased for $4,400. Axel Co. received a common stock dividend of 40 shares of this stock. What was the carrying value per share of stock after the stock dividend was received?

a. $9
b. $10
c. $11
d. $110

Use the following information in answering Questions 15 to 17. For simplicity, when calculating interest in this set of questions, assume 360 days per year and 30 days per month.

Assume that Kan Co. purchased $300,000 of Lily Corp. 12 percent bonds for face value on April 1, 20XA. The bonds pay interest on January 1 and July 1. Kan Co.'s year end is August 31. Kan Co. intends to hold these bonds to maturity.

_____________ **15.** The total amount of cash that Kan Co. paid for the bonds on April 1 was

a. $291,000.
b. $300,000.
c. $309,000.
d. $318,000.

_____________ **16.** The amount of the interest payment Kan Co. will receive on July 1 is

a. $9,000.
b. $18,000.
c. $18,540.
d. $36,000.

_____________ **17.** The adjusting entry that Kan Co. should make on August 31 is

a. debit bond interest receivable and credit bond interest revenue for $6,000.
b. debit bond interest revenue and credit bond interest receivable for $6,000.

c. debit bond interest receivable and credit bond interest revenue for $9,000.
d. No adjusting entry should be made.

Use the following information in answering Questions 18 to 20.

On January 1, 20XA, Box Co. purchased 5,000 shares (40 percent) of Bag Co.'s common (voting) stock for a total cost of $100,000. On December 31, 20XA, Bag Co. reported net income of $100,000. On January 5, 20XB, Bag Co. declared a $10,000 dividend on its common stock.

__________ **18.** The entry to record the purchase of Bag Co. stock by Box Co. would be

a. debit cash and credit investment in Bag Co. for $100,000.
b. debit investment in Bag Co. and credit cash for $100,000.
c. debit investment in Bag Co. and credit cash for $40,000.
d. debit cash and credit net income for $100,000.

__________ **19.** The entry to record the receipt of the dividend by Box Co. would be debit cash and credit

a. dividend income for $10,000.
b. dividend income for $4,000.
c. investment in Bag Co. for $4,000.
d. investment in Bag Co. for $10,000.

__________ **20.** The entry by Box Co. to record the earnings of Bag Co. would be

a. debit investment in Bag Co. and credit earnings from investment in Bag Co. for $40,000.
b. debit investment in Bag Co. and credit earnings from investment in Bag Co. for $100,000.
c. debit cash and credit earnings from investment in Bag Co. for $40,000.
d. No journal entry would be made to recognize Bag Co.'s income.

__________ **21.** Jayne Co. has the following portfolio of marketable equity securities classified as available-for-sale:

	Cost	Market
Equity security 1	$ 5,000	$ 6,000
Equity security 2	10,000	5,000
Equity security 3	6,000	6,000

The marketable equity securities should be reported on the balance sheet at

a. $16,000.
b. $17,000.
c. $19,000.
d. $21,000.

Solutions

Answer	*Refer to:*
1. (c)	[C]
2. (b)	[C-2-b(2)]
3. (b)	[C-1]
4. (c)	[C-3-a]
5. (a)	[B]
6. (d)	[D-1] Commissions paid in acquiring stock are included as part of the cost of the stock.

	Cash paid for the stock	$1,000	($10 × 100)
+	Commission paid	50	
	Amount to be debited	$1,050	

7. (b)	[D-1-a]
8. (b)	[B]

	Selling price	$22,000
−	Book value	20,000
	Gain on sale	$ 2,000

The entry to record the transaction would be as follows:

	dr	*cr*
Cash	22,000	
Gain on sale of investment		2,000
Investment		20,000

9. (a)	[D-1-b(2)]
10. (c)	[D-1-b(1)]
11. (b)	[D-1-b(1)]
12. (a)	[A]
13. (c)	[D-2-a, D-1-b(2)]

14. (b) [D-2-b]

$$\frac{\text{total original cost}}{\text{total number of shares owned after stock dividend}} = \text{cost per share}$$

$$\frac{\$4{,}400}{440} = \$10$$

15. (c) [C-2-b(2)] Since the bonds were purchased between interest dates, Kan Co. had to pay for the accrued interest as well as the face value of the bonds.

$300,000	Face value
9,000	Accrued interest ($300,000 × 0.12 × 3/12)
$309,000	

16. (b) [C-2-b(2)] The amount of the semiannual interest payment is $18,000 ($300,000 × 0.12 × 6/12).

17. (a) [C-2-c] Kan Co. must make an adjusting entry to accrue the interest earned for the months of July and August. The computation of accrued interest is $300,000 × 0.12 × 2/12 = $6,000. This entry would debit bond interest receivable and credit bond interest revenue.

18. (b) [D-1-b(2)]

19. (c) [D-1-b(2)] Dividends reduce the investment account under the equity method. Box Co.'s share of the dividend was $4,000 ($10,000 × 0.40). The entry would include a debit to cash and a credit to investment in Bag Co.

20. (a) [D-1-b(2)] Under the equity method, the investor records its proportionate share of the investee's net income as an increase in the investment account. Box Co.'s share of Bag Co.'s net income is $40,000 ($100,000 × 0.40).

21. (b) [D-1-a]

	Cost	Market
Equity security 1	$ 5,000	$ 6,000
Equity security 2	10,000	5,000
Equity security 3	6,000	6,000
Totals	$21,000	$17,000

Securities classified as available-for-sale should be presented on the balance sheet at market value.

CHAPTER 12

Accounting for Inventories

OVERVIEW

This chapter is intended to introduce the candidate to the accounting procedures used in valuing and recording inventories. Inventories are often one of the most important and largest current assets held by a company. Therefore, an understanding of the topic is important.

The candidate should understand the four methods of pricing inventories, how to apply the lower-of-cost-or-market theory, how to determine cost of goods sold, and the effects that inventory valuation and inventory errors have on net income. The candidate should review the periodic inventory system thoroughly.

KEY TERMS

FIFO
Gross profit method
LIFO
Lower of cost or market
Periodic inventory system
Perpetual inventory system
Weighted-average method

A. Types of Inventory Systems

1. *Perpetual Inventory Systems:* When a perpetual inventory system is used, a continuous record is maintained of all inventory transactions.

   a. *Merchandise inventory account:* A merchandise inventory account is kept. Inventory purchases are recorded as increases in the inventory account, and sales of inventory are recorded as decreases in the inventory account. The cost of goods sold is recorded as units are sold.

   b. *Use of perpetual inventory system:* A perpetual inventory system is often used by businesses that sell merchandise with a high per-unit value. Manufacturing firms often use a perpetual inventory system since they need accurate and timely information about costs. As computers make the processing of data easier, more companies are using perpetual inventory systems.

   EXAMPLE: Assume that Nelson Co., which sells minicomputers, has 10 units of inventory on hand on January 1, 20XA. These 10 units originally *cost $10,000. The 10 units would be included in the merchandise inventory account.*

Merchandise Inventory

1/1/XA	10,000		
2/2	7,700	6,000	2/10
Bal.	11,700		

Cost of Goods Sold

2/10	6,000		

On February 2, 20XA, the company purchased seven more units at $1,100 each. The journal entry to record the purchase would be as follows:

		dr	*cr*
Feb. 2	Merchandise inventory	7,700	
	Accounts payable		7,700
Purchased 7 units of inventory P.O. #2182			

On February 10, 20XA, the company sold six of the original 10 units for $2,500 each. The entries to record this transaction would be as follows:

		dr	*cr*
Feb. 10	Accounts receivable	15,000	
	Sales		15,000
To record sale of 6 units.			
Feb. 10	Cost of goods sold	6,000	
	Merchandise inventory		6,000
To record cost of goods sold for 6 units sold on February 10.			

c. *End-of-period inventory procedure:* At the end of the period, the balance in the inventory account should represent the cost of the inventory that is on hand. The cost of goods sold account should contain the cost of all units sold during the period. A periodic physical count of inventory is taken to verify the balance of the inventory account. This count will reveal any "shrinkage."

2. *Periodic Inventory Systems:* When a periodic inventory system is used, purchases of inventory are recorded in a purchases account. Ending inventory is determined by taking a physical count of the goods on hand at the end of the period. A value is then determined for the ending inventory that is on hand. The cost of goods sold is computed by subtracting the ending inventory from the goods available for sale. Goods available for sale is determined by adding total purchases for the period to the beginning inventory.

a. *Use of a periodic inventory system:* Many businesses that sell a variety of low-cost items use a periodic inventory system. A perpetual inventory system is more difficult and costly to maintain than a periodic inventory system.

EXAMPLE: Use the same facts as in the previous example, with the Nelson Co. using a periodic inventory system. The beginning inventory consists of 10 units which cost $10,000.

Merchandise Inventory

1/1 Bal. 10,000	

Purchases

2/2 7,700	

The entry to record the purchase on February 2 would be as follows:

		dr	*cr*
Feb. 2	Purchases	7,700	
	Accounts payable		7,700
To record purchase of 7 units of inventory P.O. #2182			

The entry to record the sale on February 10 would be as follows:

		dr	*cr*
Feb. 10	Accounts receivable	15,000	
	Sales		15,000
To record sale of 6 units.			

b. *Merchandise inventory account:* When a periodic system is used, the merchandise inventory account remains unchanged for the period. Purchases of inventory are recorded in the purchases account, and no entry is made that affects inventory when a sale is made.

EXAMPLE: Assume that Nelson Co. made no other purchases or sales during the month of February. Financial statements will be prepared as of February 28. To do so, a physical count of the inventory must be taken to determine the quantity on hand. The physical count indicated that 11 units were on hand. Nelson Co. assumed that these 11 units were made up of the 7 units purchased on February 2 and 4 units from beginning inventory (FIFO). The value of the ending inventory ($11,700) was calculated as follows:

7 units	@	$1,100	=	$ 7,700
4 units	@	$1,000	=	4,000
11 units			=	$11,700

To determine cost of goods sold, Nelson Co. made the following calculation:

	Beginning inventory	$10,000
+	Purchases	7,700
=	Goods available for sale	$17,700
−	Ending inventory	11,700
=	Cost of goods sold	$ 6,000

B. Inventory Pricing

To value ending inventory, the company must make an assumption about the cost flow of the goods out of the inventory account. Four basic inventory cost-flow assumptions are used in accounting: FIFO, LIFO, weighted average, and specific identification. (The implementation of various cost-flow assumptions with a perpetual inventory system will not be discussed in this chapter.)

1. *FIFO (First-In, First-Out):* When a FIFO inventory pricing assumption is used, the units purchased first are assumed to be the first units sold. The units left in ending inventory are made up of the units purchased last.

EXAMPLE: Petit Co. uses a periodic inventory system and uses the FIFO method of inventory pricing. The periodic inventory count indicated that 60 units were on hand on January 31. The January 31 inventory valuation and cost of goods sold for January is calculated as follows:

Units available for sale:

50 units from beginning inventory @ \$2.00/unit
20 units from January 3 purchase @ \$2.20/unit
30 units from January 5 purchase @ \$2.30/unit
50 units from January 30 purchase @ \$2.50/unit

If there are 60 units in ending inventory, 90 units must have been sold. Using a FIFO pricing assumption, the cost of goods sold would be calculated in this way:

50 units in beginning inventory @ \$2.00/unit	\$100.00
20 units from January 3 purchase @ \$2.20/unit	44.00
20 units from January 5 purchase @ \$2.30/unit	46.00
	\$190.00

Ending inventory:

10 units from January 5 purchase @ \$2.30/unit	\$ 23.00
50 units from January 30 purchase @ \$2.50/unit	125.00
	\$148.00

2. *LIFO (Last-In, First-Out):* When a LIFO inventory pricing assumption is used, the units purchased last are assumed to be the first units sold. The units remaining in ending inventory consist of the units that were acquired earliest.

   EXAMPLE: Using the facts in the previous example, assume that Petit Co. now uses a LIFO inventory pricing assumption. The cost of goods sold for January would be calculated in this way:

50 units from January 30 purchase @ \$2.50/unit	\$125.00
30 units from January 5 purchase @ \$2.30/unit	69.00
10 units from January 3 purchase @ \$2.20/unit	22.00
	\$216.00

Ending inventory:

50 units from beginning inventory @ \$2.00/unit	\$100.00
10 units from January 3 purchase @ \$2.20/unit	22.00
	\$122.00

Note: The IRS requires that if LIFO is used for income tax purposes, it must be used for financial reporting purposes. In Canada, LIFO is not acceptable for income tax purposes.

3. *Weighted Average:* When a weighted-average inventory pricing assumption is used, a weighted-average unit cost is determined by dividing the cost of goods available for sale by the total units available for sale (units in beginning inventory + total units purchased). The cost of ending inventory is determined by multiplying the total number of units in the ending inventory by the weighted-average unit cost. The cost of the units sold is determined by multiplying the number of units sold by the weighted-average unit cost.

EXAMPLE: Using the facts in the previous example, assume that the Petit Co. uses the weighted-average inventory pricing assumption. The January 31 inventory valuation and the cost of goods sold for January would be determined as follows:

	Units Available for Sale		Cost of Goods Available for Sale
Beginning inventory	50 units × \$2.00	=	\$100.00
January 3 purchase	20 units × \$2.20	=	44.00
January 5 purchase	30 units × \$2.30	=	69.00
January 30 purchase	50 units × \$2.50	=	125.00
	150 units		\$338.00

The weighted-average unit cost is computed as follows:

$$\frac{\text{cost of goods available for sale}}{\text{units available for sale}} = \frac{\$338.00}{150.00} = \$2.2533/\text{unit}$$

The cost of goods sold would be calculated as follows:

Units available for sale	150
− Units in ending inventory	−60
= Units sold	90

cost of goods sold = units sold × weighted average per unit cost
\$202.80 = 90 units × \$2.2533/unit

ending inventory = 60 units × \$2.2533/unit = \$135.20

4. *Specific Identification:* When a company is able to identify each item in inventory with a specific purchase, specific invoice prices may be used to assign costs to the units in ending inventory.

EXAMPLE: Using the facts in the previous example, assume that Petit Co. now uses specific invoice prices to cost ending inventory. Of the 60 units in ending inventory, 30 units are from the January 30 purchase, 20 units are from the January 5 purchase, and 10 units are from the January 3 purchase.

Ending inventory would be valued as follows:

30 units	@	\$2.50/unit =	\$ 75.00
20 units	@	2.30/unit =	46.00
10 units	@	2.20/unit =	22.00
		Total ending inventory =	\$143.00

Cost of goods sold:

50 units	@	\$2.00/unit =	\$100.00
10 units	@	2.20/unit =	22.00
10 units	@	2.30/unit =	23.00
20 units	@	2.50/unit =	50.00
		Cost of goods sold =	\$195.00

C. Applying Lower of Cost or Market

Inventory is normally reported in the balance sheet at cost. If a permanent decline in the value of the inventory occurs, the conservatism principle requires that the inventory be reported at a lower value than cost. A permanent decline in the value of inventory may occur when the goods become obsolete, damaged, or shopworn or if there is a general price decline for goods of that type. When the market value of inventory is lower than its cost, the inventory should be reported using the lower-of-cost-or-market principle.

D. Determining Cost of Goods Sold

1. *Periodic Inventory System:* When a periodic inventory system is used, the cost of goods sold is determined as follows:

   Cost of Goods Sold:

	Beginning inventory
+	Net purchases
	Goods available for sale
−	Ending inventory
=	Cost of goods sold

   Net Purchases:

	Purchases
+	Transportation (freight) in
−	Purchases discounts
−	Purchase returns and allowances
=	Net purchases

   EXAMPLE: Sullivan Co. had beginning inventory for 20XA of $105,000. The balance in the purchases account as of the year end was $1,120,000. The ending inventory valued at LIFO was $110,000. Cost of goods sold for 20XA is as follows:

	Beginning inventory	$ 105,000
+	Purchases	1,120,000
	Goods available for sale	$1,225,000
−	Ending inventory	110,000
	Cost of goods sold	$1,115,000

2. *Perpetual Inventory System:* When a perpetual inventory system is used, the balance in the cost of goods sold account should represent the cost of goods sold for the period, unless a physical count detects "shrinkage."

3. *Estimate as Percentage of Sales:* Cost of goods sold is sometimes estimated as a percentage of sales. This method may be used when monthly financial statements are prepared and taking a physical count is too costly. Inventory estimation may also be necessary if inventory has been stolen or destroyed by fire.

4. *Gross Profit Method:* The income statement format is as follows:

	Sales
−	Cost of goods sold
	Gross profit
−	Operating expenses
	Net operating income

   The gross profit divided by sales revenue is called the *gross profit ratio.* If a company's gross profit ratio is consistent from period to period, that ratio can be used to

Figure 12–1 Calculation/Gross Profit

Goods available for sale	$102,000		
– Estimated cost of goods sold	60,000		
Estimated ending inventory	$ 42,000		
Sales		$100,000	100%
Less: Cost of goods sold			
Beginning inventory	$ 30,000		
+ Purchases	72,000		
Goods available for sale	$102,000		
– Estimated ending inventory	42,000		
– Estimated cost of goods sold		60,000	60%
Gross profit		$ 40,000	40%

estimate the cost of goods sold. Once the cost of goods sold is estimated, ending inventory can also be computed.

EXAMPLE: Crass Co.'s gross profit ratio is 40 percent and is relatively consistent from period to period. Crass Co. wants to estimate ending inventory and cost of goods sold for the month of June. Sales for June are estimated at $100,000. Beginning inventory was $30,000 and purchases were $72,000. Figure 12–1 shows the calculation of estimated inventory and cost of goods sold.

If the gross profit percentage (ratio) is 40 percent, the average percentage for cost of goods sold is 60 percent. If sales are $100,000, cost of goods sold is estimated to be $60,000, and gross profit is estimated to be $40,000. Once cost of goods sold is estimated to be $60,000, an estimate of ending inventory can be made as follows:

Goods available for sale	$102,000
– Estimated cost of goods sold	– 60,000
Estimated ending inventory	$ 42,000

5. *Retail Inventory Method:* The retail inventory method is often used by retail businesses to compute inventory valuations. Records are kept of merchandise acquired at both cost and retail selling price. The ratio of cost to selling price is used to convert inventory from retail value to approximate cost. This method is complex, and the details of the method will not be discussed in this chapter.

E. Evaluating Effect of Inventory on Net Income

1. *Inventory Valuation:* It is important that inventory be valued accurately. An error in the ending inventory valuation will affect both the balance sheet (through inventory) and the income statement (through cost of goods sold). Since the ending inventory of one period is the beginning inventory of the next period, the income statement of the next year will also be incorrect. However, the error will cancel itself over two accounting periods.
   - **a.** *Overstatement of ending inventory:* If ending inventory is overstated, cost of goods sold will be understated, and net income for the period will be overstated.
   - **b.** *Understatement of ending inventory:* If ending inventory is understated, cost of goods sold will be overstated, and net income will be understated.
   - **c.** *Overstatement of beginning inventory:* If beginning inventory is overstated, cost of goods available for sale will be overstated, cost of goods sold will be overstated, and net income will be understated.

d. *Understatement of beginning inventory:* If beginning inventory is understated, cost of goods available for sale will be understated, cost of goods sold will be understated, and net income will be overstated.

EXAMPLE: Sullivan Corporation made an error in the ending inventory in 20XA. Ending inventory was overstated by $20,000. Because of this error, cost of goods sold for 20XA was understated by $20,000, and net income was overstated by $20,000. Figure 12–2 shows the effects of the error on the income statement for 20XA.

If it were not corrected, the error would carry through to the income statement of 20XB since beginning inventory would be overstated. Beginning inventory would be overstated by $20,000, cost of goods available for sale would be overstated by $20,000, cost of goods sold would be overstated by $20,000, and net income would be understated by $20,000. Figure 12–3 shows the effects of the error on the income statement for 20XB.

2. *Method of Inventory Valuation Used:* The method of inventory valuation used has an effect on the amount recorded in the inventory account and also an effect on cost of goods sold, which influences the amount of net income reported by the company.

Figure 12–2 Sullivan Corporation Income Statement for 20XA

		Including Error		*Without Error*
Sales		1,000,000		1,000,000
Less: Cost of goods sold				
Beginning inventory	100,000		100,000	
+ Purchases	700,000		700,000	
Goods available for sale	800,000		800,000	
− Ending inventory	100,000		80,000	
Cost of goods sold		700,000		720,000
Gross profit		300,000		280,000
Less: Operating expenses		200,000		200,000
Net operating income		100,000		80,000

Figure 12–3 Sullivan Corporation Income Statement for 20XB

		Including Error		*Without Error*
Sales		1,100,000		1,100,000
Less: Cost of goods sold				
Beginning inventory	100,000		80,000	
+ Purchases	800,000		800,000	
Goods available for sale	900,000		880,000	
− Ending inventory	110,000		110,000	
Cost of goods sold		790,000		770,000
Gross profit		310,000		330,000
Less: Operating expenses		210,000		210,000
Net operating income		100,000		120,000

a. *Rising prices:* During a period of rising prices, the use of FIFO normally results in a higher reported net income and a higher ending inventory valuation than LIFO.

b. *Falling prices:* During a period of falling prices, the use of LIFO normally results in a higher reported net income and a higher ending inventory valuation than FIFO.

c. *Use of weighted-average method:* The weighted-average method will always produce an amount of net income and an inventory valuation that is between the amounts determined using the FIFO and LIFO methods.

Review Questions

Directions: Select the correct answer from the four alternatives. Write the letter of your answer in the blank to the left of the number.

______ **1.** The type of inventory system that requires a physical count of goods on hand to determine the year-end quantity of inventory is called a/an

a. periodic inventory system.
b. perpetual inventory system.
c. merchandise inventory system.
d. accrual inventory system.

______ **2.** Which of the following businesses would most likely use a periodic inventory system?

a. A car dealer
b. A heavy equipment manufacturer
c. A piano and organ dealer
d. A drugstore

______ **3.** The method of inventory estimation that is based on the company's historical gross profit percentage is called the

a. retail method.
b. gross profit method.
c. periodic method.
d. perpetual method.

______ **4.** When the market value of inventory is less than its costs, the conservatism principle requires that inventory be reported at

a. cost.
b. LIFO cost.
c. lower of cost or market.
d. FIFO cost.

______ **5.** Jana Co. had beginning inventory of $200,000. Ending inventory is $120,000, and cost of goods sold for the year is $1,000,000. Net purchases made during the year were

a. $920,000.
b. $1,000,000.
c. $1,120,000.
d. The answer cannot be determined from the information given.

______________ **6.** Sales are $100,000, goods available for sale are $90,000, and the gross profit ratio is 40 percent. The estimate of ending inventory using the gross profit method is

a. $20,000.
b. $27,000.
c. $30,000.
d. $60,000.

______________ **7.** Merz Company had beginning inventory for 20XA of $95,000. The balance in the purchases account as of year end is $1,000,000. The ending inventory valued at FIFO is $94,000. The purchase discounts account has a balance of $5,000, the purchase returns account has a balance of $2,000, and the freight-in account has a balance of $10,000. Cost of goods sold is

a. $1,004,000.
b. $1,005,000.
c. $1,011,000.
d. $1,098,000.

______________ **8.** Obsolete or damaged inventory should be

a. excluded from inventory.
b. included in inventory at historical cost.
c. included in inventory at market value if market value is lower than cost.
d. included in inventory at its cost plus a normal markup.

______________ **9.** When prices are rising, the use of LIFO for inventory valuation normally results in

a. a higher reported net income and higher ending inventory valuation than FIFO.
b. a lower reported net income and higher ending inventory valuation than FIFO.
c. a lower reported net income and lower ending inventory valuation than FIFO.
d. the same net income and inventory valuation as FIFO.

Use the following information in answering Questions 10 to 12.

Hanes Company began a year ago and purchased merchandise as follows:

January 1	Beginning Inventory	30 units @ $10.00
February 15	Purchased	100 units @ $11.00
May 26	Purchased	50 units @ $11.50
August 10	Purchased	80 units @ $12.00
November 30	Purchased	60 units @ $12.50

Hanes uses a periodic inventory system, and 65 units are in ending inventory.

______________ **10.** Assuming that Hanes Company uses FIFO to value inventory, the amount of cost of goods sold for the year would be

a. $685.
b. $810.
c. $2,875.
d. 3,300.

_______________ **11.** Assuming that Hanes Company uses LIFO to value inventory, ending inventory for the year would be valued at

a. $685.
b. $810.
c. $2,875.
d. $3,300.

_______________ **12.** Assuming that Hanes Company uses the weighted-average method to value inventory, ending inventory for the year would be valued at (rounded to the nearest dollar)

a. $680.
b. $749.
c. $753.
d. $2,936.

Solutions

Answer	*Refer to:*
1. (a)	[A-2-a]
2. (d)	[A-2]
3. (b)	[D-4]
4. (c)	[C]
5. (a)	[D-1] The following computations show how net purchases is derived:

Beginning inventory	$ 200,000	(given)
+ Net purchases	920,000[a]	
Goods available for sale	$1,120,000[b]	
− Ending inventory	120,000	(given)
Cost of goods sold	$1,000,000	(given)

6. (c) [D-4] The estimate of ending inventory is computed as shown here:

Goods available for sale	$ 90,000
− Estimated cost of goods sold	60,000[c]
Estimated ending inventory	$ 30,000

The estimated cost of goods sold percentage is 60%. Sales % − gross profit % = 100% − 40% = 60%.

7. (a) [D-1] The following computations show how the cost of goods sold is derived:

Beginning inventory		$ 95,000
+ Net Purchases		
Purchases	$1,000,000	
Add: Freight in	10,000	
Deduct: Purchase discounts	− 5,000	
Deduct: Purchase returns	− 2,000	1,003,000
Goods available for sale		$1,098,000
− Ending inventory		− 94,000
Cost of goods sold		$1,004,000

8. (c) [C]

9. (c) [E-1-d]

[a]$1,120,000 − $200,000 = $920,000.
[b]$1,000,000 + $120,000 = $1,120,000.
[c]($100,000 × 0.6) = $60,000.

10. (c) [B-1] Goods available for sale were as follows:

		Units	$ Value
January 1	Beginning inventory	30 units @ $10.00	$ 300
February 15	Purchased	100 units @ $11.00	1,100
May 26	Purchased	50 units @ $11.50	575
August 10	Purchased	80 units @ $12.00	960
November 30	Purchased	60 units @ $12.50	750
Goods available for sale		320 units	$3,685

Under FIFO ending inventory would be as follows:

60 units @ $12.50 = $750
5 units @ $12.00 = 60
Ending inventory = $810

cost of goods sold = goods available for sale − ending inventory
$2,875 = $3,685 − $810

11. (a) [B-2] Ending inventory under LIFO would be as follows:

30 units @ $10.00 = $300
35 units @ $11.00 = 385
Ending inventory = $685

12. (b) [B-3] The weighted-average cost per unit is

$$\frac{\$3,685}{320} = \$11.5156$$

Ending inventory using the weighted-average method would be as follows:

$11.5156/unit × 65 units = $748.51, or $749.

CHAPTER 13

Property, Plant, and Equipment Records

OVERVIEW

Property, plant, and equipment accounts are the records that relate to the fixed assets of the company. This chapter is intended to introduce the candidate to the recording of transactions involving property, plant, and equipment.

The candidate should understand what is considered to be part of the cost of a fixed asset and know the procedures for calculating depreciation and depletion, accounting for repairs of fixed assets, and recording the sale or exchange of a fixed asset.

KEY TERMS

Accelerated depreciation method
Depletion
Double-declining-balance depreciation (DDB)
Extraordinary repairs
Modified accelerated cost recovery system (MACRS)
Salvage value
Straight-line depreciation
Sum-of-the-years' digits depreciation (SYD)
Units-of-production method

A. Acquisition Cost

The first thing that must be determined when a fixed asset is acquired is the cost of the asset.

1. *Cost of Fixed Assets:* Cost of a fixed asset includes all expenses necessary to acquire the asset and to prepare the asset for its use in the operations of the business. The cost of a fixed asset should include only amounts that are reasonable and necessary. Examples of items that would be included in the cost of a fixed asset are the cash paid to acquire the asset, freight-in, insurance on the asset while in transit, installation costs, and any trial runs necessary to determine the asset's readiness for use. *Freight-in* is the term used to refer to the transportation cost of an asset when it is paid by the buyer. If a fixed asset is purchased with a note that has an interest provision, any interest paid should be recorded as interest expense rather than as a part of the cost of the asset.

2. *Cost of Acquiring Land:* If land is purchased, the cost of the land must be separated from the cost of any depreciable buildings or improvements that are situated on the land since land is not depreciable. If land is purchased for use in the business and there is an existing structure on the land that must be removed, the cost of removing the structure should be included as part of the cost of the land. Any surveying or

grading costs should also be included in the cost of the land if these costs are necessary to make the land suitable for its intended use. If a building is to be constructed on the land, any excavation costs associated with the construction of the building should not be included in the cost of the land. These costs are considered part of the cost of the building. Any commissions paid to brokers, legal fees, and title fees would be included as a part of the cost of the land. Land improvements that may have a limited life, such as driveways, fences, and parking lots, should be recorded in a separate land improvements account. Land improvements have a limited life and, as such, are subject to depreciation.

B. Allocation of Costs: Depreciation and Depletion

1. *Depreciation:* Depreciation is the systematic and rational allocation of the cost of an asset over its useful life. To determine the amount of depreciation to charge to specific periods, it is necessary to perform the following steps:

a. *Cost of the asset:* The cost of the asset to be depreciated must first be determined.

b. *Useful life of the asset:* The length of the useful life of the asset is estimated.

c. *Salvage value:* Salvage value is the residual value an asset is expected to have when its estimated useful life is over. The amount of salvage value anticipated needs to be estimated. Often, no residual value is assigned because it is indeterminable.

EXAMPLE: Jones Co. purchases a truck for \$20,000. The useful life of the truck is estimated to be eight years. At the end of eight years, Jones Co. expects to be able to sell the truck for \$2,000. The salvage value of the truck is expected to be \$2,000.

d. *Selection of depreciation method to be used:* Depreciation expense is an approximation that is based on a number of estimates. There are many methods of computing depreciation. As long as a depreciation method is systematic and rational, it is normally an acceptable method. You should be familiar with the following four basic depreciation methods.

(1) *Straight-line depreciation method:* The straight-line depreciation method assumes that an equal amount of depreciation should be taken for each year of the asset's useful life. The formula for computing straight-line depreciation is

depreciation rate × (cost − salvage value)

The depreciation rate that is used with straight-line depreciation is

$$\frac{100\% \text{ (or 1.00)}}{\text{number of periods of useful life}}$$

Therefore, straight-line depreciation would be computed in this way:

$$(\text{cost} - \text{salvage value}) \times \frac{100\% \text{ (or 1.00)}}{\text{number of periods of useful life}}$$

EXAMPLE: Lox Company purchases a machine for \$10,000. Freight-in on the machine was \$100, and installation charges were \$100. The salvage value *of the machine is estimated to be $1,200. The useful life is estimated to be five years. The asset was purchased on January 1, 20XA. The calculation of depreciation for each year of useful life is shown below.*

Depreciation Schedule
Straight-Line Depreciation Method

Year	*Computation*	*Depreciation Expense*	*Accumulated Depreciation*	*Book Value*
				10,200
1	(9,000[a] × 0.20[b])	1,800	1,800	8,400
2	(9,000 × 0.20)	1,800	3,600	6,600
3	(9,000 × 0.20)	1,800	5,400	4,800
4	(9,000 × 0.20)	1,800	7,200	3,000
5	(9,000 × 0.20)	1,800	9,000	1,200
		9,000		

[a]Cost − salvage value
$10,200 − 1,200 = $9,000

[b]1/5 = 20% (or 0.20)

The journal entry to record the depreciation expense for each year would be as follows:

		dr	*cr*
Dec. 31	Depreciation expense	1,800	
	Accumulated depreciation		1,800

(2) *Double-declining-balance method:* Some assets produce more benefits in the early years of their useful life than in the later years. For example, some machines might require substantial repair as they become older. These types of assets might be depreciated using an accelerated depreciation method. Accelerated depreciation methods assign a larger amount of depreciation expense to the earlier years of an asset's useful life than to its later years. The double-declining-balance (DDB) method is an example of an accelerated depreciation method. The DDB depreciation method uses a constant depreciation rate applied to a declining asset base.

(a) The depreciation rate used in DDB depreciation is twice (200 percent of) the straight-line rate. In the previous Lox Company example, the straight-line rate was 1/5, or 20 percent, so the DDB rate would be 40 percent.

(b) To obtain depreciation expense for a period, the DDB depreciation rate is multiplied by the book value of the asset at the beginning of the period for which depreciation is to be calculated.

(c) Note that salvage value is not considered when computing depreciation using the DDB method. When the DDB method is used, however, an asset should not be depreciated below its salvage value.

EXAMPLE: Assume the same facts as were used in the Lox Company example, except that Lox Company wants to use the double-declining-balance depreciation method.

Depreciation Schedule
Double-Declining-Balance Depreciation Method

Year	*Computation*	*Depreciation Expense*	*Accumulated Depreciation*	*Book Value*
				10,200
1	(10,200 × 0.40)[a]	4,080	4,800	6,120
2	(6,120 × 0.40)	2,448	6,528	3,672
3	(3,672 × 0.40)	1,469	7,997	2,203
4	(2,203 × 0.40)	881	8,878	1,322
5		122[b]	9,000	1,200
		9,000[b]		

[a]0.40 = 2 × straight-line rate of 20% (0.20).
[b]Under DDB depreciation, we do not depreciate below the estimated salvage value amount. Note that the amount of the depreciation expense recorded each year declines from that reported in the previous year.

(3) *Sum-of-the-years' digits method:* The sum-of-the-years' digits (SYD) method is also an accelerated depreciation method. When the sum-of-the-years' digits method is used, a decreasing rate is applied to a constant asset base.

(a) The asset base to be depreciated in the SYD method is the cost of the asset minus the salvage value of the asset (as with straight-line depreciation).

(b) The decreasing rate is achieved by using a fraction, with the numerator representing the number of years remaining to be written off and the denominator representing the sum of the years' digits.

In the Lox Company example, the sum of the years' digits would be 15 years (5 years + 4 years + 3 years + 2 years + 1 year). An easy formula for calculating the sum-of-the-years' digits is $[N(N+1)]/2$, where N is the number of years of useful life. (This number is the denominator.)

In the Lox Company example, the depreciation rate in the first year would be 5/15; in the second year, 4/15; in the third year, 3/15; in the fourth year, 2/15; and in the fifth year, 1/15. By the end of the fifth year, the entire asset base will have been written off: 5/15 + 4/15 + 3/15 + 2/15 + 1/15 = 15/15.

EXAMPLE: Assume the same facts as were used in the Lox Company straight-line depreciation example, except that Lox Company now uses the SYD method of computing depreciation expense.

Depreciation Schedule
Sum-of-the-Years' Digits Method

Year	*Computation*	*Depreciation Expense*	*Accumulated Depreciation*	*Book Value*
				$10,200
1	(5/15 × 9,000)[a]	3,000	3,000	7,200
2	4/15 × 9,000	2,400	5,400	4,800
3	3/15 × 9,000	1,800	7,200	3,000
4	2/15 × 9,000	1,200	8,400	1,800
5	1/15 × 9,000	600	9,000	1,200
		9,000		

[a]Cost salvage value
$10,200 − 1,200 = $9,000

Note that the amount of the depreciation expense that is recorded declines in each successive year.

(4) *Units-of-production method:* The units-of-production method of calculating depreciation may be used when the total units of service that an asset will provide can be estimated accurately.

The formula used to calculate units-of-production depreciation is as follows:

$$\frac{\text{total units produced during the period}}{\text{total estimated units of production}} \times (\text{cost} - \text{salvage value})$$

EXAMPLE: XYZ Company bought a new truck. It is expected that the truck will have a useful life of 100,000 miles. The cost of the truck was $20,000, and salvage value is expected to be $2,000. During the first year the truck was driven 25,000 miles. The depreciation expense for the first year would be calculated as follows:

$$\frac{25{,}000}{100{,}000} \times (\$20{,}000 - \$2{,}000) = \$4{,}500$$

2. *Depletion:* Assets that are natural resources, such as timber, iron ore, gold, or oil reserves, are subject to depletion since the total quantity available will eventually be used up.

a. *Estimating quantity of natural resources:* First, the company must estimate the amount of the natural resource that will be available for use. This estimate is likely to change as time progresses and the company is more aware of the actual amount of the resource left.

b. *Calculating depletion:* The calculation of depletion is similar to the calculation of the units-of-production method.

c. *Formula for computing depletion:* The formula for computing depletion is as follows:

$$\frac{\text{quantity of resource used in current year}}{\text{estimated quantity of the resource available}} \times \text{cost} - \text{salvage value of natural resource}$$

d. *Expensing depletion cost:* Depletion is an inventoriable cost. Depletion cost should be added to the cost of extracting the resource. These costs should be expensed as the product is sold.

EXAMPLE: The Sylvan Silver Co. owns a silver mine in Alaska. It is estimated that 30,000 tons of silver ore will be able to be extracted from the mine. During the past year, 5,000 tons of silver ore were mined. The cost of the silver mine was $20,000, and the salvage value of the mine is estimated to be $5,000. The calculation of depletion for the period would be as follows:

$$\frac{5{,}000}{30{,}000} \times (\$20{,}000 - \$5{,}000) = \$2{,}500$$

C. Repairs

Ordinary repairs are amounts spent to maintain an asset in its normal operating condition. Ordinary repairs include regular maintenance, painting, cleaning, and repair of minor parts. Ordinary repairs performed on fixed assets are considered to be expenses for the period in which they are incurred. Extraordinary repairs should be capitalized and depreciated over the remainder of the asset's life. Repairs are extraordinary when they change the quality of service provided by an asset or extend its useful life beyond the original estimate.

1. *Extraordinary Repairs:* An extraordinary repair that increases the service life of an asset is recorded by debiting accumulated depreciation and crediting cash. An extraordinary repair that materially increases the productivity of the asset is debited directly to the asset account.
2. *Effect on Depreciation:* When extraordinary repairs occur, the current year's depreciation and all future periods' depreciation are affected. (No changes are made to the depreciation expense that was recorded in the past.)

EXAMPLE: Geni Co. purchased a truck for $18,000. The truck had a six-year estimated useful life. After five years Geni Co. decided to install a new engine in the truck that would extend its useful life to a total of 10 years. The new engine cost $10,000, including installation. Prior to the extraordinary repairs, the accounts appeared as follows (straight-line depreciation was used):

Truck #4

18,000	

Accumulated Depreciation

	15,000

Geni Co. recorded the extraordinary repairs as follows:

	dr	*cr*
(a) Accumulated depreciation/truck 4	10,000	
Cash		10,000
To record installation of new engine in truck 4.		

Then, the accounts appeared as follows:

Truck #4

18,000	

Accumulated Depreciation

	15,000
(a) 10,000	
	5,000

The new book value of the truck is $13,000. This amount should be depreciated over the new remaining useful life of the asset, which is five years. The depreciation expense on the truck for each of the next five years (assuming the straight-line depreciation is used) would be $13,000/5 = $2,600 per year (no salvage value is assumed).

D. Disposition of Property Items

Assets may be disposed of in one of the following three ways: sale, exchange, or abandonment. If an asset is disposed of at any time other than the end of an accounting period, depreciation should be calculated for the portion of the year for which the asset was held.

EXAMPLE: Floit Company sold a machine on June 30, 1999. The company purchased the machine on January 1, 1992, for $20,000 and estimated depreciation on the machine using the straight-line method over a 10-year period. Floit Company's year end is December 31. The entry to record the partial-year depreciation to date of sale would be as follows:

		dr	*cr*
June 30	Depreciation expense	1,000	
	Accumulated depreciation		1,000
To record 6 months' depreciation prior to disposal of machine (6/12 months × $2,000).			

1. *Sale of a Property Item:* When a property item is sold, the book value of the asset is compared to the proceeds generated by the sale of the asset.
   a. *Gain:* If an asset is sold for more than its book value, a gain is recorded.
   b. *Loss:* If an asset is sold for less than its book value, a loss is recorded.

   EXAMPLE: Assume that Floit Company sold the machine in the previous example for $10,000 cash. The book value of the asset is computed as follows:

$20,000.00	Cost
− 12,916.67	Less accumulated depreciation
$ 7,083.33	Book value

   The gain on the sale is computed as follows:

$10,000.00	Proceeds
− 7,083.33	Book value
$ 2,916.67	Gain

   The journal entry to record the sale is as follows:

		dr	*cr*
June 15	Cash	10,000.00	
	Accumulated depreciation	12,916.67	
	Machine		20,000.00
	Gain on sale of machine		2,916.67
Sold machine on June 15 for $10,000.			

2. *Abandonment of Property Items:* If fully depreciated assets are abandoned, a journal entry must be made debiting accumulated depreciation and crediting the asset account, which results in the writing off of the asset. If an asset that is not yet fully depreciated is abandoned, a loss due to the abandonment must be recorded.

   If fully depreciated assets are still being used in the business, no further depreciation should be taken on the asset, but the full amount of the asset and the accumulated depreciation related to it should be left on the records of the company.

E. Depreciation for Income Tax Purposes

In 1981, the tax provisions included a new system of depreciation known as the Accelerated Cost Recovery System (ACRS). In 1986, Congress modified the ACRS system. Under the Modified ACRS system (MACRS), an asset is assigned to a class of property that has a defined life for income tax depreciation purposes. The asset is depreciated over that statutory life at an assigned rate per year. Tables of class lives and depreciation rates for each year are published by the Internal Revenue Service.

An alternate MACRS method called the *optional straight-line method* may also be used to compute depreciation for income tax purposes. When the optional straight-line method is used, the straight-line method is generally applied to the MACRS defined life.

Although MACRS should be used for income tax purposes, it is not in accord with generally accepted accounting principles and should not normally be used for financial accounting purposes. Some small businesses may use MACRS depreciation for both financial reporting and tax purposes when the differences between MACRS and conventional methods are not material.

Review Questions

Directions: Select the correct answer from the four alternatives. Write the letter of your answer in the blank to the left of the number.

______ **1.** A depreciation method that assigns an equal amount of depreciation in each year of an asset's life is

a. double-declining-balance depreciation.
b. straight-line method.
c. units of production.
d. sum-of-the-years' digits.

______ **2.** Jones Company bought a plot of land with an old building located on it. The old building was demolished to pave the land for a parking lot. The cost of demolishing the building should be

a. capitalized as a part of the building account.
b. charged to demolition expense.
c. capitalized as part of the parking lot improvement account.
d. capitalized as a part of the cost of the land.

______ **3.** The sales tax paid when a new machine is purchased should be treated as a/an

a. tax expense item in the year the machine is purchased.
b. other expense item in the year the machine is purchased.
c. part of the cost of the new machine.
d. selling expense item in the year the machine is purchased.

______ **4.** Which one of the following items may correctly be included as part of the land account?

a. Landscaping
b. Parking lot
c. Excavation costs incurred during construction of a building
d. Brokerage commission

______ **5.** The amount a natural resource is reduced as a result of usage is called

a. depletion.
b. amortization.
c. depreciation.
d. accumulation.

_______________ **6.** A repair that is treated as an expense in the period in which it is incurred is

a. an extraordinary repair.
b. an ordinary repair.
c. a betterment.
d. a capital item.

_______________ **7.** The residual value an asset is expected to have when its useful life is over is called

a. book value.
b. accumulated depreciation value.
c. salvage value.
d. market value.

_______________ **8.** Rohas Co. purchased a new machine for $50,000 that they estimated would be able to produce 100,000 units of product C. During the current year, they produced 5,000 units of product C. The machine is expected to last eight years and have a salvage value of $2,000. Assuming that Rohas Co. uses the units-of-production method, depreciation expense for the current period is

a. $2,400.
b. $2,500.
c. $5,000.
d. $5,102.

_______________ **9.** If a fixed asset is sold for less than its book value,

a. a loss is recorded.
b. a gain is recorded.
c. no gain or loss is recorded.
d. cash is credited.

_______________ **10.** A repair that increases the service life of an asset and is recorded by debiting accumulated depreciation and crediting cash is called a/an

a. ordinary repair.
b. betterment.
c. accumulated repair.
d. extraordinary repair.

_______________ **11.** The depreciation method established by U.S. tax law is called the

a. double-declining-balance method.
b. units-of-production method.
c. modified accelerated cost recovery system.
d. Sum-of-the-years' digits method.

_______________ **12.** An accelerated method of depreciation prescribed in U.S. law for assets placed in service after 1986 is the

a. accumulated cost recovery system.
b. double-declining-balance method.

c. modified accelerated cost recovery system.
d. sum-of-the-years' digits method.

_______________ **13.** Nelson Company sold a truck for $24,000 on August 1, 20XD. The cost of the truck was $40,000, and the balance in the accumulated depreciation/truck account on January 1, 20XD, was $9,000. The truck had an estimated useful life of 10 years with no salvage value. The sale resulted in

a. a loss of $4,667.
b. a gain of $7,000.
c. a loss of $16,000.
d. a gain of $16,000.

Use the following information in answering Questions 14 to 17.

On January 1, 20XA, Hawk Co. purchased equipment for $62,000. The equipment was expected to last eight years and have a salvage value of $6,000. Hawk Co.'s year end is December 31.

_______________ **14.** Assuming that Hawk Co. uses straight-line depreciation, the balance in the accumulated depreciation account on January 1, 20XC, would be

a. $7,000.
b. $7,500.
c. $14,000.
d. $15,000.

_______________ **15.** Assuming that Hawk Co. uses the double-declining-balance method, depreciation expense for 20XB would be

a. $11,625.
b. $12,000.
c. $14,000.
d. $15,500.

_______________ **16.** Assuming that Hawk Co. uses the sum-of-the-years' digits method, depreciation expense for 20XC would be (rounded to the nearest dollar)

a. $9,333.
b. $10,000.
c. $12,000.
d. $12,444.

_______________ **17.** Assuming that Hawk Co. uses the sum-of-the-years' digits method, the book value of the equipment on December 31, 20XB (after closing) would be (rounded to the nearest dollar)

a. $10,889.
b. $25,000.
c. $32,667.
d. $36,667.

Solutions

Answer	*Refer to:*
1. (b)	[B-1-d(2)]
2. (d)	[A-2]
3. (c)	[A-1]
4. (d)	[A-2]
5. (a)	[B-2]
6. (b)	[C]
7. (c)	[B-1-c]
8. (a)	[B-1-d(4)] The calculation of depreciation using the units-of-production method is as follows: $\frac{5{,}000}{100{,}000} \times (\$50{,}000 - 2{,}000)$
9. (a)	[D-1-b]
10. (d)	[C]
11. (c)	[D-2-b]
12. (c)	[E]
13. (a)	[D-1-b] The book value of the truck was as follows:

\$40,000	Cost
− 11,333	Accumulated depreciation[a]
\$28,667	Book value

The selling price of the asset is less than the book value, so there was a loss on the sale of \$4,667 (\$28,667 − \$24,000).

14. (c) [B-1-d(1)] Straight-line depreciation expense is \$7,000 per year. [(\$62,000 − \$6,000) × 0.125] or [(\$62,000 − \$6,000)/8 = \$7,000]

Accumulated depreciation as of January 1, 20XC, would have a balance of \$14,000 (\$7,000 for 20XA and \$7,000 for 20XB).

[a]Accumulated depreciation as of January 1, 20XD + depreciation for the current year through August 1, 20XD (\$4,000/year × 7/12).

15. (a) [B-1-d(2)] Double-declining-balance depreciation would be computed as follows:

Year	*Beginning of Period Carrying Value*	*Rate*[b]	*Depreciation Expense*	*End of Period Carrying Value*
20XA	\$62,000	0.25	\$15,500	\$46,500
20XB	\$46,500	0.25	\$11,625	\$34,875

16. (a) [B-1-d(3)] Sum-of-the-years' digits depreciation would be computed as follows:

Year	*Fraction* × *Cost* − *Salvage Value*		=	*Depreciation Expense*
20XA	8/36[c]	\$62,000 − \$6,000	=	\$12,444
20XB	7/36	\$62,000 − \$6,000	=	\$10,889
20XC	6/36	\$62,000 − \$6,000	=	\$ 9,333

17. (d) [B-1-d(3)] Book value as of December 31, 20XB, is as follows:

cost	−	accumulated depreciation	=	book value
\$60,000	−	\$23,333[d]	=	\$36,667

[b]Straight-line rate = 1/8 = 0.125. Double-declining-balance rate = 0.125 × 2 = 0.25.

[c]The denominator is the sum-of-the-years' digits, which can be computed using the formula N(N+1)/2. The computation is 8(9)/2 = 36.

[d]\$12,444 + \$10,889 (sec solution to Question 16).

CHAPTER 14

Other Assets

OVERVIEW

This chapter covers the accounting for the rest of the asset categories. Some of the topics, such as the calculation of interest and treatment of prepaid expenses, were discussed in Chapter 9. The candidate should review Chapter 9 if necessary.

The candidate should be familiar with the recording of notes receivable and interest revenue for both interest-bearing and noninterest-bearing notes, the process of discounting a note receivable with a bank, accounting for accounts receivable and bad debts, types of insurance, co-insurance, and the recording of adjusting entries for prepaid insurance, accounting for office supplies, and accounting for intangible assets, including amortization of intangible assets.

KEY TERMS

Aging of accounts receivable
Amortization
Casualty insurance
Co-insurance
Contingent liability
Direct write-off method
Discounting of a note receivable
Fidelity bond
Interest-bearing note receivable
Life and health insurance
Maturity date of a note
Noninterest-bearing note receivable
Property insurance
Surety bond

A. Notes Receivable

A note receivable is a legal document signed by the borrower that promises to pay the lender the principal amount of the note. Notes receivable normally specify that a certain interest rate will be paid on the principal.

1. *Interest-Bearing Note Receivable:* A note receivable that requires payment of both the principal and a stated rate of interest is called an *interest-bearing note receivable.*

   EXAMPLE: Moomey Company accepted a $5,000 60-day 10 percent note receivable from Pone in exchange for merchandise on June 1. The journal entry to record the receipt of the note would be as follows:

		dr	*cr*
June 1	Note receivable	5,000	
	Sales revenue		5,000
Received 60-day 10 percent note from Pone in exchange for merchandise.			

The journal entry to record the collection of the note receivable would be as follows:

		dr	*cr*
July 31	Cash	5,083	
	Note receivable		5,000
	Interest revenue		83

Collected Pone note; interest =
$5,000 × 0.10 × 60/360 = $83.

2. *Noninterest-Bearing Note Receivable:* A note receivable that has no provision for the payment of interest on the principal of the note is called a *noninterest-bearing note receivable.* Since money has a time value, the principal amount received on the due date includes an amount for implied interest. Generally accepted accounting principles require that interest be imputed on long-term noninterest-bearing notes. Imputing interest refers to the process of recognizing the implied interest through an approximation process. Short-term noninterest-bearing notes are recorded at face value since the implied interest on the note is immaterial. To determine the amount of imputed interest associated with a noninterest-bearing note, the following steps are used:

   a. *Rate of imputed interest:* Determine the rate of interest that is usually charged on transactions of the same nature as the one involving the noninterest-bearing note.

   b. *Present value of note:* Find the present value of the note using the following formula:

$$\frac{\text{face value of the note}}{(1 + r)^n} = \text{present value of the note}$$

   In this formula, *r* is the interest rate and *n* is the number of interest periods.

   c. *Discount:* Find the amount of the discount to be recorded on the note using the following formula:

$$\text{face value} - \text{present value} = \text{discount on note receivable}$$

   The discount amount represents the interest that is implied in the note. This amount is recorded in a discount on notes receivable account. The discount account is a contra-asset account and is deducted from the face value of the note on the balance sheet. The balance in the discount account is written off to interest income over the life of the note. The amount of interest to be recorded in any given period is based on the beginning of the period carrying value of the note (notes receivable − discount on notes receivable) times the interest rate times the period of time for which interest is to be accrued.

   EXAMPLE: Moomey Company accepted a $10,000 two-year noninterest-bearing note receivable from Zebo Company on January 1, 20XA. The note was taken in exchange for merchandise. The interest rate normally charged in this type of transaction is 10 percent. The computation of interest to be imputed is as follows:

$$\frac{\$10{,}000}{(1+0.1)^2} = \frac{\$10{,}000}{1.21} = \$8{,}264$$

   The discount on the note would be $1,736 ($10,000 − $8,264).

The journal entry to record the receipt of the note would be as follows:

		dr	cr
Jan. 1	Notes receivable	10,000	
	Discount on notes receivable		1,736
	Sales		8,264

Received a two-year noninterest-bearing note from Zebo Co.
Interest was imputed at 10 percent.

The journal entry to record the first year's interest on the note would be as follows:

		dr	cr
Dec. 31	Discount on notes receivable	826	
	Interest income (revenue)		826

To record interest accrued on the Zebo Co. note receivable.
(Carrying value × interest rate × time) ($8,264 × 0.10 × 1 year)

The journal entry to record the collection of the note on December 31, 20XB, would be as follows:

		dr	cr
Dec. 31	Cash	10,000	
	Discount on notes receivable	910	
	Interest income (revenue)		910
	Notes receivable		10,000

To record collection of the Zebo Co. note and to write off the balance in the discount account to interest income.

d. *Imputing interest on notes:* Interest should be imputed whenever a long-term (more than one year) note is noninterest bearing or has an interest rate that is unreasonably low under the circumstances.

3. *Recording Accrued Interest Receivable:* If financial statements are prepared before a note receivable is collected, the amount of accrued interest receivable must be recorded.

a. *Interest-bearing notes receivable:* For interest-bearing notes receivable, interest is accrued in the same fashion as for bonds receivable (see Chapter 11).

b. *Noninterest-bearing notes receivable:* For noninterest-bearing notes receivable, an adjusting entry records the interest revenue that was accrued and writes off the portion of the discount that has been earned (see the December 31 entries in the example in A-2-c).

4. *Discounting of Notes Receivable:* A company may discount (sell) its notes receivable to a bank if the company needs cash immediately and does not want to hold the notes to maturity. The bank buys the note and holds it until maturity. At the time the note matures, the bank collects the principal and interest earned on the note from the maker.

The seller of the note is liable to the bank for payment of the maturity value if the maker does not pay the note. This liability to pay the bank if the maker fails to do so is called a *contingent liability.* A contingent liability might become a liability at a future date but is not a liability at the present time. Contingent liabilities are potential liabilities, but they are not currently legal obligations. Contingent liabilities are usually reported in footnotes on financial statements.

The amount that a company will receive from the bank when a note is discounted may be calculated as follows:

a. *Maturity value of note:* The maturity value of the note (the principal plus the interest) is determined.

b. *Discount on note:* The amount of interest the bank will charge for the note is calculated. This is called the *discount* on the note. The formula for calculating the discount is as follows:

maturity value × bank discount rate × portion of a year for which the bank will hold the note = discount

c. *Proceeds:* The maturity value less the discount is equal to the proceeds that the bank will pay to the seller.

maturity value − discount = proceeds

d. *Interest expense:* If the proceeds received from the bank are less than the face value of the note, the seller will record the difference as *interest expense.*

e. *Interest revenue:* If the proceeds received from the bank are more than the face value of the note, the seller will record the difference as *interest revenue.*

EXAMPLE: Lackey Co. discounted a $10,000 8 percent 90-day note receivable with the bank. The note was issued on June 1, and Lackey Co. discounted the note with the bank on July 1. The bank charges a 10 percent discount rate. The calculation of the proceeds to be received by Lackey Co. follows:

	Principal	$10,000
+	Interest ($10,000 × 0.08 × 90/360)	200
	Maturity value	$10,200
	Less: discount ($10,200 × 0.10 × 60/360)	− 170
	Proceeds to Lackey Co.	$10,030

Lackey Co. would record the receipt of the proceeds as follows:

		dr	*cr*
July 1	Cash	10,030	
	Notes receivable		10,000
	Interest revenue		30
Discounted note receivable with the bank.			

f. *Default in payment of note:* If the maker of a note defaults, the bank requests payment from the seller. The journal entry to record payment on a defaulted note would be a debit to accounts receivable and a credit to cash. The seller would then be responsible for collection of the note from the maker.

EXAMPLE: Assume that the maker of the note Lackey Co. discounted with the bank defaulted and that the bank charged a $25 protest fee. Lackey Co. would make the following entry to record the payment to the bank of the maturity value:

	dr	*cr*
Accounts receivable	10,225	
Cash		10,225
To record payment of defaulted notes receivable and bank protest fee.		

B. Accounts Receivable and Bad Debts

Accounts receivable are amounts owed to a business for sales of merchandise or services that are sold on credit. Many businesses have a credit department that analyzes prospective customers before credit is issued to them. Even if a business has a credit department that screens credit customers, some of the accounts receivable of the business will prove to be uncollectible. An allowance for uncollectible accounts (or allowance for doubtful accounts) is set up to report accounts receivable on the balance sheet at the amount that is expected to be collected.

Total accounts receivable balance
Less: Allowance for uncollectible accounts
= Net realizable value of accounts receivable

Using an allowance for uncollectible accounts results in a better matching of the expense related to uncollectible accounts with the sales revenue recorded when the initial sales took place. It also reports accounts receivable at a more conservative amount (net realizable value). There are a number of different methods for estimating the amount of bad debt expense to be recorded and the amount to be included in the allowance for uncollectible accounts.

1. *Aging of Accounts Receivable:* When an aging of accounts receivable is prepared, individual customers' account balances are categorized according to the length of time they have been outstanding. Based on past experience, the company estimates the probability of accounts not being collected for each category. The estimated losses in each category are totaled to determine the total amount of estimated uncollectible accounts. The aging-of-accounts-receivable method provides the best estimate of uncollectible accounts. Figure 14–1 shows an example of an aging-of-accounts-receivable schedule.

Figure 14–1 Aging of Accounts Receivable

Nelson Company
Aging of Accounts Receivable
December 31, 20XA

Account Name	*Account Balance*	*Not Yet Due*	*1–30 Days Past Due*	*30–60 Days Past Due*	*Over 60 Days Past Due*
Aronson	2,500	2,500			
Bellows Co.	10,122	8,000	2,122		
Bird	8,310	8,310			
Cafen Co.	503				503
Crane	12,200	10,000		2,200	
Dulow Corp., etc.	5,110		5,110		
Total	100,000	65,000	20,000	10,000	5,000
Percentage estimated to be uncollectible from past experience		1%	3%	8%	15%
Amount estimated to be uncollectible	2,800	650	600	800	750

EXAMPLE: Assume that Nelson Company's accounts receivable control account had a $100,000 debit balance and the company's allowance for uncollectible accounts account had a $200 credit balance prior to adjustment.

Accounts Receivable (Control)

Bal. 12/31	100,000		

Allowance for Uncollectible Accounts

		200	Bal. 12/31
		2,600 (adjusting entry)	12/31
		2,800	

The entry to record bad debt expense based on the aging schedule in Figure 14–1 would be as follows:

		dr	*cr*
Dec. 31	Bad debt expense	2,600	
	Allowance for uncollectible accounts		2,600
To record bad debt expense.			

2. *Percentage of Accounts Receivable:* The percentage-of-accounts-receivable method estimates the balance of the allowance for uncollectible accounts based on a percentage of the ending accounts receivable balance.

   EXAMPLE: Assume that based on past experience Nelson Company estimates that uncollectible accounts are about 2.5 percent of total ending accounts receivable. Nelson Company would estimate that its allowance for uncollectible accounts balance should be $2,500 ($100,000 × 0.025). Since the allowance account already has a balance of $200, the entry to record bad debt expense, assuming that the percentage-of-accounts-receivable method is used, would be as follows:

		dr	*cr*
Dec. 31	Bad debt expense	2,300	
	Allowance for uncollectible accounts		2,300
To record bad debt expense.			

3. *Percentage of Credit Sales:* The percentage-of-credit-sales method assumes that a certain percentage (based on past experience) of credit sales for the year will prove to be uncollectible. When the percentage-of-sales method is used, the company estimates the amount of bad debt expense rather than the amount of the allowance for uncollectible accounts as in the other two methods. The amount already recorded in the allowance for uncollectible accounts does not affect the adjusting entry when the percentage-of-credit-sales method is used. Bad debt expense might also be estimated using a percentage of net sales rather than credit sales.

   EXAMPLE: Assume that Nelson Company had credit sales of $900,000 during 20XA. Nelson Company estimates that 0.3 percent of its credit sales will be uncollectible. The entry to record bad debt expense, assuming that the percentage-of-credit-sales method is used, would be as follows:

		dr	cr
Dec. 31	Bad debt expense	2,700	
	Allowance for uncollectible accounts		2,700
To record bad debt expense ($900,000 × 0.003).			

Note: The balance in the allowance account did not affect the entry that was made since the percentage-of-credit-sales method was used.

4. *Writing Off an Uncollectible Account:* When an individual account has been determined to be uncollectible, that account must be written off. To write off an account, the allowance for uncollectible accounts is debited, and the accounts receivable account is credited. The procedure for writing off an uncollectible account is the same regardless of the method used to estimate bad debt expense and the allowance for uncollectible accounts. The writing off of a bad debt does not affect the net realizable value of accounts receivable since both accounts receivable and the allowance for uncollectible accounts are reduced by an equal amount.

   EXAMPLE: Assume that on May 1, 20XA, Nelson Company determines that Cafen Co.'s account is uncollectible. The entry to write off the account would be as follows:

		dr	cr
May 1	Allowance for uncollectible accounts	503	
	Accounts receivable		503
To write off Cafen Co.'s uncollectible account.			

5. *Collection of Uncollectible Account:* An account that has previously been written off may still be collected. When this happens, it is necessary to restore the account as a part of the accounts receivable balance before recording the collection of the account.

   EXAMPLE: Assume that on May 5, 20XB, Nelson Company collects a $300 account from J.D. Corporation that was written off in 20XA. On May 5, 20XB, the entries necessary to record the transaction would be as follows:

		dr	cr
May 5	Accounts receivable	300	
	Allowance for uncollectible accounts		300
To restore J.D. Corporation account, which was previously written off.			
May 5	Cash	300	
	Accounts receivable		300
To record collection of J.D. Corporation account receivable.			

   If a collection agency were used to help collect the account, its commission would need to be shown as a part of the cash received.

6. *Direct Write-Off:* When the direct write-off method is used, a company does not record an allowance for doubtful accounts or attempt to match bad debt expense with the related revenues. When an account is determined to be uncollectible, an entry is made directly to bad debt expense and accounts receivable. No adjusting entry is made at the end of the period. From an accounting standpoint, the direct write-off method is deficient because no attempt is made to match revenues and expenses, and the accounts receivable balance in the balance sheet is overstated, except where the company ordinarily would not have any bad accounts. This method is not acceptable under generally accepted accounting principles unless the amount is not material.

EXAMPLE: Sullivan Co. uses the direct write-off method of recording bad debts. On October 1, 20XA, the $500 account of J.B. Harding was determined uncollectible. The entry to write off the account would be as follows:

		dr	*cr*
Oct. 1	Bad debt expense	500	
	Accounts receivable		500
To write off the J.B. Harding account as uncollectible.			

C. Prepaid Expenses

Prepaid expenses consist of the cost of supplies or services bought for use in the business that are not used up at the end of the accounting period.

1. *Insurance:* Insurance policies usually cover a set period of time, and frequently they are paid for in advance. When the period of time covered by an insurance policy extends beyond one accounting period, prepaid insurance should be recorded. When payment is made on an insurance policy that covers more than one accounting period, the payment may be recorded in two alternative ways:

a. *Recording original payment:* The original payment for insurance may be recorded in either of the following ways:

(1) The original payment may be recorded as a debit to the insurance expense account. When this is done, an adjusting entry must be made at the end of the period to record any remaining prepaid insurance benefits. For an example of the recording of the adjusting entry that must be made, see Chapter 9, Section F-2-a(2)(b).

(2) The original payment may be recorded as a debit to the prepaid insurance account. When this is done, an adjusting entry must be made at the end of the period to record the portion of the benefits that have expired (i.e., have become an expense of the period). For an example of the recording of the necessary adjusting entry, see Chapter 9, Section F-2-a(1)(a).

b. *Numerous insurance policies:* A company might have a number of insurance policies that cover one or more accounting periods. When this is the case, the prepaid insurance account includes the total of all of the prepaid insurance benefits for all the policies.

c. *Types of insurance:* The major types of insurance available for businesses today include property insurance, casualty insurance, life and health insurance, fidelity bond insurance, surety bonding, and co-insurance.

(1) *Property insurance:* Insurance protection of the property (assets) of the company from damage or destruction by fire, smoke, vandalism, and so on, is provided through property insurance policies.

(2) *Casualty insurance:* Casualty insurance is insurance coverage that is primarily for the liability of a party that results from negligent acts or omissions resulting in bodily injury and/or property damage to another party.

(3) *Life and health insurance:* Business life and health insurance coverage provides funds for the normal maintenance of a business in the event of the loss of a key person. This is often called *key man insurance.*

(4) *Fidelity bond insurance:* This type of insurance guarantees that the insurance company will pay for losses of money or property that result from the dishonest acts of bonded employees. The employees are named specifically or by position. The bond covers dishonest acts, whether employees act alone or in collusion. Many organizations view bonding as beneficial. As well as paying for losses, bonding provides a deterrent to fraud. The bonding company can uncover dishonesty in the work history of a new employee, and many employees believe that the bonding company is certain to prosecute if they are caught performing dishonest acts.

(5) *Surety bond:* A surety bond is a contract under which the surety agrees to make good the debt or default of the principal.

(6) *Co-insurance:* A provision is included in some insurance contracts that requires the insured party to insure property for at least a specified minimum percentage of its fair market value or to share the loss proportionately with the insurance company.

2. *Supplies:* Office supplies are often purchased in large quantities and kept on hand for use in the business when needed. Any supplies on hand at the end of an accounting period represent a prepaid expense of the company. The original purchase of office supplies may be recorded in two alternative ways:

a. *Debit to asset account:* When the supplies are purchased, the asset account *supplies inventory* may be debited. When this is done, an adjusting entry must be made at the end of the period to record supplies expense for the supplies that were used. For an example of the recording of an adjusting entry of this type, see Chapter 9, Section F-2-a(1)(b).

b. *Debit to expense account:* When the supplies are purchased, an expense account may be debited. When this is done, an adjusting entry must be made at the end of the period to record any supplies on hand as an asset. For an example of the recording of an adjusting entry of this type, see Chapter 9, Section F-2-a(2)(a).

D. Intangible Assets and Amortization

Intangible assets are long-lived assets that have no tangible existence. Examples of intangible assets are patents, copyrights, trademarks, franchises, leaseholds, and goodwill.

1. *Value of Intangible Assets:* Intangible assets are valued at cost. A company could have intangible assets that were acquired at no cost to the company. These assets, which have no cost, should not be recorded on the balance sheet.

2. *Capitalization of Intangible Assets:* An intangible asset should be capitalized and shown on the balance sheet *only* if a future benefit can be expected to be derived from that intangible asset.

3. *Amortization of Intangible Assets:* Intangible assets should be amortized over their useful lives. Amortization expense is recorded by debiting amortization expense and crediting the intangible asset account. Amortization is always recorded on a straight-line basis.

a. *Limited legal life:* Some intangible assets, such as patents or copyrights, have a limited legal life. Patents and copyrights should be amortized over their legal life, or their useful life if it is shorter than their legal life. Patents have legal life of 17 years, and copyrights have legal life of 50 years beyond the creator's lifetime.

b. *Indefinite useful life:* Some intangible assets, such as trademarks, organization costs, or goodwill, have indefinite useful lives. If an intangible asset has an indefinite useful life, it should be amortized over a period that does not exceed 40 years.

EXAMPLE: ABC Co. has a patent that cost $10,000. The legal life of the patent is 17 years, but the expected useful life is 10 years. The journal entry to record amortization of the patent for each of its 10 years of useful life would be as follows:

	dr	*cr*
Amortization expense	1,000	
Patent		1,000
To amortize the cost of the patent over its useful life ($10,000/10 years).		

Review Questions

Directions: Select the correct answer from the four alternatives. Write the letter of your answer in the blank to the left of the number. Assume 360 days per year in all interest calculations.

______ **1.** A note receivable that requires payment of principal only with no provision for interest is called

a. an interest-bearing note receivable.
b. a noninterest-bearing note receivable.
c. an imputed note receivable.
d. a note payable.

______ **2.** What is the interest on a \$60,000 interest-bearing note at 9 percent for 120 days?

a. \$1,200
b. \$1,800
c. \$2,700
d. \$5,400

______ **3.** Arnold Company accepted a \$20,000 three-year noninterest-bearing note from Mary Mealy. The interest rate that Arnold Company charged for similar transactions was 10 percent. The amount of the discount on notes receivable that Arnold Company should have recorded is (rounded to the nearest dollar)

a. \$4,974.
b. \$6,060.
c. \$9,090.
d. \$15,026.

______ **4.** In the United States, interest should be imputed on a note receivable

a. when the note is noninterest bearing regardless of the due date of the note.
b. when the interest rate on the note is unreasonably low and the note has a due date more than one year in the future.
c. when the note is interest bearing.
d. when the interest payment date does not fall on year end.

______ **5.** When a note receivable is sold to a bank, the seller of the note is liable to pay the bank if the maker of the note does not. This is called a/an

a. unknown liability.
b. long-term liability.
c. potential liability.
d. contingent liability.

_______________ **6.** The maturity value of an interest-bearing note receivable is

a. equal to the face value.
b. equal to the face value plus the interest due on the maturity date of the note.
c. the amount a bank will pay for a note if it is discounted with the bank.
d. the principal amount of the note.

_______________ **7.** The writing off of a worthless account receivable when the allowance method of recording bad debt expense is used

a. results in a decrease in the total assets of the company.
b. should include a debit to bad debt expense.
c. decreases the net realizable value of accounts receivable for the firm.
d. should include a debit to the allowance for uncollectible accounts.

_______________ **8.** Which one of the following items would be classified as an intangible asset?

a. Inventory
b. Accounts receivable
c. Patent
d. Prepaid insurance

_______________ **9.** ABC Co. owns a patent that has a legal life of 17 years and an expected useful life of 8 years. The patent should be amortized over

a. 5 years.
b. 8 years.
c. 12 years.
d. 17 years.

_______________ **10.** Ajax Co. purchased a two-year insurance policy on June 1, 20XA, for $1,200. On June 1, Ajax Co. debited prepaid insurance and credited cash for $1,200. On December 31, 20XA (Ajax Co.'s year end), Ajax Co. should

a. include the $1,200 on the balance sheet as a prepaid expense.
b. debit prepaid insurance and credit insurance expense for $350.
c. debit insurance expense and credit prepaid insurance for $350.
d. debit insurance expense and credit prepaid insurance for $850.

_______________ **11.** On the balance sheet, the allowance for uncollectible accounts should be shown as

a. a current liability.
b. an addition to the accounts receivable balance.
c. a deduction from the balance in the accounts receivable account.
d. an income statement item.

_______________ **12.** If the interest income account has a $400 credit balance before the year-end adjustments are made and there are adjustments for $60 of accrued interest on notes receivable, the income statement should show interest earned of

a. $60.
b. $400.
c. $450.
d. $460.

_______________ **13.** Sun Co. uses the allowance method of recording bad debt expense. In 20XA, Sun Co. wrote off the account of Wendel as uncollectible. During 20XB, Wendel paid Sun Co. the amount that had been owed. Sun Co. should

a. not record the collection since the account was previously written off.
b. credit bad debt expense for the amount received.
c. first reinstate the account of Wendel and then record the collection.
d. record the amount received as miscellaneous revenue in 20XB.

_______________ **14.** After aging the accounts receivable at the end of the year, Ring Co. estimated that $200,000 of the accounts receivable would be uncollectible. The balance in allowance for uncollectible accounts prior to adjustment was a $4,000 debit. The correct adjusting entry would include a debit to bad debt expense of

a. $4,000.
b. $196,000.
c. $200,000.
d. $204,000.

_______________ **15.** Intangible assets should be amortized over

a. their useful lives.
b. a period not exceeding 50 years if they have definite lives.
c. a period not exceeding 20 years if they have indefinite lives.
d. five years regardless of their useful lives.

Use the following information in answering Questions 16 to 18. Assume 360 days per year in all interest calculations.

Millikin Co. had credit sales of $3,000,000 in 20XA. The year-end accounts receivable balance was $888,000. The allowance for uncollectible accounts had a credit balance of $12,000 prior to adjustment.

_______________ **16.** Assuming that Millikin Co. uses the percentage-of-credit-sales method of estimating bad debt expense and that past experience indicates that 1 percent of credit sales will be uncollectible, the year-end adjusting entry should include a debit to bad debt expense for

a. $18,000.
b. $30,000.

c. $42,000.
d. $50,000.

______ **17.** Assuming that Millikin Co. uses the percentage-of-accounts-receivable method of estimating uncollectible accounts and that past experience indicates that 3.5 percent of the total accounts receivable prove to be uncollectible, the year-end adjusting entry should include

a. a debit to bad debt expense for $19,080.
b. a credit to allowance for uncollectible accounts of $31,080.
c. a debit to bad debt expense for $31,080.
d. a debit to bad debt expense for $35,000.

______ **18.** Assuming that Millikin Co. uses the direct write-off method of recording bad debts, the year-end adjusting entry should include

a. a debit to bad debt expense and a credit to accounts receivable.
b. a debit to accounts receivable and a credit to bad debt expense.
c. a debit to bad debt expense and a credit to allowance for uncollectible accounts.
d. No adjusting entry would be made under the direct write-off method.

Use the following information in answering Questions 19 to 22. Assume 360 days per year in all interest computations.

Frank Co. accepted a $10,000 10 percent 90-day note receivable from Alex Co. on June 1, 20XA. On July 1, 20XA, Frank Co. discounted the note with ABC Bank. The bank discount rate is 12 percent.

______ **19.** The maturity value of the note is

a. $10,250.
b. $10,300.
c. $11,000.
d. $11,200.

______ **20.** The proceeds received by Frank Co. from ABC Bank were (rounded to the nearest dollar)

a. $9,500.
b. $10,000.
c. $10,045.
d. $10,079.

______ **21.** Assuming that the proceeds received in Question 20 were $9,500, the entry to record the receipt of the proceeds would include

a. a debit to cash, a credit to notes receivable, and a credit to interest income.
b. a debit to cash, a debit to interest expense, and a credit to notes receivable.
c. a debit to notes receivable, a credit to cash, and a credit to interest income.
d. a debit to cash and a credit to notes receivable.

_______________ **22.** On September 5, 20XA, Frank Co. received a notice from ABC Bank that Alex Co. had dishonored the note. The bank charged a $50 protest fee. The entry to record Frank Co.'s payment to the bank would include

a. a debit to notes receivable for $10,000 and a credit to cash for $10,000.
b. a debit to accounts receivable for $10,050 and a credit to cash for $10,050.
c. a debit to accounts receivable for $10,300 and a credit to cash for $10,300.
d. a debit to notes receivable for $10,250 and a credit to cash for $10,250.

Solutions

Answer	*Refer to:*
1. (b)	[A-2]
2. (b)	[A-1] Interest = principal × rate × time $1,800 = $60,000 × 0.09 × 120/360
3. (a)	[A-2] The present value of the note is computed using the following formula: $\frac{\text{face value of note}}{(1 + r)^n} = \frac{\$20{,}000}{(1 + 0.1)^3} = \$15{,}026$ The discount to be recorded is the difference between the face value and the present value of the note ($20,000 − 15,026 = $4,974).
4. (b)	[A-2-d]
5. (d)	[A-4]
6. (b)	[A-4-a]
7. (d)	[B-4]
8. (c)	[D]
9. (b)	[D-3]
10. (c)	[C-1-a(1); Chapter 9, F-2-a(1)(a)] $1,200/24 months = $50/month $50/month × 7 months = $350 insurance expense
11. (c)	[B]
12. (d)	[A-3]
13. (c)	[B-5]
14. (d)	[B-1] Since allowance for uncollectible accounts has a $4,000 debit balance, the adjusting journal entry must be made for $204,000 to have an ending balance of $200,000 in allowance for uncollectible accounts after adjustment.

15. (a) [D-3]

16. (b) [B-3] $3,000,000 × 0.01 = $30,000

17. (a) [B-2] $888,000 × 0.035 = $31,080

Since $31,080 is the ending credit balance we want to have in allowance for uncollectible accounts, the adjusting journal entry would have to be made for $19,080 ($31,080 − $12,000 credit balance already in the account).

18. (d) [B-6]

19. (a) [A-4-a] Maturity value is equal to the principal plus the interest on the note.

principal + interest = maturity value
$10,000 + ($10,000 × 0.10 × 90/360) = $10,250

20. (c) [A-4-c] The bank discount in this problem is equal to the maturity value times the bank discount rate times the length of time the bank will hold the note.

maturity value × bank discount rate × time = bank discount
$10,250 × 0.12 × 60/360 = $205

maturity value − bank discount = proceeds
$10,250 − $205 = $10,045

21. (b) [A-4-d]

22. (c) [A-4-f] Frank Co. must pay the bank the maturity value of the note plus the protest fee. Frank Co. would then record an account receivable from Alex Co. for the amount paid to the bank.

CHAPTER

15

Debt Equities or Liabilities

OVERVIEW

This chapter is intended to introduce the candidate to the accounting procedures used in recording and reporting liabilities. Many liabilities, such as accounts payable and accrued liabilities, have been discussed in earlier chapters. The accounting for notes payable and bonds payable is very similar to the accounting for notes and bonds receivable. The candidate may find it useful to review Chapter 11.

The candidate should know the accounting procedures used for interest-bearing and noninterest-bearing notes payable, the calculation of simple and compound interest, the definitions of term and installment notes payable, the treatment of accounts payable, the recording of accrued liabilities, and the accounting for long-term liabilities, including notes, mortgages, and bonds.

KEY TERMS

Bearer bonds
Bond sinking fund
Callable bonds
Compound interest
Convertible bond
Debenture
Installment note payable
Mortgage
Mortgage bond
Registered bond
Serial bonds
Simple interest
Term bonds
Term notes payable

A. Short-Term Obligations

Short-term obligations are current liabilities that will require payment within the next operating cycle. The following are the basic types of short-term obligations:

1. *Notes Payable:* Notes payable are written documents promising to pay an amount to a creditor on a specific date. Short-term notes payable can be interest bearing or noninterest bearing. Notes payable could be given in exchange for goods or services, for purchase of real estate or equipment, or to a bank in exchange for cash.

   a. *Interest-bearing notes payable:* Interest-bearing notes payable require the payment of principal and interest at their maturity date. Interest-bearing notes payable should be recorded at their face value. If the accounting period ends before the note matures, an adjusting entry should be made to record any accrued interest on the note. The following example shows the accounting entries for an interest-bearing note payable.

EXAMPLE: Assume that on May 1, Johnson Company issued a $5,000 six-month 12 percent note payable to Jones Company in exchange for merchandise. Johnson Company uses a periodic inventory system. The entry to record the issuance of the note would be as follows:

		dr	*cr*
May 1	Purchases	5,000	
	Notes payable		5,000
To record issuance of six-month 12 percent note in exchange for goods.			

Assuming that Johnson Company's year end is December 31, the entry to record payment of the note on November 1 would be as follows:

		dr	*cr*
Nov. 1	Notes payable	5,000	
	Interest expense	300	
	Cash		5,300
Paid six-month note to Jones Co. with interest ($5,000 × 0.12 × 6/12).			

If Johnson Company's year end were August 31, the following adjusting entry would be needed to record the accrued interest expense:

		dr	*cr*
Aug. 31	Interest expense	200	
	Accrued interest payable		200
To record interest accrued from May 1 through August 31 on Jones Co. note payable ($5,000 × 0.12 × 4/12).			

Assuming that Johnson Company's year end was August 31, the entry to record payment of the note on November 1 would be as follows:

		dr	*cr*
Nov. 1	Notes payable	5,000	
	Accrued interest payable	200	
	Interest expense	100	
	Cash		5,300
Paid six-month note to Jones Co.			

(1) *Simple interest:* Simple interest is calculated for a single period of time and is computed only on the amount of the principal of the note. The formula for calculation of simple interest is as follows:

$$\begin{aligned}\text{Interest} &= \text{principal}\\ &\times \text{ rate of interest for one period}\\ &\times \text{ number of periods or fraction of a period}\end{aligned}$$

Note: All examples of the calculation of interest made above are calculations of simple interest.

(2) *Compound or add-on interest:* Compound interest refers to the calculation of interest on the principal and on any interest that is earned but has not yet been paid. Any interest earned during a period earns interest in subsequent periods. Compounding of interest takes place at periodic intervals that may vary in length. For example, many savings accounts compound interest on a daily basis. Interest might also be compounded on a weekly, monthly, quarterly, or yearly basis. The more often that interest is compounded, the greater is the total amount of interest earned. Tables are available to aid in solving compound

interest problems. The following example shows the calculation of simple and compound interest.

EXAMPLE: Assume that Stein invested $1,000 at 10 percent interest for five years. The calculation of the total amount that she would earn on the investment, assuming simple interest versus compound interest (compounded yearly), would be as follows:

Year	*Interest Computation*	*Simple Interest*	*Compound Interest*
1	Interest on principal ($1,000 × 0.10)	$100.00	$100.00
2	Interest on principal ($1,000 × 0.10)	100.00	100.00
	Interest on interest ($100 × 0.10)		10.00
3	Interest on principal ($1,000 × 0.10)	100.00	100.00
	Interest on interest ($210 × 0.10)		21.00
4	Interest on principal ($1,000 × 0.10)	100.00	100.00
	Interest on interest ($331 × 0.10)		33.10
5	Interest on principal ($1,000 × 0.10)	100.00	100.00
	Interest on interest ($464.10 × 0.10)		46.41
	Total interest earned	$500.00	$610.51

b. *Noninterest-bearing notes payable:* Noninterest-bearing notes payable do not require the payment of interest. Only the payment of the principal amount is required. Since money has a time value, a portion of the payment of the note at maturity is for implied interest. Although theoretically all noninterest-bearing notes should be reported at their present value, it is acceptable to treat notes issued for a short period of time (less than one year) as noninterest bearing since any interest included in the face value is normally immaterial.

c. *Discounted note payable:* A company may issue its own noninterest-bearing note payable to a bank in exchange for cash. The bank discounts the note and pays the discounted amount to the borrower. The bank calculates the discount as follows:

Face value of note
× Discount rate
× Period of time note will be outstanding
= Discount

The face value of the note less the discount equals the proceeds the borrower will receive. The discount on the note represents interest expense to the borrower.

The following example shows the accounting entries for a noninterest-bearing note payable discounted with a bank.

EXAMPLE: Robert Corp. discounted its own 90-day note payable for $5,000 at Security National Bank. The bank discount rate is 10 percent. The proceeds received by Robert Corp. are calculated as follows:

Face value	$5,000
Less: Discount	
($5,000 × 0.10 × 90/360)	− 125
Proceeds	$4,875

The entry to record the loan would be as follows:

	dr	*cr*
Cash	4,875	
Discount on notes payable	125	
Notes payable		5,000
To record discounting of 90-day note with Security National Bank at 10 percent.		

The entry to record payment of the note when it matures would be as follows:

	dr	*cr*
Notes payable	5,000	
Interest expense	125	
Discount on notes payable		125
Cash		5,000
To record payment of loan from Security National Bank.		

d. *Term notes payable:* Term notes payable are repaid in a lump sum on a specific date. They have a specified term of life after which the principal, or principal plus interest, must be repaid.

e. *Installment notes payable:* Installment notes payable are repaid through a series of periodic payments. Each payment represents a payment of a portion of the principal plus interest. Purchase of a television set to be paid for in 20 equal monthly installments would represent an installment note payable.

2. *Accounts Payable:* Accounts payable result from the purchase of merchandise or services on open account. Accounts payable are not formal written documents and usually do not require the payment of interest. The accountant must be careful to ensure that all accounts payable are recorded. Cash (or purchase) discounts are often offered for prompt payment of accounts payable. Companies should take advantage of cash discounts whenever possible since a substantial cash savings results from doing so.

3. *Accruals:* Accruals are liabilities recorded through year-end (or monthly) adjusting entries. The recording of accrued liabilities is discussed in Chapter 9, Section F.

EXAMPLES: Accrued interest payable, accrued salaries payable, and accrued payroll taxes payable.

B. Long-Term Obligations

Long-term liabilities will not require repayment within the next operating cycle. Long-term liabilities could include mortgages, long-term notes payable, bonds payable, leases, and pensions.

1. *Notes Payable:* Long-term notes payable might be issued when large items, such as machinery, equipment, or real estate, are purchased. Long-term notes payable are accounted for in the same way as short-term notes payable.

a. *Interest-bearing notes payable:* Most long-term notes payable are interest bearing, and any applicable interest should be accrued at the end of each accounting period.

b. *Noninterest-bearing notes payable:* If a long-term note payable is noninterest bearing, the interest imputed on the note should be recorded as a discount on notes payable.

(1) The discount on the notes payable account is a contra-liability, which is shown as a deduction from notes payable on the balance sheet. By using a discount account, the note is valued on the balance sheet at its present value.

(2) If the discount were not recorded, the cost of the item obtained in exchange for the note would be overstated.

c. *Imputing interest:* Interest should also be imputed on any long-term notes payable that have unreasonably low rates of interest. The discount on notes payable account is amortized to interest expense over the life of the note.

The following example is based on the same information as the example in Chapter 14, Section A-2. Accounting for noninterest-bearing notes payable parallels the accounting for noninterest-bearing notes receivable. The candidate should review both examples together to ensure a complete understanding of the concept.

EXAMPLE: Zebo Company issued a $10,000 two-year noninterest-bearing note payable to Moomey Company on January 1, 20XA. The note was given in exchange for merchandise. The interest rate normally charged in this type of transaction is 10 percent. The computation of interest to be imputed is as follows:

$$\frac{\$10{,}000}{1.21} = \$8{,}264 \text{ (For the formula, see Chapter 14, Section A-2.)}$$

The discount (interest) on the note would be as follows:

$$\$10{,}000 - 8{,}264 = \underline{\underline{\$1{,}736}}$$

The journal entry to record the issuance of the note would be as follows:

		dr	*cr*
Jan. 1	Purchases	8,264	
	Discount on notes payable	1,736	
	Notes payable		10,000

Issued a two-year noninterest-bearing note to Moomey Co. Interest was imputed at 10 percent.

The journal entry to accrue the first year's interest would be as follows:

		dr	*cr*
Dec. 31	Interest expense	826	
	Discount on notes payable		826

To record interest accrued on the Moomey Co. note payable (carrying value × interest rate × time, or $8,264 × 0.10 × 1 year).

The journal entry to record the payment of the note on December 31, 20XB, would be as follows:

		dr	*cr*
Dec. 31	Notes payable	10,000	
	Interest expense	910	
	Discount on notes payable		910
	Cash		10,000

To record payment of the Moomey Co. note and to write off the balance in the discount account.

2. *Mortgages:* Mortgages are legal agreements that protect the lender by giving him or her the right to be paid from the sale of specific assets that belong to the borrower.

a. *Installment payments:* Mortgages usually require equal monthly installment payments. These payments include a portion for payment of interest and a portion for payment of principal on the loan.

b. *Security:* Mortgages are usually secured by the asset (often real estate) that has been purchased with the mortgage.

Mortgages and installment notes are accounted for in the same way. The current portion of any mortgage (that portion that is to be paid within the next operating cycle) should be classified as a current asset. The following example illustrates typical accounting entries used for mortgages or installment notes.

EXAMPLE: Assume that Lloyd Corp. purchases real estate for $100,000 on January 1. The firm pays $25,000 cash and obtains a four-year 12 percent mortgage for $75,000. Lloyd Corp. makes the following entry to record the purchase of the real estate:

	dr	*cr*
Land	20,000	
Building	80,000	
Cash		25,000
Mortgage payable		75,000
Purchased real estate using cash and a four-year 12 percent mortgage.		

The monthly mortgage payments are $1,975. The following schedule shows the calculation of the portion of each payment that relates to interest and to principal for three months:

Payment Date	*Monthly Payment*	*Interest of 12% on Principal Balance*	*Principal Reduction*	*Unpaid Principal Balance*
1/1				$75,000.00
2/1	$1,975.00	$750.00[a]	$1,225.00	73,775.00
3/1	1,975.00	737.75[b]	1,237.25	72,537.75
4/1	1,975.00	725.38[c]	1,249.62	71,288.13

[a](75,000.00 × 0.12 × 1/12)
[b](73,775.00 × 0.12 × 1/12)
[c](72,537.75 × 0.12 × 1/12)

The entries to record the payments in February and March would be as follows:

		dr	*cr*
Feb. 1	Interest expense	750.00	
	Mortgage payable	1,225.00	
	Cash		1,975.00
Paid monthly mortgage payment.			
Mar. 1	Interest expense	737.75	
	Mortgage payable	1,237.25	
	Cash		1,975.00
Paid monthly mortgage payment.			

3. *Bonds Payable:* When an accounting entity wants to raise a large sum of money, long-term bonds payable might be issued. Bonds are usually sold to numerous investors. Bonds normally have a face value of $1,000 each and pay interest semiannually on the face value of the bond. Bonds are usually issued by large corporations or government entities.

a. *Types of bonds payable:* There are many different types of bonds payable. The basic characteristics of some of these types are explained briefly here.

(1) *Debentures:* Debentures are unsecured bonds payable. Debentures are usually issued by large, financially sound companies.

(2) *Mortgage bonds:* Mortgage bonds are secured by specific assets.

(3) *Term bonds:* Term bonds have a single fixed date of maturity.

(4) *Serial bonds:* Serial bonds have varying maturity dates but are issued at the same time. Issuing serial bonds avoids the cash flow drain that might occur when term bonds mature.

(5) *Callable bonds:* Callable bonds may be redeemed by the issuer prior to their maturity date through payment of a stipulated call price. Callable bonds allow the company to take advantage of interest rate changes over time.

(6) *Convertible bonds:* Convertible bonds have a special provision that allows the bond holder to convert the bonds into common stock of the issuing company. Convertible bonds are often issued as inducements to the lender.

(7) *Registered bonds:* Registered bonds have the name of the owner registered with the issuing company. The issuing company mails the interest checks to the registered owner.

(8) *Coupon bonds or bearer bonds:* Bearer bonds are not registered to a specific person. The owner of a bearer bond is assumed to be the person who has possession of the bond. Bearer bonds have coupons attached to them that, when an interest payment is due, the owner sends to the issuing company or to a bank acting as trustee. The issuer then pays the bond interest when the coupon is received.

b. *Sale of bonds:* Bonds are traded regularly on securities exchanges. Bonds may be held to maturity, or they may be sold on the market prior to maturity.

c. *Interest accrued on bonds sold:* When bonds are sold between interest dates, the purchaser must pay the seller for any interest that has accrued on the bonds. When the next interest payment date arrives, the issuer then pays the holder interest for the full six-month period.

EXAMPLE: Assume that Weller Corp. sells $1,000,000 of 10-year 12 percent bonds payable on March 1, 20XA. Interest is paid on the bonds on January 1 and July 1. The bonds are sold at face value. The entry to record the sale is as follows:

		dr	*cr*
Mar. 1	Cash	1,020,000	
	Bonds payable		1,000,000
	Bond interest payable		20,000
To record issuance of $1,000,000 of 10-year 12 percent bonds at face value plus two months' accrued interest ($1,000,000 × 0.12 × 2/12).			

The entry to record the semiannual interest payment on July 1 is as follows:

		dr	*cr*
July 1	Interest expense	40,000	
	Bond interest payable	20,000	
	Cash		60,000
Paid semiannual interest on 12 percent bonds ($1,000,000 × 0.12 × 2/12).			

d. *Recording of bonds payable:* Bonds payable are always recorded in the accounts at face value. However, bonds may be sold at an amount different from their face value.

EXAMPLE: Assume that the market rate of interest for bonds of the same grade as those sold by Weller Corp. was 15 percent. When Weller Corp. attempted to sell its 12 percent bonds on the market, investors would be unwilling to pay a full $1,000 for the bonds. This is because the bonds pay interest at an amount lower than the market rate of interest.

The purchaser would be willing to pay only enough for the bond so that the effective rate of interest on the bond would be equal to the market rate of interest. Usually, the coupon rate (also called the *contract,* or *stated, rate*) is fairly close to the market rate at the time of initial issue.

(1) Bond prices are quoted as a percentage of the bond's stated face value.

EXAMPLES: A $1,000 stated value bond quoted at 98 is selling at 98 percent of face value, or $980 ($1,000 × 0.98).

A bond quoted at 104 is selling at 104 percent of face value, or $1,040 ($1,000 × 1.04).

(2) When the market rate of interest is higher than the stated rate of interest paid by the bond, the bond will sell at a discount.

EXAMPLE: Onsi Corp. issued $1,000,000 of 20-year 8 percent bonds on July 1, 20XA. The market rate of interest for bonds of the same grade was higher than 8 percent, so the bonds sold at 97 ($970 for each $1,000 bond). The bonds were sold on an interest payment date. The entry to record issuance of the bonds would be as follows:

		dr	*cr*
July 1	Cash	970,000	
	Discount on bonds payable	30,000	
	Bonds payable		1,000,000
Issued 1,000 8 percent bonds at 97.			

Note: Bonds payable are always recorded at face value, as compared to bonds receivable, which are recorded at cost. Discount on bonds payable is a contra-liability account and is shown as a deduction from bonds payable on the balance sheet.

(3) When the market rate of interest is lower than the stated rate of interest paid by the bond, the bond will sell at a premium.

EXAMPLE: Zeta Corp. issued $1,000,000 of 10-year 15 percent bonds on January 1, 20XA. The market rate of interest for bonds of the same grade was lower than 15 percent, so the bonds sold at 105 ($1,050 for each $1,000 bond). The bonds were sold on an interest payment date. The entry to record issuance of the bonds would be as follows:

		dr	*cr*
Jan. 1	Cash	1,050,000	
	Premium on bonds payable		50,000
	Bonds payable		1,000,000
Issued 1,000 15 percent bonds at 105.			

Bond premium is an adjunct account. An adjunct account is related to another account and has a balance that is on the same side of an account as the account to which it is related. Premium on bonds payable is added to bonds payable on the balance sheet to report book value of the bonds.

(4) Bond premium or discount should be amortized to interest expense over the life of the bond. There are two methods of bond premium or discount amortization: the straight-line method and the effective-interest method. The purpose of the amortization of bond premium or discount is to reflect the effective rate of interest paid by the issuer on the bonds. The effective-interest method is a more accurate method of adjusting the interest paid to the effective rate.

e. *Bond redemption:* When bonds payable mature, the issuer pays the bond holders the face value of the bonds. At maturity, all of the bond premium or discount has been amortized, and the carrying value of the bonds is equal to the face value.

EXAMPLE: Assume that Zeta Corp. redeemed the $1,000,000 of bonds on their maturity date, January 1, 20XA. The entry to record the redemption would be as follows:

		dr	*cr*
Jan. 1	Bonds payable	1,000,000	
	Cash		1,000,000
Retired 15 percent bonds at maturity.			

(1) *Sinking fund:* Some bonds provide for the establishment of a sinking fund to accumulate sufficient funds to retire the bonds when they mature. The bond issuer makes periodic cash payments into the sinking fund, and the money is invested to earn a return. The sinking fund should cover the cost of retiring the bonds when they mature. Sinking funds are reported as a long-term investment on the balance sheet.

(2) *Redemption prior to maturity date:* Bonds may be redeemed prior to their maturity date, either through payment of the call price or by purchasing the bonds on the market. A gain or loss might be reported on the early redemption of bonds payable. Gains or losses from bond retirements should be reported as extraordinary items.

Review Questions

Directions: Select the correct answer from the four alternatives. Write the letter of your answer in the blank to the left of the number. Assume 360 days per year in all interest calculations.

_______________ **1.** Interest-bearing notes payable are reported on the balance sheet at

a. market value.
b. discounted present value.
c. face value less interest accrued.
d. face value.

_______________ **2.** Which of the following statements is true?

a. Simple interest is calculated based only on the principal amount of the note.
b. If two securities with a two-year life are identical in all ways except that one earns simple interest and the other earns compound interest, with monthly compounding, the security earning simple interest will earn the larger amount of interest.
c. The more often interest is compounded, the less the total amount of interest that is earned.
d. Interest must be imputed on short-term noninterest-bearing notes.

_______________ **3.** The method of calculating interest in which interest is earned on both principal and previously accumulated interest is called

a. compound interest.
b. accrued interest.
c. simple interest.
d. double interest.

_______________ **4.** A $40,000, two-year, noninterest-bearing note payable is issued. What is the amount of the discount on notes payable that should be recorded if the interest rate for comparable transactions is 5 percent? (Round your answer to the nearest dollar.)

a. $3,719
b. $4,000
c. $18,141
d. $36,281

_______________ **5.** Discount on notes payable is

a. an asset account.
b. an expense account.
c. a contra-liability account.
d. a contra-asset account.

______________ **6.** Jones Co. discounts its own $20,000 note payable (noninterest bearing) at the Second Security Bank. The bank discount rate is 9 percent. The note is due in 180 days. The proceeds received by Jones Co. are

a. $18,000.
b. $18,200.
c. $19,100.
d. $20,000.

______________ **7.** A legal agreement that gives the lender the right to be paid from the sale of specific assets that belong to the borrower is a/an

a. bond.
b. debenture.
c. mortgage.
d. note payable.

______________ **8.** Bonds payable normally pay interest

a. monthly.
b. quarterly.
c. annually.
d. semiannually.

______________ **9.** How should a bond sinking fund established to accumulate sufficient funds to retire bonds due in 10 years be classified on the balance sheet?

a. Long-term investment.
b. Long-term liability.
c. Current liability.
d. Current asset.

______________ **10.** Zeb Co. issued $200,000 of 10 percent (contract rate) bonds on May 1, 20XA. The market rate of interest for similar bonds on May 1, 20XA, was 8 percent. The bonds were sold at

a. a discount.
b. face value.
c. a premium.
d. 98 percent of face value.

______________ **11.** When bonds sell for less than face value, the difference between the selling price of the bonds and face value is called

a. adjunct on bonds payable.
b. premium on bonds payable.
c. discount on bonds payable.
d. interest receivable.

______________ **12.** Bond premium is

a. an asset account.

b. a contra-account.
c. deducted from bonds payable on the balance sheet.
d. added to bonds payable on the balance sheet.

_______________ **13.** A bond that is quoted at 105 would sell for

a. $1,005.
b. $1,050.
c. $1,055.
d. $1,500.

_______________ **14.** The entry to record payment of a $50,000 90-day 9 percent note payable would include

a. a credit to notes payable for $50,000.
b. a debit to notes payable for $51,125.
c. a credit to cash for $51,125.
d. a debit to interest expense for $1,000.

_______________ **15.** Installment notes payable are repaid through

a. periodic payments on principal only.
b. periodic payments on interest only.
c. periodic payments that include both principal and interest.
d. a lump-sum payment of principal and interest due.

Use the following information in answering Questions 16 and 17. Assume 360 days per year in all interest calculations.

Jack Nimble invested $10,000 at 10 percent for three years.

_______________ **16.** The total interest for the three-year period, assuming simple interest, is

a. $1,000.
b. $3,000.
c. $6,000.
d. $11,000.

_______________ **17.** The total interest for the three-year period, assuming compound interest, is

a. $2,100.
b. $3,000.
c. $3,310.
d. $6,000.

Use the following information in answering Questions 18 to 20. Assume 360 days per year in all interest calculations.

Jill Sykes Company made the following journal entry to record a two-year, noninterest-bearing note payable:

	dr	cr
Equipment	24,793	
Discount on notes payable	5,207	
Notes payable		30,000

The equipment was purchased on October 1, 20XA, and the interest rate was assumed to be 10 percent. Sykes Company's year end is December 31.

______________ **18.** The amount of interest expense to be recorded on December 31, 20XA, would be (rounded to the nearest dollar)

a. \$521.
b. \$620.
c. \$651.
d. \$2,479.

______________ **19.** The entry made by Sykes Company to record the accrued interest would include

a. a debit to interest expense and a credit to interest payable.
b. a debit to interest receivable and a credit to interest income.
c. a debit to discount on notes payable and a credit to interest income.
d. a debit to interest expense and a credit to discount on notes payable.

______________ **20.** The carrying value of the note on Sykes Company's December 31, 20XA, balance sheet would be

a. \$24,793.
b. \$25,143.
c. \$29,479.
d. \$30,000.

Solutions

Answer	*Refer to:*

1. (d) [A-1-a]

2. (a) [A-1-a(1)]

3. (a) [A-1-a(2)]

4. (a) [B-1]

$$\frac{\$40{,}000}{(1+0.05)^2} = \frac{\$40{,}000}{1.1025} = \$36{,}281 \text{ (present value of note)}$$

face value of note − present value of note = discount
$40,000 − $36,281 = $3,719

5. (c) [B-1]

6. (c) [A-1-c]
discount = $20,000 × 0.09 × 180/360 = $900
proceeds = face value − discount
$19,100 = $20,000 − $900

7. (c) [B-2]

8. (d) [B-3]

9. (a) [B-3-e(1)]

10. (c) [B-3-d(3)]

11. (c) [B-3-d(2)]

12. (d) [B-3-d(3)]

13. (b) [B-3-d(1)]
$1,000 × 1.05 = $1,050

14. (c) [A-1-a]
interest expense = $50,000 × 0.09 × 90/360 = $1,125
The journal entry to record payment of the note would be as follows:

	dr	*cr*
Notes payable	50,000	
Interest expense	1,125	
Cash		51,125

15. (c) [A-1-e]

16. (b) [A-1-a(1)]
$10,000 × 0.10 = 3 years = $3,000

17. (c) [A-1-a(2)]

Year 1	$10,000 × 0.10 =	$1,000
Year 2	($10,000 + 1,000) × 0.10 =	1,100
Year 3	($10,000 + 1,000 + 1,100) × 0.10 =	1,210
Total interest		$3,310

18. (b) [B-1] Interest expense would be computed as follows:
carrying value × interest rate × time = interest
$24,793[a] × 0.10 × 3/12 = $620

19. (d) [B-1]

20. (b) [B-1]

Notes payable	$30,000
− Discount on notes payable	− 4,857[b]
Carrying value of the note	$25,413

[a]Carrying value is equal to the face value of the note less the balance in the discount on notes payable account ($30,000 − $5,207 = $24,793).
[b]Discount on notes payable = $5,207 − $620 = $4,857.

CHAPTER 16

Owners' Equity

OVERVIEW

This chapter covers accounting and reporting for owners' equity. The three forms of business entities were introduced in Chapter 6 and are elaborated on further in this chapter. In Chapter 8 we introduced the recording of owners' equity on the balance sheet. The candidate might want to first review the owners' equity section of Chapter 8, where we emphasize accounting for the owners' equity of sole proprietorships, partnerships, and corporations. Accounting for the owners' equity of a corporation is more complex than accounting for the owners' equity of a sole proprietorship or a partnership, so the majority of the material in this chapter relates to corporations.

The candidate should understand the three basic types of business entities and their advantages and disadvantages as well as the recording of transactions affecting owners' equity in a sole proprietorship and a partnership. The candidate should also understand the following topics pertaining to corporations: the rights of and accounting for common and preferred stock, accounting for treasury stock, calculation of book value of stock, securities markets, and accounting for unappropriated and appropriated retained earnings.

KEY TERMS

Appropriated retained earnings
Authorized shares of capital stock
Book value
Callable preferred stock
Convertible preferred stock
Cumulative preferred stock
Dividends in arrears
Issued shares
Limited liability
Organized stock exchanges
Outstanding shares
Over-the-counter market
Par value
Participative preferred stock
Private placement
Treasury stock
Unappropriated retained earnings
Unlimited liability

A. Sole Proprietorships and Partnerships

As discussed in Chapter 6, sole proprietorships are businesses owned by one individual. Partnerships are businesses with two or more co-owners who share profits and losses. These forms of business carry with them certain advantages and disadvantages.

1. *Advantages of Sole Proprietorships and Partnerships:* The following advantages are common to both sole proprietorships and partnerships:

   a. *Formation:* Formation is relatively easy. No legal formalities are required to create the business.

b. *Regulation:* There is less regulation of the business during its existence than that involved in a corporation.

c. *Tax advantage:* A possible tax advantage exists. There is no double taxation of the business firm since no tax is assessed at the business level. All taxable income is passed through to the owners. Losses, too, may be passed through. However, the tax laws are extremely complicated, so it is best to seek expert advice relating to tax matters before deciding which form of business organization to use.

2. *Disadvantages of Sole Proprietorships and Partnerships:* Both these forms of business enterprises do not create new legal entities, as happens when a corporation is formed. Several disadvantages are common to both sole proprietorships and partnerships.

a. *Limited life:* Because the form of business is not a legal entity, the business terminates on the death or withdrawal of an owner.

b. *Unlimited liability:* The sole owner in a sole proprietorship and each general partner in a partnership are liable for the debts of the business, not only from business assets but also from personal assets.

c. *Limited capital-raising ability:* As compared to a corporation, both sole proprietorships and partnerships have far less ability to generate capital from contributors.

3. *Accounting for Owners' Equity:* In sole proprietorships and partnerships, accounting for owners' equity may be handled in the following ways:

a. *Sole proprietorships:* The accounting for a sole proprietorship is relatively simple (see Chapter 8). Owner's equity consists of one capital account that records all increases and decreases in owners' equity.

b. *Partnerships:* The accounting for a partnership was discussed in Chapter 8. In a partnership, capital accounts for each individual partner record the increases and decreases in the owner's equity for individual partners. Since there is more than one capital account in a partnership, one of the major differences between accounting for a sole proprietorship and a partnership is in the division of profit or loss.

(1) If no agreement is apparent among partners as to the sharing of profits, the division will be made equally, even if time or capital contributions devoted to the business are not equal. Losses will also be shared equally. However, if any agreement has been reached, either oral or written, that agreement will hold for both profits and losses in the same manner unless otherwise specified.

(2) The division of profits and losses can take many forms, depending on the agreement of the partners. Division may be according to a fixed ratio (e.g., 3:2:4) or a ratio reflecting capital contributed. Salaries may be allowed as a distribution of profit as well as interest on the capital balances.

Note: If salaries and/or interest are allowed as part of the distribution of income, they are not recorded as salary expense or interest expense.

EXAMPLE: The P and Q Partnership has a net income for the period of $25,000. The written agreement between P and Q specifies that each partner is to be allowed a salary of $7,000 and interest on invested capital of 10 percent. P has *invested $40,000 capital and Q $30,000. The division of profit is to be equal after accounting for the salary and interest allowances. Division of profits is as follows:*

Net income				$25,000
Salary Allowance:	P	$7,000		
	Q	7,000	$14,000	
Interest Allowance:	P	$4,000		
	Q	3,000	7,000	(21,000)
Remaining profit to be divided:				$ 4,000
	To P			$ 2,000
	To Q			$ 2,000

Each partner will then receive:

	P	Q
Salaries	$ 7,000	$ 7,000
Interest	4,000	3,000
Remainder	2,000	2,000
Totals	$13,000	$12,000

The $25,000 net income has been divided according to the partners' agreement.

The journal entry to record the distribution of income would be as follows:

	dr	*cr*
Income summary	25,000	
P, capital		13,000
Q, capital		12,000
To record distribution of net income for the period.		

B. Corporations

As discussed in Chapter 6, corporations are entities created by state or federal law that are separate and distinct from ownership interests. A corporation can hold and dispose of property, can contract in its own name, and can sue and be sued. This type of business entity carries with it certain advantages and disadvantages.

1. *Advantages of the Corporate Form of Ownership:* Corporations have a number of advantages, including limited liability for the shareholders, continuity of existence, capital-raising capacity, and quality of management.

a. *Limited liability:* The shareholder, or owner, in a corporation risks only the amount of his or her investment. Such a shareholder's personal assets are protected from corporate creditors by the limited liability feature.

b. *Continuity of life:* Since the corporation is a creature of law, its existence does not depend on continuous ownership by one or a group of individuals. This feature leads to free transferability of ownership interests. Shares in a corporation may be bought and sold freely without the issuing corporation's interference and without affecting the operations of the corporation.

c. *Capital-raising capacity:* The corporation is efficient as a mechanism for pooling the investments of many individuals. It can not only raise large amounts of capital but also use several means of raising capital. For example, bonds and several types of capital stock may be issued.

d. *Quality of management:* Owners need not devote time and energy to managing the entity. Instead, they can employ professional executives to accept the responsibility of management.

2. *Disadvantages of the Corporate Form of Ownership:* Double taxation and regulation costs are two of the primary disadvantages of the corporate form of business enterprise.

   a. *Double taxation:* Since the corporation is considered a legal entity, it is taxed on its earnings. The distribution of these earnings to the owners in the form of cash dividends is considered to be personal income to the shareholders and is again taxed. (See comments about taxation with respect to the sole proprietor.)

   b. *Regulation costs:* A corporation is regulated by federal and state governments, securities exchanges, and other bodies. The costs of this regulation may be high compared to other types of business entities.

C. Accounting for Stockholders' Equity in a Corporation

The ownership of a corporation consists of individuals who hold the shares of capital stock originally issued by the corporation in exchange for contributions of cash, property, or services. The stockholders' equity section of the balance sheet will display this contributed capital. Contributions are not the only source of capital for a corporation. If the business is successful and has income, management may want to retain some of these earnings in the corporation. The stockholders' equity section of the balance sheet allows for the recording of the retention of earnings.

1. *Contributed Capital:* A corporation has flexibility in the amounts and types of capital stock that it offers in exchange for capital. The amount of capital stock that can be offered to individuals is determined by the corporate charter filed with the state of incorporation. This is known as the *authorized amount* and cannot be exceeded. The amount of stock that has actually been issued to investors is known as the *issued amount.* The amount that is in the hands of stockholders is the *outstanding amount.* These three amounts may be identical; however, they need not be the same. (Some authorized shares may not have been issued to investors, and some shares that were issued to investors may have been repurchased by the company and are no longer considered outstanding. When a corporation holds treasury stock, the treasury shares are still classified as issued, but they are no longer considered outstanding since they are not in the hands of shareholders.) Flexibility in the types of capital stock offered to investors exists. The two major types of capital stock are common stock and preferred stock.

   a. *Common stock:* Common stock is the basic unit of ownership in a corporation. If a corporation has only one class of capital stock, it will be common stock. Common stock carries with it four basic rights that are inherent in its ownership unless specified otherwise by the corporation on issue or waived by the stockholder after issuance. These rights are as follows:

      (1) *The right to have a voice in management:* Stockholders elect the board of directors, which is responsible for the overall management of the firm. Stockholders are also able to vote on matters such as the issuance of long-term debt or the amendment of the state charter.

      (2) *The right to share in profits on distribution:* Each shareholder is entitled to obtain a proportionate share of the earnings of the corporation in the form

of dividends based on the number of shares owned. This right does not begin until and unless dividends are declared by the board of directors.

(3) *The right to maintain percentage ownership in the corporation:* Each shareholder may have the right to purchase additional shares of stock in new issues at market value to maintain his or her percentage of ownership in the firm. This is often called the *preemptive right.*

(4) *The right to share in assets on liquidation:* Common stockholders have a residual claim: In the event of liquidation, common stockholders cannot receive any distributions unless creditors and preferred stockholders, if any, have received their claims. Once these claims have been paid, common shareholders are entitled to the remaining or residual assets in relation to proportional ownership in the firm.

b. *Basic accounting for common stock:*

(1) *Issuance of common stock:* At authorization in the corporate charter, common stock may be given a par value. *Par value* is a fixed amount printed on the face of the stock certificate. In many states, par value represents the minimum legal capital of the corporation. This means that an individual who buys stock from a corporation must give the corporation at least par value for the stock or be liable for the difference. Most states prohibit the issuance of stock at less than par value. Although par value may bear some relationship to the original price, it is often arbitrarily set and should not be confused with market value in any way. On the issuance of par value common stock, the asset cash is increased with a debit for the total amount received by the corporation. The common stock account is increased or credited for par value. The remainder, if any, is a credit and is placed in the paid-in capital in excess of par account.

EXAMPLE: Zeta Company issues 100 shares of its $10 par value stock for $28 per share. The journal entry to record this transaction is as follows:

	dr	*cr*
Cash	2,800	
Common stock		1,000
Paid-in capital in excess of par		1,800
Issued 100 shares of common stock @ $28 per share. ($10 par × 100 shares par value; $2,800 − $1,000 = $1,800 paid-in capital in excess of par).		

(a) The issuance of common stock for assets other than cash is recorded in the same manner, with the asset account increased (debited) for market value of the asset and common stock and paid-in capital increased (credited) exactly as in the Zeta Company example.

(b) At one time all stocks were required to have a par value. Since par value might mislead investors as to the "true value" of a share of stock, and since sale of stock at less than par value results in a contingent liability, the issuance of stock that does not have a par value (no-par stock) is allowed. The main advantage of no-par stock is that it may be issued at any price. When no-par stock is issued, the asset cash is debited for the amount received, and the common stock account is credited for the total amount received.

Note: These entries are only for the original issuance of stock by the corporation. Subsequent trading of the stock by investing individuals does not necessitate any entries on the part of the corporation because of the transferability characteristic of corporate stock.

(2) *Dividend payments on common stock:*

(a) *Cash dividends:* Cash dividends on common stock are not an expense of the corporation but rather a distribution of earnings to the owners. Dividend declarations are at the discretion of the board of directors. Once declared, the cash dividend amount becomes a liability of the corporation until paid.

On declaration, the debit is to dividends declared (or retained earnings). The credit increases the liability account, dividends payable. The date of payment occurs a few weeks later. At this date the liability is removed with a debit, and cash is decreased with a credit. A cash dividend, then, reduces both assets and stockholders' equity since funds are severed from the business. Dividends declared is a temporary account that is closed to retained earnings.

The entry to record declaration of a $1,000 cash dividend is as follows:

	dr	*cr*
Dividends declared	1,000	
Dividends payable		1,000

The entry to record payment of the $1,000 cash dividend previously declared is as follows:

	dr	*cr*
Dividends payable	1,000	
Cash		1,000

(b) *Stock dividends:* A stock dividend of common stock is a distribution of additional shares of common stock to existing common stockholders based on the quantity of shares currently held. A stock dividend is a distribution of earnings just as is a cash dividend. The difference lies in the payment: stock rather than cash.

On declaration, the stock dividends declared (or retained earnings) account is debited, and a stockholders' equity account, stock dividends to be distributed, is credited. There is no liability since there is no obligation to pay cash or any other asset. On payment, stock dividends to be distributed is cleared with a debit and common stock is credited. Note that the net effect of this event merely reduces one stockholders' equity account (retained earnings) and increases another (common stock). The total stockholders' equity remains unchanged as well as each stockholder's relative ownership percentage. Stock dividends declared is a temporary account that is closed to retained earnings.

A stock dividend of more than 20 to 25 percent of the number of shares previously outstanding is considered a large stock dividend. When a large stock dividend is declared, the par value per share times the number of shares to be distributed is transferred from retained earnings to common stock.

If a stock dividend is considered a small stock dividend, the market value of the shares distributed is transferred from retained earnings to common stock and paid-in capital in excess of par.

The entry to record declaration of a small stock dividend of 1,000 shares with a market value of $10.00 and a par value of $1.00 is as follows:

	dr	*cr*
Stock dividend declared	10,000	
Stock dividends to be distributed		1,000
Paid-in capital in excess of par		9,000

The entry to record the distribution of the $1,000 stock dividend declared above is as follows:

	dr	*cr*
Stock dividends to be distributed	1,000	
Common stock		1,000

c. *Preferred stock:* Preferred stock is a form of contributed capital with features that distinguish it from common stock. Generally, preferred stock will have a preference over common stock with respect to one or more of the rights of common stock (such as dividend payments or receipt of assets if the corporation liquidates) with a sacrifice of another of the rights (voting power or participation in the distribution of earnings past some specified date). The basic accounting for preferred stock involves its issuance, dividend payments, and termination of the preferred status.

(1) *Issuance of preferred stock:* The issuance of preferred stock is similar to the issuance of common stock, except that the par value, if any, is entered into a preferred stock account.

EXAMPLE: If 10 shares of Beta Company's preferred stock (par value $100) are issued for $105 each, the entry would be as follows:

	dr	*cr*
Cash	1,050	
Preferred stock		1,000
Paid-in capital in excess of par/preferred stock		50
Issued 10 shares of preferred stock for $105 ($100 par × 10 shares par value; $1,050 − $1,000 = $50 paid-in capital in excess of par).		

(2) *Dividend payments on preferred stock:* Dividend payments on preferred stock are in cash and are stated as a percentage of par value.

EXAMPLE: If par is $100 on a share of preferred stock and the dividend rate is 9 percent, the dividend payment would be as follows:

$$9\% \times \$100 \text{ par} = 0.09 \times 100 = \$9 \text{ per share}$$

This stock may also be referred to as *$9 preferred.*

(a) *Payment of dividends:* Dividends are payable only at the discretion of the board of directors. Once dividends are declared, preferred dividends normally take precedence over dividends on common stock.

EXAMPLE: The Miller Corporation has 100 shares of $9 preferred stock and 1,000 shares of common stock, and the board of directors declares a $2,000 dividend. The distribution will be as follows:

Preferred stock		$ 900
($9 × 100 shares)		
Common stock		1,100
($2,000 − 900 = $1,100		
Per share:		
Preferred stock	$9.00	
Common stock	$1.10	
($1,100/1,000 shares)		

(b) *Cumulative dividends and participation:* Two features with respect to dividends make preferred stock a more attractive investment. These two features are cumulative dividends and participation.

One reason for investment in preferred stock is the expectation of a regular stream of dividends of a fixed amount. Without a cumulative dividends feature, any dividends not declared in a period will be lost forever. Therefore, most preferred stock is issued with a *cumulative dividends* feature, which signifies that any dividends not paid in any one period to the preferred stockholders (called *dividends in arrears*) must be made up before any current dividends to preferred or common stock can be distributed. These dividends in arrears are not a liability since no liability exists until declaration. Dividends in arrears are not recorded in the accounting records.

Normally, preferred stock has no right to share in earnings above the stated rate, even if the corporation has high earnings. One desirable feature of preferred stock is *participation.* Participation means that preferred shareholders may not only receive their stated dividend but also share in earnings of the corporation when they are high. Participating preferred stock will never receive less than the stated dividend when dividends are declared. Many preferred stock issues contain the cumulative feature, with relatively few participating.

(3) *Termination of the preferred status:* Some preferred stocks carry features that make them terminable at the option of either the issuing corporation or the stockholder.

(a) *Callable preferred stock:* If a preferred stock is callable, the issuing corporation may call, or redeem, the stock at a date after issue for a stipulated price, usually slightly higher than the issue price. Callable preferred stock allows the issuing corporation to raise capital without the loss of control by the existing shareholders. The corporation has the prerogative of redeeming the stock should the funds prove unnecessary in the future.

(b) *Convertible preferred stock:* If a preferred stock is convertible, the stockholder can exchange the preferred stock at his or her option for a predetermined number of shares of common stock. Convertible preferred stock allows the shareholder to participate in periods of high growth by conversion to higher common stock dividends and market value. In this way the former preferred shareholder now has an equity interest in higher earnings, which usually translate to higher market value of the stock.

d. *Treasury stock:* The shares of its own capital stock reacquired by a corporation are referred to as *treasury stock.* Treasury stock is reacquired for various purposes (e.g., to be used in an employee bonus plan). Treasury stock can be reissued at any time or held in the treasury indefinitely. While in the treasury, the stock carries none of the rights of the other shares in its class (such as cash dividends or voting). On the acquisition of shares for the treasury, the stockholders' equity contra-account, treasury stock, is debited to increase the account, and the cash account is credited for the cost of the treasury stock.

EXAMPLE: The reacquisition of 10 shares of $100 par common stock originally issued at $115 per share for $1,300 ($130 per share) would be recorded as follows:

	dr	*cr*
Treasury stock	1,300	
Cash		1,300
To record reacquisition of 10 shares.		

Even though it has a debit balance, the treasury stock account does not represent an asset. It is deducted from total stockholders' equity on the balance sheet at its reacquisition cost since the company, in effect, has become smaller.

e. *Book value:* Book value per share of common stock is a numerical measure of the net assets of a corporation as reflected in a single share of common stock. Book value is not market value but rather is computed by referring to the accounting records. Assume stockholders' equity presented as follows:

Common stock (100,000 shares)	$ 200,000
Preferred stock (2,000 shares)	200,000
Paid-in capital in excess of par	500,000
Retained earnings	900,000
Total stockholders' equity	$1,800,000

Since the common shares have a residual claim, all of the net assets belong to the common stockholders except that which belongs to the preferred shareholders. In this example, book value per common share would be as follows:

Total stockholders' equity	$1,800,000
Less: Par value of preferred stock ($100 × 2,000 shares)	– 200,000
Equity allocated to common stock	$1,600,000
Divided by: Number of common shares outstanding	100,000
Book value per share of common stock	$16

The number of common shares that is divided into the equity allocated to common stock represents the shares outstanding, which indicates that any unissued or treasury shares would not be included in the computation.

f. *Securities markets:*

(1) *Original issues markets:* The issuing corporation offers its securities in exchange for capital. A new issue of securities may be offered to the public through an investment banker (or underwriter) who is a specialist in marketing

securities to investors. Original issues of securities may also be sold through private placement. *Private placement* is the sale of an entire issue of securities by the issuing corporation directly to one or a few large institutional investors. The offering is not open to the public.

(2) *Secondary markets:* Securities are exchanged among the general public in the secondary markets. Organized stock exchanges are markets for securities where buy and sell orders are matched at public auction. Organized exchanges may be national (New York Stock Exchange and American Stock Exchange) or may be regional or local. The *over-the-counter market* consists of all markets for securities except organized exchanges. In the over-the-counter market, securities dealers maintain inventories of over-the-counter securities and sell these to the public at bid-and-ask prices.

2. *Retained Earnings:* Retained earnings is the portion of stockholders' equity that arises from the retention of earnings in the corporation. The retained earnings account is a historical record of all net income (or loss) from the time of incorporation to the present date less any distributions of earnings to stockholders in the form of cash or stock dividends.

a. *Increases in retained earnings:* The retained earnings account has a normal credit balance but may have a debit balance should accumulated losses be large. In this case, it is presented on the balance sheet as a deficit, or negative balance. The retained earnings account is increased with a credit entry. Increases result from net income in any period. Increases will also result from releases from the appropriations account.

b. *Decreases in retained earnings:* The retained earnings account is decreased with a debit entry. Decreases will result from a net loss in any period or a transfer to an appropriations account. Decreases will also result from the declaration of cash or stock dividends.

c. *Appropriated retained earnings:* The division of the retained earnings account into two or more separate accounts is achieved by the appropriation of retained earnings. The purpose of this segregation is to inform the financial statement reader that a portion of retained earnings is not available for the payment of dividends. Since the declaration of dividends is at the discretion of the board of directors in all cases, appropriations are not a mandatory accounting procedure. Alternatively, this information may be given in a footnote, which is the most prevalent practice.

Should an appropriation of retained earnings be desired, the entry will be a debit to reduce unappropriated retained earnings and a credit to establish one or more appropriations accounts:

	dr	*cr*
Unappropriated retained earnings	xx	
Retained earnings appropriated		xx

The total amount of retained earnings remains the same. This appropriation may be voluntary, as in the case of plant expansion, or it may result from contractual or legal obligations, such as long-term loan covenants restricting the payment of cash dividends. Note that the appropriation of retained earnings does not provide cash or other assets. It is not a source of funds. Conversely, a lack of an appropri-

Figure 16–1 Owners' Equity Section/Financial Statement

Stockholders' equity			
Cumulative 10% preferred stock, $100 par, 9,000 shares authorized and issued	900,000		
Common stock, $1 par, authorized 1,000,000 shares, issued 500,000 shares of which 2,000 shares are held in the treasury	500,000		
Paid-in capital in excess of par value	3,100,000		
Total contributed capital		4,500,000	
Retained earnings			
Appropriated for contingencies	800,000		
Unappropriated retained earnings	2,524,000	3,324,000	
Total paid-in capital and retained earnings		7,824,000	
Less: Treasury stock 2,000 shares (at cost)		20,000	
Total stockholders' equity			7,804,000

ations account does not ensure that cash will be available for the declaration of cash dividends. An appropriation of retained earnings is a convention of accounting designed to provide information only. The retained earnings account has its own financial statement presentation (refer to Chapter 8).

Figure 16–1 shows an example of a complete owners' equity section shown in financial statement format, illustrating all the points discussed in this chapter.

Review Questions

Directions: Select the correct answer from the four alternatives. Write the letter of your answer in the blank to the left of the number.

_______________ **1.** An arbitrary value placed on a share of stock at the time a corporation seeks authorization is called

a. statutory value.
b. par value.
c. preferred value.
d. stock value.

_______________ **2.** Each partner in a general partnership is personally liable for

a. only the amount he or she contributed to the partnership.
b. his or her proportionate share of the partnership debts.
c. all of the partnership's business debts.
d. the amount he or she contributed to the partnership plus his or her proportionate share of income retained in the business.

_______________ **3.** Cumulative preferred stock dividends in arrears

a. are recorded as a liability.
b. are recorded as an asset.
c. must be paid before any current dividends to preferred or common stockholders can be distributed.
d. do not need to be paid before dividends for the current year can be distributed to common stockholders.

_______________ **4.** Which of the following is normally a right of common stockholders?

a. The right to vote on all decisions affecting the company.
b. The right to demand a share of the profits.
c. The right to purchase as many shares as they wish when additional shares are sold.
d. The right to share in assets on liquidation.

_______________ **5.** Treasury stock is shown on the balance sheet as

a. an asset.
b. a reduction from stockholders' equity.
c. a liability.
d. an increase in stockholders' equity.

_______________ **6.** Sood Company had a balance of $20,000 in retained earnings on 1/1/20XA. During the year 20XA, the company earned $5,000 in net income and declared $2,000 in dividends. The 12/31/20XA balance in retained earnings should be

a. $20,000.
b. $22,000.

c. $23,000.
d. $25,000.

_____________ **7.** Joseph and Alexander own a partnership. They have not made an agreement regarding how profits and losses should be split. Profits and losses will be distributed

a. in proportion to their capital contributions.
b. in proportion to the time they devote to the business.
c. equally.
d. according to a formula based on both their capital contributions and the time they devote to the business.

_____________ **8.** Preferred stock that may be exchanged by the stockholder for a predetermined number of shares of common stock is called

a. convertible preferred stock.
b. callable preferred stock.
c. cumulative preferred stock.
d. preferred stock in arrears.

_____________ **9.** The right of common stockholders to maintain their proportionate interest in a corporation is called the

a. preemptive right.
b. proportional right.
c. shareholder's right.
d. participative right.

_____________ **10.** On June 30, 20XA, XYZ Corporation declared a dividend of $2.00 per share to the common stockholders of record July 10, 20XA, to be paid July 20, 20XA. XYZ Corporation has 5,000 authorized shares and 3,000 outstanding shares. The journal entry to be made on June 30 would be

	dr	*cr*
a. Dividends declared	10,000	
Common dividends payable		10,000
b. Dividends declared	6,000	
Common dividends payable		6,000
c. Retained earnings	6,000	
Dividends declared		6,000
d. No journal entry would be made on June 30.		

_____________ **11.** Using the information from Question 10, the journal entry to be made on July 20 would be

	dr	*cr*
a. Dividends declared	6,000	
Cash		6,000
b. Common dividends payable	10,000	
Cash		10,000
c Common dividends payable	6,000	
Cash		6,000
d. No journal entry would be made on July 20.		

_____________ **12.** Zeno Corporation issued 20,000 shares of $1.00 par value common stock for $10 per share. The journal entry to record this transaction would include a

a. credit to common stock for $200,000.
b. debit to cash for $180,000.
c. credit to common stock for $20,000.
d. debit to cash for $20,000.

_____________ **13.** Original issues of stock may be sold

a. by private placement to large institutional investors.
b. on the American Stock Exchange.
c. over the counter.
d. on local organized stock exchanges.

_____________ **14.** The paid-in capital in excess of par account is

a. shown as part of the contributed capital section of stockholders' equity on the income statement.
b. credited for the excess of market price over par value on the original issuance of stock.
c. used only when stock is sold for cash.
d. shown as an asset on the balance sheet.

_____________ **15.** Failure to record the declaration and distribution of a stock dividend (dividend issued in stock) would

a. cause assets to be understated.
b. cause total stockholders' equity to be overstated.
c. cause total stockholders' equity to be understated.
d. have no effect on total stockholders' equity.

_____________ **16.** An appropriation of retained earnings

a. reduces the total retained earnings of the company.
b. is used to inform the financial statement readers that a portion of retained earnings is not available for the payment of dividends.
c. is a mandatory procedure when all the retained earnings of the company are not available for dividend payment.
d. provides cash for payment of dividends.

Use the following information in answering Questions 17 to 19.

Brown and Smith own a partnership. The written agreement between Brown and Smith specifies that each partner is to be allowed a salary of $10,000 and interest on invested capital of 12 percent. Smith has invested $60,000 in the partnership, and Brown has invested $20,000. The division of profit after salaries and interest have been accounted for is to be made equally.

_____________ **17.** Assuming that the partnership has net income of $40,000 for the period, the amount allocated to Brown would be

a. $17,600.
b. $20,000.

c. $22,400.
d. $30,000.

______ **18.** Assuming that the partnership has net income of $40,000, the journal entry to record the distribution of earnings would include a debit to

a. each partner's capital account and a credit to income summary.
b. income summary and a credit to each partner's capital account.
c. salaries expense, a debit to interest expense, a debit to income summary, and a credit to each partner's capital account.
d. cash and a credit to each partner's capital account.

______ **19.** The stockholders' equity of Martin Corporation is as follows:

Preferred stock, $100 par value	
100 shares outstanding	$100,000
Common stock, $10 par value	
10,000 shares outstanding	100,000
Paid-in capital in excess of par—common	100,000
Retained earnings	500,000
	$800,000
Less treasury stock (2,000 shares)	−150,000
Total stockholders' equity	$650,000

What is the book value per common share?

a. $25.00
b. $68.75
c. $75.00
d. $87.50

Use the following information in answering Questions 20 and 21.

Morgan Corporation has 100 shares of $100 par 10 percent cumulative preferred stock outstanding. Two years' dividends are in arrears on the preferred stock. (No dividends were paid in 20XA and 20XB.) There are 10,000 shares of common stock outstanding. Morgan Corporation declares a $10,000 cash dividend at the end of 20XC.

______ **20.** The total amount of the $10,000 dividend that will be paid to the preferred shareholders is

a. $100.
b. $1,000.
c. $2,000.
d. $3,000.

____________ **21.** The amount that common stockholders will receive per share is

a. $0.70.
b. $0.80.
c. $0.99.
d. $1.00.

Solutions

Answer	*Refer to:*
1. (b)	[C-1-b(1)]
2. (c)	[A-1-a]
3. (c)	[C-1-b(2)]
4. (d)	[C-1-a]
5. (b)	[C-1-d]
6. (c)	[C-2] \$20,000 + \$5,000 − \$2,000 = \$23,000
7. (c)	[A-3-b]
8. (a)	[C-1-c]
9. (a)	[C-1-a(3)]
10. (b)	[C-1-b(2)(a)] Dividends are paid to outstanding shares (3,000 shares × \$1.00 per share).
11. (c)	[C-1-b(2)(a)]
12. (c)	[C-1-b(1)] The journal entry to record this transaction would be as follows:

Cash	200,000[a]	
Common stock (at par)		20,000[b]
Paid-in capital in excess of par		180,000[c]

13. (a)	[C-1-f(1)]
14. (b)	[C-1-b(1)]
15. (d)	[C-1-b(2)(b)] A stock dividend results in a transfer from retained earnings to contributed capital. If this entry were omitted, total stockholders' equity would be correct, but the components of stockholders' equity would be misstated.
16. (b)	[C-2-c]

[a]20,000 shares × \$10.00 per share = \$200,000.
[b]20,000 shares × \$1.00 per share = \$20,000.
[c]Cash paid − par value = \$200,000 − \$20,000 = \$180,000.

17. (a) [A-3-b] The allocation of income would be as follows:

	Smith	Brown	Total
Income to be split			$40,000
Salary	$10,000	$10,000	(20,000)
Interest	7,200	2,400	(9,600)
Balance to be			$10,400
split equally	5,200	5,200	(10,400)
	$22,400	$17,600	0

18. (b) [A-3-b]

19. (b) [C-1-e]

Total stockholders' equity	$650,000
Less: Par value of preferred stock	(100,000)
Equity available to common shares	$550,000

$$\frac{\text{Equity available to common shares}}{\text{Common shares outstanding}} = \frac{\$550{,}000}{8{,}000^{d}} = \$68.75$$

20. (d) [C-1-c(2)(b)]

Dividends in arrears (100 × $100 × 0.10)	20XA	$1,000
Dividends in arrears	20XB	1,000
Current dividend	20XC	1,000
Total preferred dividend		$3,000

21. (a) [C-1-b(2)(a)]
$7,000[e]/10,000 shares = $0.70/share

[d] 10,000 − 2,000 = 8,000.
[e] $10,000 total dividend − $3,000 allocable to preferred stock.

CHAPTER 17

Income Statement Accounts

OVERVIEW

This chapter covers accounting for revenues and expenses. (The general accounting for revenue and expense accounts is covered in Chapter 7. The candidate should review this material if necessary.) In this chapter we emphasize accounting for payroll, payroll-related expenses, and accounting for individual federal income taxes. In studying the material related to payroll and income taxes, the candidate should focus review on definitions and methods of recording rather than tax rates or amounts of exclusions since these amounts are subject to frequent change by the federal government.

The candidate should understand the recording of revenues and expenses in general; the specific treatment of payroll, payroll taxes, and payroll fringe benefits; and the treatment of individual federal income taxes.

KEY TERMS

Capital assets	FICA tax	Short-term capital gain or loss
Capital gain	Long-term capital gain or loss	
Capital loss		

A. Revenues

Revenues are earnings resulting from the receipt of cash or other assets (or the reduction of a liability) in exchange for goods sold by an entity or services performed by an entity. (A complete discussion of revenues is presented in Chapter 7.)

B. Expenses

Expenses are the cost of goods and services consumed (used up) by an entity as a result of earning revenue. (A complete discussion of expenses is presented in Chapter 7.)

1. *Operating Expenses:* Operating expenses are those expenses related to the normal operations of a business. They include selling expenses and general or administrative expenses.

   EXAMPLES OF OPERATING EXPENSES: Salaries, payroll taxes, sales commissions, advertising, state and local taxes, telephone, legal fees, insurance, depreciation, and bad debt expense.

   a. *Payroll accounting:* Accounting for payroll expenses includes more than just recording the cash paid out for salaries. Companies must also account for health insurance (if provided), employees' income tax that is withheld, social security

(FICA) taxes, union dues (if applicable), pension plans, savings bond purchases, and employer payroll taxes.

(1) *Income tax withheld:* Employers are required to withhold a portion of their employees' gross wages for payment of federal income taxes. They are also required to keep records of the tax withheld. These taxes must be remitted to the federal government periodically. State and local income taxes might also be required to be withheld from the employees' pay. The amount withheld for federal income tax purposes is based on withholding tax tables provided by the government. These tables are based on the amount of the employees' earnings, the frequency of pay periods, and the number of exemptions to which each employee is entitled.

(2) *FICA tax:* Federal Insurance Contributions Act tax must also be withheld from each employee's pay. Employers withhold a specific percentage of each employee's earnings until a maximum limit is reached. The employer must also pay a tax at the same rate as the employee. The rate used to calculate FICA tax and the base salary (maximum amount that will be taxed) have changed frequently in recent years. The rate in effect in 1998 was 6.2 percent on the first $68,400 of gross income. For simplicity, it is assumed in this chapter that the rate is 7 percent on the first $50,000 of income.

EXAMPLE: Assume that Chase Co. has two employees, Howe and Peters. Howe earned $2,000 for the month of May. Howe's gross pay for the year as of May 1 was $10,000. Peters earned $12,000 for the month of May. Peters' gross pay for the year as of May 1 was $47,000. Chase Co. would withhold $140 of Howe's earnings for payment of FICA taxes ($2,000 × 0.07 = $140). Chase Co. would withhold $210 of Peters' earnings for payment of FICA taxes ($3,000 × 0.07 = $210). Only $3,000 of Peters' May earnings are subject to FICA tax since Peters reached the $50,000 limit in May. Chase Co. will have to match the amount paid by the employees, so they must remit a total of $700 to the federal government for FICA taxes related to payroll in May.

(3) *Federal Hospital Insurance Tax:* Both the employer and the employee pay this tax at the rate of 1.45 percent on the employee's total compensation. The combination of the FICA tax and the Federal Hospital Insurance tax are often called the *social security tax.*

(4) *Voluntary deductions from employees' pay:* The employee might also have other amounts withheld from pay such as insurance premiums, pension plan payments, and purchase of savings bonds. The employer must keep records of all voluntary deductions.

Note: Amounts withheld from employees' pay are part of salary expense to the company. The amount withheld represents a liability for the company since employees' earnings are held until payment is remitted to the appropriate party.

(5) *Employer payroll expenses:* The employer is liable for specific contributions toward social security as well as payments for state and federal unemployment insurance and fringe benefits provided for employees.

(a) *Social security tax:* The employer's portion of the FICA tax and the Federal Hospital Insurance tax are employer payroll expenses.

(b) *Federal unemployment insurance tax:* Employers must pay an amount for Federal Unemployment Insurance Tax. This tax is levied only on the employer, and no portion is deducted from the employee's pay. Like FICA taxes, the rates used to calculate federal unemployment tax change periodically. The rate in effect in 1997 was 6.2 percent on the first $7,000 paid to an employee. The employer is allowed to take a maximum credit of 5.4 percent for contributions to state unemployment programs. For most companies, the net federal tax is 0.8 percent on the first $7,000.

(c) *State unemployment tax:* The states administer distribution of unemployment insurance payments and also collect a state unemployment tax. Most states only tax the employer for unemployment tax, but a few states also tax the employee. Many states use 5.4 percent on the first $7,000 as the basic rate for unemployment taxes. Most states assign a merit rating based on the employment history of the company. A company that has a favorable merit rating will normally have its state unemployment tax rate reduced.

(d) *Employee fringe benefits:* The employer might also provide fringe benefits such as paid vacations, health insurance (the employer might pay all or a portion of the premiums), retirement plans, and paid holidays. These fringe benefits are a substantial amount for most companies.

EXAMPLE: This example illustrates the recording of payroll and related expenses for one payroll period. Nelson Company's employees earned gross pay of $10,000 for the week ending August 31, 20XA. The net cash paid out to employees was $7,000. The following amounts were withheld from the employees' gross pay:

Federal income tax	$2,000
State income tax	200
FICA tax	700
Health insurance premiums	100

The employer payroll taxes were $700 for FICA, $60 for federal unemployment tax, and $180 for state unemployment tax. The employer expenses for fringe benefits were $750 for the retirement plan and $200 for health insurance. The entries to record the payroll and related expenditures were as follows:

		dr	*cr*
Aug. 31	Salary expense	10,000	
	Federal income tax withholding payable		2,000
	State income tax withholding payable		200
	FICA tax withholding payable		700
	Insurance withholding payable		100
	Salaries payable		7,000
To record salaries for the week of August 31.			

		dr	cr
Aug. 31	Salaries payable	7,000	
	Cash		7,000
To record payment of August 31 salaries.			
Aug. 31	Payroll taxes expense	940	
	FICA tax payable		700
	State unemployment tax payable		60
	Federal unemployment tax payable		180
To record employer payroll taxes for salaries for the week of August 31.			
Aug. 31	Payroll benefits expense	950	
	Retirement plan payable		750
	Health insurance payable		200
To record expenses for benefits associated with August 31 payroll.			

(6) *Accrual of payroll-related taxes and expenses:* When payroll is accrued at the end of the accounting period, all the payroll-related taxes and expenses should also be accrued. This results in proper matching of revenues and expenses. Payroll taxes are not a legal liability until the salaries are paid. Therefore, some businesses do not accrue payroll taxes.

(7) *Payroll liabilities:* Liabilities related to payroll are recorded as current liabilities.

(8) *Filing of quarterly reports:* A business must file quarterly reports with the government showing the amounts withheld from employees' earnings for federal income taxes and FICA taxes. Payroll taxes must be accounted for on a calendar-year basis in reporting to the government. Amounts withheld from employees must be deposited periodically. The frequency of deposit depends on the amount of taxes withheld. If the total amount is very small, it may be remitted with the quarterly tax returns. If the amounts withheld are significant, they must be deposited with a Federal Reserve Bank or a designated commercial bank on a frequent basis.

2. *Federal Individual Income Taxes:* Individuals must pay federal income tax on the amount of taxable income they earn. Taxable income is calculated as follows:

Income
Less: Adjustments to income
Adjusted gross income (AGI)
Less: Personal and dependency exemptions
Itemized deductions or standard deductions (whichever is greater)
= Taxable income

a. *Income:* Some of the common items included in income are wages, salaries, tips, taxable interest income, dividend income, taxable refunds of state and local income tax, alimony received, business income, capital gains, rents, bonuses, and royalties. Some of the common items excluded from gross income include accident insurance proceeds, child support payments, cost-of-living allowances (for military), damages for personal injury or sickness, gifts, disability benefits, life insurance paid on death, a limited amount of social security benefits, certain scholarship grants, and inheritances.

b. *Gains and losses from property transactions:* When property is disposed of, a gain or loss may result. Gains are generally recognizable for income tax purposes. Losses from the disposition of property held for personal use (not for investment or used in a trade or business) are not recognizable for tax purposes. To determine the appropriate tax treatment of a recognizable gain or loss, the amount of the gain or loss must be classified as *ordinary or capital.* Usually, ordinary gains and losses result from the disposition of assets not classified as capital items.

c. *Capital gains and losses:* Capital gains and losses result from the disposition of capital assets. The U.S. Internal Revenue Code defines capital assets as any property a taxpayer holds that is not listed in Section 1221. Inventory, accounts receivable, and depreciable property or real estate used in a business are classified as Section 1221 property.

EXAMPLE: Individual capital assets include property held for personal use, such as a house or a car, and assets held for investment purposes, such as securities.

Capital gains must be classified as short term or long term in nature to determine the appropriate tax treatment.

(1) *Short-term capital gains or losses:* Short-term capital gains or losses result from dispositions of capital assets held for one year or less. Short-term gains and losses must initially be offset to determine net short-term capital gain or loss.

(2) *Long-term capital gains or losses:* Long-term capital gains or losses result from dispositions of capital assets held for more than one year. Long-term capital losses are used to offset long-term capital gains.

(3) *Net short-term capital gains or losses:* Next, any net short-term capital losses are offset against any net long-term capital gains. If the taxpayer has net long-term capital losses and net short-term capital gains, they are also offset.

(4) *Taxing of net capital gains:* The rules for taxation of capital gains change frequently. Net long-term capital gains have often been afforded special beneficial tax treatment.

(5) *Deduction of net capital losses:* Net capital losses are deductible (as a deduction from adjusted gross income) to a maximum of $3,000 per year. Any unused amount of net capital loss may be carried forward indefinitely.

d. *Deductions (business/personal):* Deductions allowed to individual taxpayers include deductions from gross income to arrive at adjusted gross income and deductions from adjusted gross income:

(1) *Adjusted gross income:* Some of the deductions from gross income to arrive at adjusted gross income are the following:

(a) Ordinary and necessary expenses incurred in a trade or business

(b) Employee business expenses that are reimbursed by the employer

(c) Penalties on early withdrawal of savings

(d) Alimony paid

(e) Capital loss deduction

(f) Some IRA payments

(g) Certain retirement plan contributions

(2) *Itemized deductions:* Certain personal expenses are allowed as itemized deductions from adjusted gross income (AGI). Some of the items that may be included as itemized deductions are the following:

(a) Medical expenses that exceed 7.5 percent of adjusted gross income (AGI)

(b) Real estate taxes

(c) Personal property taxes

(d) Interest on a home mortgage

(e) Charitable contributions

(f) Casualty and theft losses that exceed 10 percent of AGI

(g) Moving expenses

(h) Job expenses and other miscellaneous deductions (only the total amount that exceeds 2 percent of AGI is deductible): union dues, professional dues and subscriptions, job education, job travel (with limitations), tax return preparation fees, investment counsel fees, and safe deposit box fees.

Note: Items that are allowed as a deduction from gross income to arrive at adjusted gross income provide a greater potential benefit for the taxpayer than itemized deductions from AGI. This is because the taxpayer will always benefit from the deduction for AGI. Itemized deductions will benefit the taxpayer only if the total amount of itemized deductions exceeds the amount of the standard deduction allowed for the taxpayer. The amount of the standard deduction is specified by Congress and depends on the filing status of the taxpayer.

Review Questions

Directions: Select the correct answer from the four alternatives. Write the letter of your answer in the blank to the left of the number.

______ **1.** Which one of the following is legally required to be withheld from employees' pay?

a. FICA taxes
b. Federal unemployment taxes
c. Insurance premiums
d. Pension contributions

______ **2.** Which one of the following items would be recorded in the payroll taxes expense account?

a. Federal income tax withheld
b. Company pension plan contributions
c. Federal Unemployment Tax Act payments
d. State income tax withheld

______ **3.** Which one of the following items deducted from employees' pay *must* be matched by an equal contribution by the employer?

a. Insurance premiums
b. Company pension plan contributions
c. Federal income tax withheld
d. FICA tax

______ **4.** Items withheld from employees' pay should be classified by the employer as

a. current assets.
b. long-term liabilities.
c. expenses.
d. current liabilities.

______ **5.** When a company records payroll, salaries or wages expense should be

a. debited for the amount of net pay.
b. debited for the amount of gross pay.
c. credited for the amount of net pay.
d. credited for the amount of gross pay.

______ **6.** Unemployment taxes are normally levied on

a. only the employee.
b. both the employee and the employer.
c. wages that exceed $25,000.
d. only the employer.

_______________ **7.** Short-term capital gains could result from sales of

a. any asset held for one year or less.
b. capital assets held for two years or less.
c. capital assets held for one year or less.
d. capital assets held for six months or less.

_______________ **8.** In the United States, long-term capital gains

a. have never been given preferential tax treatment.
b. may be carried forward indefinitely.
c. could result from the sale of inventory.
d. could result from the sale of investments held by an individual for more than one year.

_______________ **9.** Which of the following items would normally be included in gross income for individual income tax purposes?
a. Child support payments
b. Accident insurance proceeds
c. Dividend income
d. Disability benefits

_______________ **10.** Operating expenses normally include

a. payroll taxes.
b. interest.
c. losses on the sale of buildings used in the business.
d. losses on the sale of investments.

Use the following information in answering Questions 11 and 12.

Young Company has an employee named Wiley. During the past week Wiley earned gross pay of $1,500. Wiley's federal income tax withholding based on the federal tax tables is $200, and his state income tax withholding is $20. Wiley has requested that a $10 insurance premium and $2 in union dues be withheld from his check each week. Assume that the FICA rate is 7 percent on the first $50,000, the federal unemployment tax rate is 0.8 percent on the first $7,000, and the state unemployment tax rate is 2 percent on the first $7,000. Wiley's gross pay to date for this year is $6,000.

_______________ **11.** Wiley's take-home pay (net pay) would be

a. $1,163.
b. $1,175.
c. $1,268.
d. $1,500.

_______________ **12.** Young Company's total payroll tax expense related to Wiley's earnings for the week would be

a. $105.
b. $133.
c. $147.
d. $353.

Solutions

Answer	*Refer to:*
1. (a)	[B-1-a(2)]
2. (c)	[B-1-a(5)]
3. (d)	[B-1-a(2)]
4. (d)	[B-1-a(7)]
5. (b)	[B-1-a(5)(d)]
6. (d)	[B-1-a(5)(c)]
7. (c)	[B-2-c(1)]
8. (d)	[B-2-c(2)]
9. (c)	[B-2-a]
10. (a)	[Chapter 8, B-5-a(2)]
11. (a)	[B-1-a]

Gross pay		$1,500
Less:		
Federal income tax withheld	$200	
State income tax withheld	20	
Insurance withheld	10	
Union dues withheld	2	
FICA withheld ($1,500 × 0.07)	105	337
Net pay or take-home pay		$1,163

12. (b) [B-1-a(4)]

FICA ($1,500 × 0.07)	$ 105
Federal unemployment tax ($1,000 × 0.008)	8
State unemployment tax ($1,000 × 0.02)	20
Total payroll tax expense	$ 133

CHAPTER 18

Analysis and Interpretation of Financial Statements

OVERVIEW

Users of financial statements have developed techniques to evaluate the financial data contained in published statements. To a skilled reader, the statements themselves show a wealth of information. A balance sheet can give a good indication of the amount and composition of a firm's assets and liabilities. The income statement displays the results of operations. Finally, the statement of cash flows indicates from where a firm is obtaining cash and how it is being used. When prepared on a consistent basis, comparative statements allow trend analysis, that is, how a firm is progressing through time. Ratio analysis is another widely used technique for evaluating a firm's activities.

The balance sheet, income statement, and statement of retained earnings were discussed in Chapter 8. The candidate should review those particular topics at this time.

KEY TERMS

Cash flow statement
Comparative financial statements
Financing activities
Investing activities
Operating activities
Ratio
Working capital

A. Statement of Cash Flows

The statement of cash flows explains the differences between the beginning and ending balances of cash (including cash equivalents). Cash equivalents are generally short-term temporary investments that are readily convertible to a known amount of cash *and* sufficiently close to their maturity date so that their market value is relatively insensitive to changes in interest rates. Generally, only investments purchased within three months of their maturity dates meet these two criteria. Short-term investments in Treasury bills, investments in money market funds, and some investments in commercial paper would normally qualify as cash equivalents. The statement of cash flows presents information about cash flows from operating, investing, and financing activities.

1. *Operating Activities:* Operating activities generally include transactions that relate to the calculation of net income. These items are usually related to the production and sale of goods and services.

   a. *Operating cash inflows:* Typical operating cash inflows include the following:

      (1) Cash sales to customers

      (2) Cash collections from credit sales

(3) Cash dividends received from stock investments

(4) Interest payments received

(5) Refunds from suppliers

b. *Operating cash outflows:* Typical operating cash outflows include the following:

(1) Payments for salaries and wages

(2) Payments made for goods and services used by the company

(3) Interest payments

(4) Payments to the government for taxes

(5) Payments for other normal business expenses

2. *Investing Activities:* Investing activities include transactions that involve the investment of a company's cash.

a. *Investing cash inflows:* Typical investing cash inflows include the following:

(1) Cash received from sale of investments (stocks or bonds of other firms)

(2) Cash received from the sale of property, plant, and equipment

(3) Cash received from repayment of loans made by the company to other entities

(4) Cash received from the sale (discounting) of loans made by the company to other entities

b. *Investing cash outflows:* Typical investing cash outflows include the following:

(1) Payments made to buy property, plant, and equipment

(2) Payments made in purchasing stocks of other entities as an investment

(3) Payments made to purchase debt securities of other entities as an investment (excluding cash equivalents)

(4) Payments made in making loans to other entities

3. *Financing Activities:* Financing activities include transactions with the company's owners and long-term creditors.

a. *Financing cash inflows:* Typical financing cash inflows include the following:

(1) Cash received from sale of stock

(2) Cash received from the issuance of bonds or nonoperating notes payable

b. *Financing cash outflows:* Typical financing cash outflows include the following:

(1) Payment of dividends to owners

(2) Payments of the principal amount on nonoperating loans or bonds payable

(3) Payments made to acquire treasury stock

4. *Noncash Investing and Financing Activities:* Some important investing and financing transactions do not involve cash. For example, a company might purchase equipment and issue a long-term note payable to the seller. This transaction does not involve an inflow or an outflow of cash, but both financing and investing activities are involved. Since the statement of cash flows would omit significant financing and investing activities if noncash financing and investing transactions were excluded, the FASB requires that noncash investing and financing transactions be disclosed in either a separate schedule or in a footnote to the financial statements. Examples of noncash investing and financing activities that must be disclosed are the following: conversion of bonds payable to stock, conversion of preferred stock to common stock, exchange of one noncash asset for another noncash asset, purchase of long-term assets through the issuance of a note payable to the seller, purchase of a building by securing a mortgage loan, purchase of noncash assets in exchange for stock, and leasing of assets in a transaction that involves a lease classified as a capital lease.

5. *Presentation of Statement of Cash Flows:* The cash flows from operating activities may be presented in either a direct or an indirect fashion. The FASB recommends use of the direct method. However, most companies actually use the indirect method. The financial statements (balance sheet and income statement) for Schmaus Company shown in Figure 18–1a provide the information needed to develop a statement of cash flows for both the direct and indirect methods (see Figures 18–1b and 18–1c).

a. *Direct method:* The direct method involves the calculation and presentation of individual cash inflows and outflows. These cash inflows and outflows can be calculated by converting the information in the income statement from an accrual basis back to a cash basis. The following formulas may be used to obtain the amounts necessary for the statement of cash flows, using the direct method, shown in Figure 18–1b.

(1) *Cash receipts from customers:*

Revenues from sales
- + decrease in accounts receivable
- *or*
- − increase in accounts receivable

(2) *Cash payments to suppliers:*

Cost of goods sold
- + increase in inventory *or* − decrease in inventory
- + decrease in accounts payable *or* − increase in accounts payable

(3) *Cash payments for operating expenses:*

Operating expense
- + increase in prepaid expense *or* − decrease in prepaid expense
- + decrease in accrued expenses payable *or* − increase in accrued expenses payable

(4) *Cash payments for income taxes:*

Income tax expense
- + decrease in income taxes payable
- *or*
- − increase in income taxes payable

Figure 18–1a Schmaus Company Comparative Balance Sheet for 20XA and 20XB and Income Statement for 20XB

Schmaus Company
Balance Sheet
December 31, 20XB

	20XB	20XA
Assets		
Cash	$130,000	$ 40,000
Accounts receivable	69,000	60,000
Inventory	60,000	80,000
Prepaid insurance	5,000	3,000
Land	220,000	300,000
Plant assets	600,000	500,000
Accumulated depreciation	(205,000)	(200,000)
Total Assets	$879,000	$ 783,000
Liabilities and Owners' Equity		
Accounts payable	$ 20,000	$ 25,000
Income taxes payable	22,600	20,000
Notes payable, long-term	50,000	60,000
Bonds payable	179,000	159,000
Common stock	450,000	400,000
Additional paid-in capital	60,000	50,000
Retained earnings	97,400	69,000
Total Liabilities and Owners' Equity	$879,000	$ 783,000

Schmaus Company
Income Statement
December 31, 20XB

Sales revenue		$ 300,000
Expenses		
Cost of goods sold	$180,000	
Salary expense	39,000	
Depreciation expense	5,000	
Interest expense	3,000	
Insurance expense	11,000	
Income tax expense	18,600	
Total expenses		256,600
Net income		$ 43,400

Additional information:

1. Land that originally cost $100,000 was sold for $100,000.
2. A building was purchased for cash.
3. Bonds were issued at par value in exchange for land.
4. Common stock with a par value of $50,000 was sold for $60,000.
5. Dividends of $15,000 were declared and paid during 20XB.

Figure 18–1b Schmaus Company Statement of Cash Flows (Direct Method)

Schmaus Company
Statement of Cash Flows—Direct Method
For the Year Ended December 31, 20XB

Cash flows from operating activities:		
Cash received from customers	$ 291,000	
Cash inflows from operating activities		$291,000
Less cash paid for:		
Payments for merchandise	$ 165,000	
Payments for salaries	39,000	
Payments for interest	3,000	
Payments for insurance	13,000	
Payments for income taxes	16,000	
Cash outflows from operating activities		236,000
Net cash provided by operating activities		$ 55,000
Cash flows from investing activities:		
Proceeds from sale of land	$ 100,000	
Purchase of building	(100,000)	
Net cash provided by investing activities		0
Cash flows from financing activities:		
Proceeds from sale of common stock	$ 60,000	
Payment of long-term notes payable	(10,000)	
Payment of dividends	15,000	35,000
Net cash provided by financing activities		
Net increase (decrease) in cash		$ 90,000
Cash balance, January 1, 20XA		40,000
Cash balance, December 31, 20XA		$130,000
Schedule of noncash investing/financing activities:		
Issuance of bonds in exchange for land		$ 20,000

Figure 18–1c Partial Statement of Cash Flows

Schmaus Company
Partial Statement of Cash Flows
For the Year Ended December 31, 20XB
(Indirect Method)

Cash flows from operating activities:		
Net income		$43,400
Adjustments to reconcile net income to net cash flow from operating activities		
Depreciation expense	$ 5,000	
Increase in accounts receivable	(9,000)	
Decrease in inventory	20,000	
Increase in prepaid expenses	(2,000)	
Decrease in accounts payable	(5,000)	
Increase in income taxes payable	2,600	
Total adjustments		11,600
Net cash provided by operating activities		$55,000

EXAMPLE: For the Schamus Company example, the calculations would be as follows:

Operating Activities Section

Cash received from customers = \$300,000 (sales) − \$9,000 (increase in accounts receivable) = \$201,000.

Cash payments to suppliers = \$180,000 (cost of goods sold) − \$20,000 (decrease in inventory) + \$5,000 (decrease in accounts payable) = \$165,000.

Cash payments for salaries = \$39,000 (salary expense). (There is no salaries payable amount in either 20XA or 20XB so the amount paid is equal to the amount of the expense.)

Cash payments for interest = \$3,000 (interest expense). (There is no interest payable amount in either 20XA or 20XB so the amount paid is equal to the amount of the expense.)

Cash payments for insurance = \$11,000 (insurance expense) + \$2,000 (increase in prepaid insurance) = \$13,000.

Cash payments for income taxes = \$18,600 (income tax expense) − \$2,600 (increase in income taxes payable) = \$16,000.

Investing Activities Section

Change in the land account: Two items explain the change in the land account: (a) the sale of land for \$100,000 and (b) the exchange of bonds for land. The exchange of bonds for land is a noncash financing or investing item that would be shown in a separate schedule or a footnote. The amount of the exchange of bonds for land is \$20,000. This amount is equal to the increase in the bonds account and explains the net decrease in the land account of \$80,000 (−\$100,000 + \$20,000).

Purchase of a building for cash: The amount of the purchase is assumed to be for the increase in the plant assets account of \$100,000 since no other information is given that would affect this account.

Depreciation: The change in accumulated depreciation is equal to the amount of depreciation expense.

Financing Activities Section

Notes payable: The long-term notes payable account decreased by \$10,000 indicating that the company must have paid \$10,000 on these notes.

Bonds payable: The increase in bonds payable (\$20,000) is treated as a noncash financing and investing activity.

Sale of common stock: Common stock was sold for \$60,000. This transaction explains the increase in the common stock and additional paid-in capital accounts.

Dividends paid: The dividends paid (\$15,000) are classified as a financing activity.

b. *Indirect method:* When the indirect method is used to present the operating activities section, net income is adjusted for items included in the amount that do not affect cash.

net income + additions − deductions = net cash flow from operating activities

Additions

Depreciation expense
Amortization of intangibles
Amortization of bond discount
Loss on investment in common stock using the equity method
Loss on sale of plant assets
Decrease in current receivable accounts
Decrease in inventory accounts
Decrease in prepaid expense accounts
Increase in accounts payable
Increase in accrued liabilities

Deductions

Amortization of bond premium
Income on investment in common stock using the equity method
Gain on sale of plant assets
Increase in current receivable accounts
Increase in inventory accounts
Increase in prepaid expense accounts
Decrease in accounts payable
Decrease in accrued liabilities

Figure 18–1c shows a partial statement of cash flows (the operating activities section) for the Schmaus Company example, using the indirect method. The remainder of the statement would be the same as shown in Figure 18–1b.

B. Comparative Statements

Firms often present financial data for several years in annual statements to allow comparison of current performance to previous performance. To allow such comparison, it is important that the statements be prepared on a consistent basis. Any consistency exceptions are prominently noted in the auditor's report and the financial statements themselves. A common practice is to show percentage increases or decreases in selected items. Financial analysts often get a better idea of the progress of a firm by such reports.

C. Ratio Analysis

Ratio analysis essentially studies the relationships between various amounts on financial statements. A ratio for a given firm can be compared to others in the same industry. Such ratios are printed regularly by publishing services. Ratios from the current year are often compared to the same ratios in preceding years to provide information about changes within the company.

1. *Liquidity Ratios:* Liquidity ratios are concerned with a firm's ability to meet current obligations. For purposes of short-term financing, these ratios are very important. Creditors are often interested in liquidity ratios.

   a. *Current ratio:* The current ratio is expressed as follows:

   $$\frac{\text{current assets}}{\text{current liabilities}}$$

   b. *Acid-test ratio or quick ratio:* Since inventories and prepaid expenses may be difficult to liquidate quickly, the acid-test ratio is often computed as a supplement to the current ratio. The acid-test ratio compares only the highly liquid assets of cash, marketable securities, and receivables with current liabilities:

$$\frac{\text{cash} + \text{marketable securities} + \text{receivables}}{\text{current liabilities}}$$

c. *Receivables turnover:* This ratio shows how often, or how quickly, a firm's receivables are collected. Too large a ratio may indicate too lenient a credit policy. This is important, as receivables are often interest free. A firm may be giving credit to customers at no charge for extended periods while paying interest on its own short-term debt to finance the receivables. The ratio is as follows:

$$\frac{\text{credit sales}}{\text{average receivables}}$$

If credit sales are not available, net sales may be used. Average receivables is a better number to use than year-end receivables, as the average allows for the effects of seasonal business.

d. *Inventory turnover:* Inventory turnover is identical in concept to the receivables turnover. A low ratio may indicate overstocking of inventory or the presence of obsolete inventory, usually financed with short-term debt. The inventory turnover ratio is as follows:

$$\frac{\text{cost of goods sold}}{\text{average inventory}}$$

Note that cost of goods sold, rather than sales, is comparable to inventory cost.

e. *Working capital:* Working capital is defined as current assets minus current liabilities. It represents the net amount of a company's relatively liquid resources. This amount may be used as an indicator of a company's short-run liability.

2. *Debt Ratios:* Debt ratios are more concerned with a firm's policy on long-term debt. The capital structure of a corporation is composed of both debt and owners' equity. A firm that is financed primarily by debt must be able to service that debt in a timely manner to maintain its credit standing.

a. *Debt-to-equity ratio:* The debt-to-equity ratio measures the balance between the portion of assets provided by stockholders and the portion provided by creditors:

$$\frac{\text{total liabilities}}{\text{total stockholders' equity}}$$

This ratio often is expressed as long-term debt over equity.

b. *Debt-to-total-assets ratio:* The debt-to-total-assets ratio is similar to the debt-to-equity ratio. This ratio shows the percentage of assets financed by debt:

$$\frac{\text{total liabilities}}{\text{total assets}}$$

c. *Times-interest-earned ratio:* This ratio relates to a firm's ability to service debt from earnings. Obviously, a firm that is barely able to generate sufficient earnings to make interest payments is a suspect investment. The ratio may be calculated in different ways. In general, a good representation of the ratio is as follows:

$$\frac{\text{earnings before interest expense and income taxes}}{\text{interest expense}}$$

A weakness of the ratio is that principal must also be repaid, as well as the fact that payments are made from cash rather than earnings. Nevertheless, if there aren't sufficient earnings, there will not be enough cash generation in the long run.

3. *Profitability Ratios:* Profitability ratios are designed to measure a firm's efficiency in generating profits in relation to sales and in relation to investment. Investors are generally interested in profitability ratios.

a. *Earnings per share:* This is one of the most common ratios. This ratio relates to shares of common stock only. If preferred stock exists, the earnings must be adjusted for the dividends. The ratio is as follows:

$$\frac{\text{net income less preferred stock dividend}}{\text{average shares of common stock outstanding}}$$

Treasury stock is not included in the denominator. Average shares of common stock are calculated using a weighted average. For example, if 750 shares of common stock are outstanding on January 1, 20XA, and 500 shares are issued on June 30, 20XA, average shares at the end of the year can be calculated as follows:

$$\begin{array}{rcr} 750 \times 12 \text{ months} & = & 9{,}000 \\ 500 \times 6 \text{ months} & = & \underline{3{,}000} \\ \text{Total shares} & & 12{,}000 \end{array}$$

$$\frac{12{,}000}{12 \text{ months}} = 1{,}000 \text{ average shares outstanding}$$

Such computations as primary earnings per share and fully diluted earnings per share are also calculated for firms with complex capital structures.

b. *Dividend yield:* Yield is an investor's tool for comparing the cash return by means of dividends in relation to the market value of the stock. The ratio is as follows:

$$\frac{\text{dividend per share}}{\text{market value per share}}$$

c. *Price-earnings ratio:* An investor might use the price-earnings ratio to determine whether the price of the stock is suitable for his or her purposes, considering the earnings of the stock. The price-earnings ratio compares the market price of the stock with the earnings per share of the stock:

$$\frac{\text{market price per share}}{\text{earnings per share}}$$

d. *Gross profit margin:* The gross profit margin is an indicator of a firm's efficiency at producing goods and pricing them for sale. The ratio is calculated as follows:

$$\frac{\text{sales} - \text{cost of goods sold}}{\text{sales}}$$

A net profit margin may also be calculated as follows:

$$\frac{\text{net income}}{\text{sales}}$$

Two firms may produce the same product and sell it at the same price yet have different profit margins.

e. *Return on investment:* There are many different ways to calculate return on investment. The easiest method follows:

$$\frac{\text{net income}}{\text{tangible assets}}$$

Intangible assets are usually subtracted from total assets in arriving at this figure. For purposes of evaluating management performance, the DuPont method is often employed as follows:

$$\frac{\text{sales}}{\text{tangible assets}} \times \frac{\text{net income}}{\text{sales}}$$

f. *Book value:* Book value per share is a marginally useful number that is computed as follows:

$$\frac{\text{owners' equity} - \text{par value of preferred stock}}{\text{number of shares of common stock outstanding}}$$

The reason that book value per share is not particularly useful is the reliance on historical cost in preparation of financial statements.

The ratios discussed in this chapter represent many of the most common ratios used in analyzing financial statements. Numerous other ratios might be used as well.

Figure 18–2c shows the calculation of the ratios presented in this chapter. The calculations are based on the financial statements for the XYZ Company shown in Figures 18–2a and 18–2b.

Figure 18–2a Consolidated Balance Sheet

XYZ Company
Consolidated Balance Sheet
December 31, 20XB

Assets	*20XB*	*20XA*	*Liabilities and Stockholders' Equity*	*20XB*	*20XA*
Current assets			Current liabilities		
Cash	20,000	15,000	Accounts payable	125,000	100,000
Marketable securities	100,000	80,000	Notes payable	220,000	200,000
Accounts receivable	300,000	280,000	Accrued liabilities	100,000	80,000
Inventories	280,000	260,000	Total current liabilities	445,000	380,000
Total current assets	700,000	635,000	Long-term debts		
			Bonds payable	700,000	700,000
Investments	250,000	200,000	Notes payable	25,000	50,000
Fixed assets					
Plant and equipment	2,150,000	1,800,000	Total long-term debts	725,000	750,000
Less: Accumulated depreciation	(800,000)	(600,000)			
			Total liabilities	1,170,000	1,130,000
Total fixed assets	1,350,000	1,200,000			
			Stockholders' equity		
Total assets	2,300,000	2,035,000	Common stock	150,000	150,000
			Additional paid-in capital	600,000	600,000
			Retained earnings	380,000	155,000
			Total stockholders' equity	1,130,000	905,000
			Total liabilities and stockholders equity	2,300,000	2,035,000

Figure 18–2b Statement of Income

XYZ Company
Statement of Income
For the Year Ended December 31, 20XB

	20XB	*20XA*
Revenues		
Net sales	1,500,000	1,300,000
Interest income	5,000	10,000
Other income	20,000	35,000
Total revenue	1,525,000	1,345,000
Expenses		
Cost of goods sold	750,000	670,000
Depreciation expense	200,000	160,000
Selling and administrative expenses	145,000	115,000
Interest expense	72,500	75,000
Total expenses	1,167,500	1,020,000
Net income before income taxes	357,500	325,000
Less: Income tax expense	82,500	75,000
Net income after taxes	275,000	250,000
Earnings per share	$5.50	$5.00

Additional information:

50,000 shares of common stock were outstanding during 20XA and 20XB.
Cash dividends were $50,000 or $1.00 per share.
All sales were made on credit.
Market price of XYZ's stock at the end of 20XB was $50 per share.

Figure 18–2c Summary of Financial Ratios

Ratio	*Calcuation*	*Example*
1. Liquidity ratios		
a. Current ratio	Current assets / Current liabilities	700,000 / 445,000 = 1.57 times or 1.57 to 1
b. Acid-test ratio	(Cash +Marketable securities +Receivables) / Current liabilities	(20,000 +100,000 +300,000) / 445,000 = 94 times or .94 to 1
c. Receivables turnover	Credit sales / Average receivables	1,500,000 / 290,000 = 5.17 times
d. Inventory turnover	Cost of goods sold / Average inventory	750,000 / 270,000 + 2.78 times
2. Debt ratios		
a. Debt-to-equity ratio	Total liabilities / Total stockholders' equity	1,170,000 / 1,130,000 = 1.035 or 104%
b. Debt-to-total assets ratio	Total liabilities / Total assets	1,170,000 / 2,300,000 = 60.87%
c. Times-interest-earned ratio	Earnings before interest expense and income taxes / Interest expense	430,000[a] / 72,500 = 5.93 times
3. Profitability ratios		
a. Earnings per share	Net income–preferred stock dividend / Average shares of common stock outstanding	275,000 / 50,000 = $5.50
b. Dividend yield	Dividend per share / Market value per share	$1.00 / $50.00 = 2%
c. Price-earnings ratio	Market price per share / Earnings per share	$50.00 / $5.50 = $9.09
d. Gross profit margin	Sales–cost of goods sold / Sales	(1,500,000 –750,000) / 1,500,000 = 50%
e. Return on investment	Net income / Tangible assets	275,000 / 2,300,000 = 11.96%
f. Book value	Owners' equity less par value of preferred stock / Number of shares of common stock outstanding	1,130,000 / 50,000 = $22.60

[a]Net income before income taxes plus interest expense = 357,500 + 72,500 = 430,000.

Review Questions

Directions: Select the correct answer from the four alternatives. Write the letter of your answer in the blank to the left of the number.

______ **1.** The financial statement that shows the differences between the beginning and ending balances of cash, including cash equivalents, is called the

a. statement of retained earnings.
b. statement of cash flows.
c. income statement.
d. balance sheet.

______ **2.** Which one of the following ratios would normally be used to analyze a firm's ability to repay long-term debt?

a. Current ratio
b. Times-interest-earned ratio
c. Inventory turnover
d. Acid-test ratio

______ **3.** Which one of the following transactions will result in a reduction of Y Company's current 2:1 ratio?

a. Borrowing money from the bank in exchange for a note payable due in five years
b. Selling land at a loss
c. Collection of an account receivable
d. Repurchase of common stock

______ **4.** Which one of the following ratios would normally be used to analyze a firm's ability to pay its short-term obligations?

a. Acid-test ratio
b. Book value
c. Earnings per share
d. Dividend yield

______ **5.** If equipment were acquired by signing a mortgage note payable, the transaction would be reported on the statement of cash flows in the

a. operating activities section.
b. investing activities section.
c. disclosure of noncash investing/financing activities.
d. financing activities section.

______ **6.** Which one of the following methods does the FASB recommend be used in preparing a statement of cash flows?

a. The indirect method

b. The direct method
c. The working-capital method
d. The accrual method

_______________ **7.** Current assets minus current liabilities is called

a. net assets.
b. the current ratio.
c. working capital.
d. changes in financial position.

_______________ **8.** Which one of the following items would be included in the operating activities section of the statement of cash flows?

a. Purchase of a building for cash
b. Sale of captial stock
c. Sale of bonds
d. Payments for merchandise

_______________ **9.** The term used to describe the ratio between cost of goods sold and merchandise inventory is

a. current ratio.
b. gross profit margin.
c. price-earnings ratio.
d. merchandise inventory turnover.

_______________ **10.** Which one of the following is considered to be a liquidity ratio?

a. Debt-to-total assets ratio
b. Dividend yield
c. Current ratio
d. Return on investment

Use the following information in answering Questions 11 to 13.

The following financial information for the years 20XA and 20XB is available for the ABC Company:

	20XA	20XB
Current assets		
Cash	20,000	30,000
Accounts receivable	90,000	85,000
Inventory	90,000	98,000
Prepaid expenses	5,000	6,000
Total current assets	205,000	219,000
Current liabilities		
Accounts payable	10,000	12,000
Notes payable	40,000	30,000
Accrued liabilities	12,000	11,000
Total current liabilities	62,000	53,000

_______________ **11.** What is the current ratio for 20XB? (Round your answer to two decimal places.)

a. 0.26
b. 2.00

c. 3.31
d. 4.13

_______________ **12.** If credit sales are equal to $890,000, what is receivables turnover for 20XB? (Round your answer to two decimal places.)

a. 9.89
b. 10.17
c. 10.47
d. 12.45

_______________ **13.** What is the acid-test ratio for 20XA? (Round your answer to two decimal places.)

a. 1.77
b. 1.85
c. 2.20
d. 3.23

_______________ **14.** Cargo Company had net income of $30,000, which was 10 percent of net sales. Cost of goods sold was 60 percent of sales. The dollar amount of gross profit (or gross margin) for the company was

a. $60,000.
b. $120,000.
c. $180,000.
d. $300,000.

Solutions

Answer	*Refer to:*
1. (b)	[A]
2. (b)	[C-2]
3. (d)	[C-1-a]
4. (a)	[C-1-b]
5. (c)	[A-4]
6. (b)	[A-5-a]
7. (c)	[C-1-e]
8. (d)	[A-1]
9. (d)	[C-1-d]
10. (c)	[C-1]
11. (d)	[C-1-a] current assets / current liabilities $219,000 / $53,000 = 4.13
12. (b)	[C-1-c] credit sales / average receivables $890,000 / $87,500[a] = 10.17
13. (a)	[C-1-b] (cash + marketable securities + accounts receivable) / current liabilities ($20,000 + 0 + $90,000) / $62,000 = 1.77
14. (b)	[C-3-d] The solution is calculated as follows:

Sales	$300,000[b]	100%
− Cost of goods sold	−180,000	60%
Gross profit	$120,000	40%

[a]($90,000 + $85,000) / 2 = $87,500.
[b]Net income = 0.10 × sales
$30,000 = 0.10 × sales
$300,000 = sales

CHAPTER 19

Managerial Accounting

OVERVIEW

Managerial accounting is concerned with aiding managers in planning and controlling the operations of a business. The candidate should be familiar with basic techniques used in managerial accounting.

The candidate needs to understand the difference between fixed and variable costs and the effects of different costs on the decision-making process (cost-volume profit analysis). The candidate needs to understand the differences between accounting for a merchandising firm and accounting for a manufacturing firm.

Another topic that the candidate needs to understand is the budgeting process. The candidate may already be familiar with budgeting from the standpoint of preparing a personal budget. Budgeting for a business firm is more complex, but the same basic task is being performed. A plan (budget) is prepared and used to aid in making decisions during the period. At the end of the period, actual results should be compared to the plan to see how well the business met its objectives.

KEY TERMS

Breakeven point
Budget
Contribution margin
Cost behavior
Direct labor
Direct materials
Fixed costs
Forecasting
Job order costing
Manufacturing overhead
Mixed cost
Predetermined overhead rate
Process costing
Proforma financial statement
Relevant range
Standard cost
Variable cost
Variance

A. Cost Analysis

Costs are analyzed in various ways in managerial accounting. One of the most important ways in which costs are classified in managerial accounting is by cost behavior. Cost behavior refers to changes in a cost when changes in the output of goods or services occur.

1. *Determining Unit Costs:* The per unit cost of an item is calculated as follows:

$$\frac{\text{total cost of the item}}{\text{total number of units of output}}$$

EXAMPLE: Quik-Copy, Inc., produced 10,000 copies during the month of June. The total cost of toner supplies for the month was \$1,000. The per unit cost of toner supplies would be \$0.10 (\$1,000/10,000).

2. *Variable and Fixed Costs:* Costs are generally classified as variable or fixed costs. Costs that have both fixed and variable portions are known as *mixed,* or *semivariable, costs.*

   a. *Variable costs:* Variable costs vary in total directly with the level of output. As production increases, the total amount of a variable cost will increase proportionately while the per unit cost will remain the same. Raw materials are an example of a variable cost.

      EXAMPLE: Assume that Quik-Copy, Inc., pays $0.01 for each sheet of paper used in making copies. If 10 copies are made, the total cost is 10 × $0.01 = $0.10. If 10,000 copies are made, the total cost is 10,000 × $0.01 = $100. The per unit cost remains at $0.01 regardless of the level of activity.

   b. *Fixed costs:* Fixed costs remain constant in total despite changes in the volume of output. The per unit amount of a fixed cost varies as the level of activity changes. For example, if Quik-Copy, Inc., rents a building for $500 per month, the $500 rental expense will be incurred whether Quik-Copy produces 0 copies, 100 copies, or 10,000 copies. Depreciation, insurance, and advertising are other examples of fixed costs.

      EXAMPLE: Quik-Copy, Inc., has $200 per month in insurance expense, which is a fixed cost. If Quik-Copy produced 10 copies in a month, the total cost of insurance expense would be $200, and the per unit cost would be $20 ($200/10 copies). If Quik-Copy produced 10,000 copies in a month, the total cost of insurance would be $200, and the per unit cost would be $0.02 ($200/10,000).

   c. *Mixed or semivariable costs:* Mixed costs vary with level of activity but by less than a proportionate amount. A common example of a mixed cost is electricity. The cost of electricity is not constant or fixed, yet it does not vary directly with production. The cost of electricity could be separated into fixed and variable portions. This might be done by various methods, such as regression analysis, simultaneous equations, or the high-low method.

      EXAMPLE: Quik-Copy, Inc., is able to separate the mixed cost of maintenance into the following components: $100 per month plus $0.001 per copy. If Quik-Copy produced 10,000 copies, the cost of maintenance would be $110 ($100 + [10,000 × $0.001]). If Quik-Copy produced 100,000 copies, the cost of maintenance would be $200 ($100 + [$100,000 × $0.001]).

   d. *Relevant range:* Fixed and variable costs retain their characteristics within a certain relevant range. Outside the relevant range, the assumptions made about cost behavior are not valid.

3. *Cost-Volume Profit Analysis:* Cost-volume profit analysis, also called breakeven analysis, is a powerful management tool used for budgeting, forecasting, pricing, and decision making.

   a. *Contribution margin:* In managerial accounting, the income statement is often classified in the following manner:

      Sales
      − Variable costs
      Contribution margin
      − Fixed costs
      Net income

b. *Breakeven analysis:* The central concept of breakeven analysis rests on the following equation:

$$\text{sales} = \text{fixed costs} + \text{variable costs} + \text{profit}$$

The breakeven point is the point where total revenues are equal to total expenses and net income is equal to zero. Thus, the breakeven point is calculated as follows:

$$\text{sales revenue} = \text{variable expenses} + \text{fixed expenses}$$

This equation may be rewritten as follows:

$$\text{SP(SQ)} = \text{VC(SQ)} + \text{fixed expenses}$$

where SP is selling price, VC is variable cost per unit, and SQ is sales quantity.

EXAMPLE: Quik-Copy wants to know its breakeven point in number of copies if it sells copies for $0.05 each. Costs are as follows:

Fixed costs	
Rent	$500
Electricity	150
Depreciation	100
Total fixed costs	$750
Variable costs	
Materials	$0.01/copy
Labor	0.01/copy
Total variable cost per copy	$0.02/copy

The breakeven point is then calculated:

$$\begin{aligned} \text{sales} &= \text{variable expenses} + \text{fixed expenses} \\ (\$0.05)(\text{SQ}) &= (\$0.02)(\text{SQ}) + \$750 \end{aligned}$$

Simplifying the equation, we get the following:

$$\begin{aligned} (\$0.03)(\text{SQ}) &= \$750 \\ \text{SQ} &= 25{,}000 \end{aligned}$$

The breakeven number of copies is 25,000. The breakeven amount in sales dollars is equal to the following:

$$25{,}000 \text{ copies} \times \$0.05/\text{copy} = \$1{,}250$$

c. *Contribution margin approach to breakeven analysis:* The contribution margin ratio is equal to the following:

$$\frac{\text{sales (in dollars)} - \text{variable expenses (in dollars)}}{\text{sales (in dollars)}}$$

The breakeven point (BEP) in sales dollars is equal to the following:

$$\text{breakeven point (BEP)} = \frac{\text{fixed expenses}}{\text{contribution margin ratio}}$$

EXAMPLE: The Quik-Copy breakeven problem could be solved using the contribution margin approach as follows:

$$\text{contribution margin ratio} = \frac{0.05 - 0.02}{0.05} = 0.60$$

$$\text{breakeven point (BEP)} = \frac{\$750}{0.60} = \$1{,}250$$

d. *Cost-volume profit analysis for planning:* If a company wants to use cost-volume profit analysis for planning purposes, various quantities may be inserted into the cost-volume profit equation.

EXAMPLE: To determine profit when 60,000 units are sold, multiply the unit prices by 60,000.

$$\text{sales} = \text{variable expenses} + \text{fixed expenses} + \text{profit}$$

$$60{,}000(\$0.05) = 60{,}000(\$0.02) + \$750 + \text{profit}$$

$$\underline{\underline{\$1{,}050}} = \text{profit}$$

By changing the variables for sales price, fixed expenses, and variable expenses, the effects of such changes on profitability can be forecast.

e. *Graphical analysis:* The cost-volume-profit relationships may be shown in a graphical manner as shown in Figure 19–1. Fixed costs are shown as a straight horizontal line. Since the costs do not change with an increase in volume, the slope of this line is 0. The total cost line is equal to fixed costs at zero volume and increases with volume with a slope equal to variable costs per unit. The revenue line is equal to zero at zero volume and increases with volume with a slope equal to sales price. The breakeven point is where total costs intersect total revenue. Note that volume refers to sales quantity, not to quantity produced.

Using data for Quik-Copy, Inc., the graph shown in Figure 19–1 can be prepared. The fixed-cost line is drawn at \$750. Since total costs are fixed costs at zero volume, only one other point must be calculated to draw the total cost line. At 40,000 copies, total costs are $\$750 + 40{,}000(0.02) = \$1{,}550$. Total revenue is zero at zero volume, so one other point is needed to draw a revenue line. At 40,000 copies, revenue is equal to $40{,}000(0.05) = \$2{,}000$. The intersection of the total revenue and total expense lines is the breakeven point. The distance between the lines at any given volume is the amount of profit or loss associated with sales at the volume given, assuming that all other relationships remain the same.

Figure 19–1 Breakeven Point

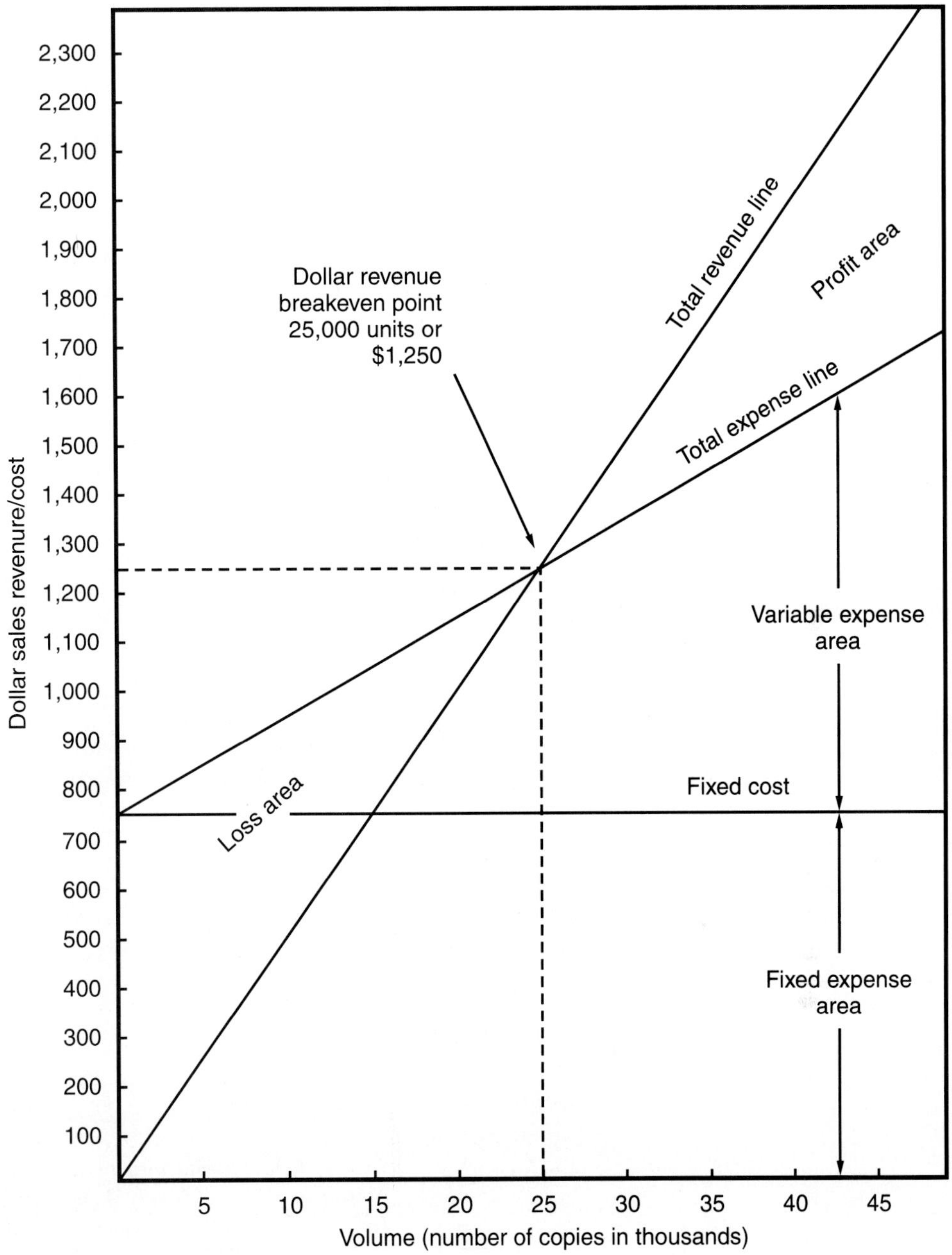

4. *Reporting for a Manufacturing Company:*

a. *Balance sheet:* The balance sheet of a manufacturing company is the same as that of a merchandising company except that three inventory accounts are shown. A manufacturing company maintains the following three inventory accounts:

(1) Raw materials inventory

(2) Work-in-process inventory

(3) Finished goods inventory

b. *Income statement:* To prepare an income statement for a manufacturing company, costs must be classified as product or period costs.

(1) *Product costs:* Product costs include direct materials, direct labor, and all manufacturing overhead costs.

(2) *Period costs:* Period costs include those costs that are not related to the manufacturing of a unit of product.

Period costs are accounted for in the same manner for both manufacturing and merchandising companies. Most period costs are treated as part of operating expenses. Product costs are summarized in a cost-of-goods-manufactured statement, and cost of goods manufactured replaces purchases in the income statement for a manufacturing company (see Figure 19–2).

5. *Cost Accounting:* Costs for a unit of product must be determined to satisfy legal and reporting requirements of the firm and to fulfill management's need for information. There are many possible methods of accumulating costs. The two most common methods, job order costing and process costing, are discussed below.

a. *Job order costing:* Job order costing is used by firms with production that is easily divided into separate projects or batches. For example, a construction firm would accumulate all costs for each building on a separate job card. Costs are sep-

Figure 19–2 Partial Income Statement with Statement of Cost of Goods Manufactured

Jones Manufacturing Co.
Partial Income Statement
For the Period Ending December 31, 20XA

Sales		200,000
Cost of goods sold		
Beginning finished goods inventory	10,000	
Cost of goods manufactured[a]	120,000	
Goods available for sale	130,000	
Less: Ending finished goods inventory	20,000	
Cost of goods sold		110,000
Gross profit		90,000

[a]From statement below.

Jones Manufacturing Co.
Statement of Cost of Goods Manufactured
For the Period Ending December 31, 20XA

Beginning work-in-process inventory			30,000
Direct materials		50,000	
Direct labor		50,000	
Manufacturing overhead			
Indirect materials	2,000		
Indirect labor	10,000		
Depreciation—factory	20,000		
Utilities—factory	5,000		
Maintenance	5,000		
Insurance	5,000	47,000	
Total manufacturing costs			147,000
Total cost of work-in-process during the period			177,000
Less: Ending work-in-process inventory			57,000
Cost of goods manufactured			120,000

arated into direct labor, direct materials, and manufacturing overhead. The combination of direct labor and direct materials is known as *prime cost.* Direct labor and manufacturing overhead together are called *conversion cost.*

(1) *Direct labor:* Direct labor is all labor performed by personnel directly involved in production. A machine operator's wage is direct labor. Salaries of production supervisors, inspectors, and maintenance personnel are not direct labor. These are not related directly to the production of a product. These costs are accumulated as indirect labor in the manufacturing overhead account. Officers' and secretaries' salaries are considered to be administrative expenses and are not considered to be part of the cost of production. They are treated as operating expenses.

(2) *Direct materials:* Raw materials that are readily identified with an individual product are known as *direct materials.* In the production of furniture, wood and cloth would be direct materials. Other items, such as the glue and nails, which are either difficult to measure or of such small value that accurate measurement is not worthwhile, are classified as *indirect materials.* Indirect materials are part of the manufacturing overhead account.

(3) *Manufacturing overhead:* Manufacturing overhead contains all other costs of production. The unique aspect of manufacturing overhead is that while direct labor and direct materials are variable costs, manufacturing overhead is composed of both fixed and variable costs. Fixed costs could include salaries, rent, and depreciation, while variable costs could include electricity, indirect materials, or any other expense that varies with volume. Manufacturing overhead is a control account in which numerous expenses are accumulated.

(4) *Cost flows in job order costing:* In job order costing, each project has a job card on which costs are accumulated. The job cards are subsidiary records of the costs that are recorded in the work-in-process inventory account. The flow of costs in job order costing is as follows:

(a) When raw materials are purchased, the raw materials inventory account is debited and accounts payable credited.

Raw Materials Inventory

(a) 15,000	

Accounts Payable

	15,000 (a)

(b) When materials are requisitioned by the production department, the raw materials inventory account is credited for the total amount requisitioned. The work-in-process inventory account is debited for the portion of the materials requisitioned that are direct materials (DM), and the manufacturing overhead account is debited for the indirect materials (IM) portion.

Raw Materials Inventory

(a) 15,000	10,000 (b)

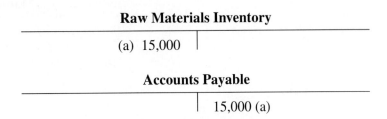

Work-in-Process Inventory

DM (b)	9,500	

Manufacturing Overhead

IM (b)	500	

The amount of direct materials used on each job is also recorded on the individual job cost sheets.

(c) When employees perform work on the product, the wages payable account is credited for the total labor cost related to the product. The work-in-process inventory account is debited for the direct labor cost (DL), and the manufacturing overhead account is debited for the indirect labor cost (IL).

Wages Payable

	12,000 (c)

Work-in-Process Inventory

DM (b)	9,500	
DL (c)	10,000	

Manufacturing Overhead

IM (b)	500	
IL (c)	2,000	

The amount of direct labor incurred on each job is also recorded on the individual job cost sheets.

(d) As items of manufacturing overhead other than indirect materials and indirect labor are incurred, the manufacturing overhead account is debited, and the related payable account (or cash) is credited.

Manufacturing Overhead

IM (b)	500	
IL (c)	2,000	
Electricity (d)	1,000	
Rent (d)	5,000	

Utilities Payable

	1,000 (d)

Cash

	5,000 (d)

(e) Manufacturing overhead is applied to individual jobs on the basis of a predetermined overhead rate. The predetermined overhead rate is used to allocate manufacturing overhead costs to the jobs included in the work-in-process inventory and to the jobs completed during the period. A predetermined overhead rate is used to avoid charging individual jobs with different overhead amounts due to seasonal variations in production volume.

To calculate the predetermined overhead rate, total overhead costs for the period as well as the total overhead application base for the period are estimated. The overhead application base chosen should be common to all jobs worked on during the period, and it should reflect each job's utilization of the manufacturing overhead incurred. Direct labor hours, direct labor cost, and machine hours are examples of commonly used overhead application bases. The formula for calculating the predetermined overhead rate is as follows:

$$\text{predetermined overhead rate} = \frac{\text{estimated total manufacturing overhead costs}}{\text{estimated total units in the application base}}$$

EXAMPLE: Assume that total manufacturing overhead costs were estimated to be \$9,000 for the period and that overhead is to be applied on the basis of direct labor hours. The total direct labor hours for the period are estimated to be 6,000 hours. The predetermined overhead rate would be \$9,000/6,000 hours, which is \$1.50 per direct labor hour. Assume that 5,800 direct labor hours were worked during the period and all jobs worked on are still in work-in-process inventory; that is, no jobs have been completed and transferred to finished goods inventory during the period. The company would apply \$8,700 (5,800 direct labor hours worked × \$1.50 per direct labor hour) of manufacturing overhead to the work-in-process inventory account. The entry to record the application of manufacturing overhead would be a debit to work-in-process inventory and a credit to manufacturing overhead.

Work-in-Process Inventory

DM (b)	9,500		
DL (c)	10,000		
ManOH (e)	8,700		

Manufacturing Overhead

IM (b)	500	8,700 (e)	Mfg. overhead applied
IL (c)	2,000		
Electricity (d)	1,000		
Rent (d)	5,000		
		200	Overapplied mfg. overhead

On the basis of the predetermined overhead rate, \$8,700 of manufacturing overhead was applied to work-in-process inventory, but only \$8,500 of actual manufacturing overhead was incurred during the period. Since *more overhead was applied than was incurred, there is a $200 credit balance in the manufacturing overhead account; this is called* overapplied manufacturing overhead. *If more manufacturing overhead was incurred than was applied during a period, the manufacturing overhead account would have a debit balance, which would be called* underapplied manufacturing overhead.

Overapplied or underapplied manufacturing overhead is normally closed to cost of goods sold at the end of the period. Overhead applied to individual jobs is recorded on the individual job cost sheet. If 200 direct labor hours have been worked on job C, $300 of manufacturing overhead would be applied to job C (200 direct labor hours × $1.50 per direct labor hour).

(f) As individual jobs are completed, the costs of producing the units within the job are transferred from the work-in-process inventory account to the finished goods inventory account. Assume that job C has been completed using $400 of direct materials, $450 of direct labor, and $300 of manufacturing overhead. The total cost of the job is $1,150, which would be transferred to finished goods by debiting the finished goods inventory for $1,150 and crediting the work-in-process inventory for $1,150. If 50 widgets were produced in job C, the per unit cost of an individual widget would be $23 per unit ($1,150/50 units).

(g) The cost of any units sold during the period is transferred from the finished goods inventory to cost of goods sold. If 20 widgets from job C were sold, cost of goods sold would be debited for $460 (20 units × $23 per unit), and finished goods inventory would be credited for $460.

b. *Process costing:* Process costing is used to cost products in companies that employ a continuous manufacturing process to produce a homogeneous product. The same accounts are utilized as in job order costing: direct labor, direct materials, and manufacturing overhead. When work is in process at the end of a period, costs may be allocated to the ending inventory on a weighted average or FIFO basis. The inventory pricing is based on equivalent units of production. The actual technique is complicated and can be found in any cost accounting textbook.

B. Budgets

A *budget* is a detailed plan that shows proposed acquisitions of financial resources and uses of financial resources during a period of time. Budgets are a powerful planning and control tool of management. Their uses are many, including cash management, inventory planning, production scheduling, profit planning, and performance evaluation. The budgeting process is sequential, beginning with the sales budget; there is great interdependence between budgets. Normally, a firm will make only the quantity of goods that it intends to sell and will purchase only the required raw materials for the quantity that it intends to make. This is the key to the planning function of budgeting. After the fact, budgets may also be used to compare actual results with planned objectives and evaluate the firm's and management's performance.

1. *Types of Budgets:*

a. *Sales budget:* The sales budget is the foundation for all other budgets. Various scientific and not-so-scientific methods of preparing a sales budget exist. This is essentially a marketing function and is passed on to management and accounting when completed. The sales budget must include the *quantity* and *timing of sales.* More sophisticated budgets also include the place where a sale is to occur.

EXAMPLE:

	Jan.	Feb.	Mar.	Apr.
Sales (in thousands)	20	24	32	50
Sales price	0.05	0.05	0.05	0.05
Total sales	$1,000	$1,200	$1,600	$2,500

Another schedule related to the sales budget is the cash collection schedule. If sales are made on an account, there may be a time lag between delivery of the product and collection of cash. Usually, depending on a firm's credit policy, a certain amount will prove to be uncollectible. These data are critical for cash planning.

EXAMPLE: Assuming that 25 percent of sales are made on account and are collected in the next month, a cash collection schedule would show the following:

	Jan.	Feb.	Mar.	Apr.
Current sales (75 percent of current sales)	750	900	1,200	1,875
Collections on account (25 percent of previous month's sales)	0	250	300	400
Total sales and collections	$ 750	$1,150	$1,500	$2,275

b. *Production budget:* The production budget is prepared next. The production budget shows the quantity and timing of units required to be produced during the period to meet sales and inventory requirements. Usually, there is a time lag between production and sales. Orders might be produced in advance, and some standard items might be kept in stock. If 20 percent of orders can be produced in advance, the production budget would appear as follows:

EXAMPLE:

	Jan.	Feb.	Mar.	Apr.	
Current requirement	20,000	24,000	32,000	50,000	Current sales
Ending inventory	4,800	6,400	10,000	?	29 percent of next month's sales
Totals	24,800	30,400	42,000		Total production needs
Less beginning inventory	0	4,800	6,400		Amount already produced
To be produced	24,800	25,600	35,600		

c. *Raw materials budget:* The timing and quantity of materials purchases can now be planned in the raw materials budget. This is important, as many materials must be ordered in advance. A shortage of raw materials will cause delays in production and sales losses in the short run and potential long-term customer dissatisfaction. The process is identical to the production budget in terms of planning ending inventory and purchases to accommodate the firm's needs.

d. *Labor budget:* The labor budget shows the quantity of labor expected to be needed during the period. The labor budget is identical to the production and materials budgets above except that labor cannot be stored in inventory. Management can plan to have sufficiently trained labor available and plan the necessary cash needed to pay them in a timely fashion. Management might plan to start with two employees and add one employee in March. If each employee earns $600 per month, the labor budget is as follows:

	Jan.	Feb.	Mar.	Apr.
Salary	$ 600	$ 600	$ 600	$ 600
Number of employees	2	2	3	3
	$1,200	$1,200	$1,800	$1,800

Another aspect, which is omitted for simplicity, is the timing and amount of withholding payments and employment taxes, usually paid no later than the following month. Large firms often must make deposits every few days.

e. *Manufacturing overhead budget:* Overhead includes both fixed and variable components. A budget is prepared for each aspect. The fixed portion is constant for any volume by definition, whereas the variable portion is largely dependent on the production schedule. Some of the costs are discretionary as to timing and even as to incurrence. Machine maintenance costs may be higher in slack periods and lower in peak periods because of management policy.

f. *Selling expense budget:* Like manufacturing overhead, selling expenses are composed of fixed and variable elements. The fixed elements remain constant, although some may be discretionary, such as advertising. The variable elements will vary with sales volume, not production volume, as manufacturing overhead does.

g. *Administrative expense budget:* Like the manufacturing overhead and selling expense budgets, the administrative expense budget has fixed and variable components. Administrative expenses are dependent on management policy for amount and timing of expenditures.

h. *Cash budget:* The cash budget is very important to the success of a firm. The timing and quantity of cash inflows and outflows need to be estimated to the best of management's ability to provide sufficient funds to continue operations. With many firms, the seasonal nature of sales will result in a cash surplus in some months and a cash deficiency in other months. In times of surplus, excess funds are invested in such a manner as to maximize returns while maintaining liquidity.

i. *Master budget:* After all the individual sales, production, and expense budgets are prepared, they are combined into a master budget that is approved by the board of directors and becomes the plan or objective for the period. Master budgets are usually prepared on a quarterly or annual basis. The master budget serves as the financial and operating plan for the period.

j. *Capital budget:* A capital budget is a long-range budget that includes plans for addition of new product lines or purchase of any new plant or equipment items. A capital budget might cover a period as long as 5 to 10 years.

2. *Factors Considered in Budget Preparation:*

a. *Participative budgeting:* Budgets are used as motivational tools to help managers understand and meet the company's goals and objectives. When the individuals responsible for implementing the budget provide input into the budgeting process, it is called *participative budgeting.* When individuals help draft a plan or budget, it is assumed that they will want to try to meet the budget goals. Participative budgeting is used to aid in getting employees to accept the budget as their goal and improve motivation within the company.

b. *Zero-base budgeting:* Zero-base budgeting is a method of budgeting where managers are required to start at zero budget levels each year. They must justify all costs as if they were first-time costs. Frequently, traditional budgets are prepared by starting with last year's budget and adding to it or subtracting from it. With zero-base budgeting, every expenditure is reviewed, not just taken for granted.

c. *Continuous budgeting:* When continuous budgeting is followed, the budget is continually updated and reviewed each month. At any time, a continuous budget covers a 12-month period since it is updated every month.

d. *Using budgets as control tools:* To use budgeting effectively, a company must use budgets not only as planning tools but also as control mechanisms. Control involves the methods through which management assures that the company is operating in such a way as to attain the goals set out in the plan. One part of the control process is budget variation and analysis.

3. *Budget Variation and Analysis:* After a period for which a budget had been prepared has ended, the performance of the firm and responsible personnel can be evaluated by comparing budgeted items to actual results. Any difference between the two is known as a *variance.* A favorable variance occurs when an actual expense is less than a budgeted expense or an actual revenue is greater than a budgeted revenue. An unfavorable variance occurs when an actual expense is greater than a budgeted expense or an actual revenue is less than a budgeted revenue.

$$\left.\begin{array}{l}\text{Actual expense} > \text{budgeted expense}\\ \text{Actual revenue} < \text{budgeted revenue}\end{array}\right\}\ \text{Unfavorable variance}$$

$$\left.\begin{array}{l}\text{Actual expense} < \text{budgeted expense}\\ \text{Actual revenue} > \text{budgeted revenue}\end{array}\right\}\ \text{Favorable variance}$$

If actual results are compared to budgeted items for only the planned level of activity, the budget is known as a *static* budget. A better means of evaluating performance is by means of a *flexible* budget. Flexible budgets have varying amounts designated for different levels of activity. Variable costs are budgeted at an appropriate amount for the attained output. Static or fixed budgets are a good planning tool but are less meaningful for control or evaluation purposes.

EXAMPLE: Assume that the following information is budgeted for ABC Company:

Fixed costs	$750
Variable manufacturing costs	0.02/unit
Variable selling costs	0.01/unit
Sales price	0.05/unit

Assume that a static budget for 60,000 units was prepared and compared to the actual results.

	Static Budget	Actual Results
Sales	60,000 × 0.05 = 3,000	65,000 × 0.05 = 3,250
Variable manufacturing cost	60,000 × 0.02 = 1,200	65,000 × 0.025 = 1,625
Variable selling cost	60,000 × 0.01 = 600	65,000 × 0.009 = 585
Fixed costs	= 750	= 750
Profit	750	290

Analysis of the static budget as compared to the actual results gives the following variances:

Sales variance	$250	Favorable	(3,000–3,250)
Variable manufacturing variance	(425)	Unfavorable	(1,200–1,625)
Variable selling variance	15	Favorable	(600–585)
Total variance	(160)		

a. *Static budget:* When a static budget is compared to actual results line by line, the variances computed may have little meaning. This is because efficiency, level of sales quantity, and changes in prices are lumped into one amount. For example, we would expect that the actual variable manufacturing cost for ABC Company would be greater than the budgeted cost per the static budget because ABC Company produced more units than it anticipated. The variance does not provide information about whether the 65,000 units were produced efficiently. Variances that provide information about cost efficiency are based on a flexible budget related to the actual level of activity. Two variances are often calculated using the master or static budget: the sales price variance and the sales volume variance.

(1) *Sales price variance:* The sales price variance is computed by multiplying the difference between the budgeted selling price and the actual selling price per unit by the number of units sold.

(2) *Sales volume variance:* The sales volume variance is determined by multiplying the difference between actual sales and budgeted sales (in units) by the budgeted contribution margin per unit. The sales volume variance is considered to be a measure of the effectiveness of management for a given period.

EXAMPLE: Using the static budget and actual results from the previous ABC Company example, the sales price variance and sales volume variance would be calculated as follows:

$$\text{Sales price variance} = \text{actual units sold (ASP} - \text{BSP)}$$

where BSP is the budgeted selling price per unit and ASP is the actual selling price per unit.

$$\text{Sales price variance} = 65{,}000(0.05 - 0.05) = 0$$

This variance is zero since the budgeted selling price and the actual selling price were equal.

$$\text{Sales volume variance} = \text{budgeted CM(ASU} - \text{BSU)}$$

where CM is the contribution margin, ASU is the actual number of units sold, and BSU is the budgeted number of units expected to be sold.

$$\text{Sales volume variance} = 0.02(65{,}000 - 60{,}000) = 100 \text{ Favorable.}$$

The budgeted contribution margin is (0.05 − 0.03) = 0.02.

b. *Flexible budget:* A flexible budget is a budget that is prepared for different levels of activity. After actual production for the period is known, a flexible budget can be prepared that shows budgeted production costs for the actual level of activity.

EXAMPLE: Assume that a flexible budget for three different levels of activity was prepared as follows:

	Level of Activity		
	50,000 Units	60,000 Units	70,000 Units
Sales	$2,500	$3,000	$3,500
Variable manufacturing costs	1,000	1,200	1,400
Variable selling costs	500	600	700
Fixed costs	750	750	750
Profit	$ 250	$ 450	$ 650

This is very similar to cost-volume-profit analysis in providing expectations of revenues and expenditures at varying levels of activity. Actual results are now compared to budgeted allowances for the actual activity level.

	Flexible Budget	Actual Results
Sales	65,000 × 0.05 = 3,250	65,000 × 0.05 = 3,250
Variable manufacturing cost	65,000 × 0.02 = 1,300	65,000 × 0.025 = 1,625
Variable selling cost	65,000 × 0.01 = 650	65,000 × 0.009 = 585
Fixed costs	= 750	= 750
Profit	550	290

Analysis of results:

Sales variance	$ 0	
Variable manufacturing variance	(325)	Unfavorable
Variable selling variance	65	Favorable
Total variance	(260)	Unfavorable

The flexible budget variances may be split into price and efficiency variances (see Section C-2 of this chapter).

C. Standard Costing and Variance Analysis

A standard cost is a predetermined estimate of the cost per unit for materials, labor, and manufacturing overhead. A *standard cost* is the cost that should be incurred to produce a product or perform an operation efficiently. When a standard costing system is used, managers compare actual results with the predetermined standard goal to determine whether performance was satisfactory.

1. *Management by Exception:* A standard costing system allows managers to direct their attention to those areas that require corrective action. This is called *management by exception.* When a standard costing system is used, managers do not spend time reviewing areas that do not differ significantly from standard cost.

2. *Variance:* The difference between standard cost and actual cost is called the *variance.* A *favorable variance* occurs when actual cost is less than standard cost. An *unfavorable variance* occurs when actual cost is more than standard cost. The following example shows the calculation of the most common standard costing variances.

EXAMPLE: Assume that Hamsmith Co. has established the following cost standards for its product Snac:

Material (1 pound per unit @ $5 per pound)	$ 5.00
Direct labor (1 hour per unit @ $10 per hour)	10.00
Overhead ($5 per standard direct labor hour)	5.00
Total standard cost of one Snac	$20.00

Direct material variances:

Hamsmith Co. produced 1,000 units of Snac. It used 1,100 pounds of raw materials, which cost $4.95 per pound to produce the 1,000 Snacs.

	Actual cost (1,100 lb. @ $4.95)	=	$5,445
−	Standard cost (1,000 lb. @ $5.00)	=	5,000
	Total direct material variance (unfavorable)	=	−$ 445

The total direct material variance (flexible budget variance) may be divided into price and efficiency components as follows:

Price variance:

	Actual units used × actual price: 1,100 lb. × $4.95	=	$5,445
−	Actual units used × standard price: 1,100 lb. × $5.00	=	5,500
	Direct material price variance (favorable)	=	+$ 55

Efficiency variance:

	Actual units × standard price: 1,100 lb. × $5.00	=	$5,500
−	Standard units allowed × standard price: 1,000 lb. × $5.00	=	5,000
	Direct material efficiency variance (unfavorable)	=	−$ 500

	Direct material price variance (favorable)	=	+$ 55
+	Direct material efficiency variance (unfavorable)	=	− 500
	Total direct material variance (unfavorable)	=	−$ 445

Direct labor variances:

Hamsmith Co. used 1,110 hours costing $10.10 per hour to produce the 1,000 units of Snac.

	Actual labor cost:		
	1,110 hours × $10.10	=	$11,211
−	Standard labor cost:		
	1,000 hours × $10.00	=	10,000
	Total direct labor variance (unfavorable)	=	$ 1,211

The total direct labor variance (flexible budget variance) may be divided into price and efficiency components as follows:

Direct labor price variance:

	Actual hours used × actual price:		
	1,110 × $10.10	=	$11,211
−	Actual hours used × standard price:		
	1,110 × $10.00	=	11,100
	Direct labor price variance (unfavorable)	=	−$ 111

Direct labor efficiency variance:

	Actual hours used × standard price:		
	1,110 × $10.00	=	$11,100
−	Standard hours allowed × standard price:		
	1,000 × $10.00	=	− 10,000
	Direct labor efficiency variance (unfavorable)	=	$ 1,100

	Direct labor price variance (unfavorable)	=	−$ 111
+	Direct labor efficiency variance (unfavorable)	=	− 1,100
	Total direct labor variance (unfavorable)	=	−$ 1,211

Overhead variances may be computed in several ways. When standard costs are used, overhead is applied to production on the basis of a predetermined standard overhead rate. The calculation of overhead variances is beyond the scope of this chapter. The candidate should refer to an elementary managerial accounting textbook for further discussion of this topic.

D. Forecasting

Forecasting is the prediction of a value of a variable in the future. This prediction may be based on past values of the variable, values of related variables, or expert judgment. Forecasts are needed in business to plan for the future development of the company.

1. *Types of Forecasts:* Forecasts may be short term, medium term, or long term in nature. Short-term forecasts cover a period of only a few months. Medium-term forecasts

cover the period from about three months to two years in the future. Long-term forecasts cover periods beyond two years into the future. Forecasts that cover a shorter time frame are generally more accurate than long-term forecasts.

a. *Sales forecast:* A sales forecast is generally the first step in preparing a budget. After sales are forecast, production needs can be estimated on the basis of the forecasted level of sales.

b. *Capital expenditures forecast:* A company also needs to forecast what its capital expenditure requirements will be in the future. Advance planning is necessary to ensure that sufficient funds are available to purchase additional capital equipment.

c. *Product demand forecast:* Forecasts of demand for a company's products are useful in preparing sales forecasts and in determining where new products should be introduced and old product lines dropped.

d. *Other forecasts:* The different types of items that might be forecast are endless. Any item of information that would aid management in meeting goals and objectives of the company might be forecast.

2. *Factors Considered in Preparing Forecasts:* A number of different methods can be used to prepare forecasts.

a. *Forecasting methods:* These methods may be quantitative or qualitative in nature.

(1) Quantitative forecasts are based on past data. It is assumed that the trends observed in the past will continue in the future. Time-series models base the forecast on past values of the variable. Regression models assume that the variable to be forecast exhibits a cause-and-effect relationship with another variable or variables.

(2) Qualitative forecasts are not based on past data but on intuitive thinking, judgment, and expert knowledge.

The type of method that should be used depends on the individual situation. In making forecasts pertaining to new products, there may be no relevant past data. Many firms use a combination of methods to prepare forecasts.

b. *Accuracy of forecast:* A forecast is usually inaccurate. It might be useful to provide more than one value for a forecasted item. For example, pessimistic, most likely, and optimistic values of the forecast might be provided, or a range might be provided (i.e., $10,000 $\pm$ 15 percent).

c. *Performance monitoring:* After a forecast is prepared, actual performance of the variable should be monitored to determine the accuracy of the forecast and to aid in preparing future forecasts.

3. *Proforma Statements:* After the budgeting process is complete, a forecasted balance sheet and income statement can be prepared. These are called *proforma financial statements* and are used for planning and evaluation purposes.

Review Questions

Directions: Select the correct answer from the four alternatives. Write the letter of your answer in the blank to the left of the number.

________ **1.** A variable cost

a. will not be affected by changes in activity from period to period.
b. will remain constant in total as the level of activity changes.
c. increases or decreases proportionately (in total) with changes in the level of activity.
d. will increase on a per unit basis as the level of activity increases.

________ **2.** Which one of the following costs is variable?

a. Double-declining-balance depreciation on machinery
b. Direct materials
c. The salary of the plant supervisor
d. Rent on the office building

________ **3.** As the number of units produced by a manufacturing company decreases,

a. the variable cost per unit decreases.
b. fixed costs per unit remain the same.
c. fixed costs in total remain the same.
d. the variable cost in total remains the same.

________ **4.** Which one of the following costs is fixed?

a. Direct labor
b. Property taxes on the office building
c. Wages of inspection employees
d. Freight-in on goods purchased

________ **5.** When a company's actual sales for a period are equal to its breakeven sales,

a. total contribution margin for the company will be equal to total expenses for the period.
b. total revenues will be equal to total fixed expenses.
c. net income for the period will be zero.
d. total fixed expenses will equal total variable expenses.

________ **6.** Janet Company produces a game that sells for $22 per game. Variable costs are $12 per game, and fixed costs total $172,000 annually. The breakeven point in units is (rounded to the nearest unit)

a. 7,818.
b. 14,333.

c. 17,200.
d. 19,111.

______________ **7.** Karl Company produces dolls. Each doll sells for $15 per unit and has a contribution margin ratio of 60 percent. Total annual fixed expenses are $240,000. If Karl Company wants to earn $30,000 of net income, how many dolls must be sold?

a. 18,000
b. 28,667
c. 30,000
d. 45,000

______________ **8.** In a job order cost system, the entry to record the requisition of direct materials for use in production would include a

a. debit to the work-in-process account.
b. credit to the wages payable account.
c. debit to the direct materials account.
d. credit to accounts payable.

______________ **9.** In a job order cost system, the entry to record the wages paid to factory maintenance workers would include a

a. debit to the manufacturing overhead account.
b. credit to the manufacturing overhead account.
c. debit to the direct labor account.
d. debit to the work-in-process inventory account.

______________ **10.** In a job order cost system, the entry to record the application of overhead to a job would include a

a. debit to the manufacturing overhead account.
b. debit to the work-in-process inventory account.
c. credit to the work-in-process inventory account.
d. credit to the cost of goods sold account.

______________ **11.** Assume that XYZ Company applies overhead to production on the basis of a predetermined overhead rate. A debit balance in the manufacturing overhead account at the end of the period means

a. the overhead cost that was actually incurred was greater than the amount applied to production.
b. the overhead cost that was actually incurred was less than the amount applied to production.
c. the amount of manufacturing overhead incurred was equal to the manufacturing overhead applied during the period.
d. more hours were actually worked during the period than were predicted in calculating the predetermined overhead rate.

_____ **12.** Which one of the following companies would be most likely to use process costing?

a. A soft-drink manufacturer
b. A manufacturer of specialized machine tools
c. A contractor building bridges
d. A company that manufactures luxury oceanliners

_____ **13.** Electricity is a mixed cost for ABC Company. ABC Company estimates that the fixed portion of the monthly electrical cost is $500 and that the variable portion is $0.10 per machine hour. If ABC Company used 12,000 machine hours in April, the estimate of total electrical cost for the month would be

a. $500.
b. $1,200.
c. $1,700.
d. $1,800.

_____ **14.** The fixed cost per unit for rent is $0.50 at a production level of 200,000 units. If 225,000 units are produced, the total fixed cost for rent would be

a. $50,000.
b. $65,500.
c. $100,000.
d. $112,500.

_____ **15.** Kilo Company applies overhead to units of product on the basis of machine hours. At the beginning of the period, Kilo Company estimated that total manufacturing overhead would be $500,000 and that the number of machine hours used during the period would be 200,000. Kilo Company actually used 220,000 machine hours during the period. The total amount of overhead applied for this period was

a. $84,000.
b. $220,000.
c. $500,000.
d. $550,000.

_____ **16.** The budget that shows the quantity of units required to be produced during the period is called the

a. sales budget.
b. cash budget.
c. production budget.
d. manufacturing overhead budget.

_____ **17.** When the individuals responsible for implementing the budget are involved in preparing the budget, it is called

a. shared budgeting.
b. collective budgeting.
c. zero-base budgeting.
d. participative budgeting.

______________ **18.** The budget that is used to plan for long-range purchases of new plant and equipment is called the

a. proforma budget.
b. cash budget.
c. capital budget.
d. production budget.

______________ **19.** Farley Enterprises has budgeted the following sales in units:

May	5,000 units
June	7,000 units
July	5,000 units

Farley Enterprises desires to have an ending inventory equal to 25 percent of next month's sales needs. The beginning inventory on May 1 was 1,250 units. The total units to be produced in May are

a. 4,750.
b. 5,000.
c. 5,250.
d. 5,500.

______________ **20.** An unfavorable variance results when

a. actual revenue is less than budgeted revenue.
b. actual expense is less than budgeted expense.
c. actual revenue is greater than actual expense.
d. actual expense is greater than budgeted revenue.

______________ **21.** A method of budgeting where managers are expected to justify all costs as if they were first-time expenditures is called

a. capital budgeting.
b. participative budgeting.
c. continuous budgeting.
d. zero-base budgeting.

______________ **22.** A predetermined estimate of the cost per unit for materials, labor, or manufacturing overhead is called

a. a standard cost.
b. management by exception.
c. a unit cost.
d. a variance cost.

______________ **23.** Which of the following variances would be used to evaluate whether a company used an appropriate amount of raw material when producing a job?

a. Direct material price variance
b. Direct material efficiency variance

c. Direct labor efficiency variance
d. Overhead variance

_______________ **24.** Forecasted financial statements are called

a. proforma financial statements.
b. historical financial statements.
c. futuristic financial statements.
d. flexible financial statements.

Use the following financial information pertaining to the sales activities of the 4R Corporation for the year 20XA in answering Questions 25 to 27.

Selling price per unit	$ 25
Variable production cost per unit	11
Fixed production cost	3,600
Selling commission per unit	2
Fixed selling expenses	24,000
Number of units sold in 20XA	6,000

_______________ **25.** The total contribution margin generated in 20XA was (rounded to the nearest dollar)

a. $50,000.
b. $57,500.
c. $72,000.
d. $84,000.

_______________ **26.** The breakeven point in dollars is (rounded to the nearest dollar)

a. $18,000.
b. $50,000.
c. $57,500.
d. $75,000.

_______________ **27.** Assuming that the cost information does not change, how many units would the company have to sell in 20XB to earn a $54,000 profit (rounded to the nearest unit)?

a. 4,460
b. 6,800
c. 10,000
d. 170,000

Use the following information in answering Questions 28 and 29.

Jones Company budgeted to sell 20,000 units at $10 per unit. Variable manufacturing costs at $5 per unit were included in the budget. Jones Company actually sold 18,000 units at a price of $11.00 per unit. Actual variable manufacturing costs were $5.50 per unit. (F = favorable; U = unfavorable)

_______________ **28.** The sales price variance would be

a. $18,000 F.
b. $18,000 U.

c. $20,000 F.
d. $20,000 U.

______ **29.** The sales volume variance would be

a. $1,000 U.
b. $10,000 U.
c. $11,000 F.
d. $20,000 U.

Use the following information in answering Questions 30 to 34.

The standard costs for a unit of finished product are as follows:

	Standard Quantity	Standard Price
Direct materials	10 feet	$ 2.00 per foot
Direct labor	2 hours	$15.00 per hour

The company actually produced 10,000 units. The actual quantity used was 105,000 feet, and the actual cost of materials was $199,500. The company actually used 18,000 direct labor hours at a cost of $279,000.

______ **30.** The direct material price variance would be

a. $500 F.
b. $10,000 F.
c. $10,500 F.
d. $15,000 U.

______ **31.** The direct material quantity variance would be

a. $950 U.
b. $10,000 U.
c. $10,000 F.
d. $11,000 F.

______ **32.** The flexible budget variance for direct materials would be

a. $500 F.
b. $500 U.
c. $10,000 F.
d. $11,000 U.

______ **33.** The direct labor rate (price) variance would be

a. $9,000 U.
b. $10,000 U.
c. $21,000 F.
d. $22,000 F.

_______________ **34.** The direct labor efficiency variance would be

a. \$21,000 F.
b. \$27,000 F
c. \$30,000 F.
d. \$30,000 U.

Solutions

Answer Refer to:

1. (c) [A-2-a]

2. (b) [A-2-a]

3. (c) [A-2-b]

4. (b) [A-2-b]

5. (c) [A-3-b]

6. (c) [A-3-b]

$$\frac{\text{fixed expenses}}{\text{contribution margin/unit}} = \text{breakeven point in units}$$

$$\frac{\$172{,}000}{\$22 - 12} = 17{,}200 \text{ Units}$$

7. (c) [A-3] The formula to solve this question is

$$\frac{\text{fixed expenses} + \text{desired net income}}{\text{contribution margin per unit}} = \text{breakeven point in units}$$

$$\frac{\$240{,}000 + \$30{,}000}{\$9 \text{ per unit}} = 30{,}000 \text{ dolls}$$

If the selling price per unit is $15 and the contribution margin ratio is 60 percent, the per unit contribution margin is $9.

Selling price	$15	100%
− Variable cost	− 6	40%
Contribution margin	$ 9	60%

8. (a) [A-5-a(4)(b)]

9. (a) [A-5-a(4)(c)]

10. (b) [A-5-a(4)(e)]

11. (a) [A-5-a(4)(e)]

12. (a) [A-5-b]

13. (c) [A-2-c]

Total cost = variable cost + fixed cost
$1,700 = $0.10(12,000) + $500

14. (c) [A-2-b]

200,000 × $0.50 = $100,000

Since fixed cost remains constant in total regardless of the level of activity (within the relevant range), the total fixed cost would be the same whether 200,000 units or 225,000 units were produced.

15. (d) [A-5-a(4)(e)]

$$\text{predetermined overhead rate} = \frac{\text{estimated total overhead}}{\text{estimated quantity of the application base}}$$

$$\text{\$2.50 per machine hour} = \frac{\$500{,}000}{200{,}000 \text{ hours}}$$

$550,000 = 220,000 machine hours × $2.50/machine hour

16. (c) [B-1]

17. (d) [B-2-a]

18. (c) [B-1-j]

19. (d) [B-1-b]

Sales	5,000
+ Desired ending inventory (7,000 × 0.25)	1,750
	6,750
− Beginning inventory already available	− 1,250
Units to be produced	5,500

20. (a) [B-3]

21. (d) [B-2-b]

22. (a) [C]

23. (b) [C-2]

24. (a) [D-3]

25. (c) [A-3-a]

sales − variable expenses = contribution margin

Sales ($25.00 × 6,000)			$150,000
− Variable expenses:			
Variable production ($11.00 × 6,000)	=	$66,000	
Variable selling ($2.00 × 6,000)	=	12,000	78,000
Contribution margin			$ 72,000

26. (c) [A-3-c]

$$\frac{\text{fixed expenses}}{\text{contribution margin ratio}} = \begin{array}{c}\text{breakeven point}\\ \text{in dollars}\end{array}$$

$$\frac{\$27{,}600}{0.48} = \$57{,}500$$

Contribution margin ratio = $72,000/$150,000 = 0.48

27. (b) [A-3-d]

$$\frac{\text{fixed expenses} + \text{desired net income}}{\text{contribution margin per unit}} = \begin{array}{c}\text{BEP in}\\ \text{units}\end{array}$$

$$\frac{\$27{,}600 + \$54{,}000}{\$12/\text{unit}} = 6{,}800$$

Contribution margin per unit = $25 − 14 = $12

28. (a) [B-3-a]

Sales price variance = actual units sold (ASP − BSP), where ASP = actual selling price and BSP = budgeted selling price.

$18,000 = 18,000 units sold (11.00 − 10.00)

The variance is favorable because the actual selling price was greater than the budgeted selling price. When actual revenue is more than budgeted revenue, the variance is favorable.

29. (b) [B-3-a(2)]

Sales volume variance = budgeted CM(ASU − BSU), where CM = contribution margin, ASU = actual sales in units, and BSU = budgeted sales in units.

−$10,000 = $5.00(18,000 − 20,000)

Budgeted contribution margin = $10.00 − 5.00 = $5.00

This variance is unfavorable because the actual cost exceeded the budgeted cost.

30. (c) [C-2] The direct material price variance is equal to AQ(AP) − AQ(SP), where AQ = actual quantity of units used, AP = actual price of units purchased, and SP = standard price per unit of material.

The actual price of the units was $1.90($199,500/105,000).

105,000($1.90) − 105,000($2.00) = $10,500

This variance is favorable because the actual price paid was less than the standard price allowed.

Note: It is also possible to base the material price variance on units purchased rather than units used.

31. (b) [C-2] The direct material quantity variance is equal to AQ(SP) − SQ(SP), where AQ = actual quantity of units used, SP = standard price per unit of material, and SQ = standard units allowed.

Standard units allowed is equal to units produced times the standard quantity of material allowed per finished unit.

SQ = 10,000 units × 10 feet = 100,000 feet

DM quantity variance = 105,000($2.00) − 100,000 ($2.00)

DM quantity variance = $10,000

This variance is unfavorable because the actual quantity of feet used was greater than the standard quantity of feet allowed.

32. (a) [C-2] The flexible budget variance is the difference between the actual cost for materials and the standard cost allowed for materials. It is also equal to the sum of the DM price variance and the DM quantity variance.

Actual cost	$199,500
− Standard cost allowed	−200,000
= Flexible budget variance	$500

Standard cost allowed is equal to the standard quantity allowed times the standard price (100,000 × $2.00).

This variance is favorable because actual cost was less than standard cost.

33. (a) [C-2] The direct labor rate (price) variance is equal to AH(AP) − AH(SP), where AH = actual hours used, AP = actual price paid per hour, and SP = standard price allowed per hour.

18,000 hours($15.50) − 18,000 hours($15.00) = $9,000

Actual price paid is equal to $270,000/18,000 hours = $15.50/hour.

This variance is unfavorable because the actual rate paid was greater than the standard rate allowed.

34. (c) [C-2] The direct labor efficiency variance is equal to AH(SP) − SH(SP), where AH = actual hours used, SP = standard price allowed per hour, and SH = standard hours allowed.

Standard hours allowed is equal to the number of units produced times the standard number of hours allowed per finished unit.

SH = 10,000 units × 2 hours/unit = 20,000 hours

DL efficiency variance = 18,000($15.00) − 20,000 ($15.00)

DL efficiency variance = $30,000

This variance is favorable because the actual number of hours used was less than the standard number of hours allowed.

Section III Business Law

CHAPTER 20 Introduction to Business Law

OVERVIEW

Law provides a consistent means of defining rights and resolving disputes. Since the business community desires an atmosphere of stability, business law in particular must be sound and predictable. To gain an adequate understanding of law, one should be familiar with the sources of law, including their hierarchy. Basic legal terminology needs to be mastered and an awareness developed of the major areas of law.

This chapter serves as a basic introduction to law. In the chapters that follow we will explore specific areas of law in greater detail.

KEY TERMS

Civil law	Misdemeanor	Statutory law
Common law	Precedent	Strict liability
Constitutional law	Procedural law	Substantive law
Criminal law	Promulgate	Tort law
Executive order	Regulation	
Felony	Stare decisis	

A. Origin of Law

The origin of our legal system is the English common law. With the signing of the Magna Charta in 1215, King John formally recognized certain rights of landowners and provided a means of adjudicating those rights. Over time, a court system evolved and judicial opinions were recorded. These opinions became precedent for future cases involving similar facts. The vast body of case law that has developed is known as *common law.*

1. *Common Law:* Common law is case law. Our common law actually includes the case law and custom of England prior to the American Revolution insofar as it has not been expressly superseded or overruled by cases or laws of the United States. Our common law also includes all published opinions of courts in the United States. Needless to say, the common law is an immense body of case law that is the subject of much legal research by attorneys and legal scholars.

   a. *Basis for common law:* Common law is based on the concept of precedent. A goal of the common law is consistency. Once a legal principle is established, it should be followed. Thus, once a case is decided, it becomes a precedent to be considered by future courts in adjudicating similar issues.

b. *The doctrine of stare decisis:* The doctrine that precedent should be followed is known as *stare decisis* (the decision stands). In applying stare decisis, a court would follow precedent and decide the same legal issue consistent with the earlier court's ruling.

2. *Constitutional Law:* Constitutional law is derived from the United States Constitution. The Constitution and the accompanying Bill of Rights are the highest law of the land. The Constitution prevails over any other law.

a. *Supreme Court opinions:* The Constitution has been interpreted in numerous cases decided by the Supreme Court. These Supreme Court opinions are part of what is commonly known as *constitutional law.*

b. *Final authority:* The Supreme Court of the United States is the final authority on what the Constitution means.

3. *Statutory Law:* Statutory law is enacted by legislative bodies.

a. *Congressional acts:* The Congress of the United States enacts federal statutes that apply throughout the United States.

b. *State legislative statutes:* The legislature of each state enacts statutes that apply within the boundaries of that state.

c. *Federal law:* Federal law governs over any inconsistent state law.

d. *An unconstitutional statute:* A statute, state or federal, may be declared unconstitutional by the Supreme Court.

4. *Regulations:* Regulations are promulgated by administrative agencies (see Chapter 25).

a. *Regulatory agencies:* Congress has created regulatory agencies and has granted rule-making authority to some of them.

(1) Agency employees are capable of acquiring a high level of expertise in a given field.

(2) Agencies can promulgate regulations only within the scope of the authority granted by Congress.

(3) Specific procedures exist for rule making by agencies (see Chapter 25).

b. *Prevailing statute:* A statute prevails over a conflicting regulation.

5. *Executive Orders:* Executive orders are laws issued by the president of the United States.

a. *Authority:* The president's authority to issue executive orders is limited. Such authority must be traceable to an act of Congress or to the Constitution.

b. *Prevailing statute:* A federal statute prevails over a conflicting executive order.

B. Classifications of Law

Although there are many subdivisions of law, in this chapter we address only several broad classifications.

1. *Civil Law:* Civil law pertains to private, as opposed to public, rights.

EXAMPLES OF CIVIL LAW: Contract law (Chapter 21) and property law (Chapter 26).

2. *Tort Law:* Tort law is a broad area of civil law. Tort law is the law of civil wrongs, which include intentional wrongs and negligence.

   a. *Negligence:* Negligence is the breach of a duty of care owed to another person.

      EXAMPLE: One who drives an automobile owes a duty of care to other motorists and to pedestrians. A breach of that duty of care may consist of driving too fast and not maintaining a proper lookout.

      If such negligent conduct results in injury, the injured party may sue and recover for his or her losses.

   b. *Strict liability:* Strict liability provides a basis for an injured party to sue for and recover damages without having to prove negligence.

      (1) *Dangerous activities:* Strict liability is limited to highly dangerous activities.

         EXAMPLE: Anderson decides to use dynamite to clear his property of old tree stumps. Blasting dynamite is a highly dangerous activity. Anderson is legally responsible for any damage caused by the blasting even if he employs all reasonable precautions.

      (2) *No real defense:* When strict liability exists, there is no real defense. The trial would focus on the extent of damage to be compensated.

3. *Criminal Law:* Criminal law defines offenses against the government and provides penal sanctions for such violations.

   a. *Criminal suit:* A criminal case is brought in the name of and on behalf of the state or federal government against the alleged violator.

   b. *Protection of individual rights:* Because the liberty of one charged with a crime is at stake, the individual's rights are carefully protected. A person charged with a crime has a right to remain silent and, if jail is a possibility, a right to free legal representation if he or she cannot afford to hire a lawyer.

   c. *Presumption of innocence:* The prosecution is required to prove guilt beyond a reasonable doubt before there can be a conviction. The person charged with a crime is presumed innocent until proven guilty.

   d. *Felony:* A felony is a crime punishable by one year or more in prison.

   e. *Misdemeanor:* A misdemeanor is a crime punishable by up to one year of incarceration.

   f. *Tort or crime:* The same act may be both a tort and a crime.

4. *Procedural Law:* Procedural law consists of rules governing the enforcement of laws and rights. Lawsuits are governed by these procedural rules.

   EXAMPLE: A statute may set forth the exact method of jury selection to be used in that state. This is a procedural law.

5. *Substantive Law:* Substantive law defines rights and duties.

   EXAMPLE: A statute may bestow a right to sue for damages in certain types of cases where no such right is specifically guaranteed by the Constitution and where no such right is recognized as common law. Such a statute is substantive law.

   Thus, while substantive law defines rights, procedural law provides the means or rules whereby these rights are enforceable.

CHAPTER 21

Contracts

OVERVIEW

Modern business transactions involve numerous agreements: employment agreements; agreements to buy or sell goods; agreements to buy, sell, or lease land; and agreements to lend or borrow money, to name just a few. Not all agreements, however, are legally enforceable. Adding to the legal complexity of modern transactions is the increased use of electronic communication (i.e., fax machines and electronic mail), which was unheard of not so long ago. The legal principles used to determine which agreements are enforceable are embodied in the law of contracts. In this chapter we present a look at the major principles of contract law.

Although knowledge of the terms and principles presented in this chapter is essential to an understanding of contract law, mere knowledge is not enough for success on the examination. The candidate must be able to apply the principles of contract law to fact situations and determine whether a contract exists. In some cases it will also be necessary to determine what type of contract is involved and what remedies are available in the event the contract is breached.

KEY TERMS

Acceptance
Assignee
Assignment
Assignor
Bilateral contract
Breach of contract
Common law
Consideration
Contract
Contractual capacity
Delegation
Disaffirmance
Duress
Express contract
Formal contract
Goods
Gratuitous assignment
Illusory promise
Implied contract
Merchant
Novation
Offer
Offeree
Offeror
Quasi-contract
Ratification
Restitution
Revocation
Simple contract
Statute
Uniform Commercial Code (UCC)
Unilateral contract
Void contract
Voidable contract

A. Common Law versus Sales Law

1. *Common Law:* The origin of contract law is the common law. Common law contract law resulted from case precedents. Although the common law evolved in each state, there are basic principles that are generally accepted in all states that will be presented in this chapter.

2. *Establishment of the Uniform Commercial Code (UCC):* To promote greater uniformity in interstate commercial transactions, the Uniform Commercial Code (UCC) was developed as a model law for state consideration and enactment. Today, the UCC has been adopted by every state. The UCC applies to a wide range of business applications, such as the sale of goods (contracts for the sale of goods), commercial paper (discussed in Chapter 22), and security interests in personal property.

3. *Application of Article 2:* Article 2 of the UCC, Sales, applies to the sale of goods. Where applicable, Article 2 supersedes the common law. Although this chapter will focus on the common law, the following sales terms and concepts should be noted.

   a. *Goods:* Goods are tangible personal property.

      EXAMPLES: A football, car, loaf of bread, this book, and similar items are all goods.

      The sale of land or the providing of a service are not goods.

   b. *Merchant:* A merchant is a person who regularly deals in the kind of goods involved.

      EXAMPLE: A hardware store owner is a merchant for goods regularly sold at his store. However, he is not a merchant for the sale of a used refrigerator at a garage sale at his house.

      Some Article 2 rules apply only to a merchant (e.g., the firm offer, discussed in Section C-2-b[2]) or to merchants (the battle of forms, discussed in Section C-3-b[2]).

   c. *Good faith:* The UCC requires good faith of all parties involved in the sale of goods. Good faith is defined as honesty in fact.

   d. *Focus on performance:* Article 2 has greater emphasis than the common law on rules and expectations of performance of a contract, including possible warranties.

Unless stated otherwise, the law presented in this chapter is common law contract law. However, many of the Article 2 provisions are similar or identical to the common law, especially with regard to the elements of a contract (discussed in Sections B-1 to B-5).

B. Elements of a Contract

For an agreement to be a legally enforceable contract, five elements must be present. First, the agreement must be legal as to both subject matter and purpose. Second, there must be mutuality of agreement. Third, there must be legal consideration. Fourth, the parties to the agreement must have contractual capacity. Fifth, the agreement must conform to any specific, additional requirements imposed by statute.

1. *Legality:* Courts will not enforce illegal agreements. If the law were otherwise, the courts would actually be facilitating the breaking of the law. Consider the absurdity of a court enforcing the following agreement:

   EXAMPLE: Atwood agrees to pay Boyd $50 in return for Boyd's promise to break Cameron's arm. Atwood cannot enforce this agreement by obtaining a court order directing Boyd to perform as promised. Similarly, Boyd, if he had actually broken Cameron's arm, could not obtain a judgment against Atwood for the promised $50.

   a. *Subject matter:* Agreements may be found to be illegal for various reasons. The subject matter may be illegal.

      EXAMPLE: Ashton agrees to sell a gram of cocaine to Booth for $200.

b. *Purpose:* The purpose of the agreement may be illegal.

EXAMPLE: Seymour promises to pay Williams $100 in return for Williams's promise to testify falsely at Seymour's criminal trial that Seymour was visiting Williams in another city at the time the crime was committed. The purpose of this agreement is for Williams to commit perjury to assist Seymour in defending himself against the charge.

c. *Violation of statute:* The agreement may violate a statute.

EXAMPLES: Simpson and Powell bet $100 on the outcome of a football game. Gambling is outlawed by a state statute. (Some states permit certain types of regulated gambling.)

Price agrees to loan Pryor $300 in return for Pryor's promise to repay the $300 with 50 percent interest at the end of one year. Most states have usury statutes regulating the maximum amount of interest that may be charged. An agreement that requires the payment of interest in excess of the statutory maximum is illegal. (Such excess interest is called usury *and is said to be* usurious.*)*

Davis hires Edwards to remove a tumor surgically from Davis's arm. Edwards is not licensed to practice medicine. Each state has laws requiring that persons practicing trades or professions, such as medicine, law, dentistry, architecture, building, and plumbing, be licensed by the state. An agreement that requires an unlicensed party to perform such work is illegal.

d. *Public policy:* The agreement may be against public policy.

EXAMPLE: The Acme Catering Company, which provides food for wedding receptions and banquets, requires its customers to sign an agreement that relieves Acme of any liability resulting from its negligence in preparing or serving food. Such an exculpatory clause is illegal because it violates public policy. The public has an interest in ensuring that the food served at such functions is safe to eat. Removing liability from the preparer and server of the food takes away a major incentive for the exercise of due care and is likely to leave the injured parties without an effective legal remedy.

e. *Partial legality:* Some agreements are only partially illegal. If the legal portion of a partially illegal agreement can be severed from the illegal part, the court will probably enforce the legal portion.

EXAMPLE: The Atlas Pharmaceutical Company agrees to sell 300 units of drug A (illegal) for $600 and 300 units of drug B (legal) for $300 to Hamilton Drug Stores, Inc. The court will probably enforce the part of the agreement pertaining to the legal drug B. Because that part carried a separate price term, the contract is severable.

2. *Mutuality of Agreement:* For there to be a contract, the words or conduct of the parties must indicate that there is an agreement between them.

a. *Intent of parties:* The law does not ordinarily delve into the minds of the parties to find what they actually were thinking; instead, it judges their intent from their words and conduct.

EXAMPLE: Knight offers to sell a new Garth Brooks compact disc to Atkins for $5. Atkins agrees. Knight then refuses to go through with their deal because he had meant his offer to be a joke. If a reasonable third party would have thought the "offer" to have been an actual offer, then Knight would be bound regardless of his subjective (persona) intent.

b. *Mutual assent:* In some situations, even though it *appears* that there is mutual assent, underlying facts make it clear that the agreement of a party was not voluntary.

(1) *Duress:* The expression of assent may be the result of duress. Duress is present when a party uses an improper threat to obtain another party's assent.

EXAMPLE: Edison threatens to break Jackson's arm unless Jackson signs a contract. As a result of the threat, Jackson signs the contract. If Edison sues Jackson to enforce the contract, duress provides a valid defense for Jackson.

(2) *Undue influence:* The expression of assent may be the result of undue influence. Undue influence is present when a party takes unfair advantage of the high level of trust and confidence another person has placed in him or her to obtain that person's expression of assent. For undue influence to apply, the relationship between the parties must be a close one built on trust.

EXAMPLE: Jenkins is an 86-year-old invalid who relies on her sister Jordan to care for her and handle her financial affairs. Jordan tells Jenkins to invest all of her savings in stock of the Green Company. Trusting Jordan, Jenkins agrees to make the investment. Jenkins does not know that Jordan and her husband operate the Green Company, which is deeply in debt. Jenkins's assent was obtained through undue influence. Jenkins, therefore, has a valid defense if Jordan attempts to enforce the agreement.

(3) *Fraud:* The expression of assent may be the result of fraud.

(a) Fraud requires that there be a false representation.

(b) The false statement must be one of fact, not of opinion.

(c) The falsely stated fact must be likely to influence the decision of the person to whom it is made. (In other words, the falsely stated fact must be material to the agreement.)

(d) The false statement must be made by one who has knowledge of its falsity and intent to deceive.

(e) The false statement must be justifiably relied on by the party to whom it was made.

EXAMPLES: Gustafson offers to sell his airplane to MacLeod. Gustafson says to MacLeod, "I think you will really enjoy owning this plane." In fact, Gustafson does not believe MacLeod will enjoy owning the plane. There is no fraud because Gustafson's statement was one of opinion, not of fact.

Gustafson offers to sell his airplane to MacLeod. Gustafson tells MacLeod that the plane has never been in a crash. In fact, the plane was damaged in a crash. Gustafson had the plane repaired. There is no apparent evidence of the earlier damage. If MacLeod agrees to buy the plane based on Gustafson's statement, fraud has occurred, and MacLeod can succeed in having the agreement set aside and may collect any damage from Gustafson.

(4) *Misrepresentation:* The expression of assent may be the result of *innocent misrepresentation.*

(a) The elements of innocent misrepresentation are the same as those of fraud, with one exception. There is no requirement that the party making the statement know of its falsity.

EXAMPLE: Gustafson offers to sell his airplane to MacLeod. Gustafson tells MacLeod that the plane has never been in a crash. Unknown to Gustafson, the plane was in a crash before he purchased it. Gustafson has made an innocent misrepresentation.

(b) The victim of innocent misrepresentation may succeed in having the agreement set aside but cannot collect punitive damages from the party making the representation.

(5) *Mutual mistake:* The expression of assent may be the result of a mutual mistake.

(a) If both parties agreed to enter into an agreement on the basis of a fundamental mistake as to the subject of the agreement, the contract may be set aside.

EXAMPLE: Allen agrees to sell her motorcycle to Sheridan. Unknown to either party, the motorcycle was totally destroyed by fire the day before their agreement. Their mistake was a mutual one that went to the very subject matter of the agreement.

(b) If the mistake is not mutual, it does not affect the expression of assent.

EXAMPLE: Allen agrees to sell her motorcycle to Sheridan for $600. Allen mistakenly believes that the motorcycle has a market value of $600. In fact, it has a market value of $800. Allen's mistake does not affect the agreement. It is not mutual. Moreover, it does not involve the fundamental nature of the subject matter but relates only to its value.

3. *Consideration:* For there to be a contract, there must be a bargained-for exchange of something of value. The legal term for this requirement is *consideration.*

a. *Exchange of value:* Consideration may consist of a party giving up a legal right in return for something else of value.

EXAMPLES: Smith agrees to refrain from smoking any cigarettes for six months in return for Gray's promise to pay Smith $100 at the end of that time. Smith has given up her right to smoke, and Gray has promised to give up $100. Consideration is present.

Adams has sued Ryan for striking him in the face and breaking his nose. Adams agrees to dismiss the suit in return for Ryan's promise to pay for his medical expenses. Adams has given up his legal right to pursue the case. Consideration is present.

b. *Bargained-for exchange:* Without a bargained-for exchange, there can be no consideration.

EXAMPLE: Feeling guilty for having injured Adams, Ryan promises to pay for Adams's medical expenses. Adams, in a gesture of forgiveness, promises to dismiss the suit he had filed against Ryan. There is no consideration. The promises were not exchanged. Each was made without a return promise.

c. *Exchange of equal value not required:* The bargained-for exchange need not involve things of equal value in order to constitute consideration.

EXAMPLE: Phillips agrees to pay Daniels $50 for a fishing pole that Daniels had recently purchased for $3. The courts are not concerned with the adequacy of what a party gets under the terms of the agreement. The courts are only concerned that there be an exchange of something of some value.

d. *Promise to pay for services already rendered:* A promise to pay for work already performed does not involve consideration.

EXAMPLE: On returning from vacation and finding that his neighbor has trimmed his hedges, Farrell promises to pay his neighbor $20. There is no consideration. At the time of Farrell's promise, the work had already been completed. Farrell's promise is unenforceable.

e. *Preexisting legal duty:* A promise to pay someone to do what that person is already legally bound to do does not involve consideration.

EXAMPLES: Dobbs promises to pay Jorgenson $35 in return for Jorgenson's promise not to break any of Dobbs's windows during the month of May. Breaking Dobbs's windows is a violation of the law. Jorgenson is obligated to obey the law. Therefore, Dobbs's promise is not legally enforceable. He has merely promised to pay Jorgenson to obey the law—something Jorgenson is already obligated to do.

Wilson contracted to paint James's house for $400. Wilson stopped painting when he was only half finished. He refused to continue unless James promised to pay him an additional $100. James made the promise. Wilson then finished painting the house. James is not legally obligated to pay the additional $100. His promise to pay it was not part of a bargained-for exchange of something of value because Wilson did nothing more than promise to do what he was already legally obligated to do. Wilson gave up nothing in return for the additional promise.

f. *Illusory promise:* An illusory promise does not provide a basis for consideration. An illusory promise is one that does not impose an enforceable obligation on the promisor.

EXAMPLE: In return for receiving a 10 percent discount, Joseph of Joe's Ice Cream Parlour promises to purchase all of the ice cream he wants from Jake's Wholesale Company. Joseph may avoid any further obligation by stating that he does not want any more ice cream from Jake's. The result would be the same if Joseph had used the word desire *instead of* want.

g. *Promise to buy one's needs:* A promise to buy all of one's *needs* or *requirements* can serve as a basis for consideration. Courts regard such a promise as being enforceable. A good faith requirement is imposed on the promisor. Needs or requirements can be determined with reasonable definiteness. The same is true of a promise to sell all of one's output to a particular customer.

4. *Capacity of Parties:* Both parties to a contract must have *contractual capacity* if the agreement is to be fully enforceable.

a. *Age of majority:* To have contractual capacity, a party must have attained the age of majority. Anyone who has not attained that age is a minor. The age of majority at common law was 21 years of age. Today in nearly all states the age of majority is 18 years of age.

(1) *Minor's right to void contract:* A minor who enters into a contract has the right to avoid (to make void) the contract if he or she elects to do so. When this happens, the minor is said to have *disaffirmed* the contract.

(2) *Minor's right to enforce contract:* A minor who has entered into a contract with an adult has the right to enforce the contract against the adult.

EXAMPLE: Donahue, who is 16 years old, contracts with Cole, who is an adult. Under the terms of the contract, Donahue is to pay Cole $20 per month for 14 months in return for Cole's jukebox. Donahue may elect to disaffirm the contract. In doing so, he must return the jukebox. Instead, Donahue might elect to treat the contract as a binding one. If Cole failed to deliver the jukebox, for example, Donahue could enforce the agreement. Only the minor has the option of disaffirming the contract.

(3) *Return of contract items:* On disaffirming a contract, a minor must return to the adult anything the minor received under the contract. If the minor no longer has what was received, however, most courts will nevertheless allow the minor to disaffirm.

(4) *Reasonable time for disaffirmance:* A minor may disaffirm anytime during minority and within a reasonable time after reaching majority.

(5) *Contract for necessary items:* On disaffirming a contract for necessary items such as food, clothing, or emergency medical care, the minor must pay the reasonable value of the necessities.

(6) *Ratification of contract by minor:* One who entered a contract while a minor may *ratify* the contract on reaching majority. Once the contract is ratified, it may no longer be disaffirmed.

(a) *Words or actions:* Ratification may result from words or actions of the minor that indicate an intent to recognize the contract as an enforceable obligation.

(b) *Majority:* Ratification can occur after the age of majority has been attained.

EXAMPLE: While 17 years old, Shafer entered into a contract to purchase a camera. Under the terms of the contract, she was to pay $15 per month for three years. Shafer made six monthly payments after her eighteenth birthday. Shafer will be deemed to have ratified the contract. Shafer can no longer disaffirm.

b. *Contractual capacity:* A party who has attained the age of majority is presumed to have contractual capacity. Not all adults, however, have contractual capacity. There are two types of situations in which an adult will be found to lack capacity.

(1) *Mental deficiency:* A person who is unable to understand the nature of the contract because of mental deficiency lacks contractual capacity.

(a) The mental deficiency must have existed at the time the contract was formed.

(b) The mental deficiency must be more severe than a mere lacking of normal intelligence. It must deprive the person of the ability to understand the subject matter of the agreement and its consequences.

(c) The lack of capacity need not be permanent.

(2) *Intoxication:* A person who is so intoxicated by alcohol or drugs that he or she is incapable of understanding the nature of the contract lacks contractual capacity.

c. *Disaffirmance of contract:* An adult who lacks capacity because of mental deficiency or intoxication may disaffirm a contract if he or she is able to substantially restore the other party to the precontractual position. The contract is said to be voidable.

d. *Ratification of contract:* One who entered a contract while suffering from incapacity because of mental deficiency or intoxication may ratify the contract after capacity is regained.

5. *Form Required by Law:* Specific statutes require that certain types of agreements be in writing or meet other special requirements as to form. The statute of frauds is discussed in Section F. Other statutes vary from state to state and have narrow application in their coverage. Negotiable instruments are discussed in Chapter 22.

C. Formation

An agreement is usually formed with an offer and an acceptance.

1. *Offer:* An offer is a communication of an intent to be bound to the terms of a specific proposed contract. The communication invites acceptance on the part of the intended recipient. A valid offer meets three basic requirements: intent, definite terms, and communication of offer.

   a. *Intent:* An offer must express an intent to enter into a contract.

   EXAMPLE: Taylor, whose new car has stalled at a busy intersection, says to Bradford, "I will sell you this heap of junk for $10." There is no offer because Taylor's words are uttered in anger and do not actually express an intent on his part to enter into such a contract.

   b. *Definite terms:* An offer must be sufficiently definite in its terms.

   EXAMPLE: If Travis says to Walker, "I offer to sell you my computer," there is no valid offer. The communication lacks definiteness.

   c. *Communication of offer:* An offer must be communicated to the intended party.

   EXAMPLES: Travis writes a note, "Dear Walker: I offer to sell you my only computer for $125." There can be no offer unless the note is communicated to Walker.

   Ordinarily, a catalog entry, newspaper advertisement, or magazine advertisement is regarded merely as an invitation for offers and is not itself regarded as an offer.

2. *Termination:* A valid offer may be terminated in the following ways:

   a. *Lapse of time:* If the expiration date contained in the offer has passed, the offer is terminated. If there is no express expiration date, the offer expires after the passage of a reasonable time.

   b. *Revocation:* As a general rule, the offeror may revoke the offer anytime prior to acceptance. There are three main exceptions to this rule:

      (1) *Option to purchase:* If the offeror has granted an option to purchase, the offer cannot be revoked for the period stated in the option. An option is a promise not to revoke an offer in return for something of value. Consideration must be present for there to be an option.

      (2) *Firm offer:* Under the UCC, if a merchant promises, in a signed writing, to hold open an offer to buy or to sell goods for any period less than three months, the offer cannot be revoked during the stated time period. If the stated

time period exceeds three months, the offer nevertheless becomes revocable after three months. This exception is known as the merchant's *firm offer.* It does not require consideration. Because this exception is statutory, each element must exist, or the exception does not apply.

(3) *Reasonable time:* If the offeror should have known that the offeree would change his or her position in reliance on the offer for a unilateral contract, the offeror will not be allowed to revoke until the offeree has had a reasonable time to complete the performance.

EXAMPLE: Peterson says to Parker, "I will pay you $5,000 if you run all the way across the state." In reliance on the promise, Parker began to run across the state. After nearly 24 hours, Peterson announces that she is revoking the offer. Peterson must allow Parker a reasonable time to complete performance. Peterson should have known that Parker would rely on the offer. It would be unfair to allow her to revoke before Parker has an opportunity to complete his performance.

c. *Rejection of offer:* When the offeree rejects the offer, the offer is terminated. A mere inquiry on the part of the offeree does not amount to a rejection.

EXAMPLE: Michaels says to Payne, "I offer to sell you my bicycle for $20." Payne responds, "$20 seems rather high. Would you consider $15?" Payne has not rejected the offer.

(1) *Rejection:* The offeree rejects an offer when he or she expresses an unwillingness to accept the offered terms.

EXAMPLE: Michaels says to Payne, "I offer to sell you my bicycle for $20." Payne responds, "No, I really don't want to buy it for that price." Payne has rejected the offer.

(2) *Counteroffer:* A counteroffer by the offeree operates as a rejection. The counteroffer stops the original offer and starts a new offer.

EXAMPLE: Michaels says to Payne "I offer to sell you my bicycle for $20." Payne responds, "I offer you $15 for your bicycle." Payne has rejected the original offer, causing it to terminate. He has also made an offer of his own, known as a counteroffer.

d. *Death or insanity:* The death or insanity of either party terminates the offer automatically (unless there is a valid option in effect).

e. *Destruction of subject matter:* If the subject matter of the offer is destroyed, the offer is terminated automatically.

f. *Illegality of the offer:* If an offer that is legal when made later becomes illegal because of a change in the law, the offer is terminated.

EXAMPLE: The Metropolis Mineral Company offers to sell four grams of cryptonite to Luthor for $20,000. Before Luthor accepts, however, the legislature enacts a law outlawing the sale of cryptonite. The offer is terminated at the time the law becomes effective.

3. *Acceptance:* A clear expression by the offeree to the offeror of an agreement to the terms of the offer constitutes an acceptance.

a. *Clarity of acceptance:* An acceptance must be positive and clear.

b. *Acceptance of terms of offer:* An acceptance cannot vary the terms of the offer in any way. Common law requires that the acceptance "mirror" the terms of the offer.

(1) *Counteroffer:* An attempted acceptance that varies from the terms of the offer will likely be interpreted as a counteroffer, which terminates the original offer.

(2) *Battle of forms:* The UCC greatly relaxes the mirror-image requirement of the common law where the sale of goods is involved. Under its battle of forms section, the UCC provides that when the sale of goods is involved, the acceptance need not mirror the terms of the offer as long as the intent to accept the terms offered is clearly expressed. This means that the offeree can add terms, modify terms, or ask that terms be deleted as long as the acceptance is not made *conditional* on the requested changes becoming part of the contract.

EXAMPLE: ABC Company offers to sell XYZ Company 100 Pluto computers for $150,000 to be shipped via Speedway Express. XYZ responds, "Accept your offer. Ship via Olympic Express." A contract for the computers now exists because the acceptance is not conditional. XYZ Company's modification would not likely be considered material, so it becomes a part of the accepted contract.

c. *Communication of acceptance:* If an acceptance is sent through an authorized means of communication, it is effective on being sent. If it is sent through an unauthorized means of communication, it is not effective until it is received.

(1) *Authorized means of communication:* Any means of communication specifically approved by the offeror is authorized. Unless the offeror indicates otherwise, any reasonable means of communication that is at least as reliable and as prompt as that used by the offeror is an authorized means. Thus, the offeree should use the same or better means of communication than the offeror used.

EXAMPLES: Palmer writes to Dunham, "I offer to sell you my camera for $30." The offer is mailed on May 1. On May 3 Dunham receives the offer and writes, "I accept." The acceptance is mailed on May 3. On May 4 Palmer mails a note to Dunham in which she says, "I revoke my offer." On May 5 Palmer receives Dunham's acceptance. On May 6 Dunham receives Palmer's attempted revocation. There is a contract. The acceptance, having been sent through an authorized means of communication, is effective on being sent (May 3). The revocation cannot be effective until it is received. Because it was received after the acceptance had become effective, it is of no consequence.

Palmer writes to Dunham, "I offer to sell you my camera for $30. Your acceptance must be by phone on or before May 5." Dunham writes, "I accept." Dunham mails the acceptance on May 4. Palmer receives the acceptance on May 6. There is no contract. The acceptance was not effective on being sent because the mail was not an authorized means of acceptance according to the terms of the offer.

Unless the offeror indicates otherwise, the means of communication used to convey the offer is an authorized means of communication for the acceptance.

EXAMPLE: Dugan faxes an offer to Parrish. Parrish may accept by fax unless Dugan expressly states in his offer that acceptance must be communicated through some other means of communication.

In many situations, electronic mail and fax transmissions will be authorized means of communicating acceptance. If offerors want to exclude these means of communication, they must either do so expressly or require acceptance through a specific means of communication as a condition of acceptance.

(2) *Receipt of first communication:* If the offeree first responds by sending a rejection and follows by sending an acceptance, the acceptance is not effective on being sent. The first communication received by the offeror is effective.

EXAMPLE: Palmer writes to Dunham on May 1, "I offer to sell you my camera for $30." On May 3 Dunham receives the offer and writes, "I will not pay $30. I offer you $20." On May 4 Dunham writes, "I accept your offer of May l." On May 5 Palmer receives Dunham's rejection. On May 6 Palmer receives Dunham's acceptance. There is no contract. The rejection was effective on receipt and terminated the offer.

d. *Silence as acceptance:* Ordinarily, silence will not constitute an acceptance.

EXAMPLE: Armstrong receives a letter from Riley offering to mow his yard this season. The letter ended with the following: "If I do not hear from you in five days, I will presume you accept." Armstrong cannot be forced to respond to avoid such an offer. Therefore, silence would not be an acceptance.

D. Types of Contracts

The basic types of contracts are quasi-contracts, unilateral contracts, bilateral contracts, express contracts, implied contracts, formal contracts, and simple contracts.

1. *Quasi-Contract:* The so-called quasi-contract is not a contract in the true sense because there is no mutual assent. The law imposes an obligation under some circumstances where there is no agreement between the parties to prevent an injustice from occurring. Frequently, a quasi-contract is found to exist to prevent unjust enrichment of a party.

EXAMPLE: Nelson owed $100 to Mitchum for the repayment of a loan from Mitchum. Without knowing that Mitchum had moved, Nelson went to Mitchum's former apartment. Finding no one home, Nelson placed the $100 in a plain folder and left it inside the door. O'Neal, the new occupant of the apartment, returned home later and found the money. On discovering what happened, Nelson demands that O'Neal return the money. The law imposes a duty on O'Neal to return the money to Nelson. O'Neal would be unjustly enriched if he were allowed to keep the money.

2. *Unilateral Contract:* A unilateral contract is one in which the offer is accepted by performance of the requested act. In a unilateral contract the offer invites acceptance only by performance of the requested act, not by a return promise.

EXAMPLE: Thompson's dog, Lassie, has disappeared. Thompson offers to pay $100 to anyone who returns Lassie to him. Jenkins learns of the offer and promises Thompson that he will find the dog and return it. There is no contract. The offer can be accepted only by actual performance. If Jenkins returns Lassie to Thompson, there is a unilateral contract.

3. *Bilateral Contract:* A bilateral contract involves an exchange of promises. The offer is accepted by a return promise from the offeree. Unless the offer provides that acceptance is to be by actual performance, a promise to perform will usually suffice as an acceptance.

EXAMPLE: Jensen says to Dixon, "I offer you $10 to shovel my sidewalk. Will you agree to do it?" Dixon says, "Yes, I accept." A bilateral contract has been formed. Jensen invited acceptance by return promise.

If it is not clear whether an offer is for a unilateral or bilateral contract, the courts will find a bilateral contract was intended.

4. *Implied Contract:* An implied contract is one in which the parties' agreement is expressed by their conduct instead of by their words.

   EXAMPLE: Hill drove his car to a self-service gas station. Without saying a word, he filled his tank with gasoline. The station attendant watched as Hill pumped the gasoline. By their conduct, the parties formed an implied contract for the sale of the gasoline. By his actions, Hill promised to pay the listed price of the gasoline he pumped into his tank.

E. Statute of Limitations

The law of each state establishes a time period within which suits for breach of contract must be brought. If the suit is not brought within the relevant time period following the breach, the right to sue for a remedy is lost. A typical statute of limitations requires that a suit based on an oral contract be brought within five years of the breach and that a suit based on breach of a written contract be brought within 10 years of the breach.

F. Statute of Frauds

The law that requires certain types of contracts to be in writing is generally known as the *statute of frauds.* When the statute of frauds applies, the contract cannot be enforced in court unless it is in writing and signed by the party being sued.

1. *Sale of Land:* Contracts for the sale of land are covered by the statute of frauds.

2. *Sale of Goods:* A contract for the sale of goods for $500 or more requires a writing.

3. *Promise in Consideration of Marriage:* A promise to give goods or money in return for a promise to marry must be in writing to be enforceable.

   EXAMPLE: Jones says to Anderson, "If you marry me, I will give you $10,000." Jones's promise is not enforceable unless it is in writing and signed by Jones.

4. *Promise to Perform for Another Party:* A promise to be responsible for the obligation of another party must be in a signed writing to be enforceable. (This promise is called a *surety promise.*)

   EXAMPLE: Sullivan accompanies Williams to the bank and tells the banker, "Give Williams the loan he wants. If he fails to pay, I will pay." Sullivan's promise is not enforceable unless it is in writing and signed by him.

5. *Contracts That Cannot Be Performed within One Year:* Contracts that cannot be performed within one year are covered by the statute of frauds.

   a. *Time for contract performance:* The time runs from the time the contract is entered into, not from the time actual performance is to take place.

      EXAMPLE: On May 1 Thorpe hires Murphy to work in Thorpe's store for six months beginning on January 2. The contract must be in writing because it cannot be performed within one year from the date it was made.

   b. *Contract performance within one year:* If the contract could possibly be performed within one year, it is not covered by the statute of frauds.

      EXAMPLE: Davis hired Pfeifer to write a program for an electronic dictionary. Even though it is most unlikely that the program can be completed within the year, it is possible. The contract, therefore, is not covered by the statute of frauds. Here the law considers possibilities, not probabilities.

6. *Promise of Responsibility for Obligation of Estate:* A promise from one who is the court-appointed manager of the estate of a deceased person to be personally responsible for an obligation of the estate must be in writing and signed.

   EXAMPLE: James died while owing money to Briggs. James's son, James Jr., was appointed by the court to manage his deceased father's estate. The estate does not have enough money to pay the debt owed to Briggs. James Jr. promised to pay the debt himself. His promise is not enforceable unless it is in writing and signed by him.

G. Assignment of Rights and Delegation of Duties

Sometimes a person who was not a party to the formation of the original contract acquires rights or undertakes responsibilities provided for in the contract.

1. *Assignment:* An assignment is a transfer of a contract right to one who is not a party to the contract. One who makes assignment is known as an *assignor.* One to whom an assignment is made is known as an *assignee.*

   a. *Assignable contract rights:* Most contract rights are assignable. The law provides, however, that certain rights are nonassignable. The contract may state that it is nonassignable. The prohibition on assignment of certain types of rights is for the protection of the nonassigning party to the contract.

      (1) An assignment that materially increases the burden or risk of the nonassigning party is prohibited.

      EXAMPLES: The Acme Pest Control Company contracted with Taft to spray Taft's house each time a roach was discovered. Taft is not permitted by law to assign his rights under the contract to Johnson, who owns a hardware store. Such an assignment changes the risk of Acme.

      Riggs, an airline pilot, contracts with Dependable On-line, Inc., for unlimited Internet use on his personal home computer for six months at $30 per month. One month later, Riggs notifies Dependable that he is assigning his contract rights to his neighbor Sutton, who operates a travel agency from her home. Dependable may legally refuse to transfer service to Sutton since its burden would be increased by the assignment.

      (2) Rights that are highly personal in nature cannot be assigned.

      EXAMPLES: Dr. Jones contracted to perform cosmetic surgery on Metcalf's face for $2,000. Metcalf cannot assign his rights under such a contract.

      Holcomb, a lawyer, contracted to make a will for Weaver. Weaver cannot assign her rights to another person.

      (3) An assignment that is specifically outlawed by a statute cannot legally be made. For example, some statutes prohibit wage assignments.

      (4) A mere statement in a contract that there can be no assignment does not necessarily mean that no assignment can be made. The assignor would be in breach of the contract and, therefore, liable for any damages caused to the nonassigning party, but an assignment could still be made.

b. *Gratuitous assignment:* The law does not require that there be consideration for an assignment to be valid. An assignment made without consideration is known as a *gratuitous assignment.*

EXAMPLE: Jacobson owes $100 to Sommers. Sommers assigns her right to receive the money to Carpenter. Even though there was no bargained-for exchange between Sommers and Carpenter, the assignment is nevertheless valid.

c. *Enforcement of assigned rights:* The assignee can enforce the assigned rights against the nonassigning party.

EXAMPLE: Amato contracted to purchase a boat from Baker for $300. Baker delivered the boat to Amato. Under the contract Amato was obligated to pay the purchase price within six months. Baker assigned his right to receive the $300 to Carlson. If Amato fails to pay within the six-month period, Carlson can sue Amato to enforce his right to receive the money.

(1) *Full performance of contractual duties:* If the nonassigning party has already rendered full performance of the contractual duties to the assignor, the assignee cannot require a second performance of them.

(2) *Notification to nonassigning party:* If, however, the nonassigning party has been notified of the assignment and still renders performance to the assignor, he or she may be required to perform again for the assignee.

EXAMPLE: Wright owes $50 to Garcia. Garcia assigns her right to receive the money to Stone. Before being notified of the assignment, Wright pays the $50 to Garcia. Wright has a good defense against a suit brought by Stone. If Wright had paid the money to Garcia after receiving notice of the assignment, Wright would not have a valid defense to a suit brought by Stone.

(3) *Assignment of contract rights only:* The assignor cannot assign greater rights than he or she has under the contract. The assignee merely stands in the shoes of the assignor.

2. *Delegation:* A delegation is a transfer of one's contractual obligation to another person. It may involve all of one's obligations under a contract or only part of them.

a. *Nondelegation of duties:* Some duties may not be delegated.

(1) *Duties requiring skill or judgment:* Duties that involve the exercise of skill or judgment cannot be delegated.

EXAMPLES: Wayne hired O'Malley to paint a portrait of Wayne. O'Malley cannot delegate his duty to paint the portrait because it involves a special skill.

Conley hired Day to mow Conley's lawn. Day can delegate his duty because it does not require special skill or judgment. However, Day is still responsible for the yard being mowed.

(2) *Delegation prohibited by contract:* If delegation is prohibited in the contract, a party cannot delegate duties.

b. *Novation:* The delegating party remains responsible for performance of the contractual duties unless there is a novation. If the nondelegating party expressly agrees to release the delegating party from further responsibility and accepts the delegating party's promise to perform, a novation has occurred.

EXAMPLES: The Gold Star Disposal Company contracted with Delaney to pick up and remove garbage from Delaney's farmhouse twice per week. Gold Star delegated this duty to the Victory Waste Management Company. Victory failed to pick up Delaney's garbage. Delaney can successfully sue Gold Star because the delegation did not relieve Gold Star of its contractual obligations.

Assume that in the above situation Delaney had expressly agreed to release Gold Star from its obligations in return for Victory's promise to perform the same duties. Delaney could then successfully sue only Victory.

H. Breach of Contracts—Remedies

When a party fails to perform its contractual obligations, the issue of what constitutes an appropriate remedy becomes relevant. A party breaches a contract when, without justification, it fails to perform its obligations under the terms of the agreement. The nonbreaching party is entitled to a remedy as compensation for the loss suffered as a result of the breach. The most commonly sought remedies are money damages, specific performance, and restitution.

1. *Money Damages:* The nonbreaching party may sue to recover the amount of money required to put the property in as good a position as it would have been in had there been no breach (i.e., had the contract been performed as promised).

EXAMPLE: Howard contracted to paint DeWitt's car for $300. Howard failed to paint the car. DeWitt hired someone else to paint the car for $450. Assuming that $450 was a reasonable price negotiated in good faith, DeWitt is entitled to recover $150 from Howard.

a. *Nominal damages:* If a party cannot prove that a loss was suffered as a result of the breach, only nominal damages are awarded. Nominal damages are a small amount, often one dollar, that the court grants to recognize that a breach of contract did in fact occur but that no real loss was proven.

EXAMPLE: If in the situation described above DeWitt hired someone else to paint his car for $300, he could recover from Howard only the value of the time and effort he expended to find someone else to paint the car.

b. *Liquidated damages:* At the time they enter into the contract, the parties may agree on the money damages to be paid in the event of a breach. These predetermined damages are known as *liquidated damages.* The courts will enforce a liquidated-damages clause only if the stated damages bear a close relationship to those that could be reasonably expected to occur in the event of a breach. If the liquidated-damages clause amounts to a penalty for the breaching party further than an attempt to compensate the nonbreaching party reasonably, it will not be enforced.

2. *Specific Performance:* The nonbreaching party may sue for a court order requiring the breaching party to perform its contractual duties. To obtain specific performance, the nonbreaching party must convince the court that no amount of money damages will put it in the position it would have been in had there been no breach.

EXAMPLES: Crawford contracted to sell her home to Williams. Crawford breached the contract. If Williams sues for specific performance to require Crawford to complete the sale, Williams will succeed. The law recognizes that no two pieces of land are the same; therefore, money damages would be inadequate.

Gates contracted to sell 20 pounds of salt to Matthews for $20. If Gates breaches the contract, Matthews will not succeed in obtaining specific performance because money damages would be adequate.

3. *Restitution:* The nonbreaching party may sue to require the breaching party to return what it received under the contract.

   EXAMPLES: Lawson contracted to sell her antique bicycle to Ferguson for $800. Under the terms of the agreement, Ferguson took possession of the bicycle and was to pay the purchase price in four installments. Ferguson breached the contract by failing to make the payments. Lawson may sue for restitution and recover the bicycle from Ferguson.

   Ames contracted to purchase a gold ring from Burke. In compliance with the terms of the contract, Ames paid $400 for the ring. Burke breached the contract by failing to deliver the ring. Ames may sue for restitution and recover the $400 she paid to Burke.

Review Questions

Directions: Select the best answer from the four alternatives. Write your answer in the blank to the left of the number.

_______________ **1.** Gray is employed by the City of Greenville as a street commissioner. In the course of his work for the city, Gray uses a concrete mixing machine owned by the city. Boyd, a citizen of a nearby town, offered to rent the machine from Gray for one day at a cost of $150. When Gray rejected the offer, telling Boyd that he feared losing his job for leasing city property to an unauthorized person in violation of a city ordinance, Boyd offered to pay a rental of $250. Gray accepted the offer. Boyd returned the machine after using it, but he refused to pay the $250 to Gray. If Gray sues Boyd to enforce the contract,

a. Gray will succeed in collecting the $250.
b. Gray will succeed in collecting only a reasonable amount.
c. Gray will succeed in collecting the fair rental value of the equipment.
d. Gray will not succeed in collecting anything from Boyd.

_______________ **2.** For months Matthews has attempted to purchase an antique car owned by Powell. Matthews' latest offer of $5,000 was rejected by Powell. The next day Matthews observed Powell leaving a theater that was showing an X-rated movie. Matthews took a picture of Powell and threatened to circulate the picture at Powell's workplace if Powell did not contract to sell the car to Matthews. Fearing that he would lose his job if the picture were circulated, Powell signed a contract to sell the car to Matthews for $5,500. When Powell refused to deliver the car, Matthews sued him for breach of contract.

a. Matthews will win because the agreement is in writing and signed by Powell.
b. Powell will win because his agreement was obtained by fraud.
c. Powell will win because his signature was obtained by duress.
d. Powell will win because his signature was obtained by undue influence.

_______________ **3.** Jordan offered to sell her television set to Booth for $200. Jordan told Booth that the television set was two years old and that a new picture tube had just been installed. Relying on these statements, Booth agreed to purchase the television. Two days later Booth learned that the set had its original picture tube. Booth sues Jordan, seeking the return of the sale price.

a. Booth will succeed in having the sale set aside. She must return the set, and Jordan must return the $200.
b. Booth will not succeed in recovering the money because the agreement involved a mutual mistake.
c. Booth will not succeed in recovering the money because of the legal principle of "buyer beware."
d. Booth could succeed in recovering the money only if she is a minor.

_______________ **4.** Michaels, who is a nurse, offered her friend Ryan $100 if Ryan would lose 25 pounds. Michaels showed Ryan a study that indicated that weight loss would improve her health. Ryan accepted Michaels' offer. She lost 25 pounds. Michaels, however, refused to pay Ryan the $100. Michaels claims that the weight loss was good for Ryan but that she received no benefit from it. Ryan sues Michaels to collect the $100.

a. Michaels will win the suit because there was no consideration.
b. Michaels will win the suit because the agreement violates public policy.
c. Michaels will win the suit because there was no bargained-for exchange of something of value.
d. Ryan will win.

______________ **5.** Jorgenson's mother was hospitalized from May 1 to June 1 while Jorgenson was in Europe on business. On her return to town, Jorgenson visited the hospital. She told the head of the hospital's billing department that she was so thankful her mother had been properly cared for over that month that she would pay the bill if her mother failed to pay. Later, however, Jorgenson refused to pay the bill. The hospital brings suit against Jorgenson on the basis of her promise to pay.

a. The hospital will win because there was no consideration.
b. The hospital will win because Jorgenson promised to answer for the debt of another person.
c. Jorgenson will win because undue influence is present.
d. Jorgenson will win because there was no consideration.

______________ **6.** Bradford hired Jenkins to panel Bradford's basement. The written contract provided that Jenkins would remove the wallpaper and install a specified kind of paneling for $1,700, including labor. After Jenkins had removed the wallpaper and paneled half of the basement, he refused to complete the job unless Bradford promised to pay him an additional $100. Jenkins realized the job was taking longer than expected. Bradford promised to pay the additional $100. On completion of the work, however, Bradford refused to pay the extra $100. Jenkins sues Bradford to collect the $100.

a. Bradford will win because there was no consideration.
b. Bradford will win because the agreement to pay the $100 was illegal.
c. Jenkins will win because there was a mutual mistake as to how long the job would take.
d. Jenkins will win because Bradford is guilty of fraud in promising to pay the $100, which he never intended to pay.

______________ **7.** The accountancy firm of Wilson, Jones, and Smith contracted to purchase all pencils that the firm needed for the coming year from the Sharp Pencil Company at a price of 7 cents per pencil. One month into the year covered by the contract, the firm began purchasing pencils from another company at 5 cents per pencil. Sharp sues the firm for breach of contract.

a. Sharp will lose because the firm's promise was illusory.
b. Sharp will lose because there was no consideration.
c. Sharp will win because the firm's promise is enforceable.
d. Sharp will win because the firm is guilty of fraudulent misrepresentation.

______________ **8.** MacLeod, who is 15 years old, contracted to buy a set of golf clubs for $85 from Seymour, who is 45 years of age.

a. The contract is void.
b. The contract is voidable by MacLeod.
c. The contract is voidable by Seymour.
d. The contract is voidable by either Seymour or MacLeod.

__________ **9.** Riggs, who is 15 years of age, ran away from home. He checked into a hotel one evening when the temperature dropped to 10°F. The next day Riggs notified the hotel clerk that he was a minor and claimed that he owed the hotel nothing because he was disaffirming the contract. The hotel clerk argued that Riggs was legally obligated to pay the $92 per night fee, which the hotel charges all its guests. Who is correct?

a. Riggs is correct. The law allows him to disaffirm.
b. The hotel clerk is correct. Because lodging was a necessary item to Riggs, he is obligated to pay the contract price.
c. The hotel clerk is correct. Riggs' minority is irrelevant.
d. Neither party is correct.

__________ **10.** Mayer, a 17-year-old high school student, contracted to purchase stereo equipment from National Sales. Under the terms of the contract, Mayer was to pay $10 per month for 45 months. After reaching 18, the age of majority in her state, Mayer continued making the monthly payments for another five months. Mayer then notified National that she was disaffirming the contract. National argued that Mayer cannot disaffirm.

a. National is correct because a minor can disaffirm only during minority.
b. National is correct because Mayer ratified the contract on making the first payment after her sixteenth birthday.
c. National is correct because the stereo equipment is a necessity.
d. National is correct because Mayer has ratified the contract.

__________ **11.** Jackson wrote a note to Travis that read, "Travis, I offer to sell you my calculator for $10. (Signed) Jackson." Jackson placed the note on a table in his own home. Later that evening Travis made an unannounced visit to Jackson's house. While Jackson was in the kitchen getting refreshments, Travis found the note and read it. When Jackson reentered the room, Travis laid out a $10 bill and said, "I accept." Is there a contract?

a. No, because there was no valid offer.
b. No, because there was no valid acceptance.
c. No, because there was no consideration.
d. Yes, there is a contract.

__________ **12.** Atwood, a college professor, offered to sell her desk to Burke for $350. Atwood promised to hold the offer open for one week. The next day, however, Atwood sold the desk to Roberts for $420. When Atwood told Burke of the sale later that same day, Burke took $350 to Atwood and said, "I accept your offer." Burke claims that she has contracted to purchase the desk. Atwood claims that the offer to Burke has been revoked. Who is correct?

a. Burke is correct. Atwood was legally obligated to hold the offer open for a week as promised.

b. Atwood is correct. The offer was revoked when Atwood told Burke of the sale.
c. Atwood is correct. The offer was revoked when Atwood refused to take Burke's $350.
d. Burke is correct. Atwood's offer was a firm offer that cannot be revoked for three months.

______________ **13.** Sheridan, a book company sales agent, wrote to Taylor, a book store purchasing agent, "I offer to sell you 300 volumes of *How to Become a Millionaire* for $900. This offer will remain open for two months. (Signed) Sheridan." A week later, however, before Taylor had responded to the offer, Sheridan phoned Taylor and told him that she revoked the offer. Taylor argues that Sheridan cannot revoke for the two-month period. Sheridan claims that she can revoke any time prior to acceptance. Who is correct?

a. Sheridan is correct.
b. Taylor is correct because there was a valid option.
c. Taylor is correct because there was a merchant's firm offer.
d. Neither party is correct. Sheridan can revoke after the passage of a reasonable time.

______________ **14.** Anderson said to Baker, "I offer to sell you this briefcase for $30." Baker responded, "I offer you $25 for it." Anderson said, "No, that is not enough." Baker then said, "O.K., I accept your offer." Is there a contract at this point?

a. Yes, there is a contract.
b. No, because there is no consideration.
c. No, because the offer was not in writing.
d. No, because the offer had terminated before Baker's attempted acceptance.

______________ **15.** Ferguson wrote to Johnson, "I offer to sell you my lawn mower for $50." Johnson wrote back, "I accept. Include a gallon of gasoline." Is there a contract?

a. No, because the attempted acceptance does not match the terms of the offer.
b. No, because the parties are not merchants.
c. Yes, because the acceptance was mailed.
d. Yes, because the acceptance was not conditional.

______________ **16.** On May 1 Simpson wrote to Bennett, "I offer to sell you my banjo for $50." On May 3 Bennett received Simpson's offer and wrote back, "I accept your offer." On May 4 Simpson sold the banjo to Edwards. She phoned Bennett on May 4 and told him the offer was revoked. On May 5 Simpson received Bennett's letter of acceptance. Is there a contract between Simpson and Bennett?

a. No, because the offer was revoked before the acceptance was received.
b. No, because performance became impossible when Simpson sold the banjo to Edwards on May 4.
c. Yes, because the acceptance became effective on May 3.
d. Yes, because the offer was made prior to May 3.

______________ **17.** Adams faxed an offer to sell Brennan two tickets to the Super Bowl for $450. Brennan responded by mailing his check for $450 to Adams. After the check was mailed, but before it was received, Adams phoned Brennan and told him the offer was revoked. Adams subsequently received the check. Brennan claims that there is a contract. Is he correct?

a. Yes, because his acceptance was effective on being sent.
b. Yes, because Adams' attempted revocation was through an unauthorized means of communication.
c. No, because the offer was not valid.
d. No, because the revocation was communicated before the acceptance was effective.

_____________ **18.** James visits Allen, who offers to sell James her television set for $200. Allen tells James that other people are interested in purchasing it and says, "Phone me on my cell phone with your answer by 6 o'clock tonight." At 5 P.M. James e-mails Allen the following message: "I accept your offer. Will come by with the money this evening." Allen spent the afternoon running errands while carrying her cell phone and did not turn on her computer. At 7 P.M. she sold the television set to Thompson. At 8 P.M. James appeared with $200 and insisted that Allen honor their deal. Is there a contract between Allen and James?

a. No, because the television set was sold before James appeared with the money.
b. No, because acceptance was through an unauthorized means of communication.
c. Yes, because acceptance was communicated before revocation.
d. Yes, because the offer was never revoked.

_____________ **19.** On June 1 Ashton wrote to Browne, "I offer to sell you my window fan for $25." On June 3 Browne received Ashton's offer and wrote to Ashton, "No, thank you. Your price is higher than I can pay." On June 4 Browne changed his mind and wrote to Ashton, "I accept your offer." On June 5 Ashton received Browne's letter of rejection. On June 6 Ashton received Browne's letter of acceptance. Is there a contract between Ashton and Browne?

a. Yes, because the acceptance was effective on being mailed.
b. Yes, because the offer had not been terminated on June 6, when the acceptance was received.
c. No, because the rejection was effective when mailed on June 3.
d. No, because the rejection was effective on June 5, before the acceptance was received.

_____________ **20.** Meyer lost his watch. He placed an ad in the local newspaper that read, "I offer $20 to anyone who returns my watch to me." It included a description of the watch and his address. Kennedy read the ad and later found the watch. He returned it to Meyer and collected the reward. What kind of contract existed between Meyer and Kennedy?

a. Unilateral contract
b. Bilateral contract
c. Quasi-contract
d. Implied contract

_____________ **21.** Cameron agreed to purchase a small strip of land from Dixon for $499. The agreement was not put in writing. Cameron later denied that he had made such an agreement. Dixon sues Cameron to enforce the agreement.

a. Dixon will win. The contract need not be in writing because less than $500 is involved.
b. Dixon will win. The statute of frauds does not apply to sales of land.

c. Cameron will win because there was no consideration.
d. Cameron will win because the agreement was not in writing and signed by him.

_______________ **22.** Cole owned and operated a restaurant. He contracted to purchase 400 dozen plates from Shafer. Shafer failed to deliver the plates. Cole sues Shafer. Cole seeks specific performance. Will the court order specific performance?

a. Yes.
b. Yes, but only if Cole proves that Shafer breached the contract.
c. No, because specific performance cannot be awarded in a breach of contract suit.
d. Yes, but only if money damages are inadequate.

Use the following information in answering Questions 23 to 25.

Ted and Mary Palmer were robbed of all their cash and belongings while vacationing in a large city. Since they had left home without traveler's checks or credit cards, they contacted Jacobson, a friend who lived in the city. On her way to work Jacobson accompanied Ted to a camera shop and told the proprietor, "Let him pick out any camera under $300, and I will pay for it on the way back home this afternoon." She then took Mary to a clothing store and told the clerk, "Mary will select the clothes she wants up to $400. If she doesn't pay, I will." The next day she accompanied Mary to a furniture store, where Mary ordered an $800 couch to be delivered in 30 days. Jacobson told the salesperson, "I will pay for it."

_______________ **23.** Assume that the camera shop sues Jacobson to recover the $250 sale price of the camera Ted selected and took home.

a. The camera shop will win because Jacobson's promise was a direct promise to pay for goods under $500.
b. The camera shop will win because the goods are valued at under $1,000.
c. Jacobson will win because her promise was to pay for the debt of another.
d. Jacobson will win because the camera's value is more than $200.

_______________ **24.** The clothing store sues Jacobson to collect the $350 sale price of the clothing Mary selected and took home. The correctly reasoned answer is

a. the clothing store will win because Jacobson's promise was a direct promise to pay for goods under $500.
b. the clothing store will win because the goods are valued at under $500.
c. Jacobson will win because her promise was to pay for the debt of another and was not in writing.
d. Jacobson will win because the promise to pay for the debt of another is never enforceable.

_______________ **25.** If the furniture store sues Jacobson for the price of the couch,

a. the furniture store will win because Jacobson's promise is a direct promise to pay.
b. the furniture store will win because the price of the couch is under $1,000.
c. Jacobson will win because her promise is indirect.
d. Jacobson will win because her promise to pay for goods over $500 is not in writing.

Use the following information in answering Questions 26 and 27.

Sommers owned an antique coffee grinder that Taft, Randall, and Kelley each wanted to buy. On June 1 Sommers mailed to each of the interested parties an offer to sell the item for $300. On June 3 each of the interested parties received the offer. On June 3 Taft mailed a note that read, "$300 is too high. I offer $250." This message was received by Sommers on June 4. On June 3 Randall mailed the following response, "Would you consider $250?" Also, on June 3 Kelley wrote, "I do not have $300 to spend. Sell it to someone else." On June 4 Sommers received Randall's note but did not receive Kelley's because it had been mailed to an incorrect address.

Also on June 4, Taft, Randall, and Kelley, acting independently of one another, each mailed the following communication: "I accept your offer of June 1. Enclosed is my money order for $300." On June 5 Sommers received Kelley's first response. On June 6 she received all the responses mailed on June 4.

__________ **26.** With whom does Sommers have a contract?

a. Taft
b. Randall
c. Kelley
d. Randall and Kelley

__________ **27.** If Sommers had hand delivered the following note to each of the other parties on June 3, "My offer of June 1 is hereby revoked," the delivery of the note would

a. revoke the offer.
b. have no effect.
c. revoke the offer only if delivered before the other party's receipt of the offer.
d. revoke the offer only as to Taft and Kelley.

Use the following information in answering Questions 28 and 29.

On May 1 Jones loaned $200 to Thorpe. The loan was payable with 5 percent interest on January 30. On July 1 Jones assigned her right to receive the money to Ames. Thorpe was not notified. On January 30 Thorpe paid the required amount to Jones. On February 1 Ames demands that Thorpe pay her.

__________ **28.** The correct outcome is

a. Thorpe must pay Ames.
b. Ames may collect from Thorpe and then from Jones.
c. Ames may recover the money from Jones.
d. Ames is not entitled to any recovery.

__________ **29.** If Thorpe had been notified of the assignment on January 29,

a. it would make no difference.
b. Thorpe could be required to pay Ames even after he paid Jones.
c. Thorpe cannot be required to pay twice.
d. Ames is not entitled to any recovery.

______________ **30.** Davis contracts with Reliable On-Line, Inc., for six months of unlimited time on the Internet for $35 per month. Two months later Davis learns that Reliable is delegating its contractual obligation to Dependable On-Line, Inc., which purchased Reliable's equipment. Davis argues that Dependable cannot delegate its duties. Is she correct?

a. Yes, because she specifically contracted with Reliable, not Dependable.
b. Yes, because duties of this type cannot be delegated.
c. No, because contractual obligations may always be delegated.
d. No, because the duties do not require unique skill or judgment.

Solutions

Answer	Refer to:
1. (d)	[B-1-c] The agreement is illegal. A city ordinance prohibits the leasing of city property to unauthorized persons. Because the agreement is illegal, it is not an enforceable contract. Gray, therefore, will lose his suit.
2. (c)	[B-2-b(1)] Matthews' threat to circulate the picture caused Powell to lose free will. His apparent agreement to the terms of the sale was obtained by duress. Powell feared the loss of his job if the picture was released. Matthews' conduct did not amount to undue influence because there was no close relationship between the parties. There was no fraud because Matthews did not make a false representation to Powell.
3. (a)	[B-2-b(3), (4)] Booth will succeed in having the agreement set aside. Jordan's statement that the set had a new picture tube was a false statement of fact. It was reasonably relied on by Booth. If Jordan knew that her statement was false, it amounts to fraud. If Jordan reasonably believed that her statement was true, it amounts to an innocent misrepresentation. In either event, Booth is entitled to have the agreement set aside. She will be required to return the television set and will be entitled to the return of the money.
4. (d)	[B-3-a] Ryan will win because all the elements required for a valid contract are present. Ryan surrendered her right to maintain her weight. She performed the act requested by Michaels. Whether Michaels received anything of value is unimportant. The fact that Ryan benefited from the weight loss is unimportant.
5. (d)	[B-3-d] Jorgenson will win because there was no consideration. The care that the hospital rendered to her mother had already been performed. There was, therefore, no bargained-for exchange. Moreover, Jorgenson merely told the hospital employee that she would pay the bill if her mother failed to pay. Since this is a promise to answer for the debt of another person, the law requires that it be in writing. There was no evidence to support a claim of undue influence.
6. (a)	[B-3-e] There was no consideration to support Bradford's promise. Jenkins was doing nothing in return for the extra $100. He was merely doing what he had already contracted to do. He was legally obligated to perform his contractual duties.
7. (c)	[B-3-g] A promise to buy all the goods that a party needs or requires is enforceable. The Uniform Commercial Code imposes a standard of good faith, thus making the quantity involved in such a promise reasonably

certain. Had the promise been to buy all the pencils the firm wanted or desired, it would have been illusory and, therefore, unenforceable. As stated, the promise provides a basis for consideration.

8. (b) [B-4-a(1), (4)] A contract entered into by a minor is voidable at the option of the minor. The minor may elect to enforce the contract against the adult. MacLeod may avoid the contract by disaffirming it during his minority or within a reasonable time after reaching his majority.

9. (d) [B-4-a(1), (5)] Riggs is allowed to disaffirm, but since lodging was a necessity to him, he must pay the reasonable value of the lodging. The reasonable value may differ from the $92 that the hotel charges its customers.

10. (d) [B-4-a(6)(a), (b)] By making five monthly payments after reaching majority and remaining in possession of the stereo equipment, Mayer has ratified the contract. It is also true that more than a reasonable time has passed since she reached her majority. Mayer, therefore, cannot now disaffirm.

11. (a) [C-1-c] The offer was not communicated to Travis with Jackson's intent. Since Jackson had not sent the note, there is a chance he would reconsider it and not communicate it to Travis. When Travis found and read the note in Jackson's house, he learned of the note's contents without Jackson intending for him to learn of it at that time. The law requires that an offer be communicated with the intent of the offeror.

12. (b) [C-2-b] As a general rule, the offeror may revoke the offer at any time prior to acceptance. Atwood told Burke of the sale to Roberts before Burke tendered the money and indicated her intent to accept.

13. (c) [C-2-b(2)] All the elements of a merchant's firm offer are present. Sheridan is a merchant; she sells books on a regular basis. Her offer is in writing. It is an offer to sell goods, signed by her, containing a promise that the offer will be held open for a period of time. The offer is not revocable for two months.

14. (d) [C-2-c(2)] Baker made a counteroffer that terminated Anderson's original offer. Answer (c) is incorrect because there is no requirement that such agreements be in writing. Answer (b) is incorrect because were it not for the termination, consideration would be present.

15. (d) [C-3-b(2)] Since this is a contract for the sale of goods, the Uniform Commercial Code applies. As long as the offeree expresses an intent to accept the offer and does not make acceptance conditional on new or different terms, acceptance is effective. In this case, the acceptance is not conditioned on the additional term.

16. (c) [C-3-c(1)] The mail was an authorized means of communication since it was used by the offeror and there was nothing in the offer to indicate that the mail would be unacceptable. The acceptance, therefore, was effective on being sent. Since the offer was accepted on May 3, the attempted revocation on May 4 was of no legal effect.

17. (d) [C-3-c(1)] Since Brennan responded to the faxed offer by sending his acceptance through a slower means of communication, the acceptance would not become effective until received. The revocation was communicated before the acceptance became effective.

18. (b) [C-3-c(1)] Allen's offer specifically provided that acceptance was to be by phone to her cellular phone before 6 P.M. E-mail was not authorized and, therefore, was not effective when it was sent. The offer expired by its own terms at 6 P.M., before the acceptance was effective. E-mail may be an authorized means of acceptance in many instances, but the specific requirement of calling the cellular phone rendered e-mail unauthorized.

19. (d) [C-3-c(2)] Because the offeree's first response was the sending of a rejection, the acceptance was not effective on being sent. In such a case, whichever communication arrives first is the one that is effective. Since the rejection was received before the acceptance was received, the rejection governs, and there is no contract.

20. (a) [D-2] The only way that Meyer's offer could be accepted was by performance. It was, therefore, a unilateral offer. When Kennedy performed the requested act, he accepted the offer.

21. (d) [F-1] A contract for the sale of land must be in writing and signed by the party being sued. The $500 requirement applies only when goods are involved.

22. (d) [H-2] Specific performance is available only in cases where money damages are inadequate. In this case Cole could get specific performance only if he could prove that the plates he contracted for were so unique that he could not purchase similar plates with any sum of money. It is extremely doubtful that Cole can prove that. He will be limited to receiving money damages in his suit.

23. (a) [F-2] Jacobson's promise was a direct promise to pay for the camera. The promise was not conditional. Since the goods are valued under $500, there is no requirement for the promise to be in writing.

24. (c) [F-4] Jacobson's promise was to pay for the debt of Mary. It was not a direct promise to pay. Rather, the promise was conditional on Mary's failure to pay. Since the promise was to pay for Mary's debt, the law requires that it be in writing.

25. (d) [F-2] Although Jacobson's promise was a direct promise to pay, the law required that it be in writing because the value of the goods exceeds $500.

26. (b) [C-3] Randall's first communication was a mere inquiry, which did not constitute a rejection of the offer. His second communication was a valid acceptance. Kelley and Taft had rejected Sommers' offer in their first communications, which Sommers received before she received their attempted acceptances.

27. (a) [C-2] Generally, an offer may be revoked by the offeror any time prior to its acceptance. Sommers' actual delivery of the revocation before any of the offerees had accepted was a valid revocation.

28. (c) [G-1-c] Thorpe was not notified of the assignment before he performed his obligation fully. He cannot, therefore, be required to perform twice.

29. (b) [G-1-c(2)] Once he is notified of the assignment, Thorpe must honor it, or risk being required to pay twice.

30. (d) [G-2-a] Unless contractual obligations require unique skill or judgment, they may be delegated in the absence of a contract clause expressly prohibiting delegation. In this case Dependable purchased Reliable's equipment and is, therefore, capable of providing the contracted-for service. If Dependable fails to perform, Davis may sue Reliable for breach of contract. If the contract contained a nondelegation clause, the outcome would be different.

CHAPTER 22

Negotiable Instruments

OVERVIEW

In the modern business world the use of checks, drafts, and promissory notes is taken for granted. Yet, if such instruments were not available, business transactions would, by necessity, be based on the actual transfer of cash. If cash were required, the risk and inconvenience of transporting the money would retard the conduct of business. Moreover, credit would become more difficult to arrange, and efforts to finance transactions would be hampered.

The use of negotiable instruments as substitutes for money makes today's streamlined transactions possible. In this chapter we present the fundamentals of the law of negotiable instruments. The candidate should become familiar with the concept of negotiability and the elements it requires, the types of negotiable instruments, the requirements for a valid transfer of such instruments, and the defenses that the law recognizes against the holder of such instruments.

KEY TERMS

Bearer
Cashier's check
Draft
Drawee
Drawer
Holder
Holder in due course
Indorsee
Indorsement without recourse
Indorser
Maker
Negotiable instrument
Negotiation
Payee
Promissory note
Restrictive indorsement
Special indorsement

A. The Significance of Negotiability

Negotiability is a valued characteristic because it is possible for the recipient of a negotiable instrument to be free of many of the defenses that the promisor could assert against the original owner of the document.

1. *Legal Requirements:* The law establishes certain requirements for negotiability (see Section B). These are contained in the Uniform Commercial Code (UCC).

2. *Effect of Negotiability:* A document containing a promise that can be transferred to another party in a manner that entitles the recipient to enforce the promise without being subject to all the defenses that could be asserted against the original owner is

said to be negotiable. To appreciate fully the effect of the transfer of a negotiable instrument, it should be compared to the ordinary assignment of contract rights.

a. *Assignable contract rights:* Most contract rights are assignable (see Chapter 21). However, the assignee is subject to the same defenses to which the assignor is subject. The assignee merely stands in the shoes of the assignor.

EXAMPLE: Ace Stereo contracted to deliver $5,000 in stereo equipment to Brown Computer Corporation in return for Brown's agreement to supply and install a certain computer system in Ace's store. Brown assigned its contract rights to Central Credit Corporation. When Central attempted to collect the stereo equipment, Ace refused on the grounds that Brown had failed to install the computer system. Brown's contract rights were assignable, but the contract was not a negotiable instrument. Thus, Central is subject to all defenses that Ace could assert against Brown.

b. *Assignable rights free of defenses:* A document that meets all the legal requirements for negotiability is worth more to other parties because, unlike an ordinary contract, its recipient, if he or she qualifies as a holder in due course (see Section B-6-c[6]), may take rights free of most defenses. It therefore involves less risk.

EXAMPLE: Allen signed a properly drawn check in the amount of $200 and delivered it to Brandt in return for Brandt's promise to carpet Allen's living room. Brandt endorsed the check and delivered it to Carlson, to whom he owed $200. Carlson cashed the check. Even if Brandt did not carpet Allen's room as he promised, Carlson, assuming that he took the check without any knowledge of Brandt's failure to perform, is free of Allen's claims.

B. Elements of a Negotiable Instrument

The UCC establishes the legal requirements for a negotiable instrument. If all these requirements are not met, a document may be a contract capable of being assigned, but it is not a negotiable instrument. The difference between a mere contract and a negotiable instrument is important to those to whom the document is transferred (see Section A-2).

1. *Writing:* A negotiable instrument must be in writing. The requirement serves two main functions:

a. *Fraud:* Having the instrument in writing minimizes the risk of fraud.

b. *Transfer:* A written instrument allows for ease and certainty in transferring the promise to other parties.

The UCC does not require that the writing be on paper. The writing requirement will be satisfied if the material on which the writing is done is in "tangible form." The material should, of course, be of the type that is likely to last for a considerable time.

EXAMPLE: Unhappy with his hotel room on his vacation to Hawaii, Lawrence paid his bill with a check that he carved on a coconut. The instrument meets the writing requirement of the UCC.

2. *Signature:* To qualify as a negotiable instrument, a writing must be signed in accordance with the UCC.

a. *Maker's signature:* If the instrument is a note, it must be signed by its maker.

b. *Drawer's signature:* If the instrument is a check or a draft, it must be signed by the drawer.

c. *Type of signature required:* A traditional signature is not required. Any mark made or adopted by a party with the intention of authenticating the writing will suffice as a signature.

(1) An *X* or other mark will serve as a signature if it was the intent of the person making the mark to authenticate the document.

(2) A rubber stamp that imprints a party's name may be used by the party or the party's authorized agent as the party's signature.

(3) The signature may appear any place on the document.

3. *Unconditional Promise:* A negotiable instrument must contain an unconditional promise or order to pay.

a. *Promise to pay:* A writing that merely recognizes a debt does not satisfy the requirement of a promise to pay.

EXAMPLE: Dawson agreed to purchase Taylor's lawnmower for $40. On receiving the lawn mower, Dawson wrote on a piece of paper, "Taylor, I owe you $40. (Signed) Dawson." The promise requirement is not satisfied.

b. *Order to pay:* A check that bears the name of a bank and words such as "Pay to the order of . . . " satisfies the order requirement.

(1) The order to pay is clear and certain.

(a) Words such as "please pay" are sufficiently clear and definite.

(b) Words such as "I hope you will pay" or "I wish you would pay" are *not* sufficiently clear and definite.

(2) The bank's name on the check identifies the party who must pay pursuant to the order and thus satisfies the legal requirement that the order to pay be directed to a specific, identifiable party.

c. *Unconditional promise:* The promise must not be conditional.

(1) If the promise states that it is subject to another agreement, the promise is conditional and does not meet the requirements for a negotiable instrument.

(2) If the promise to pay states that payment can be made *only* from a particular source or fund, the promise does not meet the requirement for a negotiable instrument.

EXAMPLE: Willis signed a document that read, "I promise to pay to the bearer of this note $5,000 on May 1, 2001. Payment is to be made only from my travel account."

(a) Because it is possible that a specified fund will not be in existence when payment becomes due, the promise is conditional.

(b) If the word *only* were omitted, the preceding promise would satisfy the promise requirement for a negotiable instrument.

d. *Reference to agreement:* A mere reference to an agreement does not render a promise to pay conditional.

(1) The instrument may contain a statement of the parties' agreement.

EXAMPLE: Green writes, "I promise to pay Jordan $100 on May 1 in payment of the desk she will deliver to me on that date. (Signed) Green." Green's promise is not conditional. He merely stated the terms of the agreement.

(2) The instrument may contain a reference to a separate agreement as long as the promise to pay is not made conditional on the other agreement.

EXAMPLE: Stewart writes, "I promise to pay Jennings $35. Jennings agrees to return the books he borrowed from me last semester. (Signed) Stewart." Stewart's promise merely refers to another agreement. Because the promise to pay is not subject to Jennings' agreement to return the books, it is not a conditional promise.

4. *Specific Sum of Money:* The promise to pay must be expressed in terms of a specific sum of money.

a. *Stated or ascertainable sum:* The sum must either be stated on the face of the instrument or be ascertainable without the necessity of referring to another source.

EXAMPLE: A promise to pay "$100 with 9 percent interest on demand" expresses a specific sum because the interest can be calculated without reference to any other source of information.

b. *Promise to pay money:* The promise to pay must not include a promise to pay in something other than money.

EXAMPLE: A promise to pay $300 and deliver a new light fixture will not suffice for a negotiable instrument because the promise includes a commitment to pay in something other than money.

c. *Promise to pay in foreign currency:* The promise may be expressed in terms of a foreign nation's money. The UCC recognizes as money "a medium of exchange authorized or adopted by a domestic or foreign government as part of its currency."

EXAMPLE: Baumgarten writes, "I promise to pay 10,000 deutsche marks on June 1." Deutsche marks are recognized as money in Germany, so Baumgarten's promise states a specific sum of money.

5. *Payable at Specific Time or on Demand:* To meet the requirements of a negotiable instrument, the promise must make the payment due at a specific time or on demand.

a. *Statement of due date:* To be considered payable at a specific time, the document must either state a certain date or express the due date in terms that allow the time to be ascertained with certainty.

EXAMPLES: Brady promises to pay "$500 sixty days after the birth of Lafferty's next child." The due date cannot be ascertained because the birth date of the child is uncertain.

Stacy promises to pay "$200 on or before July 1, 2000." The due date is sufficiently definite. Although Stacy may elect to pay before the stated date, the payment is due on July 1, 2000.

b. *Payment on demand:* Promises to pay *on demand, at sight,* or *on presentment* satisfy the requirement.

6. *Payable to Order or Bearer:* To be negotiable, an instrument must make it clear that the promisor intended for the instrument to be transferable by the promisee to another party.

a. *Acceptable word usage:* Words such as "pay to the order of Gregg Wilson" or "payable to the bearer" satisfy this requirement.

b. *Transfer of instrument:* If the instrument is simply made payable to a named party, it may still be transferred, but the rights of the transferee will be limited. The transferee will not be considered a holder (see Sections B-6-c[5] and [6]).

c. *Parties to negotiable instruments:* The parties involved in the making and transferring of negotiable instruments are known in the law by various names. Familiarity with the basic terminology employed by the UCC is helpful in understanding negotiable instruments.

(1) *Drawer:* A drawer is one who issues a check or other draft.

(2) *Drawee:* A drawee is a party who is ordered by the drawer to pay a certain sum of money to a party known as a *payee.*

EXAMPLE: Anderson writes a check in the amount of $10 payable to Bauer. Anderson is the drawer; Bauer is the payee. Anderson's bank is the drawee.

(3) *Maker:* A maker is one who signs a promissory note promising to pay a certain sum of money to another party.

(4) *Indorser and indorsee:* An indorser is a payee who transfers the instrument by signing it and delivering it to one known as an indorsee. (An indorsee can become an indorser.)

EXAMPLE: Bauer is named as the payee on a check. She signs the check and delivers it to Chapman. Bauer is the indorser. Chapman is the indorsee.

Note: The word *endorse* is commonly used in business. The word *indorse* is used in the UCC.

(5) *Holder:* A holder is one who possesses an instrument that is issued or indorsed to that person or is payable to the bearer.

(6) *Holder in due course:* A holder in due course is one who gives value for an instrument and takes it in good faith without knowledge of any defect. A holder in due course is free of many defenses to which an ordinary assignee is subject (see Section E).

C. Types of Negotiable Instruments

The UCC recognizes two types of instruments: drafts and promissory notes.

1. *Drafts:* A draft is an instrument that contains an unconditional order by the drawer, directing the drawee to pay money to a payee (see Section B-6-c).

EXAMPLE: A check.

2. *Promissory Notes:* A promissory note is an instrument that contains a promise by the maker to pay a certain sum of money to another party at a specific time or on demand.

D. Transfer of Negotiable Instruments

A negotiable instrument may be transferred by assignment or by negotiation.

1. *Assignment:* An assignment is a transfer of contract rights. Assignments are governed by contract law (see Chapter 21, Section G). Because the assignee stands in the shoes of the assignor, the assignee is subject to the same defenses as those to which the assignor is subject. Thus, one of the main advantages of a negotiable instrument is lost when it is merely assigned.

2. *Negotiation:* Negotiation is the transfer of an instrument in such form that the transferee becomes a holder (see Section B-6-c[5]). Negotiation may occur in two ways: by delivery and by indorsement and delivery.

a. *Negotiation by delivery:* If the negotiable instrument is payable to the bearer, it is negotiated by delivery.

EXAMPLE: Dickinson signed a check reading, "Pay to the order of cash, $100." He delivered the check to McCay. The act of delivery constituted negotiation. McCay became the holder.

b. *Negotiation by indorsement and delivery:* If the negotiable instrument is payable to the order of a party, the instrument is negotiated when the named party indorses it and delivers it to a holder.

EXAMPLE: Dickinson signed a check reading, "Pay to the order of Mary McCay, $100." McCay took the check to the bank, indorsed it by signing her name on the back, and received the $100. The bank became the holder.

(1) *Blank indorsement:* A blank indorsement is one that does not specify an indorsee. An instrument that is payable to the order of a payee becomes payable to the bearer once the payee indorses it in blank.

EXAMPLE: McCay signed a check that read, "Pay to the order of Debbie Black, $20." Black indorsed the check in blank by signing the back of it. The check became payable to the bearer when she indorsed it in blank.

(2) *Special indorsement:* A special indorsement is one that names the party to whom the indorser makes the instrument payable.

EXAMPLE: Edwards signed a check that read, "Pay to the order of Peter Jones, $40." Jones specially indorsed the check by writing on the back, "Pay to the order of Glen Hall. (Signed) Peter Jones."

A party who receives a negotiable instrument indorsed in blank may make it a specially indorsed instrument by writing over the signature of the blank indorser.

EXAMPLE: Green received a check that had been made payable to Lane. Lane had indorsed the check in blank by signing his name on the back. Green may write over Lane's signature, "Pay to Ed Green." Green has made the check into one that is specially indorsed.

(3) *Indorsement without recourse:* An indorsement without recourse is one in which the indorser disclaims liability in the event that the maker or drawer fails to pay.

EXAMPLE: Temple manages several apartments for Matthews. A tenant gave Temple a check for rent. The check was made payable to the order of Temple. Instead of merely indorsing the check, Temple writes "without recourse" above his signature. This ensures that Temple will not be held liable in the event the check is not paid.

(4) *Restrictive indorsement:* A restrictive indorsement is one that requires the indorsee to follow certain instructions.

EXAMPLE: Amato signed a check payable to the order of Baldwin. Baldwin indorsed the check on the back by writing, "Pay to Caldwell, provided that she graduates from college by May 30, 2000." Baldwin signed beneath the statement. Caldwell or any subsequent holder cannot collect payment until the condition is met. (Baldwin could not put such a condition in a check on which she is the drawer without making the check nonnegotiable, but she is permitted to indorse a check conditionally.)

E. Defenses

The two main categories of defenses are personal defenses and real defenses. Real defenses are specified by the UCC. Any defense not so specified is a personal defense.

1. *Real Defenses:* Real defenses are valid against all holders, including holders in due course. Real defenses are sometimes referred to as *universal defenses.*

a. *Forgery:*

(1) One whose signature is forged on a negotiable instrument may use forgery as a defense even against a holder in due course.

(2) If an agent has signed a negotiable instrument on behalf of a principal, the principal may assert the signer's lack of *any* authority as a defense even against a holder in due course.

b. *Fraud in the execution (real fraud):* See Chapter 21, Section B-2-b(3).

EXAMPLE: Baldwin, a movie star, is asked by a fan to autograph a picture. Later the fan lifts the picture off the promissory note that it was covering. Baldwin's signature appears on the note. Since Baldwin was deceived as to what he was signing, he has a valid defense even against a holder in due course.

c. *Material alteration:* A material alteration of the instrument is a real defense. A material alteration is one that changes the amount, the interest, the date, the signature, or the parties. If an alteration is material, it is a defense against any ordinary holder. A holder in due course may enforce the instrument as originally drawn or written.

EXAMPLE: Reed raises an $80 check to $800. Miller, a holder in due course, acquires the check. The drawer has a real defense to the raised amount, but Miller can enforce the check to the original amount, $80.

d. *A discharge in bankruptcy:* Federal bankruptcy prevails over the interest of a holder in due course. If the debt is discharged in bankruptcy court, the holder has no right to payment.

EXAMPLE: Moore signed a promissory note payable to Frank's Furniture Store. Frank's indorsed the note to Blackberry Finance. After the note became due, Blackberry demanded payment. Moore filed for bankruptcy. In bankruptcy court, she will prevail over Blackberry even though Blackberry is a holder in due course.

e. *Illegality that renders an instrument void:* If the instrument is merely voidable, it provides only a personal defense (see Section E-1-c).

f. *Mental incompetence:* A person who has actually been found by a court to be mentally incompetent cannot issue a negotiable instrument that is enforceable against him or her. Such a person has a real defense. If at the time the instrument is signed the person has not yet been adjudged by a court to be mentally incompetent, the instrument is merely voidable and provides only a personal defense.

g. *Threat:* If a signature was obtained by the threat of force or immediate violence, the instrument is void. This type of extreme duress provides a real defense.

EXAMPLE: Kidnappers demand $20,000 from Green for the return of his daughter, threatening to kill her if he does not comply. Brown signs and delivers a $20,000 check made payable to bearer. The kidnappers cleverly convey the check to Lane who has no knowledge of these events and qualifies as a holder in due course. Green, nevertheless, may assert the defense of duress.

h. *Minority:* Minority is a real defense to the same extent that it is a defense to the enforcement of a simple contract.

EXAMPLE: Jensen, a mature-looking 17-year-old, signs a promissory note to purchase stereo equipment. The store indorses the note to a finance company that has no knowledge that Jensen is a minor. Jensen may avoid payment by asserting her minority even against the holder in due course.

2. *Personal Defenses:* Personal defenses are valid only against an ordinary holder. Personal defenses will not allow a party to avoid paying a holder in due course (see Section B-6-c[6]). Personal defenses include the following:

a. *Breach of contract:* Negotiable instruments are usually issued as a result of a contract between two parties. If a third party gives value for that negotiable instrument and takes it without any knowledge of the breach, the third party is free from the defense of breach of contract.

EXAMPLE: Larson contracted to purchase four copy machines from True-Copy, Inc. Under the agreement Larson gave True-Copy a promissory note for $4,000 payable in two months. True-Copy sold the note to XYZ, Inc., for $3,600. When the note became due, XYZ presented it for payment. Larson claimed that because he received only three machines, he was not obligated for the full amount of the note. XYZ is free of Larson's personal defense because XYZ qualifies as a holder in due course, provided that it had no knowledge of any breach at the time it acquired the note for value.

b. *Fraud in the inducement (personal fraud):* A party who issues a negotiable instrument on the basis of a fraudulent representation (see Chapter 21, Section B-2-b[3][a]) cannot use fraud as a defense against a holder in due course.

EXAMPLE: On the basis of Lloyd's representation that a certain rock had been brought from the moon to earth by astronauts, Jacobs agreed to purchase the rock for $5,000. Jacobs issued a promissory note to Lloyd in that amount. Later Jacobs learned that Lloyd had misrepresented the rock's origin and that in fact Lloyd had found the rock in his yard. Although Jacobs would have a valid defense against Lloyd or an ordinary holder, if Lloyd has transferred the note to a holder in due course, Jacobs must pay the note. (Jacobs could still sue Lloyd for breach of contract.)

c. *Duress and undue influence:* Both duress and undue influence are considered personal defenses as long as the abuse involved did not become so outrageous that the issuer of the instrument lost his or her will as a result of threats of physical harm.

EXAMPLE: Morales threatens to organize all the local hardware-store owners and obtain their promise never to buy from ABC Manufacturing, Inc., unless ABC issues a note to him for $10,000 for his services as a consultant. When ABC issues *the note to Morales, he quickly sells it to Irving for $9,450. Irving had no knowledge of any threat. ABC cannot assert the defense of duress against Irving, who is a holder in due course.*

d. *Mental incapacity:* Mental incapacity is not a valid defense against a holder in due course unless the incapacity is so extreme that the instrument is void rather than merely voidable.

e. *Payment of the instrument:* On paying the amount of the negotiable instrument, the maker should obtain the return of the instrument or at least have it marked "Canceled." If such a precaution is not taken, the instrument may come into the possession of a holder in due course against whom payment would not be a valid defense.

f. *Writing without authority:* The defense that someone acted without authority and completed an incomplete instrument is a personal defense.

EXAMPLE: Lambert asked Gordon to go to the supermarket for her and purchase the items on a grocery list. Lambert gave Gordon a check that she had signed. The check was left blank as to the payee and the amount. Gordon wrote her name in as the payee and wrote in $200 as the amount. Gordon then indorsed the check and delivered it to a holder in due course. The unauthorized completion would constitute a valid defense against Gordon or an ordinary holder but not against a holder in due course.

Review Questions

Directions: Select the best answer from the four alternatives. Write your answer in the blank to the left of the number.

_____ **1.** After three years of monthly payments, Lee finally pays off the note he signed to purchase his car. He is so happy that he goes out to celebrate without obtaining the note or insisting that it be marked "Canceled." A bookkeeping error occurs, and the finance company sells the note to Harvey, who becomes a holder in due course. Harvey sues Lee to collect on the note. Who will win?

a. Lee, because payment is a defense even against a holder in due course.
b. Lee, provided that he can prove that he paid the finance company.
c. Harvey, because payment is a personal defense not valid against a holder in due course.
d. Harvey, because payment is a real defense, not a personal one.

_____ **2.** Weston contracted to deliver his motorcycle to Emery in return for Emery's promise to paint Weston's house. Emery assigned his rights in the contract to Taft. When Taft sued Weston to obtain the motorcycle, Weston defended on the grounds that Emery had not painted the house. Is Weston permitted to assert the defense against Taft?

a. Yes, because Taft is subject to the same defenses to which Emery would be subject.
b. Only if Taft knew that Emery had not completed painting the house at the time Taft took the assignment.
c. No, because the contract was a negotiable instrument.
d. No, because the contract contained an unconditional promise to pay a specified sum of money.

_____ **3.** Morgan owed a disputed debt to the Acme Farm Implement Company. Angry and frustrated at his inability to resolve the dispute, Morgan carved a check on a pumpkin and delivered it to Acme. Does the pumpkin qualify as a negotiable instrument?

a. No, the UCC requires the writing to be on paper.
b. No, pumpkins are among the items specifically excluded by the UCC as media for negotiable instruments.
c. Yes, if all the elements of negotiability are met.
d. Yes, because pumpkins are goods under the UCC.

_____ **4.** Alexander wrote on a slip of paper, "Briggs, I owe you $55. (Signed) Alexander." Is this a negotiable instrument?

a. Yes, because all requirements of the UCC are met.
b. No, because the signature was not notarized.
c. No, because the promise was conditional.
d. No, because the writing does not contain a promise to pay.

______________ **5.** Jackson wrote, "I promise to pay Wayne $150 if Wayne delivers his 13-inch color television set to my home by May 1. (Signed) Jackson." Is this writing a negotiable instrument?

a. Yes, because all requirements of the UCC are met.
b. No, because the sum of money is not certain.
c. No, because the promise to pay is conditional.
d. No, because it is not payable to the bearer.

______________ **6.** Lawrence wrote a check payable to the order of Seymour. The check is drawn on the First National Bank. Which of the following is true?

a. Lawrence is the drawer, Seymour the drawee, and the bank the payee.
b. Lawrence is the drawer, Seymour the payee, and the bank the drawee.
c. Lawrence is the maker, Seymour the holder, and the bank the indorsee.
d. Lawrence is the maker, Seymour the indorsee, and the bank the drawee.

______________ **7.** Williams contracted to purchase a new oven for his restaurant from the Universal Supply Company. Under the terms of the agreement, Williams gave Universal a promissory note for $6,000 payable in three months. Universal negotiated the note to Maxwell in return for $5,200. When the note became due, Maxwell presented it for payment. Williams claimed that the oven Universal had delivered did not comply with the contract. Is Maxwell subject to Williams' defense?

a. No.
b. No, provided that Maxwell had no knowledge of any breach of the contract at the time he purchased the note.
c. Yes, because breach of contract is a real defense.
d. Yes, because a promissory note is not a negotiable instrument.

______________ **8.** Which of the following is a real defense?

a. Fraud in the inducement
b. Payment on the instrument
c. Forgery
d. Breach of contract

______________ **9.** An important difference between a real defense and a personal defense is that

a. a personal defense can be asserted against a holder in due course, but a real defense cannot.
b. a real defense can be asserted against a holder in due course, but a personal defense cannot.
c. a personal defense requires two witnesses, but a real defense requires only one.
d. a real defense requires at least two witnesses, but a personal defense requires none.

______________ **10.** Simpson signed a check made payable to the order of Price. Price indorsed the check by writing on the back of it, "Pay to Lawson provided that she registers to vote by October 1, 2000." Price signed her name below the statement. Price has made

a. a restrictive indorsement.

b. an indorsement without recourse.
c. an assignment.
d. a forgery.

_______________ **11.** Which of the following would constitute a material alteration of a negotiable instrument?

a. The signer of a promissory note changes in age from minor to adult.
b. The stated rate of interest is changed from 7 percent to 7.25 percent.
c. A breach of contract takes place.
d. The stated address of the maker is changed for the purpose of correcting it.

_______________ **12.** Hughes is a holder in due course of a note made by Clark. When Hughes demanded payment on the note, Clark claimed that he had already paid the full amount to Griffin, the previous holder. Which of the following statements is true?

a. Clark may assert the defense against Hughes because payment is a real defense.
b. Clark will succeed with the defense if he can prove that he actually paid the full amount to Griffin.
c. As a holder in due course, Hughes is subject to the defense of payment.
d. Hughes is not subject to the defense of payment.

_______________ **13.** Assume that in the preceding situation Hughes sued Clark on the note. Before the case came to trial, however, Clark obtained a discharge of the debt in federal bankruptcy court. Which of the following statements is true regarding Hughes' right to collect on the note?

a. Hughes can collect only if he proves that he obtained the note prior to Clark's filing for bankruptcy.
b. Hughes can recover only if he proves that he obtained the note prior to the date on which Clark obtained the discharge in bankruptcy.
c. Hughes can recover regardless of the timing of the bankruptcy.
d. Hughes cannot collect on the note since the debt was discharged in bankruptcy court.

_______________ **14.** A material alteration of a negotiable instrument provides a defense against

a. any holder (ordinary holders and holders in due course).
b. only ordinary holders.
c. ordinary holders and holders in due course if the alteration is apparent.
d. only holders in due course.

_______________ **15.** Lange, a delivery person for a flower shop, delivered flowers to Jones. Lange showed Jones a receipt and asked him to sign on a certain line. While Jones went to get a pen, Lange substituted a promissory note for the receipt. Thinking he was signing the same document he had just examined, Jones signed the note. Lange negotiated the note to Howard, a holder in due course. When Howard demanded payment, Jones asserted the defense of fraud. May Jones' defense be used against a holder in due course?

a. No, because fraud is a personal defense.
b. Yes, because Lange's conduct amounts to fraud in the execution.

c. No, because Lange's conduct amounts to fraud in the inducement.
d. Yes, because Lange's conduct amounts to duress.

Use the following information in answering Questions 16 and 17.

Wilson had several fake diamonds that he attempted to sell as real diamonds. On May 1 he sold one of these to Ryan in return for a promissory note in the amount of $200. Also on May 1 he sold one to Mayer in return for a promissory note in the amount of $250. On May 2 Wilson transferred Ryan's note to Wiley in return for $175. Wiley had no knowledge of any misrepresentation. On May 8 Wilson transferred Mayer's note to Benson in return for $20. Benson knew at the time of this transfer that Mayer planned to sue Wilson for misrepresentation concerning the "diamond" sale.

______________ **16.** When Ryan's note became due, Wiley sued Ryan to collect the $200. Which is the correct result?

a. Ryan can use the defense of misrepresentation against Wiley.
b. Ryan will win because a promissory note is nontransferable.
c. Wiley will win if she can prove that the misrepresentation was fraud in the execution.
d. Wiley will win because she is a holder in due course.

______________ **17.** When Mayer's note became due, Benson sued to collect the $250. Which is the correct result?

a. Mayer can use the defense of misrepresentation against Benson.
b. Benson can collect $20 from Mayer but not the full amount of the note.
c. Benson will win because he is a holder in due course.
d. Benson will win because misrepresentation is no defense in a suit based on a promissory note.

Use the following information in answering Questions 18 and 19.

Adams is a holder in due course of a promissory note purportedly signed by Bruce. When Adams sued to collect on the note, Bruce claimed that the signature was forged.

______________ **18.** Which of the following is a correct statement?

a. Bruce can assert the defense of forgery against Adams.
b. Bruce cannot assert the defense of forgery against Adams.
c. As a holder in due course, Adams can collect on the note only from the party who negotiated the note to him.
d. As a holder in due course, Adams cannot collect on the promissory note.

______________ **19.** Assume that Bruce, instead of claiming forgery, claims that the note was altered after he signed it. Which of the following is correct?

a. Any alteration will be a defense against Adams.
b. Any material alteration will be a defense against Adams.
c. Any apparent alteration will be a defense against Adams.
d. Only apparent and material alterations will be a defense against Adams.

Use the following information in answering Questions 20 and 21.

Haines signed a draft that read, "Pay to the order of Wayne, $100." She delivered the draft to Wayne.

______________ **20.** To negotiate the draft, Wayne must

a. indorse it.
b. deliver it.
c. indorse and deliver it.
d. Wayne cannot indorse the draft since it is payable to him.

______________ **21.** Assume that Haines signed a draft that read, "Pay to bearer, $100." She delivered it to Wayne. To negotiate the draft, Wayne must

a. indorse it.
b. deliver it.
c. indorse and deliver it.
d. Wayne cannot negotiate the draft because it is payable to the bearer.

Solutions

Answer	*Refer to:*
1. (c)	[E-2-e] Payment is a personal defense, not valid against a holder in due course. It is essential that the note be destroyed or marked "Canceled" when it is paid. (Lee may recover from the finance company if he is required to pay twice.)
2. (a)	[D-1] Taft is merely an assignee. As such he stands in the shoes of Emery, the assignor. Since Emery would be subject to Weston's defense, Taft is also subject to that defense. The contract did not qualify as a negotiable instrument. Among other things, the contract did not contain an unconditional promise to pay a certain sum of money.
3. (c)	[B-1] The Uniform Commercial Code requires only that the writing be in tangible form. Since a carving on a pumpkin is tangible, this requirement is met.
4. (d)	[B-3-a] Alexander's writing merely acknowledges a debt. It does not contain an express promise to pay the money. There is no requirement that the signature be notarized.
5. (c)	[B-3-c(1)] Jackson's promise is conditioned on Wayne's delivery of the television set. The writing does not, therefore, qualify as a negotiable instrument.
6. (b)	[B-6-c] As the issuer of the check, Lawrence is the drawer. The bank is the party that is ordered to pay the money, the drawee. Seymour, the party to whom the check is payable, is the payee.
7. (b)	[E-1-a] If Maxwell had no knowledge of the alleged breach, he qualifies as a holder in due course and therefore takes free of Williams' defense.
8. (c)	[E-2-a] Forgery is a real defense. All the others listed are personal defenses, which cannot be asserted successfully against a holder in due course.
9. (b)	[E-2] Only real defenses can be asserted successfully against a holder in due course.
10. (a)	[D-2-b(4)] Price has made a restrictive indorsement. Lawson, the indorsee, must perform the stated act to collect payment on the check. If Price had been the drawer of the check, she could not include such a condition without making the check nonnegotiable. As the payee, however, Pamela may make such an indorsement.
11. (b)	[E-2] Changing the stated rate of interest affects the amount due and thus is considered a material alteration of the negotiable instrument.

12. (d) [E-1-f] Payment is a personal defense. Because Hughes is a holder in due course, he is not subject to such a defense. Clark should have insisted that Griffin return the note to him when he paid Griffin. At least Clark should have had the note marked "Canceled."

13. (d) [E-1-d] A discharge in bankruptcy is a real defense. It therefore applies even against a holder in due course.

14. (c) [E-1-c] A material alteration provides a valid defense against all ordinary holders. In addition, it provides a defense against a holder in due course if the alteration is an obvious one.

15. (b) [E-1-b] Since Lange actually deceived Jones into signing something other than what he thought he was signing, fraud in the execution occurred. Unlike fraud in the inducement, fraud in the execution is a real defense. It is therefore valid even against a holder in due course.

16. (d) [E-2-b] Since Wiley gave value for the instrument and took it in good faith without knowledge of any defenses, she is a holder in due course who takes free of the personal defense of fraud in the inducement.

17. (a) [E-2-b] Since Benson did not take the instrument in good faith without knowledge of the defense, he is not a holder in due course. He is therefore subject to the defense of fraud in the inducement.

18. (a) [E-1-a] Forgery is a real defense that may be asserted even against a holder in due course.

19. (d) [E-1-c] Since Adams is a holder in due course, he takes free from even a claim of material alteration unless the alteration is an apparent one.

20. (c) [D-2-b] Because this instrument is payable to Wayne, he must both indorse and deliver it in order to negotiate the instrument.

21. (b) [D-2-a] Since this negotiable instrument is payable to the bearer, it is negotiated by mere delivery.

sales clerk, she asks him how much a certain chair costs. Johnson responds by stating that the chair is on sale for $100. In fact, the chair is priced at $300. Fleming purchases the chair and takes it home. On discovering what happened, Mitchell seeks to recover the chair or the $200 difference between the actual price and what Fleming paid. Mitchell will not succeed. Johnson had apparent authority. Mitchell knowingly allowed the circumstances to exist under which Fleming could reasonably believe that Johnson had authority to sell the chair.

E. Obligations of Agent to Principal

The agent owes the highest duty of loyalty to the principal.

1. *Duty to Act within Authority:* The agent has a duty to act within his or her actual authority, that is, not to exceed power to the detriment of the principal.

   EXAMPLE: Stone leaves her bicycle with Lamont. Stone tells Lamont, "Rent my bicycle if you can to someone for $3 per day, but do not sell it." Lamont sells the bicycle to Carlson. Lamont has breached her duty to Stone by not acting within her actual authority. Lamont is liable to Stone for the value of the bicycle.

2. *Duty to Perform:* The agent has a duty to personally perform the duties undertaken in the agency agreement. The law permits the agent to delegate his or her duties only in certain limited circumstances.

   a. *Delegation of performance:* If the task is extremely simple, requiring no skill or expertise, it may be delegated.

   b. *Customary delegation:* If it is customary for such tasks to be delegated, the agent may delegate unless the agent has specifically agreed to perform personally.

3. *Duty to Exercise Care and Skill:* The agent has a duty to exercise reasonable care and skill in performing services for the principal. The agent is liable for any damages that failure to exercise reasonable care and skill causes the principal to suffer.

   EXAMPLE: Taylor hires Warren to serve as his agent for the purpose of purchasing milking cows for Taylor's dairy farm. Warren is an experienced purchaser of milking cows. Warren nevertheless fails to inspect a dozen cows that he purchases on Taylor's behalf. The cows are obviously diseased and unfit for use as milking cows. Warren has breached his duty of exercising reasonable care and skill in serving as Taylor's agent. Warren is liable to Taylor for the damage his breach of duty caused.

4. *Duty to Account to Principal:* The agent has a duty to account to the principal for all money or other property that the agent has handled on behalf of the principal.

5. *Duty Not to Commingle Property:* The agent has a duty not to commingle personal funds or other property with that of the principal.

   EXAMPLE: Blair serves as Walker's agent for purposes of renting apartments owned by Walker. Blair receives security deposits from tenants and places the money in his personal bank account along with his personal funds. Blair has breached his duty to Walker because Blair did not keep his principal's funds separate from his own.

6. *Duty to Inform Principal:* The agent has a duty to inform the principal of relevant information that comes to the attention of the agent.

   EXAMPLE: Wallace is employed as a sales agent by Modern Fashions, Inc., a corporation that manufactures and sells clothing. She discovers that Mirror Image, Inc., a competitor of Modern Fashions, has manufactured a line of clothing practically identical to Modern Fashions' latest line. Wallace is obligated to pass this information on to her employer.

7. *Duty to Avoid Conflicts of Interest:* The agent has a duty to avoid conflicts of interest.

   a. *Competition with principal:* The agent must not compete against the principal or work for a competitor of the principal.

   b. *Conflict of interest:* If a conflict of interest does develop, the agent must promptly inform the principal of the conflict. Only if the principal, with full knowledge of the conflict, consents to the agent's continued service can the agent maintain this position.

      EXAMPLE: Blomberg works as a purchasing agent for Ajax Used Auto Parts, Inc., a corporation that buys used auto parts. Blomberg takes a part-time job as a purchasing agent for Baxter, Inc., a competitor of Ajax. Blomberg has breached his duty to Ajax because he has undertaken a job that conflicts with his duty of loyalty to Ajax. Only if Blomberg fully discloses the conflict to Ajax and obtains Ajax's approval can he continue to work for Baxter.

   c. *Seizing principal's opportunity:* The agent must not seize the principal's opportunity.

      EXAMPLE: Avery serves as a sales representative for Lowell Industries, a rapidly growing company that is looking for an attractive site for a new corporate headquarters. In the course of her work for Lowell Industries, Avery has a conversation with Rodriguez, who informs her of the availability of an ideal site for such a building. Avery acts to buy the land for herself. She has breached the duty of loyalty to her principal by taking advantage of the principal's opportunity.

   d. *Divulging confidential information of principal:* The agent must not divulge confidential information of the principal.

      EXAMPLE: Jefferson is employed as a paralegal by Stearns, who is a lawyer. Jefferson releases information from a confidential file to Monroe, who is suing one of Stearns' clients. Jefferson divulged the information in the hope of obtaining a higher-paying job with Monroe. Jefferson has breached her duty of loyalty to Stearns.

8. *Duty to Make No Secret Profit:* The agent has a duty not to make a secret profit. Any money or other property obtained by the agent must be reported to the principal.

   EXAMPLE: Ayers serves as a purchasing agent for Rainbow Industries, Inc., a company that purchases 20 new cars each year for use by company executives. Ayers received a secret payment of $10,000 in return for purchasing 20 cars from Smiley Motors, a local car dealer, on behalf of the company. Ayers has breached his duty of loyalty to Rainbow by receiving this secret profit.

F. Obligations of Agent to Third Party

The obligation of an agent to a third party often depends on the type of agency involved (see Sections B-1, B-2, and B-3).

1. *Contract on Behalf of Disclosed Principal:* An agent who enters a contract on behalf of a disclosed principal incurs no liability on the contract.

   EXAMPLE: Abbott, acting within his actual authority, enters a contract with Turner, who knows that Abbott is acting merely as Prentice's agent. Abbott is not personally liable on the contract. If Prentice breaches the contract, Turner can recover damages from Prentice only.

2. *Contract on Behalf of Partially Disclosed Principal:* An agent who enters a contract on behalf of a partially disclosed principal can be held liable to the third party.

   EXAMPLE: Anderson, acting within her actual authority, enters a contract with Travis, who knows that Anderson is acting as an agent but does not know the identity of Anderson's principal, Palmer. If the contract is breached, Travis can recover damages from Anderson. Because Travis did not know of Palmer's identity, she relied on Anderson's background and reputation in contracting with Anderson. Thus, Travis is allowed to hold Anderson responsible in the event the contract is breached.

   Note: If the third party determines the identity of the principal, that party may enforce or pursue either the principal or the agent.

3. *Contract on Behalf of Undisclosed Principal:* An agent who enters a contract on behalf of an undisclosed principal can be held liable to the third party.

   If the third party suffers a loss as a result of the agent's fraud, deceit, or negligent conduct, the agent is liable, and the third party may recover such loss.

   EXAMPLE: Alexander, acting within his actual authority, enters a contract with Terry, who does not know that Alexander is acting as an agent for Phillips. Terry reasonably believes that Alexander is acting on Alexander's own behalf. If the contract is breached, Terry can recover damages from Alexander. Because Terry reasonably believed that Alexander was acting for himself, Terry relied on Alexander's background and reputation in contracting with Alexander. Terry is, therefore, allowed to hold Alexander responsible in the event the contract is breached.

G. Obligations of Principal to Agent

The principal's duties to the agent may be divided into four categories: duty to compensate, duty to honor contract terms, duty to reimburse expenses, and duty to indemnify.

1. *Duty to Compensate:* Unless it is agreed that the agent will serve without being compensated for services (a gratuitous agent), the principal is obligated to pay the agent for the services rendered.

   EXAMPLE: Ames developed new software specially designed for law offices. Bannon, an acquaintance, offered to contact every law office in his hometown in an effort to sell the software. Ames gladly provided him with samples and information. Bannon made several sales and expects to be compensated. Ames refuses by pointing out that she never agreed to pay him. Bannon is entitled to reasonable compensation because it was not agreed that he would work for nothing.

2. *Duty to Honor Contract Terms:* In addition to the duty to compensate the agent in the absence of a contrary agreement, a principal who has contracted with an agent must abide by the terms of the contract.

   EXAMPLE: Arnold agreed to serve as Payne's agent for the purpose of selling Payne's race horse, Molasses. When Arnold attempted to show the horse to a prospective buyer, Payne would not give Arnold the keys to the stable. When Arnold attempted to make other arrangements to show the horse, Payne refused. Payne has breached his implied promise not to interfere unreasonably with Arnold's efforts to sell the horse.

3. *Duty to Reimburse Expenses:* The principal is obligated to reimburse the agent for authorized expenditures the agent has made.

   EXAMPLE: Perkins hires Archer to serve as her agent in managing Perkins' clothing store. To prevent the electricity from being turned off while Perkins was vacationing in Europe, Archer paid the store's electricity bill. Perkins is obligated to reimburse Archer for the payment.

4. *Duty to Indemnify:* The principal is obligated to indemnify the agent for losses suffered by the agent in the course of the agent's duties.

EXAMPLE: Peterson hires Andrews to serve as his agent for the purpose of purchasing a yacht from Thompson. Peterson directs Andrews to make no mention of the agency relationship and to act as if Andrews is purchasing the boat for himself. Andrews follows these instructions and enters into a contract with Thompson for the purchase of the yacht on the terms that Peterson had indicated he would find acceptable. Peterson forwards the down payment to Andrews. After Peterson takes possession of the boat, however, he fails to make any further payments. Thompson sues Andrews and wins a judgment, which Andrews pays. Andrews is entitled to reimbursement from Peterson.

H. Obligations of Principal to Third Parties

The principal's liability to third parties may result from contracts entered into by an agent on the principal's behalf or from injuries caused by the agent's conduct within the scope of the agent's employment.

1. *Principal's Duty to Perform Contract:* The principal has a duty to perform on contracts entered into on the principal's behalf by an agent who acted with authority.

a. *Authorized acts of agent:* The principal is bound by the authorized acts of his or her agent whether the principal is disclosed, partially disclosed, or undisclosed (see Section B in this chapter).

(1) Even though the third party did not know the identity of a partially disclosed principal, the party may nevertheless hold the principal liable on contracts entered on behalf of the principal by an authorized agent.

(2) Even though the third party did not know of the existence of a principal at the time of entering into the contract, the party may, on learning of the principal, hold the principal liable.

EXAMPLE: Austin acted as Page's agent in dealing with Thayer. Thayer thought that Austin was acting on Austin's own behalf. Thayer entered into a contract with Austin. Later, on learning that Austin was acting on behalf of Page, Thayer elects to hold Page responsible for performing the contract. Page is responsible to Thayer.

b. *Ratification of agent's acts:* If the agent acted without authority, the principal may still be bound if he or she ratifies the acts of the agent.

(1) Ratification occurs when the principal adopts the unauthorized acts of the agent.

(2) Ratification need not be stated in words. If the principal accepts the benefits of the agent's unauthorized acts with the intent of ratifying those acts, the principal has ratified.

(3) The principal can ratify only if he or she has knowledge of all relevant facts.

EXAMPLE: While serving as Page's agent, Austin acted beyond his authority and entered into a contract with Thayer. On learning of the unauthorized act and the resulting contract, Page accepted the benefits of the contract with the intent of being bound by its terms. Page has ratified Austin's unauthorized act.

2. *Principal's Liability for Injuries to Third Parties:* The principal is liable to third parties for injuries caused by negligent or intentional acts of an employee acting within the scope of employment. This legal doctrine is known as *respondent superior.*

   a. *Injuries by independent contractor:* A principal is not ordinarily liable for injuries caused by an independent contractor (see Section C-3).

      EXAMPLE: Tracy's lawyer negligently drives his car into an intersection and strikes a pedestrian while on the way to the courthouse to file a document on behalf of Tracy. Tracy is not liable to the injured pedestrian because the lawyer is an independent contractor.

   b. *Interests served by employees:* In determining whether an employee is acting within the scope of the employee's authority, courts consider the interest the employee was serving at the time the employee caused the injury.

      EXAMPLES: Romano employs Jordan to travel from store to store in Central City to solicit sales for Romano's awning business. While driving between stores, Jordan negligently injures Moore. Romano is liable to Moore.

      Assume that at the time he negligently injured Moore, Jordan had decided to take the rest of the day off and was 20 miles outside of Central City on his way to a lake. Romano, Jordan's employer, is not liable to Moore. Jordan was serving only his own purpose. He had abandoned his duties to Romano and was outside the scope of his employment.

I. Obligations of Third Parties to Principals and Agents

Third parties are bound to perform on contracts they enter into with agents.

1. *Contract with Agent for Disclosed Principal:* A third party who contracts with an agent who is acting on behalf of a disclosed principal owes a duty to the principal to perform contractual obligations.

2. *Contract with Agent for Partially Disclosed Principal:* A third party who contracts with an agent acting on behalf of a partially disclosed principal owes a duty to the principal and to the agent to perform contractual obligations.

   EXAMPLE: Thomas contracts with Ashley, who is acting for Preston, a partially disclosed principal. If Thomas fails to perform under the contract, either Ashley or Preston may sue Thomas for breach of contract.

3. *Contract with Agent for Undisclosed Principal:* A third party who contracts with an agent who is acting on behalf of an undisclosed principal owes a duty of performance to the agent and, in most cases, to the principal.

   a. *Duty of performance to agent:* The third party owes a duty of performance to the agent because he or she contracted with the agent, thinking that the agent was acting on the agent's behalf.

   b. *Duty of performance to undisclosed principal:* The third party owes a duty of performance to the undisclosed principal unless one of the following situations exists.

      (1) If the contract requires the agent to perform contractual duties personally, the undisclosed principal cannot hold the third party liable for breach of contract.

(2) If the agent lies to the third party by denying that he or she is acting as an agent, the undisclosed principal cannot hold the third party liable for breach of contract.

(3) If the agent or undisclosed principal knows, or should know, that the third party would not agree to do business with the principal, the undisclosed principal cannot hold the third party liable for breach of contract.

4. *Third-Party Performance on Contract:* Under no circumstances can the third party be required to perform contractual duties twice. Even where both the agent and the principal can hold the third party responsible for performance, once performance is rendered or once damages are paid, the third party is relieved of further obligation.

J. Termination of Agency Relationship

An agency may be terminated in the following ways:

1. *Mutual Agreement:* The principal and the agent can terminate the agency by mutual agreement.
2. *Agency Agreement:* The agency agreement itself may provide for termination of the agency.
   - a. *Accomplishment of agency purpose:* If the purpose of the agency, as specified in the agreement, is accomplished, the agency terminates.
   - b. *Expiration of time:* The agreement may specify that the agency is to last only for a specified time. The agency terminates when that time expires.
3. *Notification of Intent to Terminate Agency:* Either the principal or the agent may terminate the agency by notifying the other party of his or her intent to terminate.
   - a. *Limited right to terminate:* While either party has the *power* to terminate the agency, the right to terminate may be limited by the agency agreement.
   - b. *Liability for damages:* If a party exercises his or her power to terminate without having the right to terminate, he or she is liable to the other party for any damages the termination caused.

     EXAMPLE: Parrish and Anthony agree that their agency relationship will last for one year. After only two months, Parrish acts to terminate the agency. Parrish is liable for any damages the termination has caused Anthony to suffer.
4. *Death:* The death of either the principal or the agent terminates the agency.
5. *Insanity:* The insanity of either the principal or the agent terminates the agency.
6. *Impossibility of Performance:* When the objective of the agency becomes impossible to accomplish, the agency is terminated.

   EXAMPLE: Redmond agrees to serve as Bryant's agent for the purpose of selling Bryant's motorcycle. When the motorcycle is destroyed by fire, the agency is terminated.
7. *Illegality of Agency Agreement:* When the agency agreement becomes illegal because of a change in the law, the agency is terminated.

   EXAMPLE: Sanford hires Burch to serve as his agent for the purpose of purchasing a certain type of hunting rifle. After Sanford and Burch enter into an agency relationship, the legislature of their state enacts a law making the purchase of such a gun illegal. The agency is terminated when the law becomes effective.

8. *Change in Circumstances:* The agency terminates when the agent should know from the change in circumstances that the principal no longer desires the agent to perform under the agency agreement.

   EXAMPLE: Donnelly agrees to serve as Harper's agent for the purpose of purchasing auto parts for Harper's 1932 Ford automobile. When Donnelly learns that Harper has sold the car, the agency terminates. Donnelly should know that Harper no longer desires him to acquire parts for the vehicle.

K. Notification of Termination of Agency Relationship

When the agency is terminated, the principal should notify all parties who had knowledge of the agency. Such notice will eliminate apparent authority. In the absence of such notice, the principal may be bound by an agent acting with apparent authority.

1. *Oral or Written Notice:* Parties who previously dealt with the agent must be notified orally or in writing.
2. *Notice Published in Newspaper:* Other parties can be notified by a notice published in a newspaper of general circulation in the area where the agent was operating.
3. *No Formal Notification Needed:* If the agency was terminated by death, illegality, or insanity, it may not be necessary for the principal to notify others of the termination.

Review Questions

Directions: Select the best answer from the four alternatives. Write your answer in the blank to the left of the number.

________ **1.** Warner agrees to offer Elliot's snowblower for sale for $150 at Warner's garage sale. Their agreement is oral. Warner is not entitled to any compensation under the terms of the agreement. An agency relationship between Warner and Elliott

a. does not exist because the agreement is not in writing.
b. does not exist because there was no consideration.
c. does exist for a definite period of time
d. does exist for the sale of the snowblower.

________ **2.** The A and B Corporation wants to hire the partnership of White and Black as its agent for locating and purchasing desirable land for A and B's new corporate headquarters. Which of the following statements is true?

a. A corporation cannot serve as a principal.
b. A partnership cannot serve as an agent.
c. This agreement must be in writing.
d. This agreement may be oral or written.

________ **3.** Cole, a 16-year-old, hired Austin, a 22-year-old, to act as Cole's agent for the purpose of purchasing some fishing equipment. Austin contracted to purchase the designated equipment as Cole's agent. Cole, however, wants to disaffirm the purchase contract. May Cole legally disaffirm the purchase contract?

a. Yes, because she is a minor.
b. No, because the capacity of the agent governs.
c. No, because she did not disaffirm the agency agreement before the purchase contract was entered into by the agent.
d. Cole can disaffirm only if the sale price of the equipment exceeded $500.

________ **4.** Avery acts as Peterson's agent in dealing with Travis. Travis knows that Avery is acting on behalf of a principal, but Travis does not know who the principal is. Peterson is

a. a disclosed principal.
b. a partially disclosed principal.
c. an undisclosed principal.
d. an illegal principal.

________ **5.** St. Peter's Church hired Michael to paint a detailed religious scene on the ceiling of its new church. Michael was authorized to select the colors and materials to be used. He was recognized as an expert in his field. Michael became very busy and delegated his duties to Angelo, a young unknown and inexperienced artist. The church claims that Michael is not legally permitted to delegate his duties. Is the church correct?

a. No, because the law permits an agent to delegate duties in all cases.
b. No, because Michael didn't know he would become very busy.

c. Yes, because Michael's duties required special skill and expertise.
d. Yes, because an agent may never delegate duties.

______________ **6.** Jensen is employed as a purchasing agent by Alpha, Inc., a company that purchases many chemicals. Jensen owns a significant amount of stock in the Beta Chemical Company. Jensen contracted on behalf of Alpha to purchase chemicals from Beta. Has Jensen breached the duty she owes to Alpha?

a. Yes, unless Jensen notified Alpha of her conflict of interest and received Alpha's authorization to contract with Beta despite her conflict of interest.
b. No, there is no evidence that the purchase from Beta was a poor deal.
c. Yes, there is no way that an agent can contract with another party on behalf of the principal when a conflict of interest exists.
d. No, the mere fact that Jennifer had an interest in Beta is irrelevant.

______________ **7.** The kind of authority an agent appears to possess that stems from circumstances the principal allows to exist is

a. express authority.
b. implied authority.
c. apparent authority.
d. emergency authority.

______________ **8.** An agent who enters into an authorized contract on behalf of the principal is liable on the contract if the agent acted

a. for a disclosed principal.
b. as an independent contractor.
c. for an undisclosed principal.
d. as an employee.

______________ **9.** Parker hired Allison as her agent for the purpose of selling Parker's ring. The ring has an imitation diamond. Allison falsely represented to Taylor that the diamond was genuine. On the basis of that representation, Taylor paid $3,000 for the ring. May Taylor recover the money from Allison?

a. Yes, an agent is liable for losses caused by the agent's fraud or deceit.
b. Yes, an agent is always liable under contracts entered into on behalf of the principal.
c. No, an agent cannot be held liable under a contract entered into on behalf of a principal.
d. No, only the principal, Parker, is liable.

______________ **10.** Which of the following is an obligation of the principal?

a. Duty to reimburse the agent for any expenditures.
b. Duty to indemnify the agent for losses suffered by the agent as a result of the principal's failure to honor an authorized contract that the agent entered on the principal's behalf.

c. Duty to indemnify the agent for losses suffered as a result of the agent's negligent conduct.
d. Duty to reimburse the agent for authorized expenditures even if the agent acts in a deceitful manner.

______________ **11.** A principal has a duty to perform on contracts entered into on the principal's behalf by an agent who acted without authority if

a. the agent is indemnified.
b. the contract is ratified.
c. the contract is fair.
d. the contract is disaffirmed.

______________ **12.** Anthony is employed as a salesperson in the Powell hardware store. Anthony negligently dropped a heavy box on the toe of Smith, a customer. Against whom may Smith recover for his injury?

a. Powell, the principal.
b. Anthony, the agent.
c. Smith may recover against Powell or Anthony.
d. Smith cannot recover against Anthony or Powell.

______________ **13.** Parrish and Daniels entered into an agency agreement that, by its terms, was to run for two years. Parrish was to serve as Daniels' agent. Parrish notified Daniels that he was terminating the agency after only two weeks had passed. Daniels claims that Parrish cannot terminate the agency. Which of the following is true?

a. Parrish has the power to terminate, but not the right.
b. Parrish has the right to terminate, but not the power.
c. Parrish cannot terminate the agency.
d. Parrish has both the power and the right to terminate the agency.

______________ **14.** Alvarez, a professional golfer, entered into a written agency agreement with Palmer, who was to serve as Alvarez's agent in negotiating product endorsement deals. The agreement was for a period of one year. Palmer successfully negotiated several endorsement deals and had just finished producing a video and a color brochure to aid in marketing Alvarez when Alvarez notified her that the agency agreement was terminated after only three months. Palmer argues that she is entitled to damages. Which of the following is correct?

a. Alvarez is not liable for any damages.
b. Alvarez is liable for commissions on the completed deals, but nothing more.
c. Alvarez is liable for all of Palmer's damages attributable to the termination.
d. Alvarez cannot terminate the agreement; therefore, there are no damages.

______________ **15.** Kohler was employed as Wilson's agent for the purpose of selling encyclopedias. Cameron had previously dealt with Kohler while she was acting as Wilson's agent. Wilson fired Kohler. After being fired, Kohler, representing herself as Wilson's agent, contracted to sell encyclopedias to Cameron. Cameron paid Kohler $100 as a down payment. Kohler then left town. Can Cameron enforce the contract against Wilson?

a. No, because the agency had been terminated.
b. No, because Cameron was not entitled to actual notice of the termination.
c. Yes, because Kohler had apparent authority.
d. Yes, because Kohler need not have authority in order to bind Wilson.

Use the following information in answering Questions 16 and 17.

Simon, president of a small advertising firm, obtained approval from the board of directors to purchase all new office furniture and to sell the used furniture. She placed an ad in the local paper announcing that used furniture would be sold on a particular Saturday. On the designated day Simon left Gilbert in charge of the sale. She told him, however, not to sell any lamps because the board had decided to keep all lamps and light fixtures.

Gilbert sold all the furniture, including seven lamps, to parties who responded to the ad. He placed the money obtained from the sale in his personal bank account without writing down the exact amount of the sale proceeds. He cannot remember how much of the deposit was from sale proceeds and how much was from his winnings at the race track that afternoon.

______________ **16.** On learning of these events, Simon's firm seeks to recover the lamps from the purchaser who has now been identified as Simpson. Which of the following statements is true?

a. The firm will recover the lamps from Simpson because Gilbert had no actual authority to sell them.
b. The firm will recover the lamps from Simpson because Gilbert had been specifically instructed by his principal not to sell them.
c. Simpson will be permitted to keep the lamps because Gilbert possessed emergency authority to sell them.
d. Simpson will be permitted to keep the lamps because Gilbert had apparent authority to sell them.

______________ **17.** Which of the following duties of an agent did Gilbert violate?

a. Duty to inform the principal of a conflict of interest
b. Duty not to commingle funds
c. Duty not to use agency-related information for personal gain
d. Duty to make no secret profit

Use the following information in answering Questions 18 and 19.

Grant started a pharmaceutical firm to market a new drug known as Tridol. He hired Allen, Barnes, and Cooper as sales agents. Each signed an agency agreement for one year. Each was given a certain sales territory. One month later, in March, Allen notified Grant that he was terminating his agency relationship. In April

Barnes died after using Tridol. The federal Food and Drug Administration declared the sale of Tridol illegal in May.

_______________ **18.** Which statement concerning Allen's agency relationship is correct?

a. The agency terminated on Allen's notification of Grant.
b. The agency terminated when the sale of Tridol was made illegal.
c. The agency will terminate at the end of the one-year period.
d. The agency will remain in effect until it is mutually terminated.

_______________ **19.** Which of the following statements is correct?

a. The agency relationship of both Barnes and Cooper terminated on Allen's notification of Grant.
b. The agency relationship of both Barnes and Cooper terminated on the death of Barnes.
c. The agency relationship of both Barnes and Cooper terminated when the sale of Tridol was made illegal.
d. Barnes' agency relationship terminated on her death, but Cooper's did not terminate until the sale of Tridol was made illegal.

Use the following information in answering Questions 20 to 22.

Warner is employed by Mediocre Foods as a sales and delivery person. He drives a company truck along a specified route and fills orders from his truck. While unloading some frozen meat, Warner bumped Armstrong, causing her to fall and injure her arm. While driving to the next store on the route, Warner bumped into the back of a garbage truck and injured Brennan, who was loading garbage into the truck. Warner decided to take the remainder of the day off and visit his grandmother at a nursing home. After driving 10 miles off his route, Warner crashed into a vehicle stopped at a red light, causing injury to Calhoun, its driver.

_______________ **20.** Which of the following statements is true?

a. Mediocre Foods is liable to Armstrong, Brennan, and Calhoun.
b. Warner is liable to Armstrong, Brennan, and Calhoun.
c. Mediocre Foods is liable only to Armstrong.
d. Warner is liable only to Calhoun.

_______________ **21.** Mediocre Foods notified Warner of his termination. Nevertheless, he later went to Able's Foods, a customer he had sold to for seven years, and took advance payment for a large order. Able's Foods now seeks to collect from Mediocre Foods because the delivery of its order was never made. Which of the following statements is accurate?

a. Able has no right to recover because Warner's agency had already been terminated.
b. Able can recover unless Mediocre published a notice of termination in a newspaper of general circulation in the area where Able does business.
c. Able can recover if it was notified both orally and in writing of the termination.
d. Able can recover unless it was notified either orally or in writing of the termination.

_______________ **22.** Two weeks after being terminated, Warner introduced himself at Bentley's Grocery as an agent for Mediocre Foods. Warner had never been to Bentley's before. He took advance payment for a large order. Which of the following statements is true concerning Bentley's right to recover its payment from Mediocre?

a. Bentley's cannot recover because the agency had already been terminated.
b. Bentley's cannot recover because it was not notified orally or in writing of the termination.
c. Bentley's can probably recover unless notice of Warner's termination was published in a newspaper of general circulation in the area where Bentley was operating.
d. Bentley's cannot recover; no notice to third parties is required when an agent is fired.

Solutions

Answer	*Refer to:*
1. (d)	[A-1, A-2-b] There is an agency relationship between the parties. As a general rule, agency agreements need not be in writing. Only if the contract that the agent is authorized to enter on behalf of the principal is legally required to be in writing must the agency agreement be in writing. In this case Warner is authorized to enter into a contract to sell a snowblower (goods) for Elliott for $150. Because this is under $500, the contract would not have to be in writing.
2. (c)	[A-2, A-3, A-4] Since a contract for the purchase of land must be in writing, an agency agreement that authorizes the agent to purchase land on behalf of the principal must also be in writing.
3. (a)	[A-3] It is the capacity of the principal that is important in determining whether a contract entered into by an authorized agent can be disaffirmed. Because Cole, the principal, is a minor, she is permitted to disaffirm. It is not necessary that the minor principal have disaffirmed the agency agreement before disaffirming the contract entered into by the agent.
4. (b)	[B-2] The third party (Travis) knows of the existence of the principal but does not know the principal's identity, so Peterson is a partially disclosed principal. If Travis had known of Peterson's identity, Peterson would be a disclosed principal. If Travis had reasonably believed that Avery was acting on his own behalf without any principal being involved, Peterson would be an undisclosed principal.
5. (c)	[E-2-a] An agent may delegate duties only in certain limited circumstances. In this case Michael's duties require special skill and therefore cannot be delegated. The mere fact that Michael became very busy does not allow him to delegate his duties.
6. (a)	[E-7-b] An agent has a duty to avoid conflicts of interest. Jensen owned stock in Beta, and a conflict of interest therefore existed. Jensen was obligated to notify Alpha of the conflict. Unless Alpha, with full knowledge of the conflict, approved of the transaction with Beta, Jensen would be in breach of her duty of loyalty.
7. (c)	[D-4] An agent who possesses apparent authority can bind the principal to a contract. Apparent authority results when a third party dealing with the agent reasonably believes that the agent has certain authority.
8. (c)	[F-3] An agent who enters into a contract on behalf of an undisclosed or partially disclosed principal is liable on the contract. Only the agent who acts for the disclosed principal can avoid liability on the contracts entered into on behalf of the principal.

9. (a) [F] An agent is liable for losses caused by the agent's fraud or deceit.

10. (b) [F] The principal is obligated to indemnify the agent for losses suffered by the agent in the course of carrying out his or her duties as an agent.

11. (b) [H-1-b] A principal may ratify an unauthorized contract and thereby become bound by its terms. Ratification requires that the principal have knowledge of all relevant facts and that the principal accept the benefits of the contract with the intent of being bound by its terms. Without ratification, a principal is not bound by an unauthorized contract.

12. (c) [F, H-2-b] Because Anthony was negligent, he is liable for the injury he caused. Because the negligent act occurred in the course of the agent's employment, the principal is also liable. Anthony was an employee, not an independent contractor.

13. (a) [J-3-a] Either the principal or the agent has the power to terminate the agency at any time. In this case the parties have limited their right to terminate. Parrish had no right to terminate for two years. Parrish therefore can terminate the agency, but he is liable for any damages that his termination causes because he exercised his power to terminate without possessing the right to terminate.

14. (c) [J-3-b] Alvarez had the power, but not the right, to terminate the agency agreement, which by its terms was to last for a year. She is liable to Palmer for all damages reasonably related to the wrongful termination.

15. (c) [K-1] Because Cameron had previously dealt with Kohler acting as Wilson's agent, he was entitled to actual notice. No notice of termination was given. Kohler had apparent authority to bind her principal. Kohler, of course, is liable to Wilson for her wrongdoing.

16. (b) [D-4] By leaving Gilbert in charge of the sale after advertising it as a furniture sale, the firm allowed circumstances to exist that would lead a reasonable person to conclude that Gilbert had authority to sell the lamps. Simpson was allowed to rely on the appearance of things, even though Gilbert lacked actual authority to sell the lamps.

17. (b) [E] Gilbert breached the duty not to commingle business funds with personal funds.

18. (a) [J-3] Although Allen lacked the right to terminate the agency after one month, he had the power to do so.

19. (d) [J] Both death and illegality cause termination of an agency. Barnes' agency was terminated when she died. Cooper's agency remained but was terminated by the FDA's action when the sale of Tridol became illegal.

20. (b) [F] An agent is always liable for his or her own negligence, whether or not the principal can also be held liable. Mediocre Foods can also be held liable for injuries to Armstrong and Brennan that occurred in the scope of Warner's employment.

21. (d) [K-1] Since Able had previously dealt with Warner in his capacity as an agent of Mediocre Foods, Able was entitled to either oral or written notification of the termination.

22. (c) [K-2] Since Bentley's had not dealt with Warner before, it was entitled only to notice by publication. Had the agency been terminated by death, illegality, or insanity, no notice would have been required.

CHAPTER 24

Basic Business Entity Law

OVERVIEW

In this chapter we provide a very basic review of the laws governing the formation, creation, and termination of sole entrepreneurships, partnerships, and corporations. A candidate should be able to visualize the life cycle of a business entity: the manner of formation, business operation, and the termination.

The agency-law concepts learned earlier may be applied to the study of business entities. For example, a partner, when acting on behalf of the partnership, always acts as an agent, not a principal. Therefore, a partner will have the authority to act that a general agent would normally possess (actual plus implied authority). In contrast, a shareholder of a corporation has no agency authority to bind the corporation. Shareholders are considered investors with very limited decision-making input. Directors determine policy; officers, as agents of the corporation, implement policy and handle day-to-day transactions.

The candidate should attempt to understand the basic similarities and distinctions between partnerships and corporations.

KEY TERMS

Articles of incorporation	Estoppel	Partnership
Bylaws	Joint and several liability	Preferred stock
Common stock	Joint liability	Promoter
Corporation	Limited partner	Sole entrepreneurship

A. Sole Entrepreneurship

A sole entrepreneurship, sometimes called a *sole proprietorship,* is a business owned and operated by one person.

1. *Formation of Sole Entrepreneurship:* An individual who wants to own and operate a business may form a sole entrepreneurship.
   a. *Single owner:* This type of business has only one owner and is *not* incorporated as a corporation is.
   b. *Variable size:* Although a sole entrepreneurship has a single owner, there can be any number of employees. A business may be large or small and still be in the form of a sole entrepreneurship.
   c. *Unlimited liability:* As the only owner, a sole proprietor can potentially be liable for all the debts of the business (plus the owner's personal debts).

2. *Creation of Sole Entrepreneurship:* A sole entrepreneurship is created subject to state law. Generally, no detailed procedures are required for the creation of a sole entrepreneurship. Generally, the true owner's name must be registered in the local courthouse, along with the trade and/or business name if the name of the business is not to be the owner's name.

   EXAMPLE: If John Doe begins a business called Lucky Pizza, he would have to register the business name (Lucky Pizza) along with his name as the sole owner. This is a sole entrepreneurship.

3. *Operation:*

   a. *Government regulation:* The sole entrepreneurship is generally subject to government regulations, just as any partnership or corporation might be. Small businesses (regardless of the business form), however, are often exempt from laws and/or regulations for reasons such as these:

      (1) The business has little impact, if any, on interstate commerce.

      (2) The size of the business is small, with few employees or a small amount of gross sales.

      EXAMPLE: Title VII of the Civil Rights Act of 1964, the basic law concerning employment discrimination, applies only to businesses having 15 or more employees.

   b. *Income tax applicable:* The sole entrepreneurship, as an entity, pays no income tax. Profits or losses are reflected on the owner's personal income tax return.

   c. *Employee benefits provided:* Workers' compensation, unemployment compensation, and FICA payments are all required of the sole entrepreneurship just as they are required of a partnership or a corporation.

   d. *Agency:* The laws of agency apply to the sole entrepreneurship.

      (1) The owner is the principal.

      (2) Any agents have whatever express authority is given by the principal plus that authority resulting from their agency position and/or standard trade practices.

   e. *Termination:* No formal procedure exists for the sole owner to terminate the business. As long as no fraud results as to creditors, the owner may simply cease doing business.

B. Partnership

A partnership is a business entity owned and operated by two or more persons who are called partners. The formal definition of a partnership is an association of two or more persons to carry on as co-owners of a business for profit.

1. *Formation of Partnerships:* Partnerships are governed by state laws (statutes). Many states have adopted the Uniform Partnership Act (UPA), a model act, as the state's partnership law. The purpose of the UPA is to achieve uniformity among states concerning partnership laws.

2. *Creation of Partnerships:* Partnerships may be created by an express partnership agreement, by determination of the courts, and by estoppel.

   a. *Express partnership agreement:* A written partnership agreement (articles of partnership) is always advisable to ensure clarity and understanding of the intent of the partners. However, an oral partnership agreement is legally enforceable as long as a writing is not required under the statute of frauds.

EXAMPLE: Andrews, Barnes, and Cummings form the ABC Partnership, which is to exist for 10 years. The agreement must be in writing because it will not be completed within one year.

b. *Determination of the courts:* Sometimes it is not clear whether a partnership exists. In these cases a court may be called on to examine the overall facts and determine whether a partnership exists. No one test need be met, but courts place the most emphasis on whether the parties agree to share profits and losses.

EXAMPLE: Adams and Burke jointly open a record shop. They agree to share profits. A court would probably find a partnership.

c. *Partnership by estoppel:* Partnership by estoppel is based on the same theory as agency by estoppel. *Estoppel* means that a party to a lawsuit will be precluded (stopped) from raising a defense. In partnership law, the fact that no partnership actually exists among persons who are involved will not be allowed as a defense by these persons. A court finds "partnership by estoppel" to avoid inequity to an innocent third party.

EXAMPLES: Andrews, Barnes, and Cummings represent to a bank that they are partners in a restaurant to facilitate the lending of monies to Andrews, the actual owner. Andrews, Barnes, and Cummings will be considered a partnership as to the bank.

Assume that Ashton and Boyd are not actual partners. In front of Ashton, Boyd tells Price that Ashton and Boyd are partners. Ashton would be liable as if she were, in fact, a partner for Price's loan to the supposed partnership of Ashton and Boyd.

3. *Types of Partnerships:* Partnerships may be general or limited, depending on the nature of the partnership formed.

a. *General partnership:* A general partnership is sometimes called an *ordinary* or *regular partnership*.

b. *Limited partnership* (created specially by state statute): The limited partnership has been established in many states to allow persons to invest in the partnership business without fear of personal loss beyond the original investment. In this type of partnership, there must be at least one general (regular) partner and one limited partner. The general partner is similar to the partner in a general partnership.

(1) Without specific state law authorizing a limited partnership, there cannot be one. A limited partnership agreement must be filed with the state (usually not required for a general partnership).

(2) A limited partner is treated as the equivalent of a shareholder in a corporation:

(a) A limited partner's potential liability for the partnership debt is limited to the limited partner's capital contribution.

(b) A limited partner may not participate in the active, day-to-day management of the partnership.

EXAMPLE: Benson is a limited partner in the ABC Partnership. Benson may not be actively involved in partnership business decisions.

(c) A limited partner shares in profits according to the partnership agreement.

(d) A limited partner may not lend his or her name to the partnership name.

(e) A limited partner has no inherent agency authority to bind the limited partnership.

EXAMPLE: Using the same example, Benson has no authority to bind the partnership to any contracts with third parties.

(f) A limited partner who acts as a general partner loses statutory protection and will be liable as any other general partner.

4. *Partnership Operations:* Five basic rules exist under the UPA in regard to the operation of a partnership.

a. *Agency:* Every partner is an agent of the partnership.

EXAMPLE: Michaels is a partner of XYZ Partnership. Therefore, he is an agent of the partnership. When Michaels acts on behalf of the partnership, he is acting as an agent, not as a principal.

b. *Profit/loss sharing:* Partners share profits and losses equally (unless otherwise stated in their partnership agreement).

EXAMPLE: The partnership agreement of Golden Company is silent as to the sharing of profits among the five partners. Accordingly, each partner will receive 20 percent of the profits even if one partner had put up 50 percent of the capital.

c. *Partners' liability:* Every partner is potentially personally liable for all the debts of the partnership.

EXAMPLE: Partner X and the XYZ Partnership become bankrupt. Partners Y and Z may be held individually liable for all the remaining debts of the partnership (but not for partner X's personal debts).

d. *Admission of new partners:* Unanimous consent is required to admit a new partner (unless a partnership agreement exists to the contrary).

e. *Management of partnership:* The partners have equal management rights (unless there is a partnership agreement to the contrary). In essence, each partner has one vote in partnership matters.

5. *Relationship of Partners to Third Persons:*

a. *Authority to bind partnership:* A partner may have the authority to act as an agent of the partnership and to bind the partnership to third persons.

(1) The laws of agency apply when a partner acts on behalf of the partnership.

(2) A partner acts as an agent, not as a principal, when acting for or on behalf of a partnership.

(3) A partner can bind the partnership as the result of using express, implied, or apparent authority, the usual types of agency authority (see Chapter 23).

EXAMPLE: Partner A visits a building for sale and signs a contract for the partnership to buy it. Unless the partnership deals in buildings in its ordinary course of business or unless specific partnership authority exists, the partnership will not be bound up to the seller.

b. *Contract liability—joint liability:* Partners have joint liability for the contract obligations of the partnership. In essence, this means that if a suit is brought against the partnership, all partners must be sued individually for partnership contract obligations.

EXAMPLE: ABC Partnership owes Phillips $5,000. Phillips must include A, B, and C if he includes any partner in conjunction with the suit against the partnership.

c. *Tort liability:* Partners have joint and several liability for tort actions of partners and/or employees occurring within the scope of employment. *Joint and several* means that the party bringing suit may sue the partnership and any combination of the partners.

EXAMPLE: Ellis brings a tort action against the ABC Partnership. Ellis may sue the partnership and any combination of the partners individually, such as ABC Partnership plus B.

An individual partner is always liable for personal tortious actions even if acting for the partnership.

6. *Partnership Dissolution:* A partnership dissolution occurs when there is a change of partners. In essence, this means that the old partnership terminates and a new one is formed (if the partnership continues after a partner's departure).

EXAMPLE: Partner A of the ABC Partnership retires, but B and C want to continue. The partnership of ABC will terminate, and the new partnership of BC will exist thereafter.

C. Corporation

A corporation is considered distinct from the individuals who own it (the shareholders). A corporation is a legal entity, which means that it can be sued or sue directly. A corporation must be formed according to procedures established by state law and must pay annual income taxes, whereas a partnership does not.

1. *Organization of a Corporation:*

a. *Ownership and management of a corporation:* The owners of a corporation are the shareholders, the directors are involved in establishing corporate policy, and the corporate officers are involved in the management functions. Figure 24–1 shows how a corporation may be organized.

(1) *Shareholders*: Although shareholders are owners, they are neither managers nor agents. Shareholders are considered to be investors, with a corporate voice only in extraordinary policy matters. Only a majority shareholder may owe fiduciary duties to the corporation and to the minority shareholders.

EXAMPLE: McCoy owns 50 shares of General Motors stock. McCoy may also buy Ford shares. If McCoy should invent a new type of battery, she would have no duty to provide it to General Motors (assuming that McCoy is not otherwise affiliated with General Motors).

(2) *Directors:* The shareholders have the power to elect and to remove the directors of the corporation. Directors have the responsibility to establish corporate policies. They are neither managers nor agents, but they do owe fiduciary duties to the corporation. Directors need not be shareholders or officers. The board of directors of the corporation is empowered to elect the officers of the corporation or, if necessary, to remove them from office.

EXAMPLE: One of the directors of Ace Corporation discovers an excellent building lot location for Ace's expansion. The director has no inherent

Figure 24–1 Corporation Organization

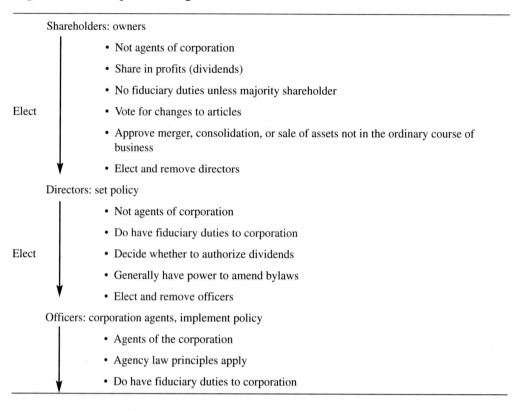

Shareholders: owners

- Not agents of corporation
- Share in profits (dividends)
- No fiduciary duties unless majority shareholder
- Vote for changes to articles
- Approve merger, consolidation, or sale of assets not in the ordinary course of business
- Elect and remove directors

Elect

Directors: set policy

- Not agents of corporation
- Do have fiduciary duties to corporation
- Decide whether to authorize dividends
- Generally have power to amend bylaws
- Elect and remove officers

Elect

Officers: corporation agents, implement policy

- Agents of the corporation
- Agency law principles apply
- Do have fiduciary duties to corporation

authority, as a director, to be able to obligate the corporation for the purchase of the lot. The director also cannot purchase the lot for personal gain and thereafter sell it to the corporation.

(3) *Officers:* Officers implement policy, manage the corporation, and serve as agents for the corporation. Officers owe fiduciary duties to the corporation.

EXAMPLE: Ace Corporation's board of directors votes to acquire a building for Ace's expansion. Corporate officers would be told to carry out the board's directive.

b. *Advantages of corporate form:* The primary advantages of the corporate form of business organization include the capital investment potential, limited liability for investors, perpetuity, and corporate control, among others.

(1) *Capital investment:* The corporation is designed to raise substantial capital from a large number of investors.

(2) *Limited liability for investors:* Shareholders' personal liability for corporation losses is limited to the original investment: the purchase price paid for the stock.

(3) *Perpetuity:* Perpetual business existence is possible.

(4) *Corporate control:* It is possible for effective control of the corporation to be vested in those with a minority of the investment (by using such techniques as nonvoting and/or preferred stock).

(5) *Employee benefits:* An investor-employee may be entitled to normal employee benefits, such as workers' compensation.

(6) *Resale of corporate stock:* Corporate stock is generally easier for the shareholder to sell than would be a partnership interest.

c. *Disadvantages of corporate form:* Some of the primary disadvantages of the corporate form of business organization include the higher cost of formation, corporate income taxes required, licensing, and government regulation affecting corporations.

(1) *High cost of formation:* The cost of formation and maintenance could be particularly significant for a small corporation because of the following:

(a) *License fees*

(b) *Franchise taxes*

(c) *Attorney fees:* An attorney must be utilized in any corporate litigation.

(d) *State corporate rules and regulations:* The numerous state rules and regulations may be more applicable to a large corporation, but even a small corporation must comply with these rules and regulations as well.

(2) *Operation:* Greater procedural rules of operation exist as to who can do what in regard to ownership (shareholders) versus management (board of directors setting policy, officers implementing policy).

(3) *Income taxes:* The corporation pays income taxes on income earned, and shareholders later pay income taxes on dividends received (double taxation).

(4) *Government regulation:* A corporation is often subject to more overall regulation than are other types of business entities.

2. *Formation of a Corporation:* Corporations are formed under state laws, not federal. The sale of stocks and bonds (both securities) may be controlled by the Securities and Exchange Commission (federal) or state laws.

a. *The role of the promoter:* A promoter is the person who organizes and forms a new corporation.

(1) A promoter assembles the necessary assets and financing for the new corporation.

(2) A promoter seeks stock purchasers, known as subscribers to the corporate stock.

(3) A promoter is not an agent of the corporation to be formed since no principal exists yet.

(4) A promoter owes fiduciary duties to fellow promoters and/or subscribers. This means that the promoter must act in good faith and without known personal gain. A promoter must disclose any situation of private gain even though the corporation may also receive a benefit.

EXAMPLE: A promoter must disclose his or her interest in a parcel of land being considered for the site of the new business.

(5) A promoter is allowed to make a profit if full disclosure is made and there is subsequent acceptance by the new corporation.

EXAMPLE: Promoter C sells an owned building to the newly formed XYZ Corporation. C is allowed to keep her profit if a full disclosure was made and appropriate approval was received.

b. *Articles of incorporation:* A new corporation is formed by the filing of articles of incorporation with a state and receiving back a corporate charter. In effect, the articles of incorporation are the corporation's constitution and, as such, contain the following:

(1) The name of the corporation being formed

(2) The address of the corporation

(3) The duration of time the corporation is to exist

(4) The corporation's purpose (often stated in very broad terms such as "any legal purpose")

(5) The names of the incorporators of the new corporation

(6) The number and types of shares of stock in the corporation

EXAMPLE: Cajun Corporation's articles of incorporation authorize 1,000 shares of voting common stock and 500 shares of nonvoting preferred stock.

(7) The name of the statutory agent (a person appointed by the incorporators who is available to receive complaints and summonses if the corporation is involved in litigation)

c. *First shareholders' meeting of new corporation:* The agenda of the first shareholders' meeting will include the issuance of stock to the subscribers and the election of the board of directors.

d. *First meeting of board of directors:* Items of business for the initial board of directors meeting should include the following:

(1) Establishment of bylaws (the internal governing rules of the corporation)

(2) Election of officers

(3) General acceptance or rejection of preincorporation contracts of the promoters

(a) The corporation is not liable on such contracts unless the directors have approved adoption (implied or express) of such contracts.

(b) The promoter continues personal liability even though a contract has been adopted unless the contract is conditional (no liability to promoter if corporation is not formed or does not adopt) or a novation occurs (third party agrees to release the promoter from liability and looks only to the corporation for performance).

3. *Corporate Finances—Stock:* The two most common types of corporate stock are common stock and preferred stock.

a. *Common stock:* Common stock represents ownership in a corporation. Each share of stock may earn a dividend only after all corporate obligations, including those to owners of preferred stock, are satisfied.

(1) *Dividends:* Common shareholders have no priority as to dividends paid.

(2) *Voting:* Generally, shareholders have one vote for each share of common stock owned.

b. *Preferred stock:* Preferred stock also represents ownership in a corporation that entitles the shareholder to certain advantages not available to owners of common stock. Owners of preferred stock are usually entitled to have priority over owners of common stock in receiving dividends.

Review Questions

Directions: Select the best answer from the four alternatives. Write your answer in the blank to the left of the number.

______ **1.** A partnership is being sued by Jackson for injuries suffered in an auto accident. The evidence shows that Burns, an employee of the partnership, was negligent in causing the accident. In a court action,

a. Jackson would win against Burns only if Burns was not acting within the scope of employment.
b. the partners would be jointly liable.
c. the partnership would be liable if Burns was acting within the scope of employment.
d. the partnership would win versus Jackson because Burns is not a partner.

______ **2.** All the following are part of the five basic rules for the operation of a partnership *except* which?

a. Every partner is an agent of the partnership.
b. Admission of a new partner must be by majority vote.
c. Partners share profits and losses equally.
d. Partners have equal management rights.

______ **3.** R, S, and T form a new partnership. R contributes $50,000, S contributes $25,000, and T contributes expertise but no money. The partnership agreement is silent as to the sharing of profits. The partnership makes $30,000 profit in its first year, which it now wants to pay partners.

a. Partner T should receive nothing.
b. Partner R should receive $10,000.
c. Partner S should receive $15,000.
d. Partner R should receive $20,000.

______ **4.** Alexander is a promoter for a new corporation to be formed, the Denver Corporation. Which of the following statements is true?

a. Alexander is an agent for the Denver Corporation.
b. The Denver Corporation will be liable for Alexander's contracts made prior to incorporation.
c. Alexander owes fiduciary duties to the new corporation.
d. Alexander is considered a corporate officer.

______ **5.** A shareholder has

a. limited liability.
b. implied authority to bind the corporation.
c. a role similar to that of partners in a partnership.
d. fiduciary duties to the corporation.

_______________ **6.** Articles of incorporation must include the

a. names of suppliers for the corporation's activities.
b. purpose of the corporation.
c. names of the promoters of the corporation.
d. human resource plans for the corporation.

_______________ **7.** The advantages of the corporate form of doing business include all of the following *except*

a. operation of the business.
b. limited liability for shareholders.
c. perpetual existence.
d. ability to raise capital more effectively from investors.

Use the following information in answering Questions 8 to 10.
Austin is contemplating opening an athletic store, Heflin Aerobics Sports, focusing primarily on running, swimming, and biking. Austin already owns the property that will be used for the store. Initially, Austin will begin the business without any other persons joining him as co-owners. From a previous business experience, Austin knows that he wants somehow to retain control if and when he does accept co-owners. He presently expects future co-owners also to be managers of new store locations.

_______________ **8.** The easiest form of business for Austin to choose to begin business would be a

a. sole proprietorship.
b. general partnership.
c. limited partnership.
d. corporation.

_______________ **9.** The form of business most compatible with Austin's goals and most appropriate for new co-owners would be a

a. sole proprietorship.
b. partnership.
c. limited partnership.
d. corporation.

_______________ **10.** Assume that Austin has formed a corporation. Austin would be considered an agent of the corporation if acting as

a. the promoter.
b. a shareholder.
c. a director.
d. an officer.

Solutions

Answer	*Refer to:*
1. (c)	[B-5-c] The employee's negligence will cause the partnership to be liable if the employee was acting within the scope of employment.
2. (b)	[B-4-d] The admittance of a new partner must generally be by unanimous vote.
3. (b)	[B-4-b] Where a partnership agreement is silent as to the manner of sharing profits and losses, the Uniform Partnership Act calls for an equal sharing. T shares in profits and losses regardless of capital contribution.
4. (c)	[C-2-a] A promoter is someone involved in the creation of a new corporation. A promoter owes fiduciary duties to both prospective shareholders and the formed corporation: full disclosure, fair dealing, and full accountability.
5. (a)	[C-1-a(1)] Unlike a partner in a partnership, a shareholder of a corporation is treated as an investor and is liable only to the extent of capital contributions. A shareholder is not an agent of the corporation and has no authority to bind the corporation.
6. (b)	[C-2-b] The articles of incorporation states the corporation's main purposes, even in general terms.
7. (a)	[C-1-c(2)] The corporate mode of operations is more involved than that of a sole proprietorship or partnership.
8. (a)	[A-2] A sole entrepreneurship is the easiest form of business to begin.
9. (d)	[C] A corporation would be best for purposes of control and the ability of co-owners to be actively involved in the day-to-day business operations.
10. (d)	[Figure 24–1] Officers are the only agents of a corporation.

CHAPTER 25

Regulation of Business and Employment

OVERVIEW

In this chapter we focus on government regulation of business and employment. The overall role of administrative agencies and antitrust laws is described and presented in detail. The candidate should review the following key points:

- The role and basic operations of an administrative agency
- The basic scope of antitrust laws (enforced by both the Department of Justice and the Federal Trade Commission)

The regulation of employment focuses on three separate parts:

- Laws of the workplace
- Laws governing employment discrimination
- Laws pertaining to labor-management relations

Laws of the workplace include such legislation as social security, minimum wage, overtime, unemployment compensation, workers' compensation, and occupational safety and health legislation. The candidate should be able to distinguish these different laws and set forth the applicable requirements of each.

Laws governing employment discrimination deal with all aspects of employment discrimination: race, color, gender, religion, and national origin (included in Title VII) as well as discrimination in regard to age or handicaps. The candidate should be familiar with the various types of discrimination, bona fide occupational qualifications, and the role of the Equal Employment Opportunity Commission in monitoring employment practices.

Labor-management relations law deals with legislation covering the private-sector workforce. The candidate should understand what the National Labor Relations Act is, the role of the National Labor Relations Board, the role of an arbitrator, how a union may be recognized, and what is meant by unfair labor practices. This subject matter area is quite broad and detailed. Included here is a basic overview of labor laws as they are most likely to be covered on the CPS Examination. Candidates from countries other than the United States are encouraged to review comparable legislation enacted in their respective countries.

KEY TERMS

Administrative agency
Administrative law judge
Age Discrimination in Employment Act (ADEA)
Americans with Disabilities Act
Bona fide occupational qualification (BFOQ)
Civil Rights Act of 1964 (Title VII)
Divestiture
Employee Retirement Income Security Act (ERISA)
Employment discrimination
Equal Employment Opportunity Commission (EEOC)
Equal Pay for Equal Work Act
Executive branch
Fair Labor Standards Act
Landrum-Griffin Act
National Labor Relations Act (NLRA)
National Labor Relations Board (NLRB)
Occupational Safety and Health Act (OSHA)
Price discrimination
Price fixing
Right-to-work law
Taft-Hartley Act
Treble damages
Unemployment insurance
Unfair labor practices
Wagner Act
Workers' compensation

A. Administrative Agencies

An administrative agency is a subdivision of the government with expertise and jurisdiction to regulate a specialized area of government operation.

1. *Relationship to Other Branches of Government:* Administrative agencies are often considered the fourth branch of government because of their significant impact on everyday life. In fact, administrative agencies fall under the jurisdiction of the executive branch (the president). Figure 25–1 illustrates the branches of government and their interrelationship with administrative agencies.

2. *Administrative Agency Functions:* Administrative agencies have been established for many specialized areas of United States government and/or government regulation. All existing agencies encompass basic similarities in the types of functions performed. Administrative agencies generally encompass similar executive, legislative, and judicial functions performed by the three branches of government.

   EXAMPLE: The administrative agency may issue regulations interpreting statutes, enforce existing statutes and regulations under the agency's jurisdiction, and/or determine liability for failure to comply with statutes/regulations.

Figure 25–1 Relationship of Administrative Agencies to Legislative and Judicial Branches

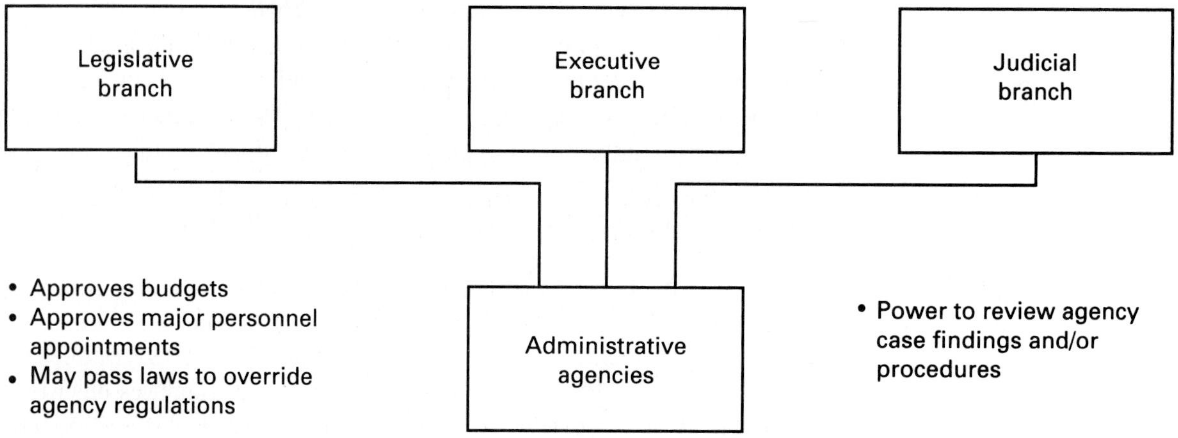

3. *Administrative Agency Configuration:*

   a. *Establishment of commission or board:* As a general rule, administrative agencies are headed by a commission or board.

      (1) The commission or board is composed of an odd number of members, usually from five to seven.

      (2) Members are appointed by the president and approved by Congress. The majority of board members are usually of the same party in control of the presidency.

      (3) Members serve set terms of office, often four years; members can be removed by the president only for wrongdoing.

   b. *General counsel:* Agencies usually have a general counsel, appointed by the president, charged with deciding which cases should be brought by the agency.

   c. *Regional agency offices:* Administrative agencies often have regional offices at different locations around the country. A regional office administers agency matters for a given geographical area.

      EXAMPLE: Anderson claims that she has been discriminated against in promotion by her employer because of her gender. Her complaint would be processed and prosecuted by a regional office of the Equal Employment Opportunity Commission (EEOC) in Chicago if she is working in the Chicago area.

   d. *Administrative law judge:* Administrative law judges (ALJs) within each agency hear administrative cases brought by the agency.

      (1) An administrative law judge hears witnesses and receives evidence in a similar manner as a court. The ALJ, however, is not a judge in the judicial branch.

      (2) An ALJ's decision is reviewable by the full board or commission of the agency.

   e. *Court review and/or enforcement:* Decisions of ALJs can be appealed to the full board or commission of an administrative agency, as discussed. An appeal is thereafter possible from the board or commission to a court of appeals. The court will not hear any witnesses or admit new evidence.

B. Relationship of Federal to State Governments

Administrative agencies administer statutes passed by Congress and promulgate regulations consistent with statutes. Sometimes a conflict occurs between federal and state laws and regulations. These conflicts must be resolved by looking to the Constitution, including judicial interpretation.

1. *Specific Federal Powers:* The Constitution gives the federal government a number of exclusive specific powers, such as to coin money, to enter into treaties with foreign governments, and to regulate interstate commerce. The federal government's power to regulate interstate commerce provides the greatest intrusion into state and local matters.

   EXAMPLE: The Civil Rights Act of 1964, including Title VII, was enacted and made applicable to employers of 15 or more employees based on the Commerce Clause. (It was presumed that an employer with 15 or more employees would have an impact on interstate commerce even if doing business primarily in one state.)

2. *Specific State Powers:* State governments, by the 10th Amendment to the Constitution, have the residual of all powers not specifically bestowed to the federal government. State governments also have police powers, the power to pass and enact statutes, and the power to promulgate regulations to protect citizens.

   EXAMPLE: The Norris-LaGuardia Act prevents federal courts in most instances from issuing an injunction to limit a federal labor dispute. However, state courts have the power to limit such a dispute where the effect of the strike is to put citizens in risk of harm or injury.

3. *Power of the Purse Strings:* The federal government gains state compliance with many federal laws or regulations by the threat of withholding specific federal money without compliance. While states could legally reject such federal "blackmail," they often choose not to forgo federal money.

   EXAMPLE: The most common example has to do with how Congress distributes federal gasoline tax revenues by requiring adherence to specific traffic speed and seatbelt rules.

4. *Stricter Law Compliance:* There are times when both the federal and the state governments have a law covering a certain matter but one law is stricter than the other. Where both laws are legal, the stricter law must be complied with.

   EXAMPLES: Both the federal government (via the Commerce Clause) and the State of California (via its police powers) have auto emissions control rules. An auto manufacturer who wants to sell new vehicles in California must comply with the stricter law (the law of the State of California).

   A state or local government may have a higher minimum wage than the required federal minimum wage. If so, an employer in that state or local area must comply with the stricter law and pay the higher minimum wage.

C. Antitrust Laws

1. *Applicable Statutes:* Three major acts make up the federal antitrust laws:
   a. *Sherman Act:* Antitrust legislation enacted in 1890 (see Section B-5).
   b. *Clayton Act:* Antitrust legislation enacted in 1914 (see Section B-6).
   c. *Robinson-Patman Act:* Antitrust legislation enacted in 1936, actually an amendment to the Clayton Act (see Section B-7).
2. *Major Objectives of Antitrust Laws:* The major objectives of antitrust legislation include the following:
   a. *A competitive society:* The preservation, protection, and promotion of a competitive society are extremely important considerations.
   b. *Economic opportunity:* Many smaller, independent businesses are favored over fewer, larger businesses in an industry.
   c. *Protection of the public:* The public is to be protected against monopolistic control of the economies (protected against monopolies).
3. *Types of Offenses:* Antitrust violations are either rule of reason violations or per se violations.

a. *Rule of reason violations:* In these types of alleged violations, the defendant(s) can attempt to show that the alleged improper conduct is not an unreasonable restraint of trade.

EXAMPLE: Favoring one buyer over another because of savings resulting from a quantity order would not be price discrimination.

b. *Per se violations:* In these types of violations, once improper conduct is shown, there can be no defense raised and recognized by the defendant(s).

EXAMPLE: Price fixing between two major competitors would be a per se violation.

4. *Possible Sanctions (Punishments) and/or Remedies:* Antitrust violations may result in sanctions or remedies like the following:

a. *Civil:* Civil remedies can be sought by the federal government (Federal Trade Commission or Department of Justice), competitors, victims, or state governments. Remedies include the following:

(1) *Injunction:* A court orders a person or company not to do something.

(2) *Treble damages:* The winning plaintiff would be awarded actual damages incurred, times three.

EXAMPLE: If actual damages were $5 million, the winning plaintiff would receive $15 million.

(3) *Divestiture:* A court orders that a corporation divest (sell) some of its particular operations and/or assets.

EXAMPLE: Procter and Gamble, because of its significant market control of the home laundry products market, was forced to divest itself of Clorox.

b. *Criminal:* Criminal prosecution can be brought only by the federal government (Department of Justice) and only for alleged violations of the Sherman or Robinson-Patman Acts. Possible sanctions include the following:

(1) Treble damages

(2) Fine(s)

(3) Prison sentence(s)

5. *Violations under the Sherman Act:* Violations under the Sherman Act can involve the sale of either goods or services. Violations include the following:

a. *Price fixing (per se violation):* Price fixing occurs when two or more competitors agree on the price at which to sell goods or services.

EXAMPLE: If two competing airlines agree to a price for the Dallas-to-Chicago air route, price fixing has occurred. (It is not a violation for one to match the other without an agreement.)

b. *Horizontal territorial allocation (per se offense):* This would take place when two or more competitors agree to divide sales territories.

EXAMPLES: It would be a per se violation for one soft drink company to agree to only sell east and another to only sell west of the Mississippi River.

It is not a violation for McDonald's to create different sales territories for McDonald's Restaurants in St. Louis. However, it would be a per se violation if McDonald's divided St. Louis with Burger King (an example of a horizontal territorial allocation).

c. *Monopoly (rule of reason offense):* An illegal monopoly results when a company has the *power* and the *intent* to control prices and/or exclude competition. A company that gains such power over the market simply from natural results and advantage of its own research and good business practices is not considered to be engaged in illegal activity.

EXAMPLES: Regional telephone companies were divested from AT&T because of the telephone company's monopoly power in the telephone market.

Microsoft has faced allegations of monopoly practices, including whether it was using its clout in software products to move into a new market area involving Web browsers. No one disputes Microsoft's clout. Microsoft has always argued that its success is a natural result of its superior research, patents, and products developed in-house by Microsoft. This issue may ultimately have to be decided by the Supreme Court.

6. *Clayton Act Violations (not applicable to sales of services):* The Clayton Act has some overlap with the Sherman Act. Common violations include the following:

a. *Tying contracts (rule of reason offense):* A tying contract occurs when the seller uses control of one market item to require buyers of that item to buy another item that the seller does not control.

EXAMPLE: Years ago IBM was found to have improperly tied the lease of IBM punchcard machines to the usage of IBM punchcards. But for this tying arrangement the lessee would have been able to acquire proper punchcards easily from a number of sources.

b. *Reciprocal dealing contracts (per se offense):* It is a violation for a stronger contracting party to require a weaker party to sell to it or buy from it as a condition of the stronger party buying or selling.

EXAMPLE: It would be a violation for General Motors to require a supplier of steering wheels to buy only GM vehicles as a condition of doing business with GM. (As a practical matter, the supplier would probably buy GM vehicles if GM were a significant customer.)

c. *Improper mergers (rule of reason offense):* A merger of two or more companies into one company is illegal where the reasonable probability or effect would be to substantially lessen competition or tend to create a monopoly.

EXAMPLE: Mobil Oil was not permitted to merge with Marathon, another oil company (which was subsequently acquired by U.S. Steel).

7. *Robinson-Patman Act (price discrimination/rule of reason offense):* The Robinson-Patman Act applies only to price discrimination—charging a buyer a different price for the same merchandise of identical grade or quality than the price charged another buyer for the same goods.

EXAMPLE: ABC Company sells the same ladder for $20 to Joe's Hardware, a small hardware store, and $18 to K-Mart, a large retail corporation. This would be an *offense unless covered by a recognized defense, such as a permissible discount because of proven savings by volume of sales.*

a. *Overview of the act:* The primary features of this legislation include the following elements:

(1) Permits criminal prosecution

(2) Is not applicable to the sale of services

(3) Does not apply to sales by retailers to consumers

b. *Violation (rule of reason offense):* It is a violation to give or receive a price discrimination knowingly.

c. *Defenses:* Appropriate defenses include the following:

(1) Meeting the price of the competitor

EXAMPLE: American Airlines matches a fare rate charged by Delta between Dallas and Chicago.

(2) Functional or quantity discount

EXAMPLE: Ladders to be sold in K-Mart stores are delivered to a central K-Mart location. From that location K-Mart trucks distribute the ladders to retail stores.

(3) Change in market conditions

EXAMPLE: Santa Claus outfits are more valuable before Christmas than afterward.

(4) Change in marketability of item involved

EXAMPLE: Fruit about to rot is worth less than fresh ripe fruit.

D. Federal Laws Regulating the Workplace

Federal laws regulating the workplace include laws regulating minimum wage and overtime pay (Fair Labor Standards Act), unemployment compensation, social security, and occupational safety and health (Occupational Safety and Health Act).

1. *Fair Labor Standards Act:* This act, also known as the Wage and Hour Law, established the requirements for an employer to pay employees a minimum wage and time-and-a-half for overtime worked over 40 hours per week. To limit child abuse, the act provides rules limiting the use of children in employment. In addition, an amendment to the act in 1963 requires equal pay for men and women who are performing equal work (the Equal Pay Act; see Section E-2).

a. *Employees covered by the act:* Employees involved in interstate commerce or producing goods for interstate commerce are covered by the act. As a practical matter, very few private employers are able to escape application of the act on this basis. Those who might will generally be covered by a similar type of state law. The act applies to both union and nonunion employees.

b. *Minimum wage:* Each year Congress reviews and sets the minimum wage employers are required to pay to employees. In figuring the minimum wage, an employer may include the reasonable value of room and board (if furnished), tips, commissions, and bonuses. In addition, an employee may be paid according to piece rate (payment for units handled or worked) as long as the probable earnings equate to the minimum wage.

c. *Overtime pay:* An employee who works over 40 hours in a week's time is due time-and-a-half by the employer. This means that if an employee makes $8 an hour, he or she will be due $12 per hour for each hour worked beyond 40 in a week. It is important to note that federal law does not require time-and-a-half pay for hours worked in excess of eight hours per day.

EXAMPLE: Smythe works 12 hours on Monday, Tuesday, and Wednesday and four hours on Thursday. Smythe would not be entitled to any overtime pay under the act. (Smythe's company may pay overtime over eight hours worked, but this is not required by the act.)

d. *Stricter rule:* An employer must comply with the stricter minimum wage or overtime rule of federal, state, or local law or an applicable collective bargaining agreement.

EXAMPLES: Until 1998, California required an employer to pay overtime wages for over eight hours of work in a single day even if the employee worked fewer than 40 hours in a given week. The employer would have to comply with the California rule.

A California employer with a collective bargaining agreement that requires time-and-a-half over eight hours a day would still have to pay this rate even though neither federal nor state law requires this.

e. *Exemptions to minimum wage and overtime payment requirements:* Employees in the following categories are not covered by the minimum wage and overtime pay provisions of the act:

(1) Fishing industry

(2) Seasonal employees

(3) Executive, professional, managerial, and supervisory personnel

(4) Outside salespersons

(5) Partial exemptions for learners, apprentices, students, and handicapped persons

f. *Child-labor laws:* To reduce the likelihood of abuse of children at work, the act generally prohibits the employment of children under the age of 16. Two exceptions apply:

(1) *Age exceptions:* Children who are age 14 or 15 may do light work, such as clerical or sales work, as long as limited hours exist that do not conflict with school hours.

(2) *Work exceptions:* Newspaper delivery, child actors, children who work for their parents, and agricultural work are work exceptions according to the act.

g. *Equal Pay for Equal Work Act:* This act, an amendment to the Fair Labor Standards Act, requires equal pay for women who are performing work substantially equal to that performed by men. A detailed explanation of the Equal Pay Act is included in Section E-2.

h. *Enforcement/remedies:*

(1) *Civil actions:* Among the available civil remedies are back pay, fines, and injunction. In addition, the government may seize goods moving in interstate commerce that were made in violation of child labor laws.

(2) *Criminal actions:* Fines and/or imprisonment may occur in exceptional cases.

2. *Unemployment Insurance (Part of the Social Security Act):* Unemployment insurance, as its name implies, is for workers who, without fault, become unemployed. The federal unemployment insurance coverage was implemented to spur the creation of such benefit programs by states at the state level. All states today have unemployment insurance programs. Employers are permitted to take as a credit a percentage of the state unemployment tax permitted.

a. *Calculation of amount owed:* An employer's tax is dependent on unemployment claims made against it. A good claims record will result in lower employer-required payments. In addition, the employer is permitted to offset a percentage of the state payment, as discussed in the preceding paragraph.

EXAMPLE: Fast-food businesses often have a very high turnover rate, which results in a higher unemployment rate than that in more stable employment businesses.

b. *Special exemptions:* Family employees working in the family business and agricultural employees for small farm operations are not covered by federal law. They may not be covered by state law.

c. *Requirements to receive unemployment benefits:* An employee who loses his or her job is entitled to compensation only if he or she has worked a minimum number of weeks and is ready, able, and willing to take equivalent new employment. It is not necessary that the terminated employee be in financial need of the benefits.

EXAMPLE: Scott, a bartender, is laid off by a bar because of slow business. Scott is eligible for unemployment benefits even if he is independently wealthy as long as he has earlier worked a minimum number of weeks.

d. *Disqualification:* In most states, an employee who was discharged for good cause, quit voluntarily (unless to take a better job), or refuses to accept equivalent work will be ineligible for benefits. In other states, the applicant may be penalized before receiving benefits if termination has been based on one of these reasons.

EXAMPLE: In the example above, if Scott refuses to take a bartender position in a similar type of bar in a similar area, he will lose his unemployment benefits.

3. *Social Security (FICA):* The social security system has undergone great scrutiny and has had many changes made by Congress because of the concern over its financial stability. The following are the basic aspects of the system:

a. *Benefits covered:* The benefits covered by the social security system include the following:

(1) Medicare

(2) Retirement

(3) Disability

(4) Death benefits to surviving family members

b. *Employees covered:* This area of the law has undergone great change. Formerly, government employees were exempt from social security taxes (except the military), but this has now been changed as to new employees in state or federal government.

(1) If covered, an employee does not have a choice to opt out of the social security system.

(2) Self-employed persons are not exempt from coverage.

c. *Computation of withholding rates:* Congress has the authority to set the rates and earning limits for the collection of the social security payments due. The following contributions are required:

(1) *Employee:* An employee has his or her FICA contribution deducted at the time of payment by the employer. If the employer should fail to deduct the employee's contribution, the government will assess the employer for the amount.

(2) *Employer:* The employer is required to pay an additional amount for each employee.

(3) *Self-employed individual:* The rate for self-employed individuals is approximately double that of the individual employee rate.

4. *Employee Retirement Income Security Act (ERISA):* ERISA was passed in 1974 in an attempt to better regulate private pension plans. ERISA does not require an employer to establish a pension plan or set any minimum level of benefits if a pension plan is established.

a. *Purposes of the act:* The primary purposes of ERISA include the following:

(1) To ensure that an employer's pension plan, if one exists, does not favor management and is sufficiently broad-based in employee coverage.

(2) To ensure that an employee will have his or her interest *vest* without the passage of an unreasonable amount of time. (*Vest* means that the employee has the legal right to receive those payments that have been contributed into the pension on his or her behalf by the employer.)

(3) To establish financial control rules relating to pension trust funds.

(4) To provide pension termination insurance via the Pension Benefit Guaranty Corporation (PBGC).

b. *Pension Benefit Guaranty Corporation (PBGC):* This federal corporation provides protection to pensions in a fashion similar to the Federal Deposit Insurance Corporation's protection of bank savings accounts. If a covered pension plan should have insufficient assets to make the required payments to beneficiaries, the PBGC would cover the deficient amounts.

c. *Health maintenance organizations (HMOs):* Although a minor focus of ERISA when enacted in 1974, ERISA provides federal oversight of employer contracts with health maintenance organizations (HMOs) for health benefits of its employees. Because of the explosion of new employer health plans tied to HMOs, ERISA has become a topic of continued congressional debate.

5. *Occupational Safety and Health Act:* This act is administered by the Occupational Safety and Health Administration (OSHA) under the secretary of labor. Established in 1970, OSHA received much media attention for its workplace rules, which were often contradictory, unclear, and unnecessary. Today OSHA has attempted to reduce its exhaustive set of miscellaneous rules and concentrates instead more on major problem areas.

a. *Purposes of the act:* The two major purposes of this legislation are the following:

(1) To ensure safe workplaces for employees

(2) To establish safety and health standards for the workplace

b. *Workplace inspections:*

(1) By law, OSHA investigators must not inform an employer of a pending investigation. The purpose of this rule is to reduce the likelihood that the employer will cover up problems that would otherwise have been detected and ordered remedied.

(2) OSHA investigations may be prompted by employee complaints or by the initiation of OSHA alone. An employee cannot be subjected to retaliation by the employer.

(3) An employer has the right to insist that an OSHA investigator secure a search warrant before being granted access to the plant. As a practical matter, a search warrant is very easily obtained by the investigator.

(4) If OSHA violations are found during the inspection, the employer is given a *citation* (notice of violation). A citation recites the alleged violations and what OSHA is demanding the employer do to rectify the situation. An employer may appeal.

c. *Potential penalties:*

(1) *Civil actions:* Fines (where greater than ten violations are found) and temporary injunctions are possible. A *temporary injunction* is issued where such danger exists that could cause great bodily harm or the possibility of death.

(2) *Criminal actions.*

d. *New directions for OSHA:* Because of the tremendous amount of criticism of OSHA operations and rules, OSHA has undergone a major reorganization.

(1) *Fewer inspections:* OSHA now permits small businesses or businesses with few problems in the past to conduct their own investigations. Results of these investigations are sent to OSHA, which always reserves the right to make an actual investigation. Inspections in the more dangerous industries have continued.

(2) *Greater focus on health standards:* OSHA initially emphasized safety standards almost exclusively.

E. State Legislation—Workers' Compensation

1. *Purpose of Legislation:* The purpose of workers' compensation is to provide coverage to employees who are incapacitated because of accidental injury, disease, or death incurred while on the job.

2. *Employer Requirements:* The state fund method requires that payments be based on claims experience and the number of employees. All states have state fund plans, but employers may be able to self-insure.

3. *Employee Eligibility for Benefits:* An employee becomes eligible for benefits if accidental injury, disease, or death was incurred while on the job.

   a. *Liberal interpretation:* Courts liberally construe "while on the job" so as to give employee compensation.

      EXAMPLE: An employee who broke an ankle sliding into second base at a company's summer picnic was found to be covered by workers' compensation.

   b. *Recovery of workers' compensation:* The employee recovers even though the injury occurred because he or she negligently failed to follow directions.

F. Employment Discrimination

Laws governing employment discrimination deal with all aspects of employment discrimination: race, color, gender, religion, and national origin (included in Title VII of the Civil Rights Act of 1964) as well as age or handicaps. Employment discrimination legislation and executive orders have been created to augment the Constitution. As such, they provide the means and/or procedures for effective redress of employment discrimination problems.

Employment discrimination laws generally prohibit discrimination in hiring, compensation, employment terms and conditions, promotion, retention, and discharge. In essence, no discrimination is to be tolerated in any aspect of employment.

1. *Title VII:* Title VII of the Civil Rights Act of 1964 brought fundamental changes to employment. The act created the EEOC to promulgate and enforce employment discrimination regulations for employers with 15 or more employees.

   a. *Coverage of act:* Title VII prohibits discrimination in any form of employment based on the following:

      (1) Race

      (2) Color

      (3) Religion

      (4) Gender

      (5) National origin

   b. *Scope of coverage:* An employer may not discriminate in hiring, retaining, promoting, or laying off persons.

      (1) In assessing the employer's conduct, a court can consider the disparate (unequal) impact on the workforce of the employer's employment practices.

      (2) A court will look with great scrutiny on any employment requirements that have the effect of eliminating a protected minority group, such as an applicant's arrest record, education (unless relevant to the position), marital status, and religion.

      (3) Applicants are not to be refused summarily simply because of preconceived notions. Applicants should be considered individually and tested against relevant work expectations.

         EXAMPLE: Formerly, utility companies often denied employment opportunities to women on work crews because the work was dangerous and/or involved hard work or lifting.

(4) Employers must attempt to make reasonable accommodations for persons claiming religious discrimination.

EXAMPLE: It is generally considered reasonable to expect an employer to accommodate a full-time employee's day of worship.

(5) Sexual harassment, a form of gender discrimination, is recognized in two situations:

(a) The traditional approach involves some personnel action made dependent on sexual favors, sometimes called the quid-pro-quo offense.

EXAMPLE: Dawson was asked by her manager to spend a weekend with her manager to get to "know her better" and to "discuss a possible promotion."

(b) The more recent type of recognized sexual harassment offense deals with a hostile working environment. A workplace where frequent sexual-innuendo jokes are permitted and/or tolerated may result in a hostile working environment. This may occur even though the person who is subjected directly to such behavior does not object but others working in the area do object.

EXAMPLE: Knight continually makes sexist jokes and remarks to Edwards who laughs and seems to encourage more of the same. For Edwards' co-workers who are subjected to this behavior and object to it, a hostile work environment is evolving.

c. *Bona fide occupational qualifications (BFOQs):* In very limited situations involving reasonable business necessity, an employer may legally discriminate on the basis of gender, national origin, or religion.

(1) This limited defense is called the *bona fide occupational qualification defense.*

EXAMPLES: A Catholic church could limit employees to Catholics.

A theater group could require that the role of Cleopatra be played by a woman.

The owner of a French restaurant could insist that French natives be employed as waiters and waitresses; however, he or she could not then reject a black French native.

(2) The BFOQ defense is *not* available for discrimination involving race or color.

d. *Enforcement/procedure for relief from discrimination:* The overall enforcement of Title VII is through the EEOC.

(1) *Filing of complaints:*

(a) Complainants must first file their complaints with a state equivalent of the EEOC, if it exists.

(b) If a complaint is filed with a state or local agency, the EEOC cannot act until that agency has had 60 days to resolve the matter.

(2) *Role of the EEOC:* The EEOC may be involved in any of the following activities designed to assist with a solution:

(a) Investigation of the complaint

(b) An attempt to reach an administrative solution with the employer

(c) Filing of suit against the employer on behalf of the claimant(s)

(d) Dismissal of the complaint

(3) *Private action:* If the complainant fails to achieve the desired relief after the preceding steps are taken, a private lawsuit may be brought against the employer by the employee(s).

e. *Burden of proof:*

(1) *Prima facie case of discrimination:* Plaintiff, whether complaining employee(s) or EEOC on behalf of complaining employee(s), must establish a prima facie case of discrimination.

EXAMPLES: Cameron, a black laborer, applied for a job with ACE Corporation. Although qualified, Cameron was not hired, and the job remained open.

Koch was qualified to receive a promotion with ACE Corporation. Kennedy was promoted instead even though he had lesser experience and poorer qualifications.

(2) *Employer accountability:* The employer has the burden to account for the apparent discrimination.

f. *Potential remedies:*

(1) Injunction prohibiting illegal action

(2) Damages (back pay)

(3) Reinstatement if fired or forced out improperly

(4) Promotion to position denied improperly

(5) Other remedies suitable to redress the employer's wrongdoing

2. *Equal Pay for Equal Work Act:* This act, a part of the Fair Labor Standards Act, requires equal pay for equal work regardless of gender. The term *equal work* means that two or more employees are doing substantially equal work under similar working conditions.

EXAMPLE: A man is paid 25 cents more per hour than the women on an assembly line because he is required to empty a 50-gallon drum twice a day. A court would probably find that this is not enough difference to justify the greater pay. (Perhaps the drum could be emptied more often, smaller drums could be utilized, or a mechanical device such as a two-wheeled cart could be used.)

a. *Permitted pay differences:* A difference in pay between men and women is permissible if due to piecework rates of production (quantity of production), seniority on the job, or merit. Pay differences based on gender, however, are not allowed. There might still be a violation of Title VII, however, because of the discriminatory effects of the seniority system.

b. *Remedy for violation:* If an equal-pay violation is found, the wages of the employees discriminated against will be raised to the wages of the favored gender. (The reverse *never* occurs: The higher wage earners are never reduced to the wage rates of the discriminated-against workers.)

3. *Age Discrimination in Employment Act (ADEA):* The Age Discrimination in Employment Act (ADEA), although not originally a part of Title VII, is enforced by the

EEOC. The ADEA originally applied to workers between the ages of 40 and 70, but the law was amended to eliminate the cap of age 70. The ADEA now applies to all workers 40 and over.

EXAMPLE: A software development company fires Eastman, age 37, and Daniels, age 45, with the expressed goal "to get some younger blood into the company." The ADEA only gives Daniels a cause of action under this specific act.

a. *Effect:* There is no mandatory retirement or discrimination in regard to hiring, promotion, and retention because of age if not at least 40 years old.

b. *Exceptions:* Exceptions include certain occupations such as airline pilots, police, and firemen, where innocent third parties rely on critical physical skills.

c. *Potential damages:*

(1) Reinstatement in position

(2) Back pay

(3) Attorney fees

4. *Rehabilitation Act of 1973:* This legislation requires employers who participate in government contracts to make reasonable accommodation to employ and to promote qualified handicapped individuals. The EEOC has the power of enforcement for this legislation even though this act is not a part of Title VII. The act seeks to have employers meet the individual needs of handicapped persons.

a. *Coverage:*

(1) Federal government employees are covered under this act.

(2) Employers with federal government contracts of $2,500 or more per year are also included within this act.

(3) Extended coverage occurs as a general contractor with a government contract is required to make its subcontractors agree to follow the act.

b. *Requirements for covered employer:* Employers who participate in government contracts of $2,500 or more per year are required to take affirmative action in employing qualified handicapped individuals.

(1) *Affirmative action:* Employers must take affirmative action to hire, promote, and retain handicapped employees.

(2) *Employment:* The legislation applies to all levels of employment.

(3) *Accessibility to work:* Working conditions and accessibility for handicapped individuals must be remedied as necessary to accommodate the handicapped person. Such remedies must not pose an undue hardship for the employer.

c. *Qualifications for employment:* For employee coverage, the handicapped individual must be able to show that he or she is otherwise qualified for the job.

(1) The individual must be able to perform the job or perform with reasonable accommodations.

(2) Alcoholics and drug abusers are specifically not covered under the act. Persons with symptomatic HIV infection (AIDS) now are covered by regulation.

d. *Damages:* The government may require the following damages as settlement:

(1) *Severance:* The government may sever the contract with the employer.

(2) *Hiring or reinstatement:* The government may require hiring or reinstatement of minority workers.

(3) *Payment of back wages:* The government may require back wages to be paid.

5. *The Americans with Disabilities Act (ADA):* The Civil Rights Act of 1964 was extended in 1992 to cover the physically and mentally disabled, including AIDS patients, cancer patients, and treated, recovering substance abusers. Individuals with emotional disorders, however, are excluded. Businesses must make reasonable accommodations to workers and job applicants with disabilities unless the required changes present an undue hardship for the business.

a. *General areas of the act:* The provisions of the act range from public services and building codes to employment practices concerning physically and mentally disabled persons.

(1) *Public services:* One of the major provisions of the act mandates that disabled persons not be excluded from participating in any municipal activities. Disabled persons cannot be denied services provided routinely for other citizens. Building codes will need to be modified to include accommodation for disabled persons.

EXAMPLE: Public transportation must be available and accessible for those citizens with disabilities.

(2) *Employment:* Employers cannot discriminate against an applicant on the basis of the disability if the person can perform the basic responsibilities of the job. Employers must make reasonable accommodation to assist the disabled employee.

EXAMPLE: Office equipment may need to be modified for the disabled person.

(3) Job duties may need to be restructured so that the employee can perform assigned duties. Such restructuring must not cause the employer an undue hardship, however.

b. *Coverage of the act:* The legislation applies to employers with 25 or more workers.

6. *The Family and Medical Leave Act of 1993:* Under certain circumstances, the provisions of the Family and Medical Leave Act of 1993 grant the opportunity for family and temporary medical leave for employees who meet the qualifications. Prior to the enactment of this legislation, employment policies were lacking that would accommodate working parents or guardians who otherwise would have to choose between job security and parenting.

a. *Rationale for the legislation:* The basic reasons for the enactment of the Family and Medical Leave Act include the following:

(1) The number of single-parent and two-parent households in which the single parent or both parents work is increasing significantly.

(2) Inadequate job security for employees with serious health conditions prevents them from working for temporary periods.

(3) If the primary responsibility for family caregiving falls primarily on women, such responsibility affects the working lives of women more than it affects the working lives of men.

(4) Employment standards that apply to one gender only have tended to encourage employers to discriminate against employees and applicants for employment who are of that gender.

b. *Purposes of the act:* The primary purposes of the legislation that are to be accomplished in a manner that accommodates the legitimate interests of employers include the following:

(1) The demands of the workplace need to be balanced with the needs of families, especially in terms of promoting the stability and economic security of families.

(2) Employees are entitled to take reasonable leave for medical reasons, for the birth or adoption of a child, and for the care of a child, spouse, or parent who has a serious health condition.

(3) The potential for employment discrimination on the basis of gender must be minimized by ensuring that leave is available for eligible medical reasons and for compelling family reasons on a gender-neutral basis.

(4) The promotion of equal employment opportunity for women and men is of primary importance to employers and employees.

c. *Eligible employees:* An employee is determined to be eligible for family or medical leave who has been employed by the employer from whom the leave is required for at least 12 months or for at least 1,250 hours of service for the employer during the previous 12-month period.

d. *Definition of employer:* The term *employer* is defined as follows:

(1) Any person engaged in commerce or in any industry affecting commerce who employs 50 or more employees for each working day during each of 20 or more calendar workweeks in the current or the preceding calendar year.

(2) Any person who acts, directly or indirectly, in the interest of an employer to any of the employees of such employer.

e. *Provisions of the legislation:* An eligible employee shall be entitled to a total of 12 workweeks of leave during any 12-month period for one or more of the following reasons:

(1) The birth of a child and in order to care for that child.

(2) The placement of a child with the employee for adoption or foster care.

(3) The care of a spouse, child, or parent of the employee because of a serious health condition.

(4) A serious health condition that makes the employee unable to perform the functions of the work position.

G. Labor-Management Relations (Private Employers)

Labor-management relations law deals with legislation covering the private-sector workforce. The National Labor Relations Act (NLRA) covers labor-management relations of private employers. This act consists of the Wagner Act (1935), the Taft-Hartley Act (1947), and the Landrum-Griffin Act (1959).

1. *The National Labor Relations Act (NLRA):*

a. *Administration of the act:* The NLRA is enforced by the National Labor Relations Board (NLRB).

(1) The board is composed of five members.

(2) A general counsel oversees operation of the NLRB and all investigations.

(3) Regional offices exist to handle NLRA matters.

b. *Coverage of the act:* Any employer engaged in private business affecting commerce is potentially covered. A business "affects commerce" if it is involved in interstate selling and/or purchasing.

c. *Purposes of the NLRA:*

(1) Protect employees in forming, joining, and being members of a union, or the alternative, their refraining from being so involved

(2) Ensure fair union election

(3) Enforce collective bargaining obligations

(4) Oversee unfair labor practices of management or the union

2. *The Wagner Act (1935):* The Wagner Act was the first comprehensive federal labor legislation. For the first time, this act set forth procedures for a union to follow to seek an election and to require an employer, if the union won the election, to recognize the union and thereafter bargain in good faith.

a. *National Labor Relations Board:* The act established the NLRB to oversee private union-management labor relations, including elections.

b. *Formation of a union:* The act gave employees the right to assist, form, and join a union at the workers' place of business.

c. *Establishment of unfair labor practices:* The act established employer, not union, unfair labor practices for inappropriate behavior, such as employer retaliation against an employee for support of a union.

3. *Taft-Hartley Act (1947):* The Taft-Hartley Act established the NLRA, a combination of the Wagner and Taft-Hartley Acts. The NLRA included the following provisions:

a. *Employer unfair labor practices:* The NLRA identified additional unfair labor practices for employers.

b. *Union unfair labor practices:* The act also identified union unfair labor practices.

c. *Union shop:* The NLRA permitted a union shop. When a union wins an election, employees are not required to join the union at that place of business as a condition of employment. However, the NLRA permits the union to negotiate with the employer to have a union shop provision put into the collective bargaining agreement.

(1) A union shop provision requires an employee to join the union in order to be employed in the shop (place of business).

(2) An employee in a union shop setting is permitted not to join the union, but the employee must pay the equivalent of union dues (generally for a charitable purpose).

d. *Free speech:* The act established the right of the employer to engage in free speech as long as "no threat of reprisal or force or promise of benefit" is made.

EXAMPLE: An employer may tell employees that he or she hopes the employees will vote against a union. It is wrong, however, to threaten retaliation.

e. *Right-to-work law:* The act established the right of states to outlaw union shops in their states (known as the *right-to-work law*).

EXAMPLE: In a right-to-work state, an employee could choose not to join the UAW, for example, even though it represents the plant employees at a General Motors plant.

Workers choosing not to belong to the union are still covered by the union collective bargaining agreement and must be represented by the union if proper grievance is filed.

4. *Landrum-Griffin Act (1959):* The Landrum-Griffin Act essentially deals with the internal operation and management of unions and establishes specific union member rights, such as the following:

a. *Election of union officers:* Union members have the right to vote.

b. *Conduct of meetings:* Union members have the right to attend and vote.

c. *Management of union funds.*

5. *Means and Effect of Union Recognition:*

a. *Voluntary recognition of union:* An employer can always voluntarily recognize a union where it is clear that the union has the support of a majority of the employees within a particular bargaining unit (group of employees). However, the employer is not required to do so. The employer can force the union to seek an NLRB union election even if it appears obvious that a majority of the employees favor the union.

b. *Union recognition:* The effect of union recognition is that the union represents all employees within the bargaining unit.

6. *The Election Process:*

a. *Order for election:* A union receiving authorization cards from 30 percent or more employees within a proposed bargaining unit will cause the NLRB to order an election.

b. *Union election:* The NLRB investigates the proposed bargaining unit and, if appropriate, orders and conducts a union election at the employer's plant.

EXAMPLE: The NLRB generally holds that a single store within a chain is still an appropriate bargaining unit.

c. *Majority vote:* The union must secure the vote of a majority of the employees of the proposed bargaining unit *who vote.*

EXAMPLE: Union A wins if it secures 150 votes to 145 no-union votes even though 20 employees abstain from voting.

d. *Union campaign:* During the union campaign period, an employer may not do the following:

(1) Spy on employees

(2) Take polls of employees

(3) Offer new benefits or change existing working conditions

(4) Fire any employee because of union sympathy

(5) Restrict or forbid solicitation or distribution of information during working hours, if similar activity allowed previously for nonunion purposes such as a charitable raffle

e. *New election ordered:* If either management or the union engages in activities that cause the other party to lose unfairly, a new election may be ordered.

EXAMPLE: An employer illegally polls employees regarding their views of the union.

7. *Unfair Labor Practices by Employer:* By law, employers are not permitted to engage in unfair labor practices, such as the following:

a. *Interference with employee's rights:* The employer may not interfere with the employee's rights to form, join, or belong to a union.

b. *Domination of union:* The employer may not dominate the union.

EXAMPLE: An employer may not establish a union for its employees.

c. *Discrimination:* The employer may not discriminate in the hiring or firing of an employee because of union activity and/or affiliation.

d. *Refusal to bargain in good faith:* The employer may be unwilling to bargain in good faith.

8. *Unfair Labor Practices by Union:* Unions are also prohibited from engaging in unfair labor practices, such as the following:

a. *Refusal to bargain in good faith:* Union representatives refuse to bargain in good faith.

b. *Striking:* Where a no-strike clause exists, the union will exhibit an unfair labor practice by striking.

c. *Picketing:* Certain types of picketing may be seen as unfair practice.

9. *The Role of the Arbitrator:* Collective bargaining agreements typically contain clauses requiring that disputes be settled by an arbitrator.

a. *Arbitration clause:* Where an arbitration clause exists and applies, a union may not strike where the matter is resolved by the arbitrator.

b. *Ruling:* An arbitrator's ruling has the same force of law as does a court decision or an NLRB decision.

10. *Potential NLRB Remedies:* The NLRB may utilize any of the following remedies:

a. *Injunction:* The NLRB may issue an injunction.

b. *New election:* The NLRB may order a new election.

c. *Union recognition:* The NLRB may require an employer to recognize a union.

d. *Good-faith bargaining:* The NLRB may order bargaining in good faith.

If the offending party refuses to comply, the enforcement will be ordered via the federal courts of appeal.

H. Emerging Employment Issues

A number of new employment issues have emerged in the United States. These issues are being addressed by both statute and court cases.

1. *Decline of the Employment-at-Will Doctrine:* At common law an employer had the power to fire any worker not subject to a term employment contract for any reason (or no reason). Employees without a contract subject to such removal were known as *employees at-will.*

EXAMPLES: Jenkins is hired as an assembler at ABC Manufacturing Company. Jenkins is not covered by a collective bargaining agreement and not hired for a set period of time. Jenkins could be freely terminated at any time under the common law.

Referring to the above example, Jenkins is covered by a collective bargaining agreement. Now Jenkins can probably not be discharged unless reasons for just cause exist.

Major league managers have contracts for term (one or more years). When a manager is fired because the team is not winning enough games, the manager will have a right to his remaining salary for the term of the contract. Such a manager is not *an employee at-will.*

a. *Limitation of employer powers:*

(1) Employment discrimination laws have greatly reduced the ability of employers to discharge employees for impermissible discriminatory reasons.

EXAMPLE: It would be a violation of Title VII for an employer to fire a person because of race or gender.

(2) Court cases and, in some states, state statutes have begun to limit employer termination rights as to other discharges that are contrary to public policy.

EXAMPLE: An employee is given a subpoena for jury duty. The employer tells the employee that he or she will be fired if the employee reports for jury duty. The employee reports to court for jury duty. The employee is subsequently fired. The court may reinstate and/or award damages.

(3) The employee handbook may define the status of probationary and permanent employees.

EXAMPLE: Assume that an employee handbook states that an employee is probationary for the first six months of service and then becomes a permanent employee. Permanent *may be interpreted as meaning that the employee cannot be removed without cause.*

b. *Emphasis on proper employment practices:* The employment-at-will doctrine is slowly eroding, primarily by state court decision precedents. The emerging abolition of the doctrine, however, has caused employers to put greater emphasis on proper employment practices policies.

2. *Employee Privacy Issues:* A number of employee privacy issues have evolved. These include the following:

   a. *Lie detector tests:* The Employee Polygraph Protection Act of 1988 forbids the usage of polygraph (lie detector) tests in most situations of employment, including hiring.

   b. *Drug testing:* Employer drug testing of employees has dramatically increased as a result of a number of reasons, including the Drug-Free Workplace Act of 1988, which requires employers with federal government contracts to maintain a drug-free workplace. Permissible ways and situations in which to test employees are still not clearly defined.

      EXAMPLE: A court is more likely to approve random drug testing for employees of an electrical utility company working at a nuclear plant than accounting personnel at the home office.

   c. *Privilege against defamation:* Many terminated employees have begun to win lawsuits against former employers who, after termination, make untrue statements about their employment, integrity, or person. As a result, many employers are limiting their exposure to lawsuits by what they will say about a former employee, good or bad.

   d. *Intrusions into personal privacy:* Employers are prohibited from unreasonable intrusions into the personal privacy of employees.

      EXAMPLES: Where an employee was provided a specific company locker and allowed to secure the lock with his or her own lock, a court found that the employee had an expectation of privacy that prohibited the employer from opening the locker without the employee's permission. (The employer, K-Mart, suspected that the employee was shoplifting.)

      Courts have consistently held that an employee does not have an expectation of privacy for personal e-mail messages received and/or stored on a desktop computer provided by the employer.

Review Questions

Directions: Select the best answer from the four alternatives. Write your answer in the blank to the left of the number.

______ **1.** Administrative agencies are

a. part of the legislative branch.
b. part of the judicial branch.
c. part of the executive branch.
d. in fact a fourth branch of government.

______ **2.** Witnesses will be heard and evidence admitted in an administrative agency matter at which stage?

a. Before the administrative law judge.
b. Before the agency board itself.
c. Before the federal court of appeals.
d. Witnesses are never heard in an administrative agency matter.

______ **3.** A criminal violation for monopoly activity is possible under the

a. Sherman Act.
b. Clayton Act.
c. Robinson-Patman Act.
d. Federal Trade Commission Act.

______ **4.** Arrow Corporation and Phoenix, Inc., have been charged with price fixing. Which of the following statements is correct?

a. Price fixing is a Robinson-Patman Act violation.
b. Arrow and Phoenix should prevail if the alleged price fixing actually resulted in lower consumer prices.
c. Price fixing is a per se rule violation.
d. Price fixing cannot result in a criminal trial.

______ **5.** A situation where a seller will sell you product A only if you also agree to buy product B, a product readily available elsewhere, is called

a. a tying contract.
b. a vertical territorial allocation.
c. a horizontal territorial allocation.
d. price discrimination.

______ **6.** Martin, Inc., has been charged with price discrimination to buyers Smith and Pace. Which defense below would be recognized?

a. Martin is not a retailer; therefore, price discrimination cannot be charged.

b. Martin's price to Pace was because the particular product was damaged by water from a flood.
c. Pace's price reduction was because of an error made in pricing the product.
d. Smith was selling Martin's product at a discount, causing Pace to lose sales.

_____________ **7.** Which antitrust act applies to both the sale of goods and the sale of services?

a. Clayton Act
b. Robinson-Patman Act
c. Securities Act of 1933
d. Sherman Act

_____________ **8.** Skyler Corporation has been charged with gender discrimination. Which defense is most likely to be recognized?

a. Lifting of heavier weights is involved in the designated men's positions.
b. Men and women are paid the same piecemeal rate.
c. The employees are represented by a union.
d. Women are excluded because the work involved is extremely dangerous.

_____________ **9.** Jordan was injured while working for Acme Manufacturing because he failed to use a machine's safety mechanism. Jordan's claim for workers' compensation will be

a. denied if Jordan was negligent.
b. denied if Jordan was grossly negligent.
c. reduced by the amount of damages attributable to Jordan's own fault.
d. paid in full.

_____________ **10.** Under the Fair Labor Standards Act, the following is required:

a. Double time on Sundays or holidays if hours worked for the week exceed 40
b. Minimum wage
c. Pay for hours worked in excess of eight hours for any day must be time-and-a-half
d. Children under the age of 16 can work only for their parent(s)

_____________ **11.** Which of the following statements about social security is correct?

a. A self-employed individual is exempt from social security coverage.
b. An employer must make contributions for each employee.
c. Social security coverage is optional.
d. An employer may decide whether to make contributions for each employee.

_____________ **12.** Cooper was laid off by Atlas Corporation. Cooper might be denied unemployment compensation

a. if he had not worked enough weeks prior to being laid off.
b. if he is wealthy and does not need it.
c. if the employer was forced to lay off Cooper because of the economy.
d. if he is an hourly employee.

_______ **13.** ABC Corporation would have to recognize union A if

a. union A had recognition cards from 60 percent of the ABC employees.
b. in an election 100 workers voted for the union, 95 voted for no union, and 7 abstained from voting.
c. an employer strongly urged employees to vote against the union.
d. union A represented ABC's major competitor.

_______ **14.** The federal agency that directly oversees private employer-union relationships is

a. the Equal Employment Opportunity Commission.
b. the National Labor Relations Board.
c. the Occupational Safety and Health Act.
d. the Department of Labor.

_______ **15.** Union A is trying to organize the employees of Huskie Corporation. In a speech to the Huskie employees, the corporation president may

a. state that the corporation wants no union.
b. tell employees that the usual Christmas bonus will be suspended pending the election.
c. poll the employees as to their preference.
d. threaten retaliation if the union should win.

_______ **16.** Which of the following is totally a matter of state law?

a. Workplace safety rules
b. Unemployment compensation
c. Workers' compensation
d. Child-labor laws

_______ **17.** The employment-at-will doctrine

a. has gained support as the result of the passage of employment discrimination laws.
b. applies to persons subject to a collective bargaining agreement.
c. prohibits removal of an employee except for cause.
d. has especially been challenged in regard to public policy matters.

Use the following information in answering Questions 18 to 20.

Tucker Corporation manufactures automobile parts. The company's former human resource manager proved to not be very astute in recognizing potential employment discrimination situations. The new human resource manager has found the following three cases on her desk.

_______ **18.** Gordon applied for a job in the warehouse shipment area of the plant. Gordon is an African-American male, 53 years of age, without a high school diploma. He was denied employment "because at the age of 53 he was not likely to have sufficient strength and energy to handle the job." Gordon's best recourse would be to allege

a. age discrimination.
b. race discrimination.

c. disability discrimination.
d. gender discrimination.

______________ **19.** Gorman, 45, applied for a position in the accounts payable section. Gorman told the accounts payable manager that she would need a double-page-size computer screen to do her work because of a vision disability. Although Gorman was the most qualified accountant, she was denied employment because the cost to provide her with the needed screen would exceed the manager's available budget and might also result in petty jealousies among section employees.

a. Gorman would likely have a good cause of action for gender discrimination.
b. The possibility of fellow employee jealousy is probably sufficient to protect the employer under the ADEA.
c. Gorman's request would likely be considered a reasonable employer accommodation under the ADEA.
d. Gorman might have a good cause of action for age discrimination.

______________ **20.** Danielson delivers mail to the various departments within the company. When he delivers company mail to the packaging department, he is often subjected to great scrutiny by women employees about his dating practices and sexual preferences with women. At first, Danielson found it kind of fun, but it has become a matter that now greatly bothers him. His supervisor has told him to just keep quiet because to say something would likely make matters worse for him.

a. Having originally not objected to the behavior of packaging department employees, Danielson would likely not now have grounds to object.
b. Being a man prevents Danielson from having a potential claim under Title VII.
c. The conduct of the women employees is often called "quid-pro-quo behavior."
d. Other employees in the packaging department might have a basis to claim a hostile working environment.

______________ **21.** One of the basic reasons for the enactment of the Family and Medical Leave Act of 1993 was to

a. enable employees to take a 12-week leave from work for educational pursuits as well as family care.
b. provide job security for employees with serious health conditions.
c. discriminate on the basis of gender only if the employee does not have a legitimate medical reason for a leave.
d. enable women to take on the major role in family caregiving while men remained the "chief breadwinners."

______________ **22.** According to the Family and Medical Leave Act of 1993, an eligible employee is entitled to a leave of up to 12 workweeks during a single year for

a. each child that must be cared for.
b. each parent that must be cared for.
c. the care of an elderly person, not necessarily a relative.
d. the care of a spouse who has a serious health condition.

Solutions

Answer	*Refer to:*
1. (c)	[A-1] Administrative agencies are often considered the fourth branch of government but actually are part of the executive branch.
2. (a)	[A-3-d] Administrative law judges act as the equivalent to trial judges in hearing administrative cases.
3. (a)	[C-4-b, 5-c] Monopoly is a violation under the Sherman Act. Criminal prosecution is possible under the Sherman Act.
4. (c)	[C-5-a] Price fixing is a per se violation under the Sherman Act. It does not matter whether the price agreed on is a fair price.
5. (a)	[C-6-a] The described actions would result in a tying contract.
6. (b)	[C-7-c] A change in the marketability of the product involved is an appropriate defense.
7. (d)	[C-5] The Sherman Act is the only antitrust act that applies to both the sale of goods and the sale of services. (The Clayton and Robinson-Patman Acts apply only to the sale of goods.)
8. (b)	[F-2-a] A bona fide piecemeal plan is a legal defense under the Equal Pay Act even if it generally results in higher net pay for men.
9. (d)	[E-3-c] An employee recovers under *workers' compensation* for all injuries suffered during work except intentional injuries. The employee recovers either the full permissible amount or none.
10. (b)	[D-1-b, D-1-e] The Fair Labor Standards Act provides for a minimum wage to be paid employees except for some specific exemptions.
11. (b)	[D-3-c] The amount deducted for FICA for an employee must be supplemented by an additional amount contributed by the employer.
12. (a)	[D-2-c] To recover unemployment compensation, an employee must show substantial past employment and involuntary severance.
13. (b)	[G-6-c] An employer must recognize a union when the union gets the majority of votes in a union-choice election.
14. (b)	[G-1] The National Labor Relations Board is the agency with the responsibility of overseeing private employer-union relationships.

15. (a) [G-3-d] Answer (a) is correct as long as no threats or inducement accompany the free speech.

16. (c) [E] Workers' compensation is the correct answer. All other choices are matters of both state and federal concern and involvement.

17. (d) [H-1-a] The employment-at-will doctrine permitted termination without any cause (or even bad cause). State court decisions are influencing the erosion of the doctrine.

18. (a) [F-3] The statement that Gordon was denied employment "because at the age of 53 he was not likely to have sufficient strength and energy to handle the job" carries the clear negative connotation of age that the ADEA attempts to eliminate. The company should instead attempt to develop an accurate, fair evaluation of the needs of the job.

19. (c) [F-5] Gorman's request would likely be considered a reasonable employer accommodation under the ADEA. The fact that the section manager might not have sufficient section capital budget would not likely be recognized as a defense for a company obligation to reasonably accommodate potential employees with disabilities.

20. (d) [F-1-b(5)] While Danielson would likely have grounds of sexual harassment, so would employees within the packaging department who object to the ongoing practices of teasing Danielson. The reason for this is that the grievant under a hostile environment claim need not be the victim.

21. (b) [F-6-a(2)] The Family and Medical Leave Act was enacted, in part, to provide the needed job security for any employee who has a serious health condition.

22. (d) [F-6-e(3)] The act provides for employees to be eligible for family and medical leave for the care of a spouse, child, or parent of the employee because of a serious health condition.

CHAPTER 26

Property

OVERVIEW

Anything that is owned or can be owned is property. Ownership means the right to possess, control use, or transfer. The most important first step is to know how to classify property. Land, including attached buildings, fixtures, and crops, is called *real property.* Property other than real property is known as *personal property.* Personal property that has a physical existence, such as a computer, is considered *tangible* property. If not, it is *intangible* property, such as a stock certificate, or *intellectual* property, which includes copyrights, patents, or trademarks. Finally, property is either public (owned by a government) or private (owned by a nongovernment owner).

Property can be acquired in a number of ways. The most common way is by purchase. The object of purchase is to receive good title: the right to possess, control, or transfer. For most purchases of personal property, however, a sales receipt will be the only evidence of proper title. In contrast, purchases of real property should always include a document of title called a *deed.* Not all deeds are the same. The buyer must understand the legal effect depending on whether the title being offered is a quitclaim, warranty, or special warranty deed. Property can be put up as collateral to support the borrowing of money. This often happens when a consumer purchases a car or a home. The consumer is said to give the lender a *security interest* in the property.

Property is often acquired jointly. To illustrate, it is common for a husband and a wife to jointly take ownership of a home. The rights of a joint owner will depend on the manner in which the joint owners take original ownership: *joint tenancy, tenancy in common, tenancy by the entirety,* or *community property* (in states where it is presumed that a husband and a wife each own one half of the property).

Intellectual property has become very important, especially with the explosion of available information on the Internet. The primary types of intellectual property protection by federal law include copyright, patent, and trademark. A copyright provides protection for a literary work, such as a book or a movie. A patent provides protection for an invention, such as a new type of lighting. A trademark provides protection for a distinctive marking, motto, or device that is placed on products to identify that source, for example, the Apple insignia on Apple computers.

Almost every piece of real property in an urban setting is subject to one or more *easements,* a right of passage over the property. Most easements are for utility lines. However, an easement may provide right of physical passage over the land of another.

Real property may also be leased by a landlord to a tenant. It is important for both the landlord and the tenant to understand the nature of their relationship and respective rights and duties.

KEY TERMS

Adverse possession	Joint tenancy	Personal property
Copyright	Literary works	Quitclaim deed
Easement	Mortgage	Real property
Fair use	Mortgagee	Security interest
Fixture	Mortgagor	Tenancy in common
Infringement	Patent	Warranty deed

A. Classification of Property

Property is classified as being either real property or personal property. Personal property that is affixed to real property becomes real property.

EXAMPLE: A sink is personal property until it is permanently installed in a new home.

1. *Real Property:* Land and any improvements on or connected with the land is *real property.* Trees and crops are considered part of the real property until severed.

a. *Rights of ownership:* An owner of real property normally owns not only the surface but what is above and below the surface as well. However, below-surface rights, known as mineral rights, can be sold separately from the real property.

(1) A prospective buyer wanting to be sure to own the oil, gas, coal, water, or other mineral rights should check the official real property records at the county courthouse to ensure that there has not been a previous conveyance of mineral rights.

EXAMPLE: A landowner might have granted either a long-term easement right to oil or have sold the right to extract oil from the subject real property.

(2) The use of airspace is limited to the amount that an owner may reasonably use. It may be further limited by government restrictions as to height of buildings and towers.

EXAMPLE: Building heights are restricted close to airports so that these buildings do not interfere with airplane takeoffs and landings.

(3) The use of the surface may also be restricted by zoning ordinances, subdivision rules (covenants), or other means.

EXAMPLE: City zoning ordinances generally prohibit most business usage of land in single-family residential areas. If applicable, a 7-11 store might be able to be built near but not actually in an area zoned for single-family dwellings.

b. *Legal interests of others:* Real property is often subject to legal interests of others, for example, utility lines, easements (right of passageway), and tenants.

EXAMPLE: If Kennedy signs a one-year lease on March 1, she will have a right to remain in her apartment for one year even if her apartment building is sold the very next day.

2. *Personal Property:* All other property that is not real property is called *personal property.*

a. *Classification of personal property:* Personal property is further classified as being either *tangible* or *intangible* personal property.

(1) Personal property having a physical existence, capable of physical possession, is known as *tangible* personal property.

EXAMPLES: A book, an automobile, and a computer Zip drive.

(2) Personal property not existing in physical form, incapable of physical possession, is known as *intangible* personal property. This property represents an ownership interest.

EXAMPLES: A stock certificate or intellectual property represented by a copyright, a patent, or a trademark.

b. *Fixtures:* Personal property that is permanently attached to real property and becomes a part of it is known as a *fixture.* Once attached, it will be sold with the real property.

EXAMPLE: Pictures hung on a wall will generally continue to be items of personal property and will not be considered as part of the real property. In contrast, a built-in dishwasher would become a fixture, part of the real property, when installed in a kitchen.

B. Types of Ownership

Real property is either owned by a sole owner (only one person or entity owns the property) or by multiple owners (more than one person or entity owns the property). When there are multiple owners of the property, ownership may be characterized by joint tenancy, tenancy by the entirety, tenancy in common, or community property.

1. *Joint Tenancy:* Joint tenancy exists when there is simultaneous (concurrent) ownership of property by two or more owners with a right of survivorship. The owners must acquire their interest at exactly the same time and must be clearly designated in the deed as joint tenants.

a. *Equal undivided interests:* Each joint tenant owns an equal undivided interest with equal rights of possession.

EXAMPLE: If there are two joint tenants for a particular piece of real property, each owns one half, regardless of which joint tenant, if either, paid greater monies toward the purchase. If there are three joint tenants, each would own one third.

b. *Conveyance of interest:* A joint tenant may convey his or her interest to another. The transferee becomes a tenant in common (see Section D-2) with the remaining joint tenant(s).

EXAMPLE: A, B, and C own a farm in joint tenancy. A sells his undivided one-third interest to X. X is a tenant in common as to B and C but as to the remaining two-thirds interest B and C remain joint tenants.

c. *Survivorship:* The surviving joint tenant(s) automatically receives the interest of a joint tenant who dies. A will has no effect.

EXAMPLE: Knight and Peters own a farm in joint tenancy. Knight's will says that Knight's son is to receive Knight's share of the farm when Knight dies. Peters would prevail.

d. *Statement of joint tenancy:* When receiving real property in joint tenancy, the joint tenants must be sure that this is clearly stated. If they do not, the ownership of the property will be presumed to be tenancy in common.

2. *Tenancy in Common:* Concurrent ownership exists by two or more owners with no right of survivorship. Surviving co-owners do not receive the property.

a. *Undivided interest:* The owners have an undivided interest (like joint tenancy).

b. *Equality of interest:* Ownership need not be equal (unlike joint tenancy).

EXAMPLE: A may own two thirds while B owns one third of a farm.

c. *Survivorship:* When a tenant in common dies, his or her share passes by will or by descent to heirs. There is no legal right by the surviving co-owner to the property unless will or descent would so direct.

When ownership interest is not clear, it is presumed to be a tenancy in common. This is the most common means of ownership where no family connection exists.

3. *Tenancy by the Entirety:* A joint-ownership interest exists between husband and wife. This type of ownership is *not* recognized in all states.

a. *Conveyance of interest:* Tenancy by the entirety is essentially like a joint tenancy except that a spouse may not sell his or her share without the consent of the other.

b. *Survivorship:* The surviving spouse receives the property as in joint tenancy.

c. *Termination:* Tenancy by the entirety is terminated by a divorce.

4. *Community Property:* Property that is owned by husband and wife is called *community property.* Community property is recognized in only eight states.

a. *Survivorship:* Owners have the right of survivorship (as in joint tenancy).

b. *Ownership:* Property acquired during marriage automatically becomes community property (one half belonging to each spouse).

C. Acquisition of Personal Property

Personal property may be acquired through purchase, gift, or finding abandoned or lost property or by will or descent.

1. *Acquisition by Purchase:* Acquisition by purchase is the most common method of acquiring personal property. Chapter 21 identifies the requirements for the purchase of personal property. A purchase requires value, usually money (whether by cash, check, or credit).

EXAMPLE: Elliot buys a gallon of paint at the local Sears store.

2. *Acquisition by Gift:* A gift involves a transfer without an exchange of value. Stated even more simply, a gift is something for nothing (or free).

a. *Parties:* The parties involved are a donor and a donee.

(1) *Donor:* The person making the gift is known as the donor.

(2) *Donee:* The person receiving the gift is known as the donee.

b. *Required elements for a gift:* To reduce the possibility of fraud or other wrongdoing, certain required elements must be met to demonstrate the existence of a gift.

(1) Present donor intent to make a gift to the donee is one of the required elements of a gift.

EXAMPLE: Gray tells Sinclair she is thinking about giving her a dining room rug that Sinclair has always wanted. This is not *present donor intent to make a gift.*

(2) The property and/or title to the property must be delivered.

EXAMPLE: Jarvis makes a gift to Murphy of an old watch she has pawned at a pawn shop. She gives Murphy the pawn receipt that will permit Murphy to retrieve the watch.

(3) The donee must accept the gift.

EXAMPLE: Hughes decides to leave behind a large desk when he vacates his apartment because the desk does not fit into the truck he is using to move his belongings. Hughes will be liable for the expenditures of removal and disposal of the desk if the landlord does not accept the desk as a gift.

c. *Types of gifts:* Gifts may be intervivos gifts, testamentary gifts, or causa mortis gifts.

(1) *Intervivos gift:* A gift made during the donor's lifetime is called an *intervivos gift.*

(2) *Testamentary gift:* A gift made through a will or trust that becomes effective on the death of the donor is known as a *testamentary gift.*

(3) *Causa mortis gift:* A gift made in contemplation of the donor's imminent death is known as a *causa mortis gift.* If the donor survives or dies of another cause, the gift is considered legally canceled.

EXAMPLE: Knudson is about to undergo life-threatening surgery. He tells his friend Sloane that if he does not survive, she is to have his Miata roadster. If Knudson survives, the gift would be nullified.

3. *Acquisition by Descent:* Personal property can be acquired by descent by relatives of a deceased person who dies intestate (without a will). Each state has its own law establishing the order of descent.

EXAMPLE: Conway, 19, dies unexpectedly during her first year of college away from home. She has no will. Her property will be distributed according to state laws of intestacy, most likely to her parents if they are still living.

4. *Acquisition by Finding Property:* It is possible to gain legal rights to property by finding it. The laws applicable to found property focus on the intent and/or actions of the person who rightfully owned the property. As the following examples demonstrate, determining intent can be very difficult. Property will be presumed to be mislaid.

a. *Abandoned property:* If property is abandoned, the finder receives full ownership rights.

(1) Property is considered abandoned when it is obvious that the previous owner intended to relinquish ownership rights.

EXAMPLE: An empty Coca-Cola can along the side of a road will be presumed to be abandoned.

(2) The manner, place, and time of the previous owner's parting with the property are relevant in determining whether abandonment has occurred where it is not obvious.

EXAMPLE: A runner, getting hot while participating in a marathon run, sheds a sweatshirt by throwing it to the side of the road. In most organized runs, this would be considered an abandonment of the sweatshirt, allowing a passerby to claim ownership.

b. *Lost property:* Personal property is considered lost when the rightful owner unknowingly leaves the property in a particular place. If the property is lost, the finder has rights superior to everyone but the rightful owner.

EXAMPLE: Carson fails to put the club cover for his driver back on tightly, and it falls off as he walks down a fairway at the golf course. A subsequent player who finds the club cover has superior rights to everyone but Carson.

c. *Mislaid property:* Personal property is considered mislaid property when the rightful owner knowingly places the property in a particular place but then forgets where it is and leaves it there. If the property is mislaid, the owner of the premises on which it is found has rights superior to all but the rightful owner. The law presumes that the rightful owner may later recall where he or she left the item of property and return to claim it.

EXAMPLE: Carson put his sand wedge golf club next to the green when he went to putt out the hole. When Carson left the green area, he forgot to pick up his sand wedge. Slater finds the club. The golf course would have a superior right to Slater.

D. Personal Property Security Interest

An owner of personal property may borrow money by putting up the personal property as collateral. When this happens, the borrower of the money gives a *security interest* to secure the debt. The lender has the right to claim against the property if the borrower should fail to repay the loan timely and/or appropriately.

1. *The Uniform Commercial Code (UCC):* Article 9 of the UCC applies to the granting of a security interest in personal property.

2. *Time of Granting Security Interest:* A security interest can be given when purchasing personal property or after the property has been purchased.

EXAMPLES: Seymour wants to finance the purchase of a new car from Bright Motors. The lender, First Bank, takes a security interest (lien) against the car title until the loan is repaid in full.

Price owns debt-free a 1957 Corvette. He wants to borrow money for his new business. He could provide the lender a security interest in the Corvette to help secure the loan he wants.

3. *Specific Action Required:* To give a security interest in personal property, the person doing so must make a specific action (the actual granting of a security interest). A purchase by credit does not in itself give the seller any specific rights in the financed property.

EXAMPLES: Summers purchases a refrigerator from Sears on her Sears credit card. No other action is taken by Summers . If she fails to pay her Sears credit card debt, Sears will have no security interest in the refrigerator to repossess it or have a higher claim in bankruptcy court than other general creditors (creditors without a security interest).

Sears has Summers sign a security agreement under the UCC, giving Sears a security interest in the refrigerator that Summers purchases with her Sears credit card. Now Sears has a right of repossession and a higher, secured credit standing in bankruptcy court.

E. Copyrights

A *copyright* is legal protection available to the author of a literary work. A copyright gives the author the exclusive right to use the work subject to certain legally recognized exceptions.

1. *Protection of Rights in Literary Works:* Copyright protection is available to the author of a literary work. A literary work may take various forms.

EXAMPLES: Books, magazines, journals, and newspapers; plays, lectures, and musical compositions; artworks, photographs, and graphic designs; motion pictures and recordings; computer programs and databases; audiovisual displays; and any other verbal or numerical symbols

2. *Protection Is Not Automatic:* The author of a literary work must take certain precautions to qualify for copyright protection.

a. *Release of work:* The author must not allow the work to be released to the public unless it bears an indication of the author's intent to copyright the work.

(1) *Intent:* The intent may consist of the word *copyright,* the year the work is released, and the name of the author.

(2) *Copyright symbol:* The copyright symbol © should be used on all works the author intends to copyright because it is recognized in many countries besides the United States.

b. *Registration of copyright:* To enforce his or her rights fully in court, the author must register the copyright with the Copyright Office in the Library of Congress in Washington, D.C. This requires filing an application form, which is accepted by the Register of Copyrights.

3. *Duration of Copyright Protection:*

a. *Author known:* Copyright protection lasts for the lifetime of the author plus 50 years.

b. *Author unknown:* If the author is unknown or if the work is done under the name of a fictitious person, the duration of copyright protection is 75 years from the date the work was first released to the public (or 100 years from the date the work was created if its creation preceded its release by more than 28 years).

c. *Work created prior to January 1978:* If the work was created before January 1, 1978, its copyright protection is for only 28 years. (An additional 47 years of protection may be applied for on the expiration of the first 25 years.)

4. *Nature of Copyright Protection:* The author of a copyrighted work has the right to the exclusive use of the work subject to certain legal exceptions.

a. *Permission to use copyrighted work:* The holder of a copyright may grant permission to another party to use the copyrighted work. The permission might be obtained in return for the payment of a fee, or it might be granted without payment.

b. *Fair uses of copyrighted work:* The law recognizes certain fair uses as exceptions to the copyright holder's exclusive right to the copyrighted work.

(1) Copying a copyrighted work for purposes of studying it or using it in the course of one's research is permissible.

(2) Using copyrighted material for limited purposes in a classroom for instructing students is permissible if the work is relatively short and it would be impractical to obtain the consent of the copyright holder. If the material is a major part of the class material or if it is used from year to year, the author's consent may be required.

(3) Other fair uses are permitted if they do not affect the potential market for the work or otherwise decrease the value of the work. If there is a question whether a particular use is permitted under copyright laws, a legal expert should be consulted.

5. *Enforcement of Copyrights:* A party who has violated copyright law may be prosecuted for a criminal offense or sued by the copyright holder for damages.

a. *Criminal violation:* In a criminal case, the intentional violator may be fined or imprisoned.

b. *Civil violation:* In a civil suit for damages, the violator will be ordered to pay damages to the copyright holder.

c. *Court orders:*

(1) A court may enter an order directing a party to stop a practice that constitutes a copyright violation. If the party defies the order, he or she will be subject to contempt of court proceedings.

(2) A court may order a party to turn over or destroy all illegal copies of copyrighted material.

d. *Prosecution:* A violator may be prosecuted in a criminal case and sued for damages in another suit for the same violation.

F. Patents

A *patent* is legal protection available to the inventor of a machine, process, product, chemical, a new variety of nonpollinating plant life, or other new useful invention. A patent gives the inventor the right to prevent others from using the patented invention in the United States and its territories and possessions.

1. *Protection of Rights of Inventors:* One who invents or discovers a new process or machine may qualify for patent protection.

EXAMPLES: Patent protection is also available for an inventor who manufactures a new product.

One who discovers a new chemical, a new chemical compound, or a plant may apply for patent protection.

One who invents or discovers useful improvements in existing machines, processes, products, chemicals, or plants may also apply for patent protection.

2. *New and Useful Requirement:* An invention must be new and useful to qualify for a patent.

a. *Known or used:* If the invention has been known or used by others or if it is merely an obvious extension of an existing invention, it does not qualify for a patent.

b. *Nonperformance:* If the invention does not perform the intended purpose or is otherwise not useful, it does not qualify for a patent.

3. *Obtaining a Patent:* To obtain a patent, the inventor must apply to the Patent and Trademark Office in Washington, D.C. The law does not require that the inventor be represented by a lawyer, but it is highly advisable that the inventor obtain expert assistance.

4. *Duration of Patent Protection:* Patent protection lasts for 17 years from the date the patent is granted.

5. *Nature of Patent Protection:* A patent gives the inventor the right to prevent others from making, using, or selling the invention in the United States and its territories and possessions.

   a. *No right to make:* A patent does not give the inventor the right to make, use, or sell the invention. The invention must comply with all relevant state and federal laws.

   EXAMPLE: Foster invented a new kind of lawn mower and obtained a patent for it. The mower, however, does not comply with the standards of the Environmental Protection Agency. Foster cannot legally market the mower unless he complies with all relevant laws. Mere possession of a patent does not give him the right to market the product. It only gives him the right to prevent others from using his invention.

   b. *Outside the United States:* It may be possible to obtain a patent protection in other countries. The United States has entered into a treaty with many other nations for the purpose of making international patent protection easier to obtain. Expert assistance should be obtained to expand patent protection beyond the United States and its territories and possessions.

   c. *Licensing:* The patent holder may grant a license permitting another party to use the invention.

6. *Enforcement of Patent Rights:* A patent holder may sue one who infringes on the patent.

   a. *Stop practice:* The court may enter an order directing a party to stop a practice that constitutes patent infringement. If the party defies the order, it will be subject to contempt of court proceedings.

   b. *Pay damages:* The court may order the infringing party to pay damages to the patent holder.

   c. *Challenge validity:* In a patent-infringement suit, the party being sued may challenge the validity of the patent.

   d. *Countersuit:* One who is threatened with a patent-infringement suit may sue the patent holder to obtain a court ruling on the issue.

   e. *Government use:* The government may use patented inventions without permission from the patent holder. The patent holder is entitled to receive fair compensation, however, for the use of the invention.

G. Trademarks

A *trademark* is a distinctive marking, motto, or device that is placed on products to identify their source.

1. *Qualification as a Trademark:* To qualify as a trademark, the marking, motto, or device must be distinctive and must not be merely descriptive of the product or its use.

   EXAMPLE: The maker of a new soft drink places the words A Refreshing Drink *on its beverage containers. This phrase does not qualify as a trademark because it is descriptive of the product. It would be unfair to prevent competitors from describing their beverages as refreshing drinks. If the phrase was accompanied by a distinctive design, it could, with the design, qualify as a trademark.*

2. *Registration Not Required:* A trademark need not be registered with the government to be protected from infringement. Registration does add to the protection of a trademark, however, by providing proof of the date of the trademark's use.

   EXAMPLE: Two businesses use the same symbol on their products. Each claims the symbol as a trademark. One of the businesses had registered its trademark with the government in 1961. The other never registered the symbol as a trademark and cannot prove that it used the symbol on products prior to that time.

3. *Infringement:* The holder of a trademark is entitled to sue anyone who infringes on it and to recover lost profits and a court order prohibiting further unauthorized use of the trademark.

H. Acquisition of Real Property

Real property is most commonly acquired through purchase, gift, or descent or by adverse possession.

1. *Purchase:* The most common manner in which real property is transferred is through purchase. To complete the purchase of real property, the following are required:

   a. *A writing:* A signed writing (written contract) from the seller is required under the statute of frauds for the sale of real property. The writing should set forth the terms and conditions of sale.

      EXAMPLE: Jenkins orally promises to sell his townhouse to Adams for $125,000. The promise is unenforceable.

   b. *Conveyance by deed:* A deed represents title to real property. It is conveyed from the seller to the buyer at the time of the real estate closing. The type of deed will depend on the seller's promise contained in the contract.

   c. *Recording of deed:* A deed does not become binding on third parties until properly filed in the courthouse of the county where the real property is located. Failure to record the deed properly will permit the seller to continue to have the appearance of ownership (meaning that the seller could resell the property that he or she no longer actually owns).

2. *Gift:* The elements required to make a valid gift are similar to those concerning the gift of personal property except for the requirement to deliver a deed.

3. *Acquisition by Descent:* Real property, like personal property, can be acquired by descent by relatives of a deceased person who dies intestate (without a will). Each state has its own law establishing the order of descent.

4. *Adverse Possession:* The taking of property from another without consent or payment may legally be accomplished by adverse possession. Acquisition by adverse possession must be the following:

   a. *Notorious:* The adverse possessor is actually using the property.

   b. *Open:* The adverse possession is obvious in actual usage. If the usage is not sufficiently visible, adverse possession is not possible.

EXAMPLE: James erects a garage that extends four feet onto his neighbor's property. If no consent and/or objection occurs, the land belongs to James after the number of years set by statute.

c. *Adverse:* The possession is without permission. In essence, the taker by adverse possession is a squatter who is trespassing. Therefore, no adverse possession may occur where the person is present with consent.

EXAMPLE: Allen was a tenant for 23 years in a house owned by Johnson. Allen has no right to the house.

d. *Hostile:* The adverse possessor is a trespasser, using the property without permission of the owner.

e. *Under a claim of right:* The adverse possessor must actually claim ownership over a period of time. The statutory requirement of years of adverse possession before the property may legally be taken varies by state from 5 to 20 years. The "tacking" of years toward meeting this statutory requirement is possible.

EXAMPLE: James (see example in Section B-3-b) lived at his property for 11 years and then sold it to Ellsworth. If the adverse possession period is 20 years total, Ellsworth would have to possess the property only 9 more years.

I. Types of Deeds

Deeds represent the giving of written title from the seller to the buyer. Specific types of deeds include quitclaim deeds, warranty deeds, and special warranty deeds.

1. *Quitclaim Deed:* The grantor (seller) conveys all he or she owns, if anything, in the property.

EXAMPLE: Kelley could give Sheridan a quitclaim deed to the White House. Sheridan would get no legal interest, however, because Kelley does not have any legal interest to give.

a. *No warranties made:* If the grantor owns nothing, the grantee (buyer) receives nothing. If the grantor owns a house and conveys by quitclaim deed, the grantee receives good and rightful title.

b. *Representation of ownership:* The grantor could be independently liable from the deed for misrepresentation or fraud in the inducement concerning false representations of ownership, if any exist.

EXAMPLE: Brooks has no real-property warranty obligations to Edison if she gives Edison a quitclaim deed to a farm that she claims to own but actually does not own and wants to convey to him legally. Brooks may, however, yet face tort liability for fraud.

2. *Warranty Deed:* In essence, a warranty deed represents a warranty by the grantor (the property seller) that the property is transferred free from all unknown defects or claims.

a. *Warranties by grantor:* In the warranty deed, the grantor warrants the following:

(1) That he or she owns the property being transferred

(2) That he or she has the right to convey the property

(3) That the property is free from undisclosed encumbrances such as easements or mortgages

(4) That the grantee's legal right to possession will not be disturbed

(5) That the title to the property is good

EXAMPLE: Carlson acquires Black Acre, a farm, from Roberts by warranty deed. If Roberts did not actually own Black Acre, Carlson would have a right of recovery against Roberts.

b. *Purchaser's knowledge of legal interests:* A purchaser of property is charged with knowledge, whether actually known or not, of any legal interest properly recorded against the property in the county courthouse, any defect in title evident from an inspection of the property being sold, or the zoning.

EXAMPLES: An electric power line runs across the back lot line of Anderson's property. If the power line is evident, the buyer would be charged with knowledge. Thus, a buyer should carefully inspect the property.

If the electric power line (above) was a buried cable, the purchaser of the property would be charged with knowledge of it if the easement (right of passage) was recorded in the county courthouse. Thus, a buyer should carefully inspect the legal title at the county courthouse.

3. *Special Warranty Deeds:* These instruments are also known as bargain and sale deeds. All warranties of the general warranty deed described above are covered. The warranties, however, apply only to the time during which the grantor actually owned the property.

J. Real Property Security Interests

In general, a mortgage represents a nonpossessory interest (lien) in real property that is given to secure a debt. People often confuse mortgages so as to believe that lenders are giving home mortgages. In fact, lenders are lending money that is secured by the real estate, the mortgaged property. Thus, the borrower is the *mortgagor* because he or she is giving a mortgage (interest in the property to secure a loan) to the lender, the *mortgagee.* A mortgage must be in writing because an interest in land is being conveyed. If the mortgagor defaults on the mortgage, not making required payments, a mortgagee may foreclose on the mortgage.

Property that is already subject to a mortgage may be mortgaged again if a lender is willing to take a second mortgage for security. The second mortgage is, of course, junior to the original mortgage. Only if the first mortgage is fully satisfied can the holder of the second mortgage recover anything.

K. Easements

In general, an easement is a nonpossessory interest in the land of another either to use (affirmative easement) or prevent usage (negative easement) in a particular manner.

EXAMPLES: As shown in Figure 26–1, Jerrard has a right to cross Stone's land to reach his cabin on a lake. This right is called an affirmative easement.

Jerrard has the right to receive sunlight crossing Stone's property. This is a negative easement, referring to the prevention of land usage by the grantor in a way detrimental

Figure 26–1 Illustration of Easement

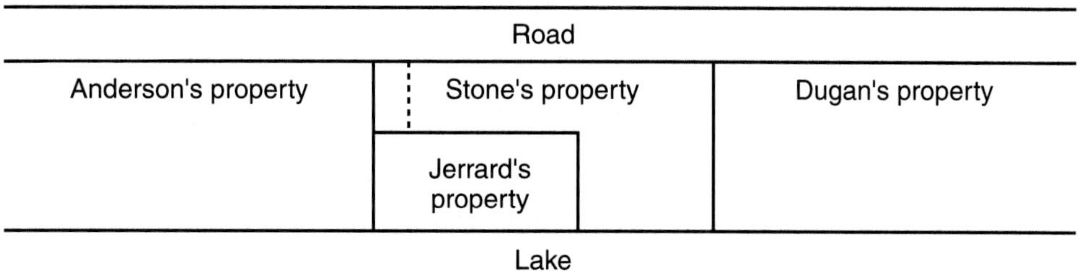

to the grantee. Stone would not be allowed to build a tall structure that would block the sunlight crossing Jerrard's property.

1. *Characteristics of an Easement:*

a. *Nonpossessory:* The easement only provides access across another individual's property.

EXAMPLE: In the example illustrated in Figure 26–1, John may use his access right across Sarah's property but could not erect a garage, plant a garden, or substantially alter the passageway as to usage or size.

b. *Maintenance:* The easement must be maintained by the individual who has the right to use the property.

EXAMPLE: Jerrard must maintain the easement.

c. *Interference:* The property owner may not interfere with the use of the easement.

EXAMPLE: Stone may not interfere with Jerrard's use of the easement passageway.

2. *The Nature of Easements:* The creation of an easement interest may occur in one of three ways:

a. *Express grant or resolution:* This easement must be in writing.

b. *By necessity:* This is possible only where an owner of land divides the land into two or more parcels without providing a means of access. (A buyer is not to be left landlocked by the seller.)

EXAMPLE: If Stone had sold Jerrard his property without mention of any right of passageway across her property, he would still have a legal right because of a necessity (see Figure 26–1).

c. *By prescription:* By continuous adverse passage, the adverse passer secures a right of passage over property of another without consent or payment. Although not an interest in land, this right of passage is achieved in a similar manner as adverse possession of land. The adverse passage must be the following:

(1) *Notorious:* The adverse passer must be actually using the property, and it is publicly known that the adverse passer is doing so.

(2) *Open:* The use of the property must be sufficiently visible.

(3) *Adverse:* The use of the property is without permission of the owner.

(4) *Hostile:* The adverse passer is a trespasser, using the property without the permission of the owner.

EXAMPLE: Hamilton gives Perez permission to go across his property on her horse. Perez can get no adverse passage right (prescriptive easement) as her passage is with Hamilton's consent.

The required number of years necessary to secure a prescriptive easement may be gained by "tacking" as in adverse possession cases. The adverse passer gets the right of passageway, a nonpossessory interest, versus actual possession rights that the adverse possessor gets.

EXAMPLE: If Barnes builds his garage five feet over onto Hogan's property without permission and the required years go by without action by Hogan, Barnes is actually considered to own the five feet. Thereafter, Barnes can do anything with it that one normally can do with land. A prescriptive easement would have given Barnes a right of passageway forever over Hogan's land but not legal title to the land or usage other than passage alone.

3. *Termination of an Easement:*

a. *Lapse:* The termination of time permitted to the passer has occurred.

b. *Abandonment:* Nonusage of the easement has occurred. Generally, abandonment requires an affirmative act besides nonusage.

c. *Merger:* Dominant and servient parcels of land have been united.

EXAMPLE: Stone purchases Jerrard's property.

d. *Misuse of easement:* The easement is being used for an improper purpose.

L. The Landlord-Tenant Relationship

Property owners may lease or rent property to others. A contract known as a lease outlines the conditions of such a relationship. Most states have specific statutes regulating the landlord-tenant relationship. Below appear the general common law rules that have been changed in many places by statutes.

1. *The Nature of the Lease:* A lease is both a contract and a conveyance of *real property.* The *lessee* (the renter) secures possession rights for a given period of time from the *lessor* (the landlord). A lease is not required to be in writing if it will be completed within one year's time. The lease is not terminated by the death of either the lessor or the lessee. A purchaser of a building takes subject to any existing leases.

2. *Types of Leasehold Estates:*

a. *Estate for years:* Tenancy is for a fixed time only, but not necessarily for only one year.

EXAMPLE: A lease of a warehouse for 60 days is an estate for years as a lease for a set period of time.

b. *Periodic tenancies:* Tenancy for a specified period of time, which will continue for similar periods of time until terminated, is known as *periodic tenancy.* Timely notice must be provided to terminate such leases.

EXAMPLE: A month-to-month lease.

c. *Tenancy at sufferance:* This type of tenancy occurs when a tenant holds over (stays) beyond the lease termination date or date otherwise agreed as to the termination date.

3. *Rights of Landlord:*

a. *Rent:* The landlord receives the rent.

b. *Lease term:* If the tenant stays beyond the lease, the landlord may do the following:

(1) Evict the tenant

(2) Treat the tenant as a holdover with period-to-period lease

c. *Abandonment of lease:* If the tenant wrongfully abandons the lease, the landlord may do the following:

(1) Nothing and sue for rent as it comes due, or

(2) Rent the property and hold the tenant liable for any deficiencies in rent money.

Note: In some states, a landlord must show evidence of having tried to rent the lease premises (known as mitigation of damages).

4. *Duties of Landlord to Tenant:*

a. *Implied warranty of habitability:* The landlord must warrant to the tenant that the premises are fit for human occupancy (generally applies only to residential leases).

EXAMPLE: The warranty is breached when the landlord rents an apartment without heat in the winter.

b. *Providing safe common areas:* The landlord must provide safe areas such as stairways and hallways.

c. *Warranty of quiet enjoyment:* The warranty of quiet enjoyment is a warranty to the tenant that the landlord has the legal right to lease out the premises and that the tenant will not be removed without just cause during the term of the lease.

d. *Termination of lease by tenant:* A breach of the landlord's duties does not legally permit the tenant to terminate the lease. Many courts, however, are finding *constructive eviction* where an apartment becomes uninhabitable. In essence, this means that the tenant may move out without further legal duties to the landlord.

5. *Tenant's Transfer of Interest:*

a. *Assignment:* The transfer of a tenant's entire interest in a lease is an assignment.

(1) *Novation:* The original tenant, the assignor, is still liable unless there is a novation from the landlord. *Novation* is the release of a party to a contract in exchange for another being liable.

(2) *Tenant liability:* The new tenant, the assignee, becomes personally liable to the landlord.

b. *Sublease:* The transfer of less than the tenant's entire interest to the sublettor is known as a sublease.

(1) *Tenant liability:* As in assignment, the assignor (the original tenant) is still liable on the lease.

(2) *Binding terms:* The assignee is not personally liable to the landlord for a sublease. The terms and conditions of the lease are still binding on the assignee, however.

A landlord may prohibit either subleasing or assignment, or both, if so stipulated in the lease. If just subleasing is prohibited, however, the tenant may still assign the lease and vice versa.

EXAMPLE: Garcia's lease prohibits her from assigning the lease to her apartment. She is not prohibited from subleasing, however.

Review Questions

Directions: Select the best answer from the four alternatives. Write your answer in the blank to the left of the number.

______________ **1.** In making a valid intervivos gift, the donor must

a. have present donative intent.
b. reserve the property for the donee.
c. be fearful of imminent death.
d. make the gift through a will or trust.

______________ **2.** Copyright protection may be obtained for which one of the following original works?

a. A newly developed production process
b. A chemical discovered for use in dental care
c. Photographs
d. A motto developed for a specific product

______________ **3.** Copyright protection lasts for

a. 17 years.
b. 50 years.
c. life of the author plus 50 years.
d. forever.

______________ **4.** Thomas invented a new engine for automobiles that makes it possible to get 73 miles per gallon. Thomas was granted a patent by the Patent and Trademark Office in Washington, D.C. When Thomas attempted to sell cars with his new engine in them, however, he was informed by the Environmental Protection Agency that the engine did not conform to the applicable standards. Thomas claims that the patent permits him to sell the engines. Is Thomas correct?

a. Yes, because patent law prevails over other applicable regulations.
b. Yes, because patent law prevails over administrative agency regulations but not over other federal legislation.
c. No, because patent laws merely give the inventor the right to prevent others from using the invention.
d. No, because he should have obtained copyright protection.

______________ **5.** Patent protection lasts for

a. 17 years.
b. 50 years.
c. the inventor's life plus 50 years.
d. the inventor's life plus 17 years.

______________ **6.** Simmons obtained a patent on a new ballpoint pen she invented. She discovered Hoffman making and selling similar pens without permission. Simmons sued Hoffman. Which of the following is true?

a. In the suit Hoffman may not challenge the validity of Simmons' patent.
b. The court may order Hoffman to stop making and selling the pens if he is found to be violating Simmons' patent rights.
c. The court may order Hoffman to pay damages to Simmons whether or not he is found to be violating Simmons' patent rights.
d. Simmons can only collect damages if her business has suffered as a result of Hoffman's sales of the pens.

______________ **7.** Archer and her niece Stewart were passengers on an airplane. The pilot announced that the plane had run out of gas and that an emergency landing would be attempted. Archer began crying and removed her diamond ring and gave it to Stewart saying, "Here, this is for you. I'm going to be dead in a few minutes." The plane made a miraculous landing, and Archer suffered only a sprained ankle. Stewart refuses to return the ring. Which of the following statements is true?

a. Stewart is entitled to keep the ring because the gift was completed.
b. Stewart is entitled to keep the ring because the ring was mislaid property.
c. Archer is entitled to the return of the ring because it was a gift in contemplation of death.
d. Archer is entitled to the return of the ring because it was a fixture.

______________ **8.** Howard signs a 10-year lease for a building with Anderson. Howard agrees in the lease not to assign it. The lease could be terminated if

a. Howard dies.
b. Anderson sells the building to Quincy.
c. Howard sublets the building to Morkle.
d. Howard assigns the lease without permission.

______________ **9.** Fitzpatrick has a year's lease with Malone, the landlord. Craig has agreed to take over Fitzpatrick's lease, and Malone has agreed to release Fitzpatrick from his lease obligations.

a. Fitzpatrick received a novation.
b. Fitzpatrick would not have been liable any longer to Malone regardless of her release.
c. Craig would not have been personally liable on the lease if Fitzpatrick had not been released.
d. This is an example of a sublet.

______________ **10.** Cross just purchased a cabin on a lake from Milton. Although there was a passageway to the highway via Milton's property, Milton had traveled the old hunter's path across Jackson's property. Jackson has now erected a barrier across this passageway.

a. Since Cross would not have used the hunter's path for sufficient time, no prescriptive easement could exist.
b. If Cross's own passageway got washed out, he could use Jackson's path because of necessity.

c. Milton could have gained a prescriptive easement only if he was an adverse passer.
d. A prescriptive easement would have to be in writing to be effective.

______________ **11.** Which one of the following must be created by a writing, if created by an express grant?

a. An easement
b. A six-month lease
c. The purchase of a new suit
d. A causa mortis gift

______________ **12.** A six-month lease is an example of

a. periodic tenancy.
b. tenancy at sufferance.
c. estate for years.
d. an easement.

______________ **13.** Which one of the following actually represents legal title to property (meaning ownership of the property)?

a. A contract to sell the property
b. An easement to cross the property
c. A deed received at closing
d. Title insurance

______________ **14.** Assuming that you have the choice about which deed you will receive from a seller, your best choice would be

a. a quitclaim deed.
b. a general warranty deed (sometimes simply called *warranty deed*).
c. a special warranty deed.
d. an implied warranty deed.

______________ **15.** All of the terms listed below are elements of adverse possession, *except*

a. notorious.
b. open.
c. hostile.
d. permission.

______________ **16.** Cindy and David Brix, newlyweds, are buying their first home together from Ben Smith, who is being transferred to a new location. Cindy and David are to receive a special warranty deed. This means that

a. defects in title prior to Ben Smith's ownership will not be covered.
b. it is likely that defects existed prior to Ben Smith's ownership.
c. their deed will be considered more valuable than both a general warranty deed and a quitclaim deed.
d. the deed ensures the same ownership interest as if a quitclaim deed had been received.

_______________ **17.** Real property can be acquired through

a. novation.
b. leasing.
c. adverse possession.
d. easement.

Use the following information in answering Questions 18 to 20.

Bates invented a low-calorie chocolate candy formula. He called it Light Chocolate. He also wrote a book describing his seven-year ordeal in developing and perfecting the formula.

_______________ **18.** If Bates wants to apply for legal protection of his new formula, he should apply for

a. copyright protection.
b. patent protection.
c. trademark protection.
d. civil rights protection.

_______________ **19.** If Bates wants to obtain maximum legal protection for the term *Light Chocolate* that will appear on his product, he should apply for

a. copyright protection.
b. trademark protection.
c. patent protection.
d. civil rights protection.

_______________ **20.** If Bates wants to obtain maximum legal protection for his book, he should apply for

a. copyright protection.
b. trademark protection.
c. patent protection.
d. civil rights protection.

Solutions

Answer	*Refer to:*
1. (a)	[C-2-b(3)] A valid intervivos gift is one made during the donor's lifetime. The donor must have present donative intent.
2. (c)	[E-1] Photographs are one category of original works protected by copyrights.
3. (c)	[E-3] Copyright protection lasts for the life of the author plus 50 years.
4. (c)	[F-1, F-5] The inventor must still comply with all other applicable laws and regulations. Patent protection only allows the inventor to prevent others from using the invention.
5. (a)	[F-4] Patent protection lasts for 17 years.
6. (b)	[F-6] If Hoffman is found to be infringing on Simmons' patent, the court may order Hoffman to stop making and selling the pens.
7. (c)	[C-2-c] A gift made in contemplation of death is canceled if the donor does not die as he or she anticipated. Since Archer survived, the gift is canceled, and she is entitled to the return of the ring.
8. (d)	[L-5] A lease that restricts assignment can be terminated by the landlord if the tenant assigns the lease without the landlord's approval.
9. (a)	[L-5-a] Fitzpatrick received a novation when Malone agreed to release him and look only to Craig.
10. (c)	[K-2-c] To gain a prescriptive easement, one must be an adverse passer, not having consent. There may be "tacking," the adding of the years Milton used the property to Cross's time. To tack, there must not have been any interruption of usage.
11. (a)	[L-1] A writing is not required for the lease because it will be completed within one year's time nor for the purchase of clothes. A causa mortis gift may be orally presented. An express grant easement must be in writing.
12. (c)	[L-2-a] A lease for a stated duration is an *estate for years* even though it may be less than a year in length.
13. (c)	[I] A deed represents the seller's passing of ownership to the buyer. The buyer records the deed in the courthouse for the county where the property is located to give official notice to third parties.

14. (b) [I-2] A general warranty deed, often simply called a warranty deed, provides the greatest protection to the buyer and is the most respected by lenders.

15. (d) [H-4] No adverse possession may occur where the person is present with consent.

16. (a) [I-3] The special warranty deed operates exactly like the warranty deed except that it applies only to the time during which the grantor actually owned the property.

17. (c) [C] Real property can be acquired by adverse possession. Novation and leasing refer to property rental. An easement merely assures passageway over someone else's property.

18. (b) [F-1] Patent protection includes protection to the inventor of a process, product, or chemical.

19. (b) [G-1] Trademark protection is available for distinctive markings or slogans attached to products to identify their source.

20. (a) [E-1] Copyright protection is available for literary works.

Glossary

Absolute advantage The ability of one country to produce a commodity at a cost lower than that of other countries. (5)[1]

Accelerated depreciation method A depreciation method that assigns a larger amount of depreciation expense to the earlier years of an asset's useful life than to its later years. (13)

Acceptance A clear expression of agreement to the terms of the offer by the offeree to the offeror. (21)

Account A device used to collect and summarize information. (7)

Account balance The difference between the total debits and total credits recorded in an account. (7)

Accounting The process of recording, measuring, summarizing, analyzing, and interpreting financial information and communicating this information to various users. (6)

Accounting cycle All the procedures performed during an accounting period, including analyzing and recording transactions, posting, taking a trial balance, preparing a worksheet, preparing financial statements, journalizing and posting adjusting entries, closing the temporary accounts, and taking a post-closing trial balance. (9)

Accounting entity Any business, individual, or not-for-profit organization whose financial affairs can be viewed as being distinct from those of any other entity or unit. (6)

Accounting equation Assets = liabilities + owners' equity or, stated another way, assets − liabilities = owners' equity. (7)

Accounts payable The account used for recording the liabilities a company has incurred for goods or services purchased on credit for use in its business. (7)

Accounts receivable The account used to record the right a company has to collect payment for sales made on open account. (7)

Accrual The concept that states that revenues should be reported when earned rather than when cash is received and that expenses should be reported when incurred rather than when paid. (7)

[1]The number in parentheses after each entry indicates the chapter location in the text.

Ad valorem "According to value"; tariff rates based on the value of the commodity (a percentage of the invoice value, not on weight or quantity). (5)

Adjusting entries A journal entry made at the end of an accounting period to bring an account balance to the correct amount. (9)

Administrative agency A subdivision of the government with expertise and jurisdiction to regulate a specialized area of government operation. (25)

Administrative law judge An official who hears cases brought by an administrative agency. (25)

Adverse possession The taking of real property belonging to another, without consent or payment, by notorious, adverse, open, hostile, or continuous possession for a period of years, often 10 to 20 years. (26)

Age Discrimination in Employment Act of 1967 (ADEA) The law prohibiting employment discrimination by employers with 19 or more employees on the basis of age for persons age 40 or over in the hiring, compensation, working conditions, and privileges of employment. (4, 25)

Agency A relationship in which one party acts for and on behalf of another party. (23)

Agent One who has authority to act for and on behalf of another party (the principal). (23)

Aggregate demand (aggregate expenditures) The total amount consumers, business, government, and foreign countries spend in the economy. (2)

Aggregate supply The amount of goods and services that the economy will make available at various price levels. (2)

Aging of accounts receivable A method of estimating the amount of the allowance for uncollectible accounts and bad debt expense when individual accounts are grouped according to the length of time they have been outstanding. The amount of uncollectible accounts is then estimated for each group. (14)

Allowance for uncollectible accounts Contra-account to the accounts receivable account used for reporting accounts receivable that is estimated to be uncollectible. (8)

Americans with Disabilities Act (ADA) The extension of the Civil Rights Act of 1964 that first became effective in 1992 to provide public services, building codes, and employment accommodations for physically and mentally disabled individuals. (4, 25)

Amortization The systematic writing off of the balance in an account as an expense over a period of time; usually associated with intangible asset accounts. (14)
Antitrust laws A set of laws designed to control monopolistic practices and monopoly power. (4)
Apparent authority Authority that a third party reasonably believes an agent possesses based on circumstances that the principal has allowed to exist, even though the agent in fact does not have the express or implied authority. (23)
Appropriated retained earnings Retained earnings that have been segregated into two or more separate accounts to inform the financial statement reader that a portion of retained earnings is not available for the payment of dividends. (16)
Articles of incorporation The legal framework of a new corporation that is filed with the state at the time of incorporation. (24)
Assets Economic resources from which an entity can expect to receive benefits now or in the future; a thing of value owned. (1) Economic resources from which an entity (owner) can expect to receive benefits now or in the future. (6, 7)
Assignee One to whom an assignment is made. (21)
Assignment A transfer of a contractual right to one who is not a party to the original contract. (21)
Assignor One who makes an assignment. (21)
Audit (independent external) An examination of the financial statements of an entity by an independent accountant to determine the fairness of the financial statements. The accounting records are referred to in assessing the fairness of the financial statements. (6)
Authority The power granted to an agent by a principal to enter into contracts. (23)
Authorized shares of capital stock The number of shares of capital stock that may legally be sold as indicated in the corporate charter. (16)
Available-for-sale securities Investments in debt or equity securities that are not classified as held-to-maturity or trading securities. (11)
Average propensity to consume (APC) The level of consumption divided by the level of income. (2)
Balance of payments An international summary of all economic and financial transactions between one nation and the rest of the world for one year. (5)
Balance sheet A financial statement that shows the financial position of an entity as of a specific time. Although *balance sheet* is the common term for this financial statement, the formal title is the *statement of financial position.* (8)
Bank reconciliation A report that explains the difference between the balance per the bank statement and the balance per the general ledger cash account. (10)
Bearer One who is in possession of a negotiable instrument. (22)
Bearer bonds Bonds that are not registered in the name of the owner and are assumed to be owned by the individual who possesses the bonds; also known as *coupon bonds.* (15)
Bilateral contract A contract in which the parties make a bargained-for exchange of promises. (21)
Bona fide occupational qualification (BFOQ) In limited situations, an employer is permitted to discriminate on the basis of gender, religion, or national origin if any of these characteristics are required as occupational qualifications. (25)
Bond A debt security issued by the government or a corporation to raise large sums of money. The bond is issued in stated dollar denominations with a stated interest rate and maturity date. The most commonly stated dollar value is $1,000. (11)
Bond discount The difference between the face value of a bond and the amount it sells for when the bond sells for less than its face value. (11)
Bond premium The difference between the face value of a bond and the amount it sells for when the bond sells for more than its face value. (11)
Bond sinking fund An investment fund established to ensure that sufficient funds are available to retire the bonds at maturity. (15)
Bonds payable Long-term liabilities consisting of securities normally issued in stated denominations with a stated interest rate and maturity date. There are numerous types of bonds. (8)
Bookkeeping The record-keeping phase of accounting. (6)
Book value or carrying value The original cost of an operational asset less the accumulated depreciation related to that asset. (8) A numerical measure of the net assets of a corporation as reflected in a single share of common stock. (16)
Breach of contract A failure by a party to a contract to perform the obligations imposed by the terms of the agreement. (21)
Breakeven point The point where a company has zero profit or loss (total revenues for the company equal total expenses). (19)
Budget A detailed plan that shows proposed acquisitions of financial resources and uses of financial resources during a period of time. (19)

Built-in stabilizers Automatic forces that moderate fluctuations in business cycles and the level of inflation and unemployment. (2)
Bylaws Regulations of the corporation that govern internal management and day-to-day operational structure. (24)
Callable bonds Bonds with a provision stating that the issuer may redeem the bonds prior to maturity by payment of a stipulated call price. (15)
Callable preferred stock Preferred stock that may be redeemed by the issuing corporation at a stipulated call price, usually slightly higher than the issue price. (16)
Capital Those human-made resources that are used in the production of other goods and services; capital should not be confused with monetary capital (money value of capital goods). (1)
Capital assets Any property a taxpayer holds that is not listed in Section 1221 of the U.S. Internal Revenue Code. Section 1221 property includes inventory, accounts receivable, and depreciable property or real estate used in a business. Examples of capital assets are investments in stocks, bonds, or real estate that are not used in a trade or business. (17)
Capital consumption allowance The use of part of the output to replace the capital goods that were used (consumed) during the production of other goods and services. (2)
Capital gain A short- or long-term gain resulting from the disposition of a capital asset. (17)
Capital loss A short- or long-term loss resulting from the disposition of a capital asset. (17)
Capital stock Ownership of a corporation as evidenced by shares of capital stock. Capital stock is also the title of the account used to record the total investment in shares of stock of a corporation. (7)
Cash Coins, paper money, checks, money orders, and money on deposit in bank accounts. (10)
Cash disbursements journal A special journal used to record all payments of cash. (10)
Cash discount A reduction in the total amount due on an invoice offered if the invoice is paid within a designated period of time. (10)
Cash flow statement A financial report that accounts for the increase or decrease in a company's cash during a period by showing where the company received cash and the uses made of the cash. (18)
Cash receipts journal A special journal used to record receipts of cash. (10)
Cashier's check A check drawn by a bank on itself. (22)
Casualty insurance Insurance coverage that is primarily for the liability of a party that results from negligent acts or omissions resulting in bodily injury and/or property damage to another party. (14)
Certified check A check for which the depositor's bank guarantees that the depositor has enough funds in the bank account to cover the check when it is presented for payment. (10)
Ceteris paribus A Latin phrase meaning "other things being equal." (2)
Check register The form of the cash disbursements journal used in conjunction with a voucher system in which all checks issued are recorded. (10)
Civil law Law pertaining to private, as opposed to public, rights. (20)
Civil Rights Act of 1964 This act created the Federal Fair Employment Practice Law covering all industries involved in interstate commerce. The fair employment practice law bars discrimination by employers, unions, employment agencies, and others on the basis of race, color, gender, religion, or national origin. (4)
Classical school of economics Pioneered by Adam Smith, David Ricardo, and Alfred Marshall, the classical school of economic thought advocates concepts such as economic freedom of choice and private property and the general principle that individuals in a society are more prosperous without government intervention into the economy. (2)
Closing entry A journal entry made at the end of an accounting period that transfers the balance of a temporary account to the owners' equity or retained earnings account. (9)
Co-insurance A provision in some insurance contracts that requires the insured party to insure property for at least a specified minimum percentage of its fair market value or to share the loss proportionately with the insurance company. (14)
Command economy A type of economic system in which the basic decisions of what, how, and for whom to produce are answered by an individual or small group of individuals. (1)
Common law A vast body of law, consisting of decided case law, that includes the case law and custom of England prior to the American Revolution to the extent that it has not been expressly superseded or overruled by cases or laws of the United States. Common law includes all published opinions of courts in the United States. (20) A vast body of recorded cases that have been decided by courts (past decisions). (21)

Common market (European Economic Community) An economic, social, and political organization of some of the European countries (Belgium, England, France, Germany, Greece, Italy, Luxembourg, the Netherlands, and Spain). (5)

Common stock A classification of capital stock that has no preferences relative to the corporation's other classes of stock. Common stockholders have rights to all residual assets left after the claims of creditors and preferred stockholders have been met. (8) Stock that represents ownership in a corporation. Each share of stock may earn a dividend only after all corporate obligations, including those to owners of preferred stock, are satisfied. (24)

Comparative advantage A principle that explains why one country would specialize in producing certain goods and importing others rather than producing all goods domestically. (5)

Comparative financial statements Financial reports that show financial data for a series of years in adjacent columns for comparison. (18)

Complementary goods Goods that are used together (e.g., tennis balls and tennis rackets). (1)

Compound interest The calculation of interest on the principal of a security and on any interest that has been earned but has not yet been paid. (15)

Compound tariff A tariff based both on ad valorem and physical units; increases the price of the foreign good in the country imposing the tariff. (5)

Comprehensive income All changes in owners' equity during a period except those that result from investments by or distributions to owners. (8)

Conflict of interest A conflict between personal interest and the official responsibilities of a person in a position of trust, such as an agent. (23)

Consent decree An agreement whereby the defendant admits no guilt but agrees to pay damages, cease an action, and/or other remedial action. (26)

Conservatism The principle that requires that the accounting method that is least likely to overstate income and financial position be used. (6)

Consideration The bargained-for exchange of something of value; an essential element of an enforceable contract. (21)

Consistency The principle that requires that once an accounting or reporting method is selected, it should be used from one period to another. (6)

Consolidated statements The combination of two or more accounting entities into one entity for financial reporting purposes. This is done when one entity possesses a controlling interest over the other entity or entities. (11)

Constitutional law Law derived from the United States Constitution and the Bill of Rights. (20)

Consumer price index (CPI) The most common price index created to measure changes in the cost of living of households throughout the years by comparing the cost to purchase a "typical market basket" of commodities by households. (2)

Consumerism A movement for the enhancement of consumer welfare; corporations and other organizations need to consider the interests of consumers and general public interests as well as those of stockholders. (4)

Consumption The act of using goods and services to satisfy wants and needs. (1) The expenditure incurred by households for final goods and services that yield direct satisfaction to consumers. (2)

Contingent liability A potential liability that could become an actual liability only if certain events occur. (14)

Contra-asset account An account that is related to a specific asset account and has a credit balance. Contra-assets are reported as deductions from the related asset on the balance sheet. Allowance for uncollectible accounts and accumulated depreciation are examples of contra-asset accounts. (8)

Contract A legally enforceable agreement. (21)

Contract rate The fixed interest rate paid by a bank. (11)

Contractual capacity The ability to understand the subject matter and consequences of an agreement; only adults are presumed to possess this kind of capacity. (21)

Contribution margin Sales minus variable expenses. (19)

Control account An account with a balance representing the total of all the account balances of a related subsidiary ledger. (10)

Convertible bond A bond with a provision allowing the holder to convert the bond into common stock of the issuing company. (15)

Convertible preferred stock Preferred stock that may be exchanged by the stockholder for a predetermined number of shares of common stock. (16)

Copyright Legal protection available to the author of a literary work. A copyright gives the author the exclusive right to use the work subject to certain legally recognized exceptions. (26)

Corporation A business entity that is created by state or federal law and has a separate legal existence from that of its owners. (6, 24)

Cost behavior Changes in a cost when changes occur in the output of goods or services. (19)
Cost of goods sold The cost of merchandise sold to customers shown as a deduction from sales on the income statement to arrive at gross margin (gross profit). (8)
Cost-push inflation Price increases caused by increases in the cost of the factors of production. (2)
Credit An entry recorded on the right side of an account. (7)
Criminal law Law that defines offenses against the government (representing all of society) and provides penal sanctions for violators. (20)
Cumulative preferred stock Preferred stock with a provision that any dividends not paid in one period must be made up before any current dividends may be paid to preferred or common shareholders. (16)
Currency Coins and printed paper used as money (medium of exchange), stamped by a government to certify their value. (3)
Current assets Those assets expected to be used in the operations of an entity within its operating cycle or one year, whichever is longer. (8)
Current liabilities Obligations of a business that are due to be paid within the next operating cycle or one year, whichever is longer. (8)
Cyclical unemployment A type of unemployment caused by declines in the business cycle that exist when people who are willing and able to work at prevailing wage rates are jobless. (2)
Debenture An unsecured bond backed only by the general credit of the company. (15)
Debit An entry recorded on the left side of an account. (7)
Delegation A transfer of one's contractual obligation to another party. (21)
Demand The quantity of goods or services that individuals will buy at various prices within a given time period. (1)
Demand-pull inflation (inflationary gap) Increase in the price level caused by excessive aggregate demand for goods and services when the level of employment is near full employment. (2)
Depletion The amount a natural resource is reduced due to usage (e.g., cutting timber, mining ore, or pumping oil). (13)
Deposits in transit Bank deposits that have been recorded on the books of the depositor but have not yet been received and recorded by the bank. (10)
Depreciation The systematic and rational allocation of the original cost of an asset over its expected useful life. (8)
Direct labor All labor performed by employees directly involved in production. (19)
Direct materials Raw materials that become a part of the company's end product and can be identified easily with that end product. (19)
Direct write-off method A method of recording bad debt expense that does not use an allowance for uncollectible accounts or attempt to match bad debt expense with related revenue. When an account is determined to be uncollectible, an entry is made to debit bad debt expense and credit accounts receivable. This method does not conform to GAAP. (14)
Disaffirmance An expression by a person lacking contractual capacity of an intent not to be bound by the terms of an agreement. (21)
Disclosed principal A principal whose identity is known to the third party with whom the principal's agent deals. (23)
Discount rate The rate at which member banks can borrow from the Federal Reserve System. (3)
Discounting of a note receivable The selling of a note receivable to a bank for cash. The seller remains contingently liable for payment of the note if the maker defaults. (14)
Discrimination Equals are treated unequally, or unequals are treated equally. (4)
Disposable personal income (DPI) The amount of income available to households for buying consumer goods, saving (personal income minus taxes), and paying interest. (2)
Divestiture A court order that a corporation divest (sell) some of its particular operations and/or assets. (25)
Dividend A distribution of assets by a corporation to its owners (stockholders). (7)
Dividends in arrears Dividends earned on cumulative preferred stock that have not yet been declared. (16)
Double-declining-balance depreciation (DDB) An accelerated depreciation method that uses a depreciation rate that is twice the straight-line rate. (13)
Double-entry accounting The recording of an equal amount of debits and credits in the accounts for an accounting transaction; also called the duality concept. (7)
Draft A negotiable instrument that contains an unconditional order by the drawer, directing another party to pay a certain sum of money. (22)

Drawee A party who is ordered by the drawer of a draft to pay a certain sum of money to a payee. (22)
Drawer One who issues a check or other draft. (22)
Duress The use of a wrongful threat that causes a person to enter into an agreement that the person would otherwise have rejected. (21)
Earnings per share The amount of net income earned per share of common stock during an accounting period. (8)
Easement The right of a nonowner to use a piece of land in a specific way (affirmative) or to prevent the owner from using his or her own land in a specific way (negative). (26)
Economic efficiency The production of goods and services in the most efficient (least costly) manner. (1)
Economic equity The distribution of resources in society and the degree of equality that is proper for the distribution of resources and income. (1)
Economic freedom The ability of individuals to choose how to use income to buy goods and services that they need or want and use owned resources in the production process. (1)
Economic growth An increase in the output of goods and services per capita over a period of time. (1) An increase in the per capita output of an economy. (2)
Economic security The absence of fear of losing possessions as a result of unexpected events. (1)
Economics of pollution A study to evaluate and compare the cost of pollution and benefits of controls to individuals, firms, and institutions in society. (4)
Economic stability The existence of low rates of inflation (price increases) and low rates of unemployment within a society. (1)
Elasticity The degree of responsiveness of buyers (sellers) to changes in the price of a commodity. (1)
Embargo The prohibition of shipping to or receiving products from a country. (5)
Emergency authority A type of implied authority that exists during a sudden, unexpected happening or unforeseen combination of circumstances that requires immediate action. (23)
Employee An employed person without legal authority to bind the employer; an agent may be, but need not be, an employee. (23)
Employee Retirement Income Security Act (ERISA) A federal pension law; an employer is not required to have a pension plan for employees, but ERISA applies if the employer does have a pension plan for employees. (25)
Employment discrimination Workplace decisions based on race, color, gender, religion, national origin, age, or disabilities that affect employed individuals adversely. (25)
Entrepreneur One who owns and assumes the risk of running a business for the purpose of making a profit. (1)
Entrepreneurial ability The ability and risk taken to organize the factors of production (land, labor, and capital) to produce goods in such a way as to make a profit. (1)
Environmental Protection Agency (EPA) A federal agency founded in 1970 to develop and enforce standards for clean air and water and establish standards to control pollution of any sort. (4)
Equal Employment Opportunity Act of 1972 A series of amendments to the Civil Rights Act of 1964; the most significant amendment created the Equal Employment Opportunity Commission (EEOC). (4)
Equal Employment Opportunity Commission (EEOC) The administrative agency that oversees the enforcement of Title VII of the Civil Rights Act and other employment discrimination laws. (4, 25)
Equal Pay for Equal Work Act An amendment to the Fair Labor Standards Act that requires equal pay for women who are performing work substantially equal to that of men; also known as the *Equal Pay Act.* (25)
Equilibrium price The price at which the quantity demanded and the quantity supplied are equal. (1)
Equity method A method used to account for investments in common stock where the investor has significant influence over the operations of the investee. (11)
Estimation Much of what is included in financial reports is the result of an estimate. (6)
Estoppel A party to a lawsuit will be precluded (stopped) from raising a defense. (24)
Excess reserves The amount of reserves that are held by a commercial bank in excess of the legally required reserves. (3)
Executive branch The president or governor and the administrative agencies thereunder (the bureaucracy). (25)
Executive order A law issued by the president of the United States. (20)
Expenses The costs of goods and services consumed (used up) by an entity as a result of earning revenue. (7)
Explicit costs Costs incurred by business for which direct monetary payment is made. (1)

Express authority Authority granted by the principal to an agent in words, whether they be written or oral. (23)
Express contract A contract in which the agreement is put into words, either written or oral. (21)
External financial reports The standard financial reports (balance sheet, income statement, and statement of cash flows) issued by entities primarily for the use of decision makers other than the management of the entity. (6)
External users Users of accounting information who are not part of the management of the company (e.g., bankers, creditors, and investors). (6)
Extraordinary repairs Repairs that either increase the service life of an asset or change the quality of service provided by the asset. (13)
Factors of production Land, labor, capital, and entrepreneurial ability; the resources used to produce other goods and services. (1) Land (land and raw materials), labor, capital, and entrepreneurial ability. (2)
Fair Labor Standards Act Legislation, known as the Wage and Hour Law, that established the requirements for an employer to pay employees a minimum wage and "time and a half" for overtime worked over 40 hours per week; provided for limited use of children in employment. (25)
Fair use Legally recognized exceptions to copyright protection that allow those other than the copyright holder to use the copyrighted work for certain limited purposes. (26)
Federal Aviation Administration (FAA) An agency chartered to provide for the regulation and promotion of civil aviation in such a manner as to best foster its development and safety and to provide for the safe and efficient use of the air space by both civil and military aircraft. (4)
Federal Deposit Insurance Corporation (FDIC) A government insurance institution that guarantees the payment of the amount deposited in banks (up to $100,000) to the depositor in case of the bank's failure. (3)
Federal Food and Drug Administration (FDA) An agency established in 1930 by federal legislation to develop standards and conduct research with respect to reliability and safety of drugs, evaluate new drug reaction programs, establish a nationwide network of poison control, and advise the Department of Justice on the results of its research. (4)
Federal Housing Administration (FHA) The government agency that helps finance housing projects for low-income families and makes loans available to families at lower-than-market interest rates. (3)
Federal Power Commission (FPC) A government agency established in 1930 to regulate interstate operation of private utilities in matters of their issuance of securities, rates, and location of sites. (4)
Federal reserve note A paper bill issued by a Federal Reserve Bank that is not backed by any commodity. (3)
Federal Reserve System (FED) The network of 12 Federal Reserve banks in the United States responsible for the regulation of most nationally chartered financial institutions and the regulation of the country's money supply. (3)
Federal Trade Commission (FTC) A national agency created in 1914 whose main tasks are to promote free and fair competition by prevention of price-fixing agreements, boycotts, and unlawful price discrimination. (4, 26)
Felony A crime punishable by one year or more of incarceration. (20)
FICA tax The Federal Insurance Contributions Act (FICA) tax paid by both employer and employee; commonly called social security tax. (17)
Fidelity bond Insurance that guarantees that the insurance company will pay for losses of money or property that result from the dishonest acts of bonded employees. (14)
FIFO The *first-in first-out* method of valuing inventory that assumes that the earliest units purchased are sold first and that ending inventory is made up of the latest purchases. (12)
Financing activities Transactions with the company's owners and long-term creditors. (18)
Fiscal policy Policy implemented to affect consumption, investment, or level of government spending. (2)
Fixed assets Long-lived assets used in the operations of the business and not held for sale to customers. (8)
Fixed costs Costs that remain constant in total despite changes in the volume of output. (19)
Fixture Personal property so attached to real property as to become a part thereof (e.g., paneling in a family room or a built-in dishwasher. (26)
Forecasting The prediction of a value of a variable in the future. (19)
Foreign exchange rate A rate at which the currency of one country can be exchanged for the currency of another country. (5)

Formal contract A contract that complies with a specific form required by law for contracts of that particular type. (21)

Fraud A misstatement or misrepresentation of a material fact made with knowledge of its falsity. (23)

Frictional unemployment People in the labor force who are unemployed as a result of changing jobs, entering the labor force, or being laid off seasonally. (2)

Full disclosure The accounting principle that requires all information that may be relevant to decision makers to be included in the financial statements. (6)

Gains Revenues generated from an activity that is not part of the normal operations of the business. (8)

GDP implicit price deflator index An index computed once a year using the prices of all goods and services produced in the United States to present the most accurate measure of price increases. (2)

General agent An agent who is authorized to represent the principal in a number of transactions over a period of time. (23)

Generally accepted accounting principles (GAAP) The standards governing the recording and reporting of information published in external financial statements. (6)

Geographic specialization A situation whereby natural resources, geographic location, climate, or market conditions of a certain region of a country might create certain advantages to producing a certain good or goods. (5)

Going concern The assumption that an entity will exist for an indefinite period of time. (6)

Goods Tangible personal property. (21)

Gratuitous assignment An assignment made without consideration. (21)

Gresham's law When two kinds of money of equal commodity value but of unequal use value are in circulation, the one of lesser use value tends to drive the one of better use value out of circulation. (3)

Gross domestic product (GDP) The market value of the nation's total output of new final goods and services within a period of time (usually one year). (2)

Gross margin (or gross profit) The amount that remains after deducting the cost of goods sold from sales of goods. (8)

Gross profit method A method of inventory estimation based on the use of past gross profit ratios experienced by the company. (12)

Historical cost The concept that assets should be recorded at their original purchase cost. (6)

Holder One who possesses an instrument that is issued or indorsed to that person or is payable to the bearer. (22)

Holder in due course A holder who has given value for an instrument and has taken it in good faith without knowledge of any defect. (22)

Illusory promise A promise that does not impose an enforceable obligation on the promisor. (21)

Imperfect competition The production environment in which one of the four conditions for perfect competition is not met; imperfect competition typically results in higher prices and less production than under perfect competition. (1)

Implicit costs The value of resources used by businesses for which direct payment is not made because resources are owned by entrepreneurs. (1)

Implied authority Authority to do those things that are reasonably necessary to exercise the express authority of an agent and to achieve the objectives of the agency. (23)

Implied contract A contract in which the parties' agreement is expressed by their conduct instead of by their words. (21)

Import quota A maximum limit imposed on the amount or value of imports to protect an industry and its workers. (5)

Import tariff A set of taxes imposed on the importation of foreign goods on behalf of national interest. (5)

Income statement A financial report that summarizes the operations of the business resulting in revenues, expenses, gains, and losses over an accounting period. (8)

Independent contractor One who is retained to achieve desired results and who is given substantial freedom in deciding the manner to be used to accomplish the objective. An agent may be, but need not be, an independent contractor. (23)

Indorsee One who receives an indorsed instrument. (*Note:* the word *endorse* is commonly used in business. The word *indorse* is used in the UCC.) (22)

Indorsement without recourse An indorsement in which the indorser disclaims liability in the event that the maker or drawer fails to pay. (22)

Indorser A payee who transfers an instrument by signing it and delivering it to an indorsee. (22)

Inelastic demand A large change in price resulting in a small change in quantity bought. (1)

Inelastic supply A large change in price resulting in a small change in quantity supplied. (1)

Inflation The increase in prices of all goods and services. (2)

Infringement Illegal use of patented or copyrighted work. (26)

Installment note payable A note payable that is due in equal periodic payments consisting of a portion of principal plus interest. (15)

Intangible assets Long-lived assets that do not have any tangible existence and represent rights that the company owns (e.g., patents, copyrights, goodwill, and trademarks). (8)

Interest-bearing note receivable A note receivable that requires payment of both the principal plus a stated rate of interest on the maturity date. (14)

Internal controls The procedures and rules used by a company to ensure that its assets are being used for legitimate business purposes. (10)

Internal financial reports Reports issued for use by managers of an entity that are usually more detailed than external reports; also called managerial accounting reports. (6)

Internal users The managers of an entity who use accounting information. (6)

International finance The movement of monies from one country to another. (5)

Inventory An asset account that is comprised of goods or merchandise held for future sale. (7)

Investing activities Transactions that involve the investment of a company's cash. (18)

Investment Expenditures for capital goods that are, in turn, used by business firms to lead to new productive capacity. (2) Asset held by the company for investment purposes for longer than one year rather than for use in the operations of the business. (8, 11)

Issued shares Shares that have actually been issued to shareholders at any time. (16)

Job order costing The form of product costing used most often by firms with production that is easily divided into separate projects or batches; costs are assigned to the specific product. (19)

Joint and several liability In partnership law, a party suing the partnership on a tort claim may include the partnership and any number of partners in the suit; responsibility either as a group or individually. (24)

Joint liability In partnership law, a party suing the partnership on a contract claim must sue all partners individually if any partner(s) is (are) included in the suit; responsibility as a group. (24)

Joint tenancy Co-ownership of property whereby a deceased party's interest goes to the surviving party or parties. (26)

Journal An accounting record in which business transactions are recorded in chronological order; also known as the *book of original entry.* (7)

Keynesian economics A school of economic thought advanced by the British economist John Maynard Keynes, who developed the concept of unemployment theory that relies on government to take an active step in the economic stabilization of a country. (2)

Labor One of the four factors of production that encompasses the human resources available in the labor force to perform work functions. (1)

Laissez faire An individualistic economic organization that emphasizes the free operation of market forces. (1)

Land One of the four factors of production. To an economist, land includes all natural resources that come directly from the land (e.g., iron ore and coal). (1)

Landrum-Griffin Act Federal legislation that deals with the internal operation of management and unions and establishes specific union member rights. (25)

Law of demand The law that indicates an inverse relationship between price of a good or service and quantity demanded. (1)

Law of supply The law that indicates a direct relationship between the price of a good or service and the quantity supplied. (1)

Ledger A collection of all the accounts of a business. Information contained in the journal is transferred periodically to the ledger. (7)

Liability An obligation or debt of an entity owed to another party. (7)

Life and health insurance Business life and health insurance coverage that provides funds for normal maintenance of a business in the event of a loss of a key person; often called *key man insurance.* (14)

LIFO The *l*ast-*i*n *f*irst-*o*ut method of valuing inventory that assumes that the latest units purchased are sold first and that ending inventory is made up of the earliest units purchased. (12)

Limited liability Shareholders of a corporation are liable for the debts of the corporation only to the amount of their investment in the corporation. (16)

Limited partner A partner who is treated as an investor only and may not engage in active day-to-day management of the business or lend his or her name to the partnership name. A limited partner is potentially liable on partnership debts only to the extent of capital contribution. (24)

Liquidity A measure of the speed with which an asset can be converted into cash. The more easily an asset can be converted to cash, the more liquid it is considered to be. (8)

Literary works Works such as books, magazines, newspapers, plays, musical compositions, artwork, photographs, motion pictures, recordings, computer programs, databases, and other verbal or numerical symbols that can be copyrighted by the author. (26)

Long-term capital gain or loss A gain or loss resulting from the disposition of a capital asset held for more than one year. (17)

Long-term liabilities Obligations of an entity that will not come due during the next operating cycle. (8)

Losses Expenses or decreased in owners' equity that do not result from normal operations of the business. (8)

Lower of cost or market The rule that requires that certain assets (such as inventory and temporary investments) be recorded at market value if their market value is below their cost. (12)

Maker One who signs a promissory note promising to pay a certain sum of money to another party. (22)

Manufacturing overhead All costs of production except direct materials and direct labor. (19)

Margin requirements The percentage of a stock purchase price an individual must deposit with a broker or a bank before the difference can be made up by a loan. (3)

Marginal propensity to consume (MPC) Change in consumption resulting from a given change in disposable income. (2)

Marginal tax rate The proportion of a unit of income paid into taxes. In the case of federal income tax, there is an increasing marginal tax rate. The proportion of income paid into taxes increases as income increases, resulting in decreases in take-home pay. (2)

Market An environment in which exchange of goods and services takes place. (1)

Marketable securities Short-term investments the company intends to hold for less than one operating cycle. (11)

Matching The accounting principle that states that expenses incurred in earning revenues should be matched with those revenues to determine net income. (7)

Materiality The accounting principle that states that insignificant items need not be accounted for in the same manner as more relevant or significant items. (6)

Maturity date of a note The date on which the principal and any interest are due and payable. (14)

Merchant A person who regularly deals in the kind of goods involved. (21)

Misdemeanor A crime punishable by up to one year of incarceration. (20)

Mixed cost A cost that consists of both variable and fixed elements. (19)

Mixed economy A combination of laissez-faire and command economic systems in which individuals within the system and the government have an impact on basic decisions; the United States is an example of a mixed economy. (1)

Modified accelerated cost recovery system (MACRS) An accelerated method of depreciation required for income tax purposes that assigns an asset to a class of property with a defined life. (13)

Monetary policy Activity of the Federal Reserve System designed to control the money supply. (2) A policy enacted to influence the course of the national economy by the Federal Reserve System through the use of monetary tools, such as reserve requirements and open-market operations, to control the money supply. (3)

Money Anything used as a medium of exchange, a store of value, and a standard of deferred payment. (3)

Money measurement A common unit of measure (money) used to record all information in the accounting records. (6)

Moral suasion An attempt by the Federal Reserve System to influence member banks to adopt what the Fed regards as more socially beneficial policy. (3)

Mortgage A long-term obligation that is usually secured by real estate and is usually repaid in installments made up partially of interest and partially of repayment of the principal of the loan. (8) A legal agreement that gives the lender the right to be paid from the sale of specific assets that belong to the borrower if the borrower does not repay the loan. (15) The legal document used when the collateral for securing a loan is real or personal property. (26)

Mortgage bond A bond secured by specific assets of the issuing company. (15)

Mortgagee The lender; the party to whom the mortgage is given. (26)

Mortgagor The borrower; the party who is giving a mortgage on property to secure a loan. (26)

National income A measurement of the sum of payments to the factors of production that results from production that occurred. (2)

Nationalism Under any economic circumstances, a way of acting to maximize the national interest and patriotism; a belief that one's country should be self-sufficient and should not depend on other countries for goods and services. (5)

National Labor Relations Act (NLRA) The federal act that deals with private employer-union relations. (25)

National Labor Relations Board (NLRB) The administrative agency established by the Wagner Act (1935) that oversees and monitors union-management relations in the private sector. (25)

Negligent conduct Careless behavior that results in injury to another person or organization. (23)

Negotiable instrument A written document containing a signed, unconditional promise or order to pay a certain sum of money at a specified time or on demand to the order of a named party or to the bearer. (22)

Negotiation The transfer of an instrument in such form that the transferee becomes a holder. (22)

Net income The excess of total revenues over total expenses of an entity during an accounting period. (7)

Net national product (NNP) A measurement of the value of the goods and services available for consumption during a given time period. (2)

Non-interest-bearing note receivable A note with no provision for the payment of interest; only the payment of principal is required. (14)

Notes payable Obligations of an entity consisting of signed documents that promise to pay specific amounts of money plus interest on specific future dates. (8)

Notes receivable Signed documents given to an entity by its customers promising to pay specific amounts of money plus interest on specific future dates. (8)

Novation An agreement by a party to a contract to release the other party from its contractual obligation and to accept another party's promise to perform those duties. (21)

NOW account A transaction account on which negotiable orders of withdrawal can be written. (3)

NSF check A check that has been written on a bank account in which there are insufficient funds deposited to cover the amount of the check; commonly called a *bad check.* (10)

Objectivity The accounting principle that requires that financial information be factual, verifiable, and unbiased. (6)

Occupational Safety and Health Act (OSHA) Federal law that provides for the establishment of health and safety standards for the workplace. (25)

Offer A communication of an intent to be bound to the terms of a specific proposed contract. The communication invites acceptance on the part of the intended recipient. (21)

Offeree One to whom an offer is made. (21)

Offeror One who makes an offer. (21)

Open-market operations The buying and selling of domestic government securities by the Federal Reserve System. (3)

Operating activities Transactions related to the production and sale of goods and services resulting in the calculation of net income. (18)

Operating cycle The period of time it takes for a firm to buy or produce merchandise, sell the merchandise, collect the accounts receivable resulting from the sale of the merchandise, and pay the accounts payable of the firm. (8)

Opportunity cost The value of the opportunity forgone when a decision is made. (1)

Organized stock exchanges Established markets for securities where buy and sell orders are matched at public auction. Examples of organized stock exchanges are the New York Stock Exchange and the American Stock Exchange. (16)

Other assets The balance sheet classification used for assets that do not fit the criteria for classification in another area. (8)

Other liabilities The balance sheet classification used for liabilities that do not fit the criteria for classification in another area. (8)

Output per capita A nation's total output divided by its population. (2)

Outstanding checks Checks written and recorded on the books of a depositor that have not yet been presented to the bank for payment. (10)

Outstanding shares The shares of stock that are currently in the hands of stockholders. (16)

Over-the-counter market All markets for securities except organized stock exchanges. (16)

Owners' equity The resources invested in the business by owners plus profits from successful operations that have been retained in the business; also called capital, net worth, or proprietorship. (7)

Parent company An investor company that owns more than 50 percent of the voting stock of the investee company. (11)

Partially disclosed principal A principal whose existence is known but whose identity is unknown to the third party with whom the principal's agent deals. (23)

Participative preferred stock Shares of preferred stock that may enable the stockholders not only to receive stated dividends but also to share in dividend distributions of earnings of the corporation. (16)

Partnership A business entity owned and operated by two or more persons who carry on the business for profit as co-owners. (6, 24)

Par value A fixed amount printed on the face of the stock certificate at the time the corporation seeks authorization of the stock. (16)

Patent Legal protection available to the inventor of a machine, process, product, chemical, a new variety of nonpollinating plant life, or other new, useful invention. A patent gives the inventor the right to prevent others from using the patented invention in the United States and its territories and possessions. (26)

Payee The party to whom a check or draft is made payable. (22)

Perfect competition An environment in which business firms produce under circumstances where no one producer can have an effect on the market price, there is freedom of entry and exit, homogeneous goods are produced, and complete information is available to all producers and consumers. Perfect competition guarantees economic efficiency in production at a given level of technology. (1)

Periodic inventory system A system of accounting for inventory that requires the use of a physical count of inventory at the end of the accounting period in order to determine ending inventory and to calculate cost of goods sold. (12)

Periodicity The concept in accounting that requires that the life of a business be broken down into specific time periods for periodic reporting purposes. The normal accounting period is one year. (6)

Permanent accounts Asset, liability, and owners' equity accounts included on the balance sheet of an entity; may also be called *balance sheet accounts* or *real accounts.* (7)

Perpetual inventory system A system of accounting for inventory that maintains a continuous record of all inventory transactions. (12)

Personal income (PI) Total income received by households from all sources. (2)

Personal property Property owned other than real property. (26)

Petty cash fund A fund established to pay for small expenditures that would be inconvenient to pay by check. (10)

Pollution Use of the environment (air, land, and water) by producers and consumers as a dumping ground for waste. (4)

Posting The process of transferring the information contained in the journal to the ledger accounts. (7)

Power of attorney A document that formally authorizes one person to act on behalf of another person as to matters stated in the document. (23)

Precedent A previously decided case. (20)

Predetermined overhead rate The rate that is determined in advance and used to allocate manufacturing overhead costs to the jobs in the work-in-process inventory and to the jobs completed during the period. The predetermined overhead rate is calculated by dividing estimated total manufacturing overhead costs by estimated total units in the overhead application base. (19)

Preferred stock A form of capital stock of a corporation that entitles its owners to certain preferences, such as receipt of a specified but limited amount of dividends before distribution of dividends may be made to common shareholders. (8) Stock that represents ownership in a corporation entitling the stockholder to certain advantages not available to owners of common stock. (24)

Prepaid expenses The cost of goods or services bought for use in the business that are not used up by the end of the accounting period; assets as long as future benefits may be obtained from them. (8)

Price ceiling A legal maximum price that can be charged for a product. (4)

Price discrimination A seller's sale of identical goods at different prices to different buyers without legal justification (Robinson-Patman Act). (25)

Price fixing The agreement by one party with one or more others as to the setting of a price for a good or service (Sherman Act). (25)

Primary deposit The initial deposit placed in a transaction account by an account owner. (3)

Principal One on whose behalf the agent is acting. (23)

Private goods Goods and services that can be used only if purchased. (1)

Private placement The sale of an entire issue of securities by the issuing corporation directly to one or a few large institutional investors. (16)

Private property Individual ownership of property and other resources; the right of individuals to own the factors of production and to do with these resources what they see fit. (1)

Procedural law Law that specifies rules governing how rights are to be enforced. (20)

Process costing The method of product costing most often used by firms that produce a homogeneous product using a continuous manufacturing process. (19)

Producer price index (PPI) An index that attempts to measure average changes in the producer's cost of goods throughout the years. A representative sampling of goods is used. (2)

Production possibility curve (PPC) The maximum amount of goods and services that can be produced at a given time with a given level of technology and full, efficient use of resources. (1) All the alternative combinations of commodities that can be produced with fixed amounts of product inputs and fixed technology. (2)

Productivity The amount of output produced per unit of input. (4)

Profit The revenue received minus the cost of production (both explicit and implicit). (1)

Proforma financial statement A forecasted (or budgeted) balance sheet or income statement. (19)

Promissory note A negotiable instrument that contains a promise by the maker to pay a certain sum of money to another party at a specified time or on demand. (22)

Promoter The person(s) who organizes (creates) a new corporation and solicits stock subscriptions. (24)

Promulgate A term describing the act of an administrative agency in creating a regulation. (20)

Property insurance Insurance protection of the assets of the company from damage or destruction by fire, smoke, vandalism, and other causes. (14)

Protective tariff A tariff placed on imported goods to protect the sale of domestically produced goods. (5)

Public goods Goods anyone can consume without diminishing the amount available for others to consume; goods provided or controlled by government. (1)

Purchases journal A special journal used to record purchases of inventory and supplies on account. (10)

Quasi-contract A legally enforceable obligation that does not stem from the agreement between the parties but rather from the court's interest in preventing an injustice. (21)

Quitclaim deed Grantor (the party conveying the property) transfers entire interest, if any, without any warranty of title. (26)

Ratification An expression of an intent to be bound by the terms of an agreement that was entered into at a time when the party was lacking in contractual capacity. Ratification can occur only after capacity is attained. (21)

Ratio The relationship of one amount to another. (18)

Real income (purchasing power) The measurement of a household's income in terms of constant dollars; the amount of goods and services that can be purchased. (2)

Real property Land and any improvements on or connected with the land, such as crops, buildings, and fixtures. (26)

Registered bond A bond that has the owner's name registered with the issuing company. (15)

Regulation A rule promulgated by an administrative agency. (20)

Relevant range The range within which assumptions made about the nature of cost behavior (i.e., fixed or variable) are valid. (19)

Required reserves A requirement that banks keep a portion of their assets on reserve with the Federal Reserve bank in addition to cash kept in the vaults of the banks. (3)

Reserve ratio The percentage of deposits required by law to be held in reserve. (3)

Restitution A remedy for a breach of contract that involves the return of what was received under the contract in an effort to put the parties in the position they were in before the contract. (21)

Restrictive indorsement An indorsement that requires the indorsee to accept the instrument subject to certain specified conditions. (22)

Retained earnings The portion of the stockholders' equity consisting of earnings of the corporation that have been retained in the corporation rather than paid out as dividends. (7)

Revenue Earnings resulting from the receipt of cash or other assets (or the reduction of a liability) in exchange for goods sold by the entity or services performed by the entity. (7)

Revenue realization The principle that states that revenue is usually recognized only after an exchange has taken place or a service has been performed. (7)

Revenue tariff A tariff with the major purpose of producing revenue for the country levying the tariff. (5)

Revocation The withdrawal of an offer by the offeror. (21)

Right-to-work law One of the provisions of the National Labor Relations Act that permits states to decide whether union shops may exist and whether an employee can be forced to join a union as a condition of continued employment. (25)

Sales journal A special journal used to record sales of merchandise on account. (10)

Salvage value The residual value an asset is expected to have when its estimated useful life is over. (13)

Scarcity A condition that exists whenever society's desire for goods or services exceeds society's ability to produce those goods and services; whenever wants exceed resources. (1)
Secondary deposit Money placed in a transaction account by a paper transaction within the financial institution, such as granting a loan and placing those funds in an account. (3)
Security interest The giving of a legal interest (lien) in one's property to another to secure a loan. (26)
Serial bonds Bonds issued at the same time but coming due at various maturity dates to alleviate some of the cash flow drain that occurs when bonds mature. (15)
Shortage Excess quantity demanded at a given market price. (1)
Short-term capital gain or loss A gain or loss resulting from the sale of a capital asset held for one year or less. (17)
Simple contract A contract that does not come within the narrow category of formal contracts. (21)
Simple interest Interest that is computed only on the principal of the loan for a single period of time. (15)
Small Business Administration (SBA) A federal agency established in 1953 to advise and assist the nation's small businesses; provides loans, loan guarantees, and other financial assistance and offers loans to victims of natural disasters; also conducts research on conditions affecting small businesses. (3)
Sole entrepreneurship A business owned and operated by one person. (24)
Source document The document that is usually prepared when an accounting transaction occurs; the source of information for making journal entries. (7)
Special agent An agent who is authorized by a principal to perform a single task or to achieve a narrow goal on behalf of the principal. (23)
Special indorsement An indorsement that names the party to whom the indorser makes the instrument payable. (22)
Special journal A journal used to record routine transactions that occur frequently. The use of special journals simplifies the posting procedure. (10)
Specific tariff A per unit tariff tax on an imported commodity. (5)
Standard cost The cost that should be incurred when producing a product or performing an operation efficiently. (19)
Stare decisis The doctrine that precedent should be followed. (20)
Statement of cash flows The financial statement that shows the operating, investing, and financing cash flows of a business. (8)
Statement of changes in capital The financial statement that explains the changes in the capital (owners' equity) account from one period to another. (8)
Statement of retained earnings The financial statement that shows the changes in retained earnings from one period to another. (8)
Statute A law passed by a legislative body. (21)
Statutory law Law enacted by legislative bodies; also referred to as *statutes.* (20)
Stock dividend A dividend distributed in the form of additional shares of stock instead of cash. (11)
Stockholders' equity The term used for the owners' equity in a corporation. (7)
Straight-line depreciation A depreciation method that assigns an equal amount of depreciation expense to each year of the asset's useful life. (13)
Strict liability A legal doctrine that requires one engaged in a highly dangerous activity to compensate those injured as a result of the activity even in the absence of any negligence. (20)
Structural unemployment A type of unemployment that occurs when there is a change in the types of labor needed in the economy (i.e., a change in technology requiring a different mix of skills) to which the labor force cannot readily adapt. (2)
Subsidiary account An individual detailed account of balances due from individual customers or balances owed to individual suppliers. (10)
Subsidiary company An investee company that is controlled by a parent company. (11)
Substantive law Law that defines rights and duties. (20)
Substitute goods Products that can satisfy the same want of an individual as other products. (1)
Sum-of-the-years' digits depreciation (SYD) An accelerated depreciation method that uses a decreasing fraction as the depreciation rate to allocate the cost less salvage value of an asset over its useful life. (13)
Supply The maximum quantity of a good that will be made available for sale by producers within a given period of time at various price levels. (1)
Supply of money Total amount of money (coins, currency, and transaction accounts in financial institutions) in the economy. (3)
Supply-side economics A contemporary school of thought advocating the idea that policies undertaken to

alter aggregate supply are more influential in the economy than policies influencing demand. (2)

Surety bond A contract under which the surety agrees to make good the debt or default of the principal. (14)

Surplus The business state that exists when the quantity supplied is greater than the quantity demanded at a given market price. (1)

T-account A representation of an account that is used for instructional or problem-solving purposes. (7)

Taft-Hartley Act Federal legislation that established free-speech rights for employees and identified union and employer unfair labor practices. (25)

Tariff A tax levied on commodities as they move through a custom boundary. (5)

Tariff quota Placement of a low tariff or no tariff on goods imported into the country up to a certain amount. (5)

Technological unemployment Unemployment as a result of displacement of employees because of technological advance. (2)

Temporary accounts Revenue, expense, and drawing accounts; temporary accounts are closed to owners' equity at the end of an accounting period. (7)

Temporary investments Marketable securities that are expected to be held for less than one year or operating cycle; can be converted into cash very quickly. (8, 11)

Tenancy in common Co-ownership of property whereby a deceased party's interest passes according to the will and/or inheritance laws. (26)

Term bond A bond that has a single fixed maturity date. (15)

Term notes payable A note payable repaid in one lump sum on a specific maturity date. (15)

Third party One who deals with an agent who is representing a principal. (23)

Tort law The law of civil wrongs, including intentional acts, negligence, and strict liability. (20)

Trade discount A reduction from the retail list price of catalog items given by manufacturers or wholesalers to their dealers; a method of determining the sales price. (10)

Trading securities Investments in debt securities or investments in equity securities that are bought and held principally for the purpose of selling them in the near term. (11)

Transaction account An account in a financial institution on which one can write checks, negotiable orders of withdrawal, or share drafts. (3)

Transfer payments Disbursements from government or private firms for which no products or services are received in exchange. (2)

Treasury stock The shares of a corporation's own capital stock reacquired by the corporation. (16)

Treble damages Triple the amount of actual damages given in some lawsuits to strongly discourage certain kinds of wrongful actions. A statute must authorize treble damages; most antitrust statutes do just that. (25)

Trial balance A listing of all the account balances in the general ledger that is used to verify that the total dollar amount of debits is equal to the total dollar amount of credits. (9)

Unappropriated retained earnings The portion of the retained earnings of a corporation that has not been appropriated for a specific purpose. (16)

Undisclosed principal A principal whose existence is unknown to the third party with whom the principal's agent deals. (23)

Unemployment insurance Payments made to employees because of involuntary severance from work; to qualify, the employee must have worked a minimum number of weeks and be ready, able, and willing to take equivalent new employment. (25)

Unfair labor practices Management and union practices that are deemed to be illegal as set forth in the National Labor Relations Act. (25)

Uniform Commercial Code (UCC) A body of law that governs many commercial transactions; it has been adopted in every state. (Louisiana has adopted major parts of the UCC but not all of it.) (21)

Unilateral contract A contract in which the offer is accepted by performance of the requested act. Only one promise is involved. (21)

Units-of-production method A depreciation method that computes depreciation expense based on the total estimated productive output of the asset. (13)

Unlimited liability The liability of sole proprietors and partners for business debts not only from business assets but also from personal assets. (16)

Usury laws Laws that limit the maximum interest rate that can be charged. (3)

Utility A measure of the satisfaction derived from consumption of goods and services. (1)

Variable cost A cost that varies in total in direct proportion to changes in the level of output. (19)

Variance The difference between the amount budgeted for an item (revenue or expense) and the amount that actually results for that item (revenue or expense) at the end of the accounting period. (19)

Vocational Rehabilitation Act of 1973 An act that specifically eliminated job-related discrimination against handicapped individuals. (4)

Void contract An attempt at forming a contract that failed because of the absence of an essential element. (21)

Voidable contract A contract that may be set aside at the option of one of the parties. (21)

Voucher A document used to summarize a transaction for authorization to pay a liability. (10)

Voucher system A system of internal control over cash disbursements, purchases, and receipts that requires that a voucher be prepared and verified before any payments may be made. (10)

Wagner Act The first comprehensive labor act to regulate private employment; this act provides protection for employees to engage in concerted union activity. (6, 25)

Wants Individual desires that can be satisfied by consuming goods and services. (1)

Warranty deed In essence, a warranty by the grantor that the property is transferred free from all unknown defects or claims. (26)

Weighted-average method The method that uses a weighted-average unit cost to value ending inventory and cost of goods sold. (12)

Workers' compensation Laws passed in most states to pay money to employees who are injured on the job even though the employee failed to follow directions and/or was negligent as long as there was no intentional infliction of injury. (25)

Working capital The net amount of a company's relatively liquid resources; current assets minus current liabilities. (18)

Worksheet An accounting tool used to make the end-of-period accounting processes easier. (9)